DEVOURING TIME

DEVOURING TIME

Nostalgia in Contemporary Shakespearean Screen Adaptations

PHILIPPA SHEPPARD

McGill-Queen's University Press
Montreal & Kingston · London · Chicago

© McGill-Queen's University Press 2017

ISBN 978-0-7735-5019-3 (cloth)
ISBN 978-0-7735-5020-9 (paper)
ISBN 978-0-7735-5021-6 (ePDF)
ISBN 978-0-7735-5022-3 (ePUB)

Legal deposit second quarter 2017
Bibliothèque nationale du Québec

Printed in Canada on acid-free paper that is 100% ancient forest free (100% post-consumer recycled), processed chlorine free.

McGill-Queen's University Press acknowledges the support of the Canada Council for the Arts for our publishing program. We also acknowledge the financial support of the Government of Canada through the Canada Book Fund for our publishing activities.

Library and Archives Canada Cataloguing in Publication

Sheppard, Philippa, 1966–, author
    Devouring time : nostalgia in contemporary Shakespearean screen adaptations / Philippa Sheppard.

Includes bibliographical references and index.
Issued in print and electronic formats.
ISBN 978-0-7735-5019-3 (hardcover). – ISBN 978-0-7735-5020-9 (softcover). – ISBN 978-0-7735-5021-6 (ePDF). – ISBN 978-0-7735-5022-3 (ePUB)

    1. Shakespeare, William, 1564–1616 – Film adaptations. 2. English drama – Film adaptations. 3. Film adaptations – History and criticism. 4. Motion pictures and literature. 5. Nostalgia in motion pictures. I. Title.

PR3093.S55 2017   791.43'6   C2017-900545-6
                                       C2017-900546-4

This book was typeset by True to Type in 10.5/13 Sabon

For Ken

Contents

Figures   ix

Acknowledgments   xi

Introduction: Remembrance of Things Past   3

PART ONE   DEFINING TERMS

1 Why Shakespeare Films Now?   31
2 The Drive to Realism in Shakespearean Adaptation to Film   57

PART TWO   REMEMBERING ORIGINS

3 Shakespeare's Prologues on Page and Screen   103
4 Nostalgia for the Stage in Shakespearean Films   133
5 Death Rituals in Shakespeare, Almereyda, and Luhrmann   153

PART THREE   DISGUISE, GENRE, AND PLAY

6 Gothic Aspects of Kenneth Branagh's *Hamlet*   179
7 Art and the Grotesque in Julie Taymor's *Titus* and Peter Greenaway's *Prospero's Books*   198
8 Five English Screen Directors' Approaches to Cross-Dressing in *As You Like It* and *Twelfth Night*   223
9 Propaganda and the Other in Branagh's *Henry V* and Fiennes's *Coriolanus*   254

PART FOUR MUSIC AND MEMORY

10 "Sigh No More Ladies": Shakespeare, Branagh, and Whedon Tackle Issues of Gender and Fidelity in *Much Ado About Nothing* 285

11 "O Mistress Mine": Intercutting in Trevor Nunn's *Twelfth Night* 303

12 Nostalgia in Hoffman's *William Shakespeare's A Midsummer Night's Dream* and Branagh's *Love's Labour's Lost* 320

13 Ariel's Singing Body as Interpreted by Greenaway and Taymor 338

Conclusion 356

Works Cited 367

Index 409

Figures

1 Jessica (Zuleikha Robinson) keeps her mother's turquoise ring in Radford's *The Merchant of Venice*, 2004. Sony Pictures.   69

2 Macbeth (Sam Worthington) watches his wife (Victoria Hill) arrange roses on their son's grave in Wright's *Macbeth*, 2007. Mushroom Productions.   123

3 Macbeth (Michael Fassbender) and Lady Macbeth (Marion Cotillard) grieve at their baby's pyre in Kurzel's *Macbeth*, 2015. Studiocanal.   124

4 Imogen (Dakota Johnson) and Posthumous (Penn Badgley) kiss goodbye under the bleachers in Almereyda's *Cymbeline*, 2014. Lionsgate.   137

5 Duke Senior (Brian Blessed) and his court watch a Kabuki performer (Takuya Shimada) in Branagh's *As You Like It*, 2006. Lionsgate.   147

6 Gertrude (Diane Venora) and the court attend Ophelia's funeral in Almereyda's *Hamlet*, 2000. Miramax Films.   170–1

7 Hamlet (Kenneth Branagh) surprises Polonius (Richard Briers) wearing a skull mask in Branagh's *Hamlet*, 1996. Castle Rock Entertainment.   195

8 Viola (Imogen Stubbs) surveys her transformation into a man in Nunn's *Twelfth Night*, 1996. Fine Line.   243

9 Volumnia (Vanessa Redgrave) kneels at the feet of her son, Coriolanus (Ralph Fiennes), in Fiennes's *Coriolanus*, 2011. Alliance Films.   278

10 Kai Cole sings "Sigh No More, Ladies" at Leonato's party in Whedon's *Much Ado About Nothing*, 2012. Lionsgate.   294

11 Don Armado (Timothy Spall) kicks at the moon in Branagh's *Love's Labour's Lost*, 2000. Miramax Films.   329

12 Ariel (Ben Whishaw) sets fire to the king's ship in Taymor's *The Tempest*, 2010. Miramax Films.   352

Acknowledgments

To members of the Shakespeare Association of America, I am indebted for feedback on some of the chapters in this book, which I presented in embryonic form during seminars at the yearly conventions. I am grateful to *Literature/Film Quarterly* and *Shakespeare Bulletin* for publishing earlier, shorter versions of chapters 10, 11, and 6 respectively. I would also like to thank the Centre for Reformation and Renaissance Studies for giving me an academic home when I started research for this book.

My heartfelt thanks go to the staff of McGill-Queen's University Press, Ryan Van Huijstee, Kathleen Fraser, and especially Mark Abley and Maureen Garvie. It was a great pleasure working with you. Thank you also to my kind friends Marlo Spence Lair, for musical advice on chapter 13, and Jane Freeman and Nicole Langlois, for recommending me as a lecturer, moderator, and writer of program notes for the Stratford Festival, which has been a real highlight of recent years. To drama gurus Jill Levenson and Brian Parker, thank you very much for general mentorship over the years. Obviously, any mistakes in this book are my own responsibility.

To my siblings, Gregory and Clare, thank you for patiently listening to me enthuse about Shakespeare adaptations during the whole process. I am grateful to my three children, Sophia, Nathaniel, and Julia, for cheerfully tolerating my absent-mindedness when in the throes of writing. My greatest debt of gratitude is owed to my stellar husband, Kenneth Oppel, for unflagging support of my career, even when it wrested him from his beloved Toronto to Oxford, Newfoundland, and Dublin.

I have used *William Shakespeare, The Complete Works*, edited by Stanley Wells and Gary Taylor (Oxford: Clarendon Press 1988), as the source for my quotations, unless stated otherwise.

DEVOURING TIME

Survivors of the twentieth century, we are all nostalgic for a time when we were not nostalgic. But there seems no way back.

Svetlana Boym

INTRODUCTION

Remembrance of Things Past

"Yea, from the table of my memory / I'll wipe away all trivial fond records / All saws of books, all forms, all pressures past / That youth and observation copied there" (1.5.98–101).

So Hamlet swears to his dead father, but he fails to keep his extravagant promise. Artists today must often feel something like this Hamletian desire to start with a clean slate, so that their art might be truly original, not bound to all the influences of the art of the past. Filmmakers, manipulating a relatively new medium, might seem to have the best chance of avoiding the charge of being derivative, and yet now more than ever, their work bears the unmistakable signs of nostalgia. Christopher Borrelli of the *Chicago Tribune* commented that the Oscar season of 2012 was dominated by films that looked to the past (*Midnight in Paris, The Help, War Horse, Moneyball*), and some to the specific past of filmmaking itself (*Hugo, The Artist*). Furthermore, the award ceremony was held in a theatre decorated to ape an old-fashioned movie hall. Borrelli sees this film nostalgia as "spurred by a concern that a cold, alienating digital future will replace the warm, recognizable pleasures of the past" (2). I argue that Shakespeare represents, to his filmmakers and their audiences, such a pleasure. Linda Hutcheon, in *A Theory of Adaptation*, also acknowledges the pleasure principle in relation to old familiar forms: "There must be something particularly appealing about adaptations as adaptations. Part of this pleasure ... comes simply from repetition with variation, from the comfort of ritual combined with the piquancy of surprise" (4). The "comfort of ritual" is, I contend, a nostalgic comfort.

This book is a collection of essays on Shakespearean adaptation to film from 1989 to the present. I have selected 1989 as the start date for two reasons. First, Kenneth Branagh's film *Henry V*, which premiered that year, both a critical and financial success, lent confidence to studios to return to Shakespeare for source material. Second, the Shakespearean adaptations made prior to 1989 have already received much critical attention. The essays in this book focus on the way in which the translation from Renaissance play to contemporary film highlights and comments on aspects of contemporary culture, particularly revealing our attitudes to art, identity, and the past. Philosopher Mikhail Bakhtin writes, "Every age reaccentuates in its own way the works of [the past]. The historical life of classic works is in fact the uninterrupted process of their social and ideological reaccentuation" ("Discourse," 45). This reaccentuation throws into sharp relief social shifts from the time that Shakespeare wrote the plays to the present day of their adaptations. The unifying theme in these essays on a wide variety of aspects of many Shakespearean adaptations is nostalgia. The growing presence of studies on nostalgia in academic libraries suggests that scholars believe it is more of an issue now than in the past. Yiannis Gabriel, writing about the arts and entertainment industries, states that "whole sectors of the economy are fuelled by nostalgia" (119).

Ginette Vincendeau sees all literary adaptations as partaking in the "nostalgic turn to the past (twinned with a denial of history) and a delight in allusions, self-referentiality and pastiche," key aspects of postmodern culture (2001, xvi), according to Frederic Jameson. Vincendeau adds that "paradoxically, under their overt nostalgia, the films respond to changes in social and cultural mores, re-interpreting texts in ways which echo new agendas, be they of politics, gender or ethnicity" (xxiv). This observation holds true for Shakespeare adaptations as much as for films generally classified as "heritage." I argue that it is an act of nostalgia to select a work from the sixteenth or seventeenth century to turn into a contemporary film. Most obviously, selecting a Shakespearean script is an acknowledgment by the filmmaker that there is something extraordinary about Shakespeare's plays. The filmmakers discussed here have not modernized the language of the plays, even though they have of necessity shortened the texts (except in the case of Branagh's 1996 *Hamlet*). This fidelity to the original is in itself a tacit recognition that there is something unique about Shakespeare's language that would be missed if it were jettisoned and only his plot and characters maintained. At the same time, these directors cannot help but bring to bear on their adaptations attitudes shaped by the present time. Some instances: Michael Radford gives context for the anti-Semitism we find in *The Merchant of Venice*; Kenneth Branagh adds physical intimacy to Hamlet and Ophelia's relationship; and Julie Taymor in her *Titus* makes explicit an anti-violence agenda.

Nevertheless, it is undeniably an act of homage on the part of filmmakers to spend at least a year of their lives on a work of Shakespeare. It is for this reason that my book's title quotes Shakespeare's Sonnet 19. The voice in the sonnet vows to preserve the beloved's image in verse, just as these directors preserve Shakespeare in film for current and future generations in what must, given the unlikelihood of reaping a profit, be seen as an act of love:

> Devouring time, blunt thou the lion's paws,
> And make the earth devour her own sweet brood;
> Pluck the keen teeth from the fierce tiger's jaws,
> And burn the long-lived phoenix in her blood.
> Make glad and sorry seasons as thou fleet'st,
> And do whate'er thou wilt, swift-footed time,
> To the wide world and all her fading sweets.
> But I forbid thee one most heinous crime:
> O, carve not with thy hours my love's fair brow,
> Nor draw no lines there with thine antique pen.
> Him in thy course untainted do allow
> For beauty's pattern to succeeding men.
> Yet do thy worst, old time; despite thy wrong
> My love shall in my verse ever live young.

In their films, these directors keep Shakespeare's works young, at least for a couple of generations, until the next group of directors take up the baton.

Scholars like Cairns Craig have identified the heritage film's "yearning and even conservative view of the past," while Andrew Higson characterized the genre as "the reproduction of literary texts, artefacts and landscapes which already have a privileged status within the accepted definition of the national heritage ... and the *reconstruction of a historical moment* [my italics] which is assumed to be of national significance" ("Waving," 27). Many examples of filmed Shakespeare share characteristics with these descriptions. All of them use as their basis plays that have the most privileged status of any literary works. Some treat important moments in British history: Branagh's *Henry V* reenacts the Battle of Agincourt, Richard Loncraine's *Richard III* features both the Battle of Bosworth and an imagined fascist pre–World War II Britain, Branagh's *Love's Labour's Lost* refers to World War II and Christine Edzard's *As You Like It* to Thatcherism. Film scholar Claire Monk notes that Loncraine's 1930s *Richard III* was among the top three most widely seen films by her Heritage Audience Survey respondents, liked by most "perhaps precisely because it was a Shakespeare film" (*Heritage Film Audiences*, 104). In our global marketplace, adaptors of Shakespeare draw on significant moments of other nations' history as well. Julie Taymor (American) in her *Titus* alludes, at least in her choice of locale, to the Serbian-Bosnian war, as does Ralph Fiennes (British) in his *Coriolanus*. Baz Luhrmann (Australian) in his *Romeo + Juliet* obliquely recalls the 1992 race riots in Los Angeles. These instances are nostalgic only in that they suggest that sixteenth-century plays can be employed to speak to us about recent political events. The nostalgia lies in the persistent promotion of Shakespeare's universalism in the face of recent literary criticism that would argue for intense cultural and temporal specificity.

What exactly is nostalgia? The term is a seventeenth-century neologism marrying two Greek words, *nostos*, meaning return, and *algia*, meaning pain – thus, the pain or longing for return. It was invented in 1678 as a disease by a Swiss doctor, Johannes Hofer, after examining soldiers, mercenaries in particular (Janelle Wilson, 21). While originally indistinguishable from homesickness, by the nineteenth century it was categorized with other *maladies de la memoire* like amnesia (Ritivoi, 19). The nostalgic, in contrast to the amnesiac, clings to the past for fear that if one forgets, one's identity will be lost. Theodule Ribot, a nineteenth-century psychologist, claimed that "our self at each moment – this present perpetually renewed – is in large part nourished by memory. That is to say, our present state is associated with other states that, rejected and localized in the past, constitute our person as it appears at each instant ... the identity of the self rests entirely on memory" (83).

This linking of memory to identity might go some way to explaining why we adapt Shakespeare to the screen, often maintaining his language: with the onslaught of information about today, we are anxious that we may lose or forget our cultural past. An adaptation provides some continuity with our heritage. In particular, in multicultural societies like the United States and Britain, where most of the English Shakespearean adaptations of the past twenty-eight years have been made, pundits have observed in some quarters a sense that traditional English literary culture is threatened. This feeling of having one's culture threatened is akin to losing a sense of home. Jan Willem Duyvendak, in his excellent book *The Politics of Home: Belonging and Nostalgia in Western Europe and the United States*, describes this zeitgeist: "Not feeling at home is a powerful emotion – perhaps not a primary one, but, as both American and West European politics have revealed in recent years, connected to primordial sentiments of who 'belongs' where: in one's house, neighborhood, city or country. 'Home' and 'feeling at home' are central within the emotionalization of politics and the culturalization of citizenship (Hooks, 2009; Isin et al., 2008; Schinkel, 2008) and now stand at the heart of public and political debate" (41).

One of the symptoms of nostalgia, the disease, was that "memories of home and a happier time ... substitute for real experience" (Ritivoi, 20). In adaptations of Shakespeare to the screen, the sanctioned art of the past substitutes for contemporary art. An adaptation of a Shakespeare play is at several removes from "real experience." Dr Hofer viewed nostalgia as a disease of the imagination, in which fantasies of home eventually crowded out any other thoughts from the victim's mind (16). As an affliction of the imagination, it is no surprise that it became associated with writers and musicians in the nineteenth century, and so it seems apt that I apply it now to film directors.

By the twentieth century, the term had become more and more distant from its original meaning of homesickness, according to Susan J. Matt. She asserts that by the 1970s it had lost the negative connotation that still clings to the term "homesickness," which, with the rise of rugged American individualism in the late 1800s, accrued associations of maladjustment and immaturity: "Whereas the homesick may believe they can return home, the nostalgic knows that moving backward in time is impossible. Nostalgia offers a way to establish connections with the past and with home that does not seriously undermine the present" (253). The shifting definitions of the term suggest the ambiguous nature of the state, but they all have two aspects in common – attachment to the past and a sense of loss in the fact of change – which do not necessarily obliterate hope for the future.

The weight of cultural history, now so accessible to us through the Internet, has rendered us, as Frederic Jameson has observed, "unable today to focus on our own present, as though we have become incapable of achieving aesthetic representations of our current experience" (*Anti-Aesthetic*, 43). Bruce Sheridan, chair of the film program at Columbia College, has noted the same trend among his students: "I've tried to figure out why this is happening, why no one is blazing trails, only going back. I think they're working in older sensibilities because their options, ironically, have exploded with digital [filmmaking], so every reference, every era, is available, ready for mimicking. And rooting yourself in the past takes away the uncertainty you feel when blazing trails" (qtd in Borrelli, 2).

Apparently we find the past more convincing than the present. Kierkegaard expresses it thus: "To live in recollection is the most perfect life imaginable; recollection is more richly satisfying than all actuality, and it has a security that no actuality possesses" (qtd in Illbruck, 21). Our films and television shows excel at pastiche and allusion, creating an expression of our times that is at best self-referential and at worst completely derivative. American cinema, as always, represents this tendency at its most excessive. The 1990s and the first decade of the twenty-first century saw a plethora of literary adaptations and, often regrettably, remakes of films and television shows that premiered as recently as the 1980s (for example, *Miami Vice*, the feature film, 2006; *The Smurfs*, 2011). Consequently, as film critic Pam Cook remarked, "One of the most significant developments in film studies over the last fifteen years or so has been the growing preoccupation with memory and nostalgia" (1).

Studies in nostalgia assert that the urbanization and globalization of our current western society accounts in part for the wistful looking to the past, a time when tight-knit rural communities were more the norm (Sprengler, 15). Certainly Shakespeare writes about such communities, and even expresses this particular kind of yearning himself in his characteristic shift of setting from the court or city to the country (as instances, Arden in *As You Like It*, the forest outside Athens in *A Midsummer Night's Dream*, Prospero's island in *The Tempest*, the heath in *King Lear*). It is always in the country that the characters find renewal or experience an epiphany. As Donald Beecher observes, many Renaissance texts focus on the "return to a place or community that constitutes refuge, family, origins, reunion, reconciliation, in sum an anchored social context for the future after a long periods of wandering, danger, exile, and emotional suffering. Implicit in this orientation toward home are all the attendant emotions and desires that make this destination so intensely important" (281).

The films I consider here are all based on plays that explore some aspect of Beecher's description. In Branagh's *Henry V* (1989), during the French campaign, the king delivers orations harping on the idea of home and family to galvanize his troops to fight for England so that they can return there. In the three adaptations of *Hamlet* considered here – Zeffirelli's (1990), Branagh's (1996), and Almereyda's (2000) – the hero pines for the time when his father was alive and his family intact. His nostalgia makes him idealize his dead father, seeing him as "Hyperion" in contrast to his current father figure, Claudius, whom he views as a "satyr." Three adaptations of *As You Like It* – Basil Coleman's (1978), Edzard's (1992), and Branagh's (2006) – focus, as does the original play, on characters in exile, who, while stoical about their pastoral retreat, return to the court at the conclusion. Branagh's and Whedon's adaptations of *Much Ado About Nothing* (1993 and 2013) focus on two young women who have lost their sense of belonging (Beatrice, an orphan, through past heartbreak at Benedick's hands, and Hero through slander) but regain it after some real suffering. *Othello*, adapted by Oliver Parker in 1995, is set mostly in Cyprus, where both protagonists, Othello and Desdemona, are far from home and constantly poisoned by remarks from those around them insisting that that have married someone from an alien culture. Both characters express a wish that life could return to what it was before Iago soured it. *Richard III*, adapted in 1995 by Richard Loncraine, opens with the famous soliloquy in which Richard yearns for the time of war in which he had a purpose, while later in the play the English long for England to go back to a period of peace and stability. *Twelfth Night*, brilliantly filmed by Trevor Nunn in 1996, and made for television by Tim Supple in 2003, again focuses on exiled characters, the shipwrecked twins Viola and Sebastian, who are reunited with each other and regain their pre-tempest identities at the conclusion. The three adaptations I consider here of *A Midsummer Night's Dream* – Noble's (1996), Hoffman's (1999), and Edzard's (2001) – are based on Shakespeare's play in which four young Athenians leave their home for the woods only to return to the city. While in the forest, they endure some (comical to us) suffering. Bottom too is restored to his Athenian friends at the end. Baz Luhrmann's *Romeo + Juliet* (1996) makes it clear that the young tragic protagonists are only at home with one another; Verona Beach is a violent and alien place to them. That is why they "reunite" through suicide. Romeo also endures an official exile from Juliet in Mantua. Julie Taymor's *Titus* takes on one of Shakespeare's bloodiest plays, about a family whose conquests in war abroad set in motion on their return home a chain of revenge and retribution that ends only when twelve people have been slain. It is left to Titus's sole remaining son, Lucius, to re-create Rome as home for his own young son. *Love's Labour's Lost* opens with a kind of nostalgia for simple, innocent schoolboy days, free from the torments of love and the puzzling ways of women, represented by the vow set by the king of Navarre, and by the pedagogical atmosphere of the court in general (the presence of the pedantic schoolmaster Holofernes and the priest, Sir Nathaniel). Branagh in his film of 2000 adds to this wistfulness by resetting the play on the eve of the World War II. The film pays direct homage to the musical films of the 1930s and concludes with VE day – lovers reunited and heading home. Michael Radford's *Merchant of Venice* (2004) ends with an extradiagetic scene of longing – Antonio gazes mournfully at the retreating form of Bassanio entering his wedding chamber with his bride, while Shylock stares yearningly into the synagogue as the doors close upon him. The bond they submitted to together has forever barred them from what they love most. Almereyda's *Cymbeline* (2015) treats the eventual return home of a lost "princess" and her brothers.

Even Geoffrey Wright's *Macbeth* (2007), a quasi-pornographic bloodbath set in contemporary Melbourne, has moments of nostalgia. Lady Macbeth grieves for her dead child; Macbeth mourns for her love that died with their child; and, near the conclusion, the film itself remembers its own origins, having its present-day protagonist don a kilt and do a Scottish jig before Dunsinane is invaded. Justin Kurzel's *Macbeth* (2015) posits the same grief over a dead child as the motivating factor for the protagonists' murderous trajectory. Fiennes's film of *Coriolanus* (2011) centres on a protagonist who exiles himself from Rome in order to wreak revenge on his home. The chief confrontation of the play is between the avenging Coriolanus and his mother, Volumnia, who compares attacking his home-city to attacking the womb that bore him. His capitulation to his mother represents a Freudian kind of homesickness.

The Tempest, as a romance, fulfills most of Beecher's criteria. Its main characters, Prospero and Miranda, are in exile from Milan, and

Prospero is magically scheming to effect a return home. The play's two most recent adaptors, Peter Greenaway (*Prospero's Books*, 1991) and Julie Taymor (*The Tempest*, 2009), add to the inherent hearkening to the past. Greenaway makes numerous visual allusions to the great art of the sixteenth and seventeenth centuries, nestling Prospero/Shakespeare among tableaux that recall old masters to suggest that we too can vicariously experience the invention of these great works of art: Shakespeare's play, and De la Tour's, Bronzino's, and Veronese's canvases among others. Taymor, in her introduction to the screenplay of her *Tempest* (2009), explains that this film was influenced by a stage production she directed; she missed the make-believe of the stage, from the sandcastle used in both productions onwards. Shakespeare's play was influenced by accounts of the Virginia Company's shipwreck on Bermuda and their exploration of it. These were just some of the many narratives describing efforts to colonize the New World, and most, not surprisingly, were dominated by details of homesickness. Susan J. Matt summarizes: "In 1585, English settlers made the first of two ill-fated attempts to establish the colony of Roanoke. They lasted only a year and then, according to reports, grew homesick, and imposing on the goodwill of Sir Francis Drake, managed to return to England. An attempt in 1607 to colonize along the Kenebec River in Maine lasted for just a year. A seventeenth century report explained, 'They after a winter stay dreaming to themselves of new hopes at home returned backe with the first occasion' ... Captain John Smith reported that members of his company attempted to commandeer a ship and sail back to England [from Virginia]" (14).

It is not unreasonable to assume that Shakespeare himself must have had firsthand experience of homesickness when he arrived in London from the country, leaving his family and friends back in Stratford-on-Avon. What is more, many of the directors studied here have spent much of their lives away from their native lands. Kenneth Branagh (*Henry V, Much Ado About Nothing, Hamlet, Love's Labour's Lost, As You Like It*) was raised in Belfast but moved to England at the height of the Troubles, when having an Irish accent was like shaking a red flag in front of the proverbial bull. His biographer, Mark White, claims that Branagh grapples with "long-standing Anglo-Irish identity issues that had affected him since the move" (17), as well as a sense of a loss of community (126). Christine Edzard (*As You Like It, The*

Children's Midsummer Night's Dream), with a German-born father and a Polish-born mother, has lived all over the world. Julie Taymor (*Titus, Tempest*) grew up in New York but spent much of her young adulthood living in Sri Lanka, India, France, Japan, and Indonesia. Michael Radford (*The Merchant of Venice*) was born in New Delhi to a British father and Austrian Jewish mother. Michael Hoffman (*A Midsummer Night's Dream*) grew up in Hawaii, went to university in England, and settled in Idaho. Franco Zeffirelli (*Hamlet*) is chiefly an Italian director of opera, but Shakespeare gave him an entrée to English-speaking Hollywood in a way that Verdi and Puccini never would have. Baz Luhrmann (*Romeo + Juliet*), Geoffrey Wright, and Justin Kurzel (*Macbeth*), as Australians, reach a broader audience with Shakespeare's stories than with narratives specific to Australia; witness the far greater success of Luhrmann's *Romeo + Juliet* than his *Australia*. Joss Whedon (*Much Ado About Nothing*), though American, spent three years of his young adulthood in England. Using biographical information to discuss authorial intentions of the playwright and his adaptors may seem old-fashioned, but as Linda Hutcheon argues, "Adaptation teaches that if we cannot talk about the creative process, we cannot fully understand the urge to adapt and therefore perhaps the very process of adaptation" (107).

Shakespeare may have furnished a familiar locus for the uprooted directors – his works, like the brand-name stores and restaurants that are ubiquitous and provide solace for immigrants and travellers – are familiar to everyone, all over the world. Susan J. Matt writes, "Perhaps somewhat surprisingly, immigrants also admit to finding comfort in American chains that were present in their native countries. Because they first became acquainted with these chains in their homelands, they are reminders not of the United States but of Mexico, or India, or wherever they were first encountered" (263). Though it may seem a strange comparison, Shakespeare, first met by many in school, is such a successfully exported product, like McDonald's, that his name is recognizable to most people. The film *Scotland, PA* (2001) and the variety show *MacHomer* (2011) both slyly make this point by substituting the fast-food chain's name with MacBeth, retaining the characteristic arches on the "M." Now more than ever, Shakespeare is not only familiar from school curricula but also from satellite television and the Internet; viewers have access to the same television and film productions of Shakespeare, no matter where they live.

Of course, most of the directors who adapt Shakespeare for the screen are British. Of the nineteen directors I consider here, eleven are British, four American, three Australian, and one Italian. The British are still the most interested in Shakespeare; it is their cultural heritage. Perhaps their interest also suggests a yearning for their great literary and historical past, for the time when their country was the most powerful in the world. As Claire Monk points out, period films, such as the Shakespearean adaptations considered here, "have come to be perceived by many ... as *particularly* 'British'" ("British Heritage-Film Debate," 176). She also notes that "the pleasures of nostalgia" were acknowledged by *Time Out* (a London entertainment magazine) respondents to her Heritage Audience Survey as being the thirteenth priority in their enjoyment of heritage films. Very high on the list of pleasures for her National Trust respondents were looking at period costumes, buildings, and furnishings, and reliving the pleasures of the original novels/plays, all of which feed into a yearning for both a national and personal past (*British Heritage Audiences*, 215).

Nostalgia has been seen as both a negative and positive force. It can be negative, in that it can describe a stagnant state of living in the past, looking backwards instead of forwards. As Alastair Bonnett wryly observes, "Any attempt to take nostalgia seriously, to see it as unavoidable, perhaps even an occasionally creative force, is likely to make us appear discontent with modernity. It rips us from some basic assumptions, not just about progress and change, but what it is to be a happy, optimistic, and 'well-balanced' citizen" (2). It is easy to fall into assumptions that the past was always somehow preferable to the present. This form of the condition idealizes, in the case of Tudor England, the intimacy and simplicity of a pre-Industrial age, or the adventure and excitement of a time of buccaneers, New World exploration, and court conspiracies, while downplaying the filth, disease, poverty, and injustice that also characterized that time. (For a list of recent films and television shows set in this period, see the next chapter.) In the debate about heritage film in the late 1980s and '90s, it was exactly this kind of wistfulness that was seen to characterize period movies, particularly the E.M. Forster adaptations, and films like *Chariots of Fire*. In depicting the past as "an attractively packaged consumer item" (Hewison, 144), these films peddled a skewed image of historical reality. Frederic Jameson comments on postmodernism's reduction of the past to "a vast collection of images" and continues by pinpointing our culture's "fascination with surfaces" (*Postmodernism*, 18). Certainly, looking at Tudor clothes and interiors contributes to the viewer's pleasure when watching some Shakespeare films. No doubt the box-office takings of Justin Kurzel's *Macbeth* (2015) benefited from the popularity of *Game of Thrones* (2011–), both featuring political intrigue, grand castle settings, and medieval costumes and jewellery. However, many Shakespeare adaptations are not set during his chosen period, including Baz Luhrmann's hit, *William Shakespeare's Romeo + Juliet*, which would seem to suggest that the longing is not for images of Shakespeare's temporal settings alone.

Nostalgia can also be a positive force, manifesting itself as a searching the past for lessons that may have been forgotten with the passage of time. Ricardo J. Quinones in *The Renaissance Discovery of Time* could be describing nostalgia's usefulness when he writes about looking back at the completed story of J.F. Kennedy that the "perception of coherence can be fulfilling since it represents an important victory over time. From the turmoil of experience, the flux of continuity, a pattern is perceived, and the lines of a life stand revealed" (363). Christine Sprengler, in *Screening Nostalgia*, summarizes writer Jeffrey St. John's positive analysis: "St. John urged his readers to 'welcome the national nostalgia boom as a long overdue backlash and rebuke to irrational art forms.' His problem was with film, theatre, literature, music and art that foregrounded as its subject 'irrational despair' and manifested an 'antiromantic and antilife' attitude. For him: 'It is not escape from reality the nostalgia lover seeks, but the desire to see the expression of ideas and values which have elevating moral values. What nostalgia offers is a sense that life is not what modern intellectuals and artists tell us it is; it is not a collective sewer in which all are condemned to swim and suffer" (St. John, 1971, qtd in Sprengler, 30). Sprengler contrasts St. John's point of view with the other side of the debate, a debate that grew in importance in the 1980s and '90s. The opposing point of view characterized the condition as "falsifying the past; severing the past from the present; preventing historical continuity; fostering disillusionment with the present; hindering attempts to improve present circumstances; stifling creativity, innovation and progress; commodifying history; and exploiting emotions for profit" (31).

Sprengler argues that the very definition of nostalgia now incorporates the notion of falsifying the past. The two distinct views of the term have tended to become associated with the political right and left respectively – the right yearning for past values, the left suspicious of them. However, as Alastair Bonnett points out, the fact that nostalgia was critically marginalized, especially by left-leaning intellectuals in the past century, now means that it can be rehabilitated as a counter-cultural critique of modernity (11). Sprengler contends that while the possibility of idealizing the past can only be seen as detrimental, this aspect is balanced by its "therapeutic potential. It can help society and the individual cope with change, endure loss, deal with alienation and quell feelings of anxiety and uncertainty" (32). These therapeutic and counter-cultural aspects may account in part for the plethora of Shakespeare films (film critic Lisa Rosman claimed on the website *Signature* that "Shakespearean adaptations are a dime a dozen") made towards the end of the millennium, which many scholars describe as a period of extreme stress. *Shakespeare, Film, Fin de Siecle*, edited by Mark Thornton Burnett and Ramona Wray, posits that millennial angst inspired directors to turn to Shakespeare, particularly as many of his plays were written at the turn of his own century in a similar climate of change. The essay writers characterize the 1990s as another era of familial crisis, social estrangement, and urban blight – issues that are prime contributors to the state of nostalgia. Peter Greenaway explains that this transitional quality was part of his attraction to *The Tempest* as a play for adaptation to the screen, "a play all about beginnings and endings, which makes it perhaps very relevant to the end of the century, the end of the millennium. Miranda is given those words which Huxley used, 'O brave new world'" (Rodgers, 138). *Apocalyptic Shakespeare*, edited by Melissa Croteau and Carolyn Jess-Cooke, also treats the notion that directors of Shakespearean adaptations are channelling their society's anxiety about impending global devastation.

Shakespeare films display both aspects of the term: naïve idealization of the past, or the past used as a kind of escape for the audience for a pleasant couple of hours, and the past looked to for lessons, as Shakespeare's language and insight into human nature are unique and rightly celebrated as such. Of course, history is neither an inexorable path upward towards what is better, nor a lamentable decline. Nostalgia can be a retreat from the now, a failure to engage with it, write about it, film it. On the other hand, artists may see adapting Shakespeare as a way to participate in what is generally perceived as an otherwise unreachable pinnacle of art that no contemporary writer can rival. His work has certainly been more often adapted into other forms than that of any other English writer. As Emma French observes, "He alone of Western culture's literary heavyweights exhibits such polysemic celebrity status" (15).

Roger Manvell in his seminal book *Shakespeare and the Film* in 1971 viewed Shakespeare's achievement as unique: "The great range of Shakespeare's humane understanding, a product of the European Renaissance of which his writings are a part, has substantially helped to create the modern era" (8). Manvell wrote at a time of drought for Shakespearean film. Laurence Olivier and Orson Welles had by then stopped making their Shakespearean films, and Franco Zeffirelli was to take a twenty-two-year hiatus between his *The Taming of the Shrew* (1968) and his *Hamlet* (1990). Yet Manvell's comment has been proven even more prescient by the past two decades. Shakespeare played a substantial role not only in creating modern western culture but also in creating postmodern western culture. As the twentieth century rushed to its close, studios returned to Shakespeare. Between 1989 and 2017, over forty films based on Shakespeare's plays were produced in English for cinema release. Even since the 1980s, then, the number of people able to watch a performance of a Shakespeare play, albeit in adapted form, has exponentially increased.

When artists adopt the art of the past for their use, they reveal more clearly than ever their contemporary perspective. Their attempts to breach the distance between Shakespeare and ourselves in terms of time and culture throw into sharp relief our views of the past and, more significantly, the way we see ourselves. This is, of course, true of both theatre directors and film directors of Shakespeare, but because film is truly a modern art form, and because Shakespeare's plays, with their assumption of Elizabethan and Jacobean stage conventions, must undergo a bigger transformation than a modern theatrical production to reach the audience, Shakespeare on film holds a mirror up to our current nature better than Shakespeare on stage.

Furthermore, Shakespeare plays an iconic role in both popular and elite culture, and so Shakespeare on film is one place where high and low culture meet. Shakespeare has for some time been a means by which, as Alan Sinfield observes, "certain ways of thinking about the world may be promoted and others impeded" (Dollimore and Sinfield, 155). This use of Shakespeare dates back at least as far as Garrick, starting the Shakespeare tourist industry with his Jubilee celebrations in Stratford-on-Avon in 1769, and in Victorian poet Matthew

Arnold's dragooning of Shakespeare to stem the tide of dehumanization set in motion by the Industrial Revolution. Once largely used to signify Anglo high culture, "Shakespeare" may now trigger very diverse associations – in some minds, with the rock band Butt Surfers (Luhrmann's *Romeo + Juliet*), or with Japanese Samurai (*Ran*), or with Maori excursions into filmmaking (*The Maori Merchant of Venice*, 2002), as much as with the bastion of colonial cultural power. Mark Thornton Burnett's *Shakespeare and World Cinema* proves that Shakespeare is a universal commodity.

In the twentieth century, film gave great nourishment to the Shakespeare industry; it was film that, as a relatively new art form, made so many people think again about these four-hundred-year-old dramas. Shakespeare films proliferated in the silent era, starting in 1899 with the flickering images of Beerbohm Tree writhing in agony from fatal poison in *King John*, directed by William Kennedy Laurie-Dickson. In France, then the centre for filmmaking, Sarah Bernhardt's performance of Hamlet dueling with Laertes was captured in 1900, the vivacity of her style preserved for posterity. Jean Mounet-Sully, equally lofty in reputation, enacted Hamlet in the graveyard scene for film at about the same time. These early films were really records of beloved theatrical performances, with little that is now considered truly "filmic" about them. The imaginative French filmmaker George Méliès also attempted a scene from *Hamlet* on screen, as well as playing Shakespeare himself in *Shakespeare Writing Julius Caesar*, both in 1907. Many abridged versions of Shakespeare's plays appeared thereafter in silent films in France, Italy, England, and the United States until about 1914, when World War I and rumours of sound film intervened. Of interest then is Forbes-Robertson's 1913 *Hamlet*, directed by Hepworth, captured on celluloid. Also of note is *Hamlet: The Drama of Vengeance*, in which the prince was played by Asta Nielsen. One of the first "talkies," *The Taming of the Shrew* (1929), featured Mary Pickford and Douglas Fairbanks in the leading roles.

After that, Shakespeare films were produced in a steady trickle, with Laurence Olivier's and Orson Welles's adaptations dominating the 1940s and '50s and Franco Zeffirelli's the 1960s, until the relative drought in the 1970s and '80s, brought about in part by a trend towards gritty urban realism, and by the box-office failure of Roman Polanski's *Macbeth* (1971). When Branagh's 1989 *Henry V* was nominated for best picture at the Academy Awards in 1990, and reaped a tidy profit on a modest production budget, skittish Hollywood moguls started creeping back to Shakespeare as a source of exciting stories, available for free, which could add a lustre of prestige to their studio.

Literary adaptations in general are a safe bet for studios. Janet Wasko in her useful study *How Hollywood Works* asserts, "The prevailing wisdom is that around 50 percent of Hollywood films are adaptations" (16). Desmond and Hawkes elaborate: "The majority of films nominated for Academy Awards in the category of best picture are adaptations ... Most of the all-time top-grossing films are adaptations." They also remark on the "large number of prominent film directors who have made adaptations" (2). Shakespearean adaptations have the advantage of being cheaper than the average major studio film, which costs "$55 million to produce with an extra $27 million to advertise and market" (qtd in Wasko, 3). Of course, as media analyst Harold Vogel has observed, "The lack of access to real numbers in this industry is astounding and it's getting worse" (quoted by Wasko, 5). Furthermore, it is important to keep the appeal of Shakespeare adaptations to studios in perspective. Even after the critical success of *Henry V*, and the huge profit made by *Dead Again*, Branagh still had to package *Peter's Friends* as a companion to *Much Ado About Nothing* to secure financing for the Shakespeare film (Mark White, 130).

Many of the Shakespeare films made in the 1990s had a prior life in the theatre. Branagh's first three Shakespeare films (*Henry V*, 1989; *Much Ado About Nothing*, 1993, *Hamlet*, 1995) were based on productions in which he himself was involved. Loncraine's *Richard III* was based on a very successful National Theatre production. Baz Luhrmann's background in opera is everywhere apparent in his *Romeo + Juliet*. Trevor Nunn (*Twelfth Night*) has made only a few departures from his life in the theatre into the realm of celluloid. Julie Taymor, director of *Titus* (1999) and *The Tempest* (2011), has directed plays and big budget musicals (*The Lion King* and *Spiderman*), as well as several critically acclaimed Shakespeare productions, including *The Tempest*. Ralph Fiennes, director of *Coriolanus*, is a trained Shakespearean actor, with a history with the Royal Shakespeare Company. Zeffirelli has a history of directing revolutionary stage productions of Shakespeare, his 1960 *Romeo and Juliet* at London's National Theatre in particular. Justin Kurzel (*Macbeth*, 2015) worked on a stage production in which his wife played Lady Macbeth. What is interesting about these crossovers from theatre into film is not that they are new – the early days of cinema depended on such cross-fertilization – but that they move from what is perceived as an elitist form (director's theatre) to a populist form (film). Directors' Shakespeare, as many critics before me have noted, assumes the audience's familiarity with the plays, even with their performance history. The Shakespeare theatre directors' goal is just as often innovation as accessibility. Some of this innovativeness is carried over by these directors into their film projects – an aspect of Shakespearean adaptation that separates it from other adaptations.

According to Kenneth Rothwell's invaluable filmography, more than 750 films were based on Shakespeare from the beginning of sound pictures until 1989 when Branagh's *Henry V* opened and changed the immediate future of Shakespeare on screen. With so many films produced, this book needs some firm parameters. It thus encompasses only films from 1989 to the present that start with Shakespeare's script as a basis for their own, rather than films that use Shakespeare's plot, themes, or characters as a point of departure. In the latter category are *10 Things I Hate About You* (a modern analogue for *The Taming of the Shrew*, 1999), *O* (a basketball *Othello*, 2001), *My Own Private Idaho* (a modern fable based on *Henry IV*, 1991), *She's the Man* (a college *Twelfth Night*, 2006), *Warm Bodies* (a zombie *Romeo and Juliet*, 2013), and even *Private Romeo* (2011), in which the play is brought to life in a cadet school; the leads, both young men, fall in love in real life as well. Further, only English-language films are part of my discussion, as my focus is on the way in which English-speaking culture has changed from Shakespeare's era to the present. Generally, I consider in detail only films released in the cinema, because these are the performances that have had the greatest impact on the largest number of people. The exception to this rule is video releases that bear the unmistakable marks of having been influenced by a widely released film and also have been extensively used for educational purposes. For example (see chapter 8), the Channel 4 film of *Twelfth Night* has been undeniably influenced by Trevor Nunn's film, a fact that becomes readily apparent when comparing the text-editing choices. It also was used extensively by British high schools for A-level consideration. I incorporate BBC Television's *As You Like It* into that chapter as well to suggest changes in attitude over the past few decades.

The advantage of a collection of this kind is that it allows a single scholar to try myriad entry points into the films, suggesting to the reader the range of possible approaches to studying Shakespearean adaptation. As Stephen M. Buhler writes of adapting Shakespeare to the screen, "The attempt to mediate between that [four-hundred-year-old] text and either a specialized or mass audience forces filmmakers to confront the nature of film, its relations to viewers, and its relation to cultural norms of art, gender, power, and profit" (3). Like filmmakers, scholars interpreting these films have to examine these aspects too in order to facilitate for their readers an understanding of the way in which these films impact our understanding of Shakespeare, his society, and, most important, perhaps, our own.

In this book, I attempt to avoid "fidelity discourse" – that is, slapping a director on the wrist for his lack of fidelity to Shakespeare's text. Adapting a work without changing it, as Alain Resnais has quipped, is like reheating a meal. However, I do not hesitate to use what is useful about comparisons to the original text. The fact that some adaptations are judged to be better than others often has much to do with the adaptation's success or failure in realizing prized aspects of the source play. Geoffrey Wright's *Macbeth*, for instance, which strips the title character of the introspection Shakespeare gave him, is therefore considerably less emotionally and intellectually engaging than Shakespeare's play. Nunn's *Twelfth Night*, on the other hand, beautifully captures the complex tone and rich themes of Shakespeare's original, despite, or even because of, cuts to the script and rearrangements of the structure.

My evaluative position is that a film of a Shakespeare play should be judged by the same criteria as any other adaptation. Films are lauded for strong dialogue, compelling performances, effective narrative structure, professional production values, engaging pacing, and thematic complexity and/or subtlety. The more of these qualities a film is thought to have, the more praised it will be by critics and discerning viewers. A film's widespread popularity (like that gained by Whedon's *The Avengers*) will garner financial success but does not guarantee its longevity as a text to be reviewed and re-evaluated. There is no such thing as a perfect film, of course; a film may compensate for the lack of one strength by providing an abundance of another. Greenaway's *Prospero's Books*, despite rendering most of its characters mute, is worth studying for its rich visual imagery and thematic suggestions, inspired by Renaissance masters, and its intriguing score.

A compelling performance, in my view, includes the ability to understand and convey the meaning of the script, whether it is written in verse or prose, and to suggest emotional depth. In my opinion, Kenneth Branagh as Iago in Parker's *Othello*, Emma Thompson as Beatrice in Branagh's *Much Ado About Nothing*, and Sam Shepard as the ghost in Almereyda's *Hamlet* are three stellar Shakespearean film performances. In each case, the actors achieve emotional intensity while maintaining the integrity of the verse. There is room for both stylized and naturalistic performances in Shakespeare adaptation; indeed, Baz Luhrmann successfully integrates both kinds in his *Romeo + Juliet*, although some critics have complained about his leads' insensitivity to the rhythms of the verse. In the comedies, a command of comic timing is advantageous. Devoutly to be wished is a sense that the characterization conveyed by the actor fits with the temporal setting of the film (so nothing jarringly modern in a pre-twentieth century setting). The urban, Southern Californian accent that characterizes Leonardo DiCaprio's speaking voice as Romeo thus works perfectly well in a twentieth-century Verona Beach but might seem out of place in a sixteenth-century Verona.

A film's narrative structure, though not necessarily the same as Shakespeare's, should be clear and engaging. One of the flaws of Almereyda's recent *Cymbeline* is that the already unwieldy Shakespearean plot is made even more bewildering by being crammed into the space of ninety minutes. In addition, the updating of the original setting of ancient Britain to contemporary United States is explained away by awkward and slightly cryptic intertitles. Ideally, a film's structure should allow the commentary and parallelism between the main story and subplot (if both are maintained in the adaptation) to be registered by the audience. Trevor Nunn's *Twelfth Night* is particularly successful in this regard. As well, the structure and pacing of the film should provide enough variety – by juxtaposing the serious and the comic, the epic and the personal, the action-packed and the contemplative – to keep the audience engaged. Branagh's *Henry V* reaches a pinnacle of achievement for this, although Branagh cannot claim all the credit as he followed Shakespeare's play fairly closely.

The camera work, editing, costumes, and set should attain a level of professionalism so that at the very least they do not draw attention to themselves as substandard compared to other feature films (given that the budgets for most Shakespeare films are small). Almereyda's *Hamlet* left itself open to criticism because of the use of the Pixel camera, engaged in part as a result of budgetary restrictions. By contrast, Taymor's *Titus*, innovative in its use of set and costumes, and Luhrmann's *Romeo + Juliet*, pioneering in terms of editing and camera work, won aesthetic kudos for these elements (although in the latter case not in all quarters).

Ideally, a film should also boast some complexity of theme and characterization so that it merits the longevity it will, by its very nature as a Shakespeare adaptation, enjoy. Fiennes's *Coriolanus*, despite being based on a very pared-down script, gained complexity of theme for a contemporary audience by its setting, which raised disturbing parallels with recent military events. In short, a Shakespeare adaptation should be able to stand alone as a film, so that anyone stumbling upon it without any knowledge of the play on which it was based will have a fulfilling experience, including, as a bonus, a somewhat more intellectual challenge than with an average movie.

Adaptations are particularly vulnerable to criticism. A very faithful rendition of a Shakespeare play can be criticized as dull or uncreative (the BBC TV series was accused of this), while a freer adaptation, like Baz Luhrmann's *Romeo + Juliet*, can be excoriated for trashing or trivializing the original. The word "original" is fraught, as Shakespeare himself used other people's stories as the basis for most of his plays, often following them quite closely. If film directors and their audiences today are nostalgic for Shakespeare's originality, what exactly does that mean? Complete originality was no more possible for Shakespeare than for his adaptors. Nor are adaptations alone amongst films in being based on a prior text; as Robert Stam points out in his introduction to *Literature and Film*, "Virtually all films, not only adaptations, remakes, and sequels, are mediated through intertextuality and writing ... they are all on some level 'derivative'" (Stam and Raengo, 45).

Stam also writes of "the nostalgic exaltation of the written word as the privileged medium of communication" (6). This exaltation has an elegiac quality precisely because in contemporary western culture the printed word is now seen as threatened by the many alternative forms of communication and entertainment available. Articles in newspapers and journals lamenting widespread addiction to Facebook, iPods, smart phones, and other personal technology proliferate, and make the tacit or explicit assumption that reading would be a better way for people, especially the young, to spend their time. Velma Bourgeois Richmond, in *Shakespeare as Children's Literature*, writes: "The excitement and challenges of the digital world are likely only to increase and much can be said in favor of technological development. However, concurrent with this is a general loss of quiet, thoughtful reading, and a valuing of the humanities" (5). Richmond then cites an article in the *Sunday Telegraph* of 23 April 2006 ("Brush Up Your Shakespeare") that reports that British students can score zero on the Shakespeare section of their English exam and still pass. A questionnaire given to a million primary school students (grades 5 to 8) in North Carolina revealed that those who did not have access to a computer at home scored highest in reading and math assessments (Katie Ash; see also George A. Panichas, and Kenneth Lindblom). Statistics quoted recently in *The Atlantic* claim that the number of non-book readers has tripled since 1978, and one-quarter of Americans had not read a single book in the past year (Weissman). The promotion of reading as an improving leisure activity (which may be part of the problem – people tend to avoid activities that are supposed to be "good for them" rather than "fun") is part of a larger argument, often aired in the media, that young people are not as adept at problem-solving as they used to be (see Stuart Wolpert, John Cassidy, and "The United States Falling Behind"). This is an argument voiced by the older generation in every society from the dawn of literacy, but, sadly, testing suggests that this time it is accurate.

The presupposition that reading is better for us than other forms of entertainment strangely also contributes to the making and financing of Shakespeare films. Studios recognize a prevailing sense in current western society that Shakespeare is good for us. Films are therefore the practical compromise for teachers and parents who may not have access to theatrical performances. The underlying thought is that students will find watching a Shakespeare film, with excellent production values and perhaps a popular star thrown in, far more palatable than reading the play. Filmed Shakespeare is the spoonful of sugar to help the medicine go down. (See websites aimed at teachers of Shakespeare, such as "Shakespeare Uncovered" or "A Teacher's Guide to Websites, Books, and Films.")

A Shakespeare film not only demonstrates a nostalgia for the printed word, or the reading habits of the past, but also exposes a class-conscious yearning for high culture. Film in its infancy was the entertainment of the poor and ignorant, even the illiterate. In contrast to reading, watching a film is often viewed as completely intellectually non-challenging; people speak of "vegging out with a movie" on the weekend. So to overcome the vestige of class or intellectual distaste that still accompanies the watching of a film for some, a studio can pair it with the prestigious name of Shakespeare. Thus, a studio like Warner Brothers, which in the 1930s had the reputation of cranking out fairly low-brow gangster films, makes a "prestige picture" like *A Midsummer Night's Dream* (1935) to raise its status. Although its status has improved, Warner Brothers used the same technique more recently in 1990 with Zeffirelli's *Hamlet*, rated by the International Movie Database as one of the studio's top twenty most popular films of that year along with *Batman*, *Nightmare on Elm Street*, *Gremlins 2*, and *Teenage Mutant Ninja Turtles*.

Adaptors of Shakespeare must decide whether to set their film in the original period of the play or to update it to make it easier for a contemporary audience to follow. Of the twenty-five films considered here, eight are set roughly in the period of the play (medieval/Tudor), five in a more recent past (Victorian/Edwardian), and twelve – the majority – in the twentieth or twenty-first centuries (two during the late 1930s). Plays of a more serious character, and demonstrating attitudes to women or minorities that are no longer thought acceptable, tend to be set in their original period: Branagh's *Henry V* and *Much Ado About Nothing*, Zeffirelli's *Hamlet*, Greenaway's *Prospero's Books*, Taymor's *The Tempest*, Oliver Parker's *Othello*, Radford's *Merchant of Venice*, and Kurzel's *Macbeth*. Victorian and Edwardian settings (Branagh's *Hamlet* and *As You Like It*, Nunn's *Twelfth Night*, Hoffman's and Noble's *Dreams*) are popular because the formal, rhetorical language seems more at home in the past than in the present, but class distinctions shown in Victorian costume and lifestyle are more recognizable to a contemporary audience than Tudor equivalents would be. The eve of World War II, the setting chosen by two directors (Loncraine in *Richard III*, Branagh in *Love's Labour's Lost*), has the advantage of being a familiar past setting, while still allowing the more formal language to seem somewhat plausible. After all, Winston Churchill's rhetoric bears a marked Shakespearean influence. The pre–World War II setting also permits the adaptor to suggest very high stakes, lending an air of importance to his adaptation.

Location is another choice the adaptor must make. Often cost-effectiveness will be the most important factor in the selection of locale. For instance, Luhrmann chose to set his *Romeo + Juliet* in "Verona Beach," really Vera Cruz, Mexico, because it was less expensive to shoot there than in Verona, Italy. This location had a huge impact on the finished product, including a dramatic backdrop of a storm during Mercutio's fatal fight with Tybalt. Similarly, Julie Taymor shot her *Titus* in Croatia, where there is a Roman amphitheatre that resembles the Coliseum. But the recent ethnic war there added resonance to the performances and brought home the themes of the play as the actors were confronted with the consequences of real violence all around them.

Ricardo J. Quinones writes that in the 1590s "a spate of English works appeared with time as a vital concern" (297). Stanley Wells concurs, observing that conjuring yearning reminiscence was characteristic of Shakespeare at a certain period in his working life: "Nostalgic recollection is in part a method of self-examination, an exercise of conscience in the effort to apportion responsibility and, if possible, to exorcize guilt. It is more poetically also an exploration of the effects of the passage of time on people, and it is typical of Shakespeare's technique at this stage in his career [*2 Henry IV*] that the most emotionally subtle and complex passages concerned with this theme are written in prose which is simultaneously funny and touching in a way that, outside Shakespeare, we are most likely to associate with Chekhov. Our sense of the reality of the present is enhanced by recollections of the past" (*Dramatic Life*, 148). Of the films treated in this book, more than half are based on plays written in the very period Wells singles out – roughly 1596 to 1600. Filmmakers seem drawn to the plays in which Shakespeare treats the theme of nostalgia most directly.

My chapters treat a wide variety of subjects. I often adopt Hamlet's method in his soliloquies of moving from the particular to the general; close scrutiny of a specific aspect of a film or several films leads towards wider theories. The first section of the book, "Defining Terms," provides background. In chapter 1, I evaluate existing theories about the proliferation of Shakespearean adaptations to the screen since 1989 and suggest some of my own. I consider the rise of the multiplex, the conservatism of Hollywood, Branagh's box-office success with *Henry V*, and the need on the part of directors for lasting prestige. This chapter also begins to examine which plays have appeared on screen and why. Chapter 2 looks at the prevalence of the conventions of realism in film adaptations of Shakespeare, even adaptations of plays that include much fanciful material, such as *The Tempest* and *A Midsummer Night's Dream*. It provides a brief background on the genre of realism and on the most commonly used filmic strategies. It acknowledges the challenges faced by adaptors; the drive for realism is obviously at odds with the conventions of Elizabethan and Jacobean stages.

The second section, "Remembering Origins," groups together essays that look back to Shakespeare's time for their exploration of recent films. In chapter 3, on opening scenes, I consider the fact that adaptors almost invariably introduce a kind of frame to ease the viewer's entrance into Shakespeare's world and language in a way that is distinct from most other sorts of adaptation. As it is possible for a Shakespeare adaptor to have seen all the previous films based on the chosen play, the concerns around influence are more acute than with adaptations of other published works. Consequently, the pressure to make the play seem new or the interpretation unique is all the heavier; the opening scene trumpets to the audience what is different about this particular adaptation. Chapter 4, "Nostalgia for the Stage in Shakespearean Films," investigates moments in the films in which direct allusions are made to the stage arts. Even today, when the audience for Shakespearean films is so much more film literate than theatre literate, directors still choose to bridge the gap between the two art forms by inserting representations of the stage. In chapter 5, "Death Rituals in Shakespeare, Almereyda, and Luhrmann," I examine two film directors' nostalgia for death rituals in their adaptations. Even though the directors have cut the texts quite freely and reset the plays in contemporary cities, they retain from the original plays much of the religious language and some of the consoling ceremony surrounding death.

The third section, "Disguise, Genre, and Play," looks at what these adaptations owe to genres like the gothic, grotesque art, gender-bending comedy, and the buddy/war movie. Chapter 6, treating Branagh's *Hamlet*, investigates the director's use of setting and imagery to comment on Branagh's gothic sensibilities as a director and then expands this commentary to incorporate Shakespeare's embrace of a kind of gothicism: late medieval *copia* over classical perfection. Chapter 7, "Art and the Grotesque in Julie Taymor's *Titus* and Peter Greenaway's *Pros-*

pero's Books," explores two painterly films that nevertheless revel in the grotesque. Both directors respond to grotesque aspects of the plays because they express our own society's uncomfortable sense that violence and entertainment are inextricably linked. Both directors take refuge from their reality in the visual art of the past, also frequently referenced in their films. Chapter 8 compares approaches to cross-dressing in Trevor Nunn's Pre-Raphaelite *Twelfth Night* and Tim Supple's multicultural Channel 4 adaptation of the same play with BBC's conventional *As You Like It*, Christine Edzard's anti-Thatcherite version, and Branagh's Japanese fantasy. The chapter focuses on the way in which the directors' interpretation of the cross-dressing role comments on a particular moment of recent English history. In chapter 9, "Propaganda and the Other in Branagh's *Henry V* and Fiennes's *Coriolanus*," I address the national-political aspect of nostalgia and the way it connects to adaptation of Shakespeare to the screen. In interviews, both directors reveal anxiety about possible offence to minority groups and demonstrate awareness of their vulnerability to criticism for making films about warrior-heroes. Under the surface of both films lies a yearning for an era when political leaders could, at least temporarily, be viewed without irony as heroes, and when most citizens had a clear sense of home/nation to which they could devote their loyalty. All the chapters in this section focus too on the notion of play or pretend, from the most obvious form, the disguise of the cross-dressed heroine (chapter 8) to the make-believe that is an integral part of the gothic genre (chapter 6), the grotesque (chapter 7), and the carefully created rhetoric and pose of the politician (chapter 9).

The fourth and final section, "Music and Memory," treats the use of song and soundtracks in seven films. Chapter 10, "'Sigh No More Ladies': Shakespeare, Branagh, and Whedon Tackle Issues of Gender and Fidelity in *Much Ado About Nothing*," takes a close look at the preoccupation with female chastity and, more unusually, male fidelity in this play, particularly as reflected in Balthasar's central song. Shakespeare's use of the song and Branagh's and Whedon's different interpretations of it manifest surprising attitudes to sexual double standards. Chapter 11, "'O Mistress Mine': Intercutting in Trevor Nunn's *Twelfth Night*," argues that Nunn's editing technique makes the counterpoint between the main plot and subplot more immediate, reinforcing Shakespeare's themes of gender, identity, and the inexorable march of time. Chapter 12 explores the nostalgic use of music in Hoffman's *A Midsummer Night's Dream* and Branagh's *Love's Labour's Lost*. In both cases, the past is painted in an idealized Merchant-Ivory or musical-theatre style that obfuscates truths about the period settings (nineteenth-century Italy and 1930s Navarre). The soundtracks, based on existing forms, and the pastiche nature of the films' structure, make them perfect examples of postmodernism. Chapter 13 examines the depiction of Ariel's singing body in Greenaway's *Prospero's Books* and Taymor's *Tempest*. Both directors follow cues provided by Shakespeare and exhibit a yearning for the visual art and theatrical productions of the past. This sense, coupled with the underlying guilt regarding the colonial content of the play, contributes to a prevailing melancholy mood in both films. The concluding chapter attempts once again to bring together the many different approaches and films under the overarching theme of nostalgia.

PART ONE

Defining Terms

I

Why Shakespeare Films Now?

Most adaptations of Shakespeare to the screen emerged in the late twentieth and early twenty-first century, a rich period for Shakespearean adaptations, and have chosen to use the conventions of realism. Chapters 1 and 2 in this section, "Defining Terms," put forward theories to explain these developments.

Not since the silent era have so many Shakespeare-related films been produced as in the past three decades. The proliferation of Shakespeare films in the silent era is perfectly explicable: then, cinema and theatre existed in a close economic and aesthetic relationship. The absence of the spoken word meant that filmmakers could churn out films with Shakespeare's exciting plots and characters without worrying about the Elizabethan language alienating their largely immigrant audiences. That set of conditions no longer exists, although as already mentioned, many of the Shakespeare films considered here have of course had a specific pre-life in the theatre. Why, then, are we making so many Shakespeare films now? It is a question that basked in the spotlight of media attention in the mid-1990s, when prominent stories ran in *Time*, *Newsweek*, and the *New Yorker* and in major English-language newspapers (e.g., Philip Jackman, *Globe and Mail*) regarding the sudden boom. None of these stories came up with a thorough set of hypotheses.

Between 1989 and 2016, twenty-five English-language films based closely on Shakespeare's playscripts were released in the cinema – on average, almost one a year. This number does not count films loosely based on Shakespeare, which use excerpts from his original script (e.g., *Looking for Richard*, 1996; *Shakespeare in Love*, 1999), films that use his story but no more than the occasional phrase from his scripts (e.g., *Men of Respect*, 1990 and 1999; *Scotland, PA*, 2001; *Warm Bodies*, 2012), films made in a foreign language, based on the plots and characters of his plays (e.g., *Maqbool*, 2003; *Omkara*, 2006), Shakespeare on television (e.g., BBC's *Shakespeare Retold*, 2005), or Shakespeare for children (e.g., *Shakespeare, The Animated Tales*, 1992). Shakespeare has never been so accessible to the masses and therefore so significant, in English-speaking cultures and globally.

TECHNOLOGICAL ADVANCES

As always with film, technological progress has had a huge impact on its content, aesthetics, and reception. For example, the arrival of sound in 1927 utterly changed the nature of filmmaking, giving birth to significant new genres like the musical film (David Cook, 259). The invention of video was almost as momentous for the direction of film, and certainly very important for the course of literary adaptations, particularly of Shakespeare.

Video and DVD

With the invention of videotape, and the increasing affordability of videocassette recorders in the early 1980s, the experience of watching a film changed radically. There was a shift from viewing films in the cinema to watching them at home. While this phenomenon sounded the death knell for the old cinemas with one screen and huge auditoria, it meant that movies could be viewed regularly by people who previously seldom took advantage of the cinemas – the poor and the housebound. Suddenly, a whole family could watch a film for the cost of admitting one member to the cinema. Teachers who might have been daunted by the paperwork and hassle of organizing a class trip to a cinema could now show whole videos or clips whenever appropriate. DVDs then added commentaries, interviews with cast and crew, and deleted scenes to stimulate the viewers to think about the way the film was constructed (Jess-Cooke, 38).

The availability of videocassettes and later DVDs contributed to renewed studio interest in Shakespeare because of potential sales to schools, universities, and libraries. Institutions invest in Shakespeare films. (A filmed production of a play has more educational relevance than a film version of a novel, which was not originally designed to be performed.) Many teachers and professors started assigning essays on filmed versions of the plays, which was even more of an incentive for educational institutions to purchase copies of the cassette or DVD. Michael Anderegg refers to this trend as early as 1976 in his article, "Shakespeare on Film in the Classroom" (165).

It is no coincidence that Shakespeare began reappearing on screen more often after the invention of video technology. Even an institution with money might have flinched at the cumbersome aspects of film reels, projectors, and screens. Renting films from a company was so expensive that schools had to arrange to team up together and then agree on a date. The film was therefore typically shown only once. Film stocks were often old and unreliable. The film could not easily be stopped to point out salient features. With the advent of videocassette recorders in the mid-1970s, a more convenient method of showing Shakespeare became available. However, the machines were not widely purchased by schools until the 1980s.

During the 1980s, not much in the way of adaptations was available. The BBC Shakespeare (1978–85) and the Hallmark Hall of Fame Shakespeare (1953–70) series were for the most part not likely to entertain Shakespeare novices. The 1990s saw a sudden explosion of Shakespeare adaptations, and today teachers can show students exciting films and even have several versions of the same play to compare. Studios now can rely on residuals from the sale of Shakespeare DVDs to institutions. As Russell Jackson, textual scholar for Branagh's Shakespeare films, points out, "The better part of these profits is often mortgaged in advance to pay for the making of a low-to-middle budget film" (5). In other words, these adaptations might not have been made at all, were it not for the anticipation of sales of videos and DVDs to educational institutions.

Rise of the Multiplex/Cineplex

As Shakespeare-on-screen scholar Samuel Crowl has observed, the rise of the multiplex has been another boon to independent filmmakers. In the past, an art film like a Shakespeare adaptation had to fill a huge cinema. Now, it merely has to fill one of the smaller rooms in the multiplex while the blockbusters in the larger rooms pay for it. This means that the owner of a multiplex might well be willing to show an art film, while the bijou theatre owner of the past would have shied away from the risk. Furthermore, the fact that most cinemas now have multiple screens has actually meant that more films need to be made to fill them – a further boost to the independent filmmaker.

The Internet

The rise of the Internet has also encouraged the production of Shakespeare films by yet again increasing audience exposure to his works. Shakespeare fans, whose hobby was previously only known to their closest friends, now create homepages accessible to any idle surfer. Christy Desmet in her article "Teaching Shakespeare with YouTube" opens with the observation that this platform "supports a lively community devoted to the performance of Shakespeare and Shakespearean adaptations" (65). Most Shakespeare films now boast their own websites, so a surfer tracing, for instance, the career of his or her favourite actor, might be linked up with a Shakespeare site if that actor appeared in an adaptation of a Shakespearean play. Websites like the International Movie Database display comprehensive filmographies, so a teen wanting to learn more about an actress like Julia Stiles, who appeared in the Oscar-nominated *Silver Linings Playbook* (2012), would discover that she has been in three Shakespeare adaptations: Michael Almereyda's *Hamlet*, *10 Things I Hate About You*, and *O*.

There is also, of course, a vast intellectual side to the use of Shakespeare on the Internet. Christie Carson in her essay "Shakespeare Online" acutely observes: "The debate about Shakespeare online has become fascinatingly meta-argumentative. Shakespeare has become in this discussion symbolic of the usefulness of the humanities and of a creative approach to education and to life" (97). Carson also extols the multimedia nature of the Shakespearean explorations on the web.

BETTER TEACHING METHODS

The availability of several versions of a Shakespeare play on video and then DVD changed the way that teachers introduced Shakespeare to their students. Gradually, Shakespeare was less likely to be taught like a novel-writer, a hangover from Edwardian times and the influence of A.C. Bradley (author of *Shakespearean Tragedy*, 1904). Artistic issues like performance, set, costumes, and editing are being increasingly explored in the classroom, and students typically become more engaged, judging by the comments of my undergraduates. Students can now compare two or more adaptations and discuss the decisions made by actors, directors, and crew. Shakespeare is now associated with aspects of life with which they are familiar and in which they are interested: filmmaking and celebrities. There is all the difference in the world between discussing with teenagers the performances of Joseph Fiennes and Leonardo DiCaprio and listening to John Gielgud recite Shakespeare on a scratchy LP. Shakespeare has entered the world of *Entertainment Tonight*, and even *Rolling Stone* magazine (with film soundtracks, for example). Young urbanites can go to Shakespeare camp in the summer and put on a rock and roll version of one of his plays (the Upper Canada Repertory Company, which operates out of Toronto, is an example of this), thanks in part to what Baz Luhrmann did in his *Romeo + Juliet* to revolutionize the way Shakespeare is perceived.

Teachers now have unlimited inspiring tools at their disposal to galvanize students studying Shakespeare. The TEACH act in the United States (2002) allows classroom use of films without the school having to secure any additional licence or permissions. Pedagogical boards now consider the use of film in the classroom standard. For example, Alberta's senior high school English language arts guide has a long section on the use of film in the classroom. Film Education, "a body funded by the British Film Industry to foster understanding and love of film," prepared a schools' pack on Branagh's *Henry V* (Quinn and Kingsley-Smith, 169). The British Film Institute also has educational resources available to teachers, including an expensive online course on film theory to prepare them to introduce film to students fourteen years and older (BFI website). Manga, comic, and children's versions of Shakespeare texts abound. Interactive websites and trivia games are readily available. YouTube videos no longer than ten minutes, easily found on an instructor's laptop, are a simple way to incorporate a clip in the classroom. Teachers around the world are able to share and discuss the same video. Professional troupes can be hired for reasonable fees to workshop plays in schools using an attractive blend of performance and pedagogy (Shakespeare-in-Action and Shakesperience are two such companies in Toronto). Self-contained kits for a group of students to perform the plays either live or with puppets are available at good bookstores for a sensible price (e.g., "Masterpuppet Theatre: The World of Shakespeare"; "The Romeo and Juliet Finger Puppet

Set"). The *New York Times* has produced a pedagogical resource on the Internet for teaching using Shakespeare in the classroom, with prepared lessons. Shakespeare is much more a part of a student's extracurricular world than he was even thirty years ago. He is used in novelty books, like *Shakespeare's Insults*, and in advertising. His heroines have a series of chocolates named after them (Sweet Theatre Chocolates; for example, Miranda Sea Salt Milk Chocolate and Titania Dark Chocolate), and he is quoted or alluded to in rock lyrics. Madonna, Indigo Girls, Dire Straits, Hard Target, Elvis Costello, Bruce Springsteen, Fey, Vox Vermilion, Sting, James Harvest, Hollerado, the Lumineers, Max Webster, Mary Prankster, and Bob Dylan are just a few of the bands and singers to feature lines or references to Shakespeare. Teachers can draw on these popular cultural references to spark their students' interest in Shakespeare.

INCREASING PROFESSIONALIZATION OF THE SHAKESPEARE INDUSTRY

Shakespeare has long been more than just a staple of the English curricula of high schools and universities: he is at the centre of an ever-expanding industry. Numerous academic societies and conferences are organized around his work, including the Shakespeare Association of America, which holds an annual conference; the International Shakespeare Association, which hosts a congress every five years; the British Shakespeare Association, which also organizes conferences and produces a magazine entitled *Teaching Shakespeare*; the Shakespeare Society of America, which collects books and memorabilia related to Shakespeare, among other activities; and the Shakespeare Society of India, which sponsors intercollegiate drama competitions and hosts international seminars. Special courses and summer schools are offered for unconventional students such as the retired, businesspersons wanting to improve their rhetorical or leadership skills, and teachers wanting to enrich their teaching, in addition to the usual classes geared to young people. Examples include summer schools run by the Stratford Festival in Canada, the University of Cambridge, NYU, LAMDA, RADA, Bard on the Beach in Vancouver, the Globe Theatre in London, business leadership training offered by Movers and Shakespeares, Oxford Said Business School, and HEC Management School (Paris). Theatres increasingly offer pre-show lectures and post-show question-and-answer sessions (two local instances include Stratford Festival in Stratford, Ontario, and Soulpepper Theatre in Toronto).

It is not only in the realm of education that the pursuit of Shakespeare has become professionalized. The tourist and cultural industries have honed their use of him. Stratford-on-Avon and Stratford, Ontario, largely depend on Shakespeare for their financial solvency. The marketing of Shakespeare in these towns has been greatly ramped up in recent years. Now, it is not only the shops attached to the theatres that offer Shakespeare paraphernalia – every bookshop and clothing shop has some evidence of the dominant industry. It is possible to dress oneself almost exclusively in clothes that bear the bard's name, face, or the title of one of his works, from baseball cap to socks and even jewellery. One can redo one's bathroom with tiles illustrated with scenes from his plays; decorate one's living room with Shakespearean busts, throws, cushions and posters; check the time with a Shakespeare watch, drink and eat using mugs, plates and utensils that allude to him; and play with one's children using puppets, action figures, and puzzles related to his plays and person. This kind of exposure means that audiences find him more accessible – Shakespeare, like Tommy Hilfiger, is a name on T-shirts and totes. The Shakespeare film creates a further plethora of connected products that contribute to the marketing of the playwright in general as well as the film in particular. Gerard Genette calls the extra material associated with a text "paratextuality" (28). While the paratext of a Shakespeare film will never be as extensive or as lucrative as the paratext of blockbuster productions like the Harry Potter, Twilight, Hunger Games, or Divergent series, it adds to the feasibility of making an independent film. Ginette Vincendeau observes that Peter Greenaway "produced no fewer than three publications to accompany *Prospero's Books*: a companion novel (*Prospero's Creatures*), the film script, and extracts from the apocryphal books featured in the film" (xxiii). These are in addition to Michael Nyman's soundtrack and copies of the film on videocassette and DVD.

OPENING WIDE

It is no coincidence that the Shakespeare films that opened "wide," as they say in Hollywood (Luhrmann's *Romeo + Juliet*, Zeffirelli's *Hamlet*, Branagh's *Much Ado*, and Michael Hoffman's *A Midsummer Night's*

Dream), also fared best at the box office (Crowl, *Cineplex*, 4). Luhrmann's film tops the bill, being shown in just under two thousand theatres at once. Film critic Wheeler Winston Dixon remarks wryly that opening wide is the "'saturation hooking' method of distribution, in which a film is released in thousands of theatres simultaneously for maximum audience penetration, before any negative word of mouth can set in. Everyone gets the chance to participate in the newly released spectacle together, as a pre-constituted group; professional reviewers are thus reduced to the margins of critical discourse, and it is the public's appetite alone that ensures the success or failure of a given film" (129–30).

The benefits of "saturation hooking" were certainly proven true with Luhrmann's *Romeo + Juliet*, which received many hostile reviews but is still used today in classrooms. Joss Whedon's *Much Ado About Nothing*, in contrast, opened on only five screens in the first weekend, and from June to October 2013 had so far only grossed US$4,327,763. It fared much better, however, than Carlei's *Romeo & Juliet* (2013), which opened on 461 screens, yet only made US$520,116 that weekend, not even a full five times what *Much Ado* made in its inaugural weekend on just five screens. By 1 December 2013, Carlei's film had only grossed $US1,161,089 in the United States.

TEENAGED AUDIENCES

The dominance of teenagers in the cinema audience may also, surprisingly, be a contributing factor to the rise of the Shakespeare adaptation. Dixon reports, "It really doesn't matter how much money one spends to produce a hit film. The only overriding question is simply this: *will the finished film appeal to teens?*" (128). This assertion is corroborated by the United Kingdom Film Council's 2015 report, available on its website, which shows that the 15-to-24-year-old age group formed 31 per cent of the cinema audience, the largest proportion. Teenagers might not at first seem the most likely audience for a Shakespeare film, but when you consider that they are the most likely people to be reading and studying the plays, either at school or university, they are worth targeting. It is surely teen audiences that contributed to the greater box-office success of Zeffirelli's *Hamlet*, Branagh's *Much Ado*, Luhrmann's *Romeo + Juliet*, and Michael Hoffman's *A Midsummer Night's Dream* than of the other Shakespeare films based closely on his playscript (as opposed to loose adaptations). Two out of four of these plays are also almost invariably on high-school curricula in English-speaking countries.

The loose adaptations that jettison Shakespeare's language are particularly popular with teens, not merely because they are more accessible but also because they often star teen actors and are reset in a high-school situation. Only Luhrmann's *Romeo + Juliet* (1996 gross, US$46,338,728) outperformed the more popular examples of the loose adaptations, *10 Things I Hate About You* (1999 gross, US$38,176,108), and *She's the Man* (2006 gross, US$33,741,133) (IMDB).

Dixon contends that "genres aren't the crucial audience-producing factor they once were" (128), which may be true of Shakespeare adaptations as a whole. While those very loosely based on tragedies (like *Men of Respect*, based on *Macbeth*, and *O*, based on *Othello*) fared worse at the box office than those based on comedies (like *10 Things I Hate about You*, based on *Taming of the Shrew*, and *She's the Man*, based on *Twelfth Night*), amongst the four top-grossing adaptations based closely on Shakespeare's scripts, two were tragedies (Luhrmann's *Romeo + Juliet* and Zeffirelli's *Hamlet*) and two were comedies (Branagh's *Much Ado* and Hoffman's *A Midsummer Night's Dream*; Hoffman's film at least made a small profit, which for a Shakespeare adaptation is the exception rather than the rule). Radford's *Merchant of Venice*, both tragic and comic, performed quite well worldwide but was so expensive to make ($30 million) that it is still in the red. Once again, so many variables are at work that it is difficult to pin down the reason for success or failure. Certainly Dixon's assertion that "opening wide" is crucial to creating a hit seems borne out by the figures for these four loose adaptations. *She's the Man* grossed $57 million worldwide, and its widest release was 2,631 cinemas. In contrast, *Men of Respect*, which bombed, grossing only $139,155, was released simultaneously in only thirty-two cinemas. Similarly, as stated earlier, Luhrmann's *Romeo + Juliet* was shown in just under two thousand cinemas simultaneously, whereas Nunn's *Twelfth Night*, a box office failure, was shown in only thirty-one. The successful films here considered, both loose and close adaptations of Shakespeare, also generally boast popular and attractive stars: Mel Gibson (*Hamlet*), Keanu Reeves (*Much Ado*), Leonardo DiCaprio and Claire Danes (*Romeo + Juliet*), Christian Bale, who holds cult status on the Internet (*A Midsummer Night's Dream*), Josh Hartnett and Julia Stiles (*O*), Heath Ledger and Julia

Stiles (*10 Things I Hate about You*), and Amanda Bynes, who starred in the popular television series *What I Like about You* (*She's the Man*). The less popular films featured somewhat older leads who were largely unknown to mass international audiences (Imogen Stubbs, who was thirty-five in *Twelfth Night*, John Tuturro, who was thirty in *Men of Respect*).

In addition to wanting to see their own generation dominating the silver screen, teenagers will be drawn to see a film if it has had enough "buzz" generated about it ahead of time, which may explain the success of Luhrmann's *Romeo + Juliet* over any other Shakespeare film. The two leads of the film had garnered a loyal teen following from their respective TV sitcoms, *Growing Pains* (1985–92) and *My So-Called Life* (1994–95) long before the film was released. The advance publicity was no doubt crucial to its popularity. Many movie magazines and newspapers covered the shoot, which had more than the usual number of disasters – among them Montezuma's revenge rampant among cast and crew, and a tornado (Ascher-Walsh, 28). Today, the advance excitement is generated online rather than in magazines. Emma French contends that marketing on websites and DVDs is a decisive factor in a film's box-office takings. Branagh's films in the 1990s did not take advantage of these relatively new modes of marketing in the same way that the teen films mentioned did (65). According to the International Movie Database, the teen adaptation of *The Taming of the Shrew*, *10 Things I Hate About You* (1999), made on a budget of $16 million, grossed over $38 million in the United States, while *Love's Labour's Lost* (2000), made for a budget of $13 million, grossed under $US300,000. The former, of course, is more accessible as it jettisoned Shakespeare's language. It also "opened wide" on 2,271 screens.

Romeo + Juliet fits Dixon's description of the requirements for a teen hit: "You needed an exploitable angle, an aggressive marketing campaign, and stars borrowed from television to make your film a success at the box office. And above all, the film must not partake of the real world, but rather of a construct having nothing to do with contemporary teen reality" (130). Verona Beach, Luhrmann's setting, while it shares characteristics with Miami and Los Angeles, is a fabricated composite. A kitschy version of Catholicism mingled with Shakespeare's poetry plastered on billboards forms the basis for the culture of this fantastical, postmodern city. Emma French, crediting Michael Bristol's *Big Time Shakespeare*, argues that this hybridity is key to a

Shakespeare adaptation's success, citing Luhrmann's film and *Shakespeare in Love* as examples. Films that combine Shakespeare with current trends appeal to a wider audience (16, 35). The showcasing of a star like Gwyneth Paltrow in *Shakespeare in Love* must have sealed its triumph, even before the Academy's seal of approval. Paltrow was much in demand, starring in four other feature films that year (1998).

Shakespeare's familiarity is also key to his appeal for studios in the last two decades. In an age of remakes, exploiting Shakespeare's free scripts makes sense. And, unlike an adaptation of a novel, the dialogue is ready made. Furthermore, if the road to success is to make a film that appeals to teens, retellings seems to work: "The teen movies of the late 1990s are, for the most part, contemporary retellings of films that once starred adults ... Contemporary, narrative-driven audiences want continuity and predictability in their entertainment above all other considerations" (Dixon, 138, 131). Herbert Coursen observes that the teenaged audience now also influences what the older spectators want to see: "Shakespeare, no doubt, is an adjunct of the profound narcissism of America. Since he is 'good,' association with him is also 'good.' Narcissism nowadays, according to Christopher Lasch, involves the imitation of successful behaviour. That means that association with Shakespeare in advertising or teenage 'culture' is inevitable. And since adults, it seems, imitate teenagers, the association filters upwards" (*Translated*, 3–4).

Appeal to teens is not a feature of all Shakespeare adaptations, however, especially those set in the past, such as the Edwardian era and before. These productions share enough characteristics with "period drama" that surveys conducted on that latter genre are somewhat useful. The Cinema and Video Industry Advertising Report (CAVIAR) from the first half of the 1990s, a dense era for Shakespeare film production, reveals that the audience for period dramas tended to be predominantly middle class, female, and over 45 years of age. Viewers aged 25–34 formed the second-largest group (Monk, *Heritage Film Audiences*, 49).

TRENDS IN FILMMAKING:
NOSTALGIC RELIANCE ON FAMILIAR STORIES

In the past twenty years, Hollywood has shown itself to be very conservative in its choice of scripts. As Janet Wasko in *How Hollywood Works* observes, "There are economic factors that contribute to this ongoing reliance on recycled ideas, already-proven stories and movie remakes and sequels" (16). Stars are so expensive to hire that most studios crave scripts that have already been tested and proven popular. To take only a few examples, *Willie Wonka and the Chocolate Factory* (1971), *Charlie and the Chocolate Factory* (2005), *Bewitched* (TV, 1964; film, 2005), and *Mamma Mia* (music, 1972–84; stage show, 1999, film, 2008) all target families. Baby-boomer grandparents and Generation X parents, feeling a yearning for their youth, are delighted to share the entertainment of the past with their own grandchildren and children. The children are willing to go along, not only because these scripts are new to them but because they are acted by the current stars. Shakespeare plays boast similar advantages. Parents may remember with some nostalgia the first production of Shakespeare they attended, whether in the theatre or the cinema. They believe they are helping to cultivate and educate their children by encouraging them to attend the contemporary equivalent: "93% of Americans believe that the arts (including theatre) are essential to a complete education" ("Effects of Theatre Education"). Branagh jokes about parents' aspirational motives for seeing Shakespeare adaptations, justifying his inclusion of the flashback showing Ophelia and Hamlet having sex by saying that if "he were a thirteen year old who'd been dragged to a bloody four-hour *Hamlet*, he'd be very grateful for an occasional nude scene" (Andrews, 62). This quotation acknowledges the two reasons people generally see a Shakespeare film – education/culture (parents think it is improving for their children) and entertainment (the nude scene). Claire Monk reports "that there are concrete connections between the heritage film, formal education, and notions of what it is to be 'educated'" (*Heritage Film Audiences*, 63). This statement must be even truer of an adaptation of a play like *Hamlet*, generally viewed as one of the most important literary works. If, in addition to nude scenes, a Shakespeare adaptation includes trendy actors like Amy Acker and Alexis Denisof, is directed by a blockbuster director (Whedon's *Much Ado About Nothing*), and features the hippest bands on the soundtrack, young viewers are unlikely to express any objections.

Shakespeare films are produced knowing that many members of the audience will have some acquaintance with the script, which can have both positive and negative sides. Reviewers and scholars may well go to the film with high expectations. The general audience, however, may be attracted by the fact that the story is vaguely familiar to them, or that they feel they should have more of an acquaintance with Shakespeare than they do, especially given, as scholar Douglas Lanier puts it, "the currently hip" image of Shakespeare (*Shakespeare and Modern Popular Culture*, 3). Alternatively, they could be turned off completely by remembering some tedious or baffling experience with Shakespeare at school.

Acknowledging the positive connections, the marketing of Shakespeare film often emphasizes Shakespeare as much as a thrilling movie. The full titles of Luhrmann's, Branagh's, and Hoffman's films *William Shakespeare's Romeo + Juliet*, *William Shakespeare's Hamlet*, and *William Shakespeare's A Midsummer Night's Dream*, which all premiered in the late 1990s, are obvious examples. Michael Andregg observes that this kind of branding is true of literary adaptations in general. Unlike other adaptations, the literary adaptation "wants to be seen as an adaptation or, even better, as the text itself" (3). Andrew Higson also writes of "the desire to establish the adaptation ... as an authentic reproduction of the original" (*Waving*, 27). Coppola's *Bram Stoker's Dracula* (1992) and Branagh's *Mary Shelley's Frankenstein* (1994) are other instances of this phenomenon. By the late 1990s and into the new millennium, however, Shakespeare's name had apparently lost star status: it is no longer highlighted in the title, trailers, or posters for the films (French, 32). The posters for *Coriolanus* (2011) and *Tempest* (2011) reserve mention of Shakespeare for the fine print at the bottom. Joss Whedon's marketing team were braver in the tagline under the title of his *Much Ado About Nothing* (2012): "Shakespeare knew how to throw a party." Even they, however, do not refer to Shakespeare in the trailer. Whedon's film also has the advantage of a director/writer and actors known for their recent television work in such successful shows as *Angel* (1999–2004), *Firefly* (2002–3), *Buffy the Vampire Slayer* (2004), and the blockbuster movie *The Avengers* (2012) and its sequel, *Avengers: Age of Ultron* (2015).

Michael Almereyda may be turning the tide back towards acknowledging Shakespeare. His two-minute official trailer ends with the words "this spring ... experience a bold new vision ... the undiscovered masterpiece ... by William Shakespeare ... Cymbeline ... written and directed for the screen by Michael Almereyda." The poster, however, lets the *Hollywood Reporter* provide its tagline: "Mashup of *Sons of Anarchy* with *Game of Thrones*." *Macbeth* (2015), directed by Justin Kurzel, acknowledges Shakespeare neither in the trailer nor in the posters. Perhaps it was thought that in the case of this very famous play, the author was understood. The aesthetic of one of the posters is very pared down – just a close-up of Michael Fassbender's face, painted with war stripes, looking very sinister, with his name, the title of the film, and the words: "From the Academy Award winning producers of *The King's Speech*." This same phrase appears prominently in the trailer. Clearly, the chief selling features of the film are seen to be the leading actor and the association with another British film that won best picture at the Oscars. The alternate poster for English-speaking viewers replaces Fassbender with Marion Cotillard, who plays Lady Macbeth. The text is the same. Cotillard herself won best actress at the Academy Awards for her portrayal of Edith Piaf, so both posters emphasize the prestige factor.

Variety magazine claimed that "studios have found that ... you can't go wrong" when you adapt the works of William Shakespeare and Jane Austen (Thompson, 1). The author of the article may have been generous to Shakespeare. When *The Merchant of Venice* and *Pride and Prejudice* both premiered in 2005, the Austen adaptation grossed $121 million worldwide, while the Shakespeare adaptation brought in a modest $21 million. Of course, the major selling points of these films are not only Shakespeare's and Austen's statuses but also that of the actors, and the lavishness of the production. Keira Knightley, who played Lizzie Bennett, was a hot young star famous for her role in the hugely popular *Pirates of the Caribbean* series (2003–). Al Pacino, who plays Shylock, was a star from the 1970s, and Joseph Fiennes (Bassanio) an art-house actor. Radford's choice for Portia, Lynn Collins, was a complete unknown. Add to these variables the fact that the widest release for *Pride and Prejudice* was 1,335 theatres, while for *Merchant* it was 107, and it becomes clear that the films' fates were sealed before they even opened.

In addition to the mainstream appeal of headlining actors and extravagant production values, Shakespeare films are marketed, as one might expect, to the intellectual crowd. Many adaptations using Shakespeare's dialogue in recent years have had a scholar of some kind as part of their crew. Branagh has availed himself of Russell Jackson's expertise for all his Shakespeare adaptations. Michael Almereyda only consented to provide a DVD commentary for *Cymbeline* on the condition that Anthony Holden would speak with him. As Andregg writes, "Although this scholarly presence, in some instances, may be little more than window dressing, the point is that the studios and filmmakers think this window dressing is necessary or, at the least, desirable" (11).

KENNETH BRANAGH'S TRAILBLAZING *HENRY V*

As suggested earlier, Branagh can also be largely credited for studios' willingness to return to Shakespeare by showing that an award-winning and relatively popular film based on a Shakespeare play could be made for a modest budget. His *Henry V* was nominated for best picture at the 1990 Academy Awards and garnered the Oscar for best costume design. It also won the BAFTA for best direction and the Chicago Film Critics award for best foreign film, among numerous other awards and nominations. The film was made for $9 million, and grossed $10 million in the United States alone. It also managed to achieve all this without using any headlining stars. In fact, its popularity in Britain reflected the impression made by Branagh's touring Renaissance Theatre Company: the film did better in the towns in which the company had recently played (Mark White, 96). Its success encouraged investors to turn back to Shakespeare. Zeffirelli's *Hamlet* (1990) starring Mel Gibson, and grossing almost $21 million in the United States, reinforced the trend. In the same year, *Men of Respect*, a loose adaptation of *Macbeth*, also premiered. In 1991, Greenaway brought out his *Prospero's Books*, based on *The Tempest*. Christine Edzard then followed with her Thatcher-era *As You Like It* in 1992. Branagh's 1993 *Much Ado About Nothing* was a consummate financial success. Made for $8 million, it grossed $22.5 million in the United States and more than £4 million in Britain. This time Branagh had leavened his British cast with American stars: Denzel Washington, Robert Sean Leonard, Michael Keaton, and – perhaps most enticing to the young audience – Keanu Reeves. At this juncture, studios had the confidence to fund Parker's *Othello* (1995). In fact, Branagh's involvement in Parker's *Othello* was what secured its funding; the director remarked that Branagh was "instrumental in raising the money" (Mark White, 191). Branagh's inclusion gave the project instant credibility as a Shakespearean adaptation. When he agreed to play Iago, Parker was able to recruit Laurence Fishburne to take on the title role. Luhrmann's *Romeo + Juliet* (1996) and John Madden's *Shakespeare in Love* (1998) followed, the latter one of only four romantic comedies in film history ever to snag the Best Picture Oscar (Crowl, *Cineplex*, 224).

NOSTALGIA

Plots, Themes, and Characterization

The cliché used to explain the enduring interest in Shakespeare is that his plays treat universal themes like love, revenge, ambition, and jealousy relevant in any age and place. This premise is, I think, unsatisfying, because surely most works of literature treat these themes. Shakespeare's contemporaries Francis Beaumont and John Fletcher, who for a decade were more popular than he, certainly explored all these tropes, yet we do not turn their plays into films, ballets, sculptures, paintings, cartoons, and symphonies. On the contrary, outside of academe, we leave them severely alone.

The other cliché is that Shakespeare is eternal because of his three-dimensional characters. This for me is a more credible explanation. John Barton, long-time artistic director of the Royal Shakespeare Company, observes in his book *Playing Shakespeare*, "I think that [Shakespeare] is the unconscious inventor both of characterisation in depth and of naturalistic speech. There's not much of it in the theatre before him" (13). Barton illustrates this point with examples from the work of Marlowe, Kyd, and Lyly (13–14). This aspect of Shakespeare's talent does present all kinds of practical advantages to a film producer. The plays are star vehicles in which a top-billing actor might be willing to take a pay cut just to have the honour of enacting a famous and challenging role. A Shakespeare film foregrounds the performances of the star, especially in the tragedies and histories like *Othello* or *Richard III* that are dominated by the eponymous hero. Thus it is no coincidence that in the renaissance of the 1990s of Shakespeare on screen, star power once again dominated Hollywood. If a studio could get the likes of Mel Gibson or Al Pacino to play the leading role, cold feet might be warmed. Of course, catering to stars is no new phenomenon; Shakespeare had Richard Burbage in mind when he wrote many of his great parts. Many of Shakespeare's plays are about being a star – a king, a prince, a general – and how the individual fares under the pressures of the job. This theme fits with the preoccupations of the Nineties and "Noughties" with power and celebrity and the way they are used. One only has to think of the number of films about national leaders and film stars to make the connection: *Air Force One* (1997), *Celebrity* (1998), *Notting Hill* (1999), *The Queen* (2008), *Frost vs. Nixon* (2009), *The Iron Lady* (2011), and so on. Consider also the number of pop songs that treat the theme of celebrity (e.g., "Money for Nothing" by Dire Straits; "I Wanna Be a Movie Star" by Nickelback, "I'm Just a Troublemaker" by Wheezer, "Don't Let Me Get Me" by Pink). Neither is Shakespeare alone among greater and lesser writers in focusing on one charismatic character. Tolstoy's *Anna Karenina*, also recently made into a film (2012), does just that, as does Mario Puzo's *The Godfather* (1972, 1974, 1990).

Language/Poetry

What is it that motivates directors to adapt a Shakespeare play, maintaining his dialogue, even though it usually jars with their chosen setting (only six out of twenty-five of the feature films using Shakespeare's script are set in the time selected by Shakespeare) when they could have commissioned a similar story in contemporary English? Many take this easier route; witness *O*, *10 Things I Hate about You*, *Men of Respect*, *She's the Man*, and *Warm Bodies*. These films pay homage to Shakespeare's plot, structure, and characters but leave his language behind, apart from occasional quotations. The directors considered here maintain the language.

The commonplace explanation is that it is Shakespeare's poetry, the words he uses to express his themes, that makes him immortal. This explanation has some merit. Shakespeare was trained in rhetoric as no modern playwright or screenwriter is. At the same time, his language is less alienating than that of his contemporaries, who were similarly schooled. The several-page-long monologues Christopher Marlowe gives to Tamburlaine, for instance, could never work in film. The intense topicality of some of Ben Jonson's work, treating issues like the humours or Puritanism in some detail, date his plays as well. Shakespeare's plays are sprinkled with topical allusions but these are never at their heart and are easily excised. As Crowl puts it, "What opens them [the plays] up for endless reinterpretation yet makes them recognizably Shakespearean is the way they circulate around core myths and ideas in a vibrant metaphoric language that opens up rather than closes up" (*Cineplex*, 220–1). Shakespeare's immense verbal flexibility is part of the reason for his popularity. His language is also cited as an aid to actors. Sheila Hancock enthuses, "I found that if I let it flow, just happen, it [his language] seemed the most natural thing in the world. And what's more the language was so potent that I felt I had to make less effort than I'd ever had to make before" (qtd in Barton, 15).

Nostalgia too may be at the root of the appeal of Shakespeare's language. We like to spend a few hours in a world in which people had the leisure to construct elegant speeches and to listen to them with pleasure and without impatience (and a time when "R U going 2?" would not be an acceptable invitation to a dance). Peter Greenaway explains that this is partly why three of his films are set in Shakespeare's period: "Since I employ a cinema of metaphor, of fable, of symbolism, I have more room when I distance myself from the contemporary, from the mimetic quality of surrounding reality. My dialogue is intentionally declamatory, artificial – it has nothing to do with conversation. I feel more comfortable with the literature from the period starting with Shakespeare and concluding with the theatre of the Restoration, which facilitates tirade, word play, enigmas, allegory" (Ciment, "Interview," 154).

In other words, Greenaway yearns for a heightened language with immense possibilities for complex layers of meaning. The "realistic" dialogue of most contemporary films seems impoverished to him. Several reviewers during the mid 1990s, the height of the renaissance in Shakespearean film adaptation, explained the trend using the same motivation. As Peter Howell, film critic of the *Toronto Star*, observed, "The more English has gone global, the more it has been stripped of its nuances. Most Hollywood blockbusters consist of little more than an endless series of one-liners, separating the big special effects. The major studios want their movies to play everywhere with the least amount of dubbing and subtitles. A car crash is the same in any language ... Which is all the more reason for native English speakers to rejoice at the lyricism of Tom Stoppard's screenplay for *Shakespeare in Love*. Stoppard isn't ashamed to quote from Shakespeare at length, and to use constructions that delight the ear." Kenneth Rothwell concurs, pointing out in his *Cineaste* review that *Shakespeare in Love* "nostalgically yearns for the transcendent power of words to represent human emotion."

The Grand Passions

Maurice Charney in *All of Shakespeare* writes of Shakespeare's *Antony and Cleopatra*, "We glory in the grand passions and the poetic speeches of the protagonists" (294). Directors often comment on the emotions in Shakespeare's plays as being more intense and requiring more intensity from actors than do other plays. Oliver Parker, director of *Othello*, observes, "The passions are tidal, deep and uncontrollable as the ocean" ("Shakespeare in the Cinema," 51). Actress Lisa Harrow, quoting Barton, affirms this: "You said that the emotion in Shakespeare has to be bigger in order to actually create those words. That was a terrific note, because the moment I actually felt something more intense and bigger and then had to say those particular words, I found that they did fit in with what I was feeling. And it was real" (Barton, 15). Sensational news items of cuckolded husbands murdering their unfaithful wives prove that we still have the extreme emotions expressed by Shakespeare's characters but are generally without the soaring language to voice them. Fidelity in love, a major theme in so many of Shakespeare's plays, is, as Quinones observes, "a means of continuity. In its renewing and creative energies it represents a triumph over time" (366). Thus, when Shakespeare's characters look back nostalgically to the time when the beloved was assumed faithful, the audience members' searing memories are given eloquent music.

His Originality

In their use of Shakespeare, directors also expose their nostalgia for the notion of originality. So much of postmodern art is a composite of something from the past, a patchwork quilt of allusions to older works, at best an ironic take on what has gone before. Shakespeare's achievement, which is always seen as unique, therefore seems even more desirable – a capacity for original thought and expression, for true innovation, that we feel we have lost, inundated as we are by information. Also, the fact that Shakespeare, like most writers today, started with old stories, is reassuring. He managed to make old stories fresh, give them his inimitable twist – so what is stopping today's artists from doing the same? Even when he recycles elements from his older plays, as with the plot of *Cymbeline*, it is seen (perhaps solipsistically) as speaking to our time. Film critic Lisa Rosman, assessing Almereyda's film of the play, remarks: "Even the onslaught of Shakespearean self-references doesn't hurt; what could be more culturally relevant than 'meta' these days?" (*Signature*).

Of course, the notion of "originality," a slippery term, is not something that Shakespeare would have understood or prized as we do. At school, Shakespeare was taught chiefly to imitate the Classical masters, and the closest imitation would have been the most highly rewarded. As a playwright, he shamelessly stole from his sources. If he were writing now, he might well be accused of plagiarism, a word not used until 1598. It was the Romantics who hailed Shakespeare as a true original, a natural genius, and their influence prevails. What is closer to the truth is not that we admire Shakespeare because his plots were original but that we credit him with original plots because we admire him. However, even though most of his plots were derived from earlier sources, this does not diminish his innovations in other creative areas of composing a play. Barton (above) credits him with inventing complex characters and naturalistic dialogue. Shakespeare is also justly famous as an inventor of words. Furthermore, Emrys Jones has written eloquently on Shakespeare's pioneering ways with scenic form. Shakespeare's work is, then, remarkably original.

Shakespeare's Time:
Escape from the Everyday

If spectators watch films to escape from the quotidian – and the enormous popularity of film series like Harry Potter (2001–11), Twilight (2008–12), Hunger Games (2012–15), and Divergent (2014) suggests they do – then Shakespeare also fits the bill. Wheeler Winston Dixon, in his essay "Teen Films in the 1990s," writes, "Teens ... in the 1990s, want escapism without risk, and when it gets too close [to their reality] they lose interest. Hyper reality is not the issue here; the key is unreality, unrelenting and unremitting. The movie viewer, ensconced in her/his seat in the darkness, seeks above all to avoid reality, to put off for as long as possible the return to normalcy" (Dixon, 131).

Shakespeare's plays are filled with the extraordinary: witches, ghosts, fairies, gods, prophecies. Directors do not have to concern themselves with plausibility to the extent that would be necessary with a modern script, as the audience knows these plays were written long ago. Again, the appeal of Shakespeare is a nostalgic one; the supernatural aspects of his dramas remind us of the fairytales of our childhood and the fantasy novels of our youth.

In addition to our yearning for the fantastic is our longing for Shakespeare's time, or rather, for a popular, idealized image of it: "Merrie Olde Englande," the Golden Age of Good Queen Bess, when men were brave swashbucklers like Sir Francis Drake and Sir Walter Raleigh, women were decorative in ruffs and powder, speech was eloquent, visual art was realistic, dramatic, and easy to understand, and politics was rife with exciting conspiracies and assassination plots. The English Renaissance is probably the most popular period of history in contemporary western culture. Witness television series like *The Tudors* (2007–10), *The Other Boleyn Girl* (2003), *Elizabeth I* (2005), and *Wolf Hall* (2015) and the films *Elizabeth* (1998), *Elizabeth: The Golden Age* (2007), *The Other Boleyn Girl* (2008). Our desire to escape the mundane into what we view (erroneously) as a more fascinating, turbulent time is partly what inspired the Shakespeare revival in film. Almereyda, commenting on the DVD of his adaptation of *Cymbeline*, expresses his sense that "the American Empire is fatigued and confused" and contrasts this with the time in which Shakespeare wrote the play, when James was newly acceded to the throne and Great Britain was born.

In *Shakespeare, Film, Fin de Siecle*, editors Mark Thornton Burnett and Ramona Wray observe that "recent Shakespearean films are key instruments with which Western culture confronts the anxieties upon the transition from one century to another" (book cover). They cite as examples of *fin de siècle* concerns the disintegration of the family, social alienation, multiculturalism, urban blight, the impact of technology, and the threat of environmental Armageddon. Some of these themes occur in Shakespeare's plays, and those most popular with filmmakers do seem to come from the last decade of the sixteenth century, Shakespeare's own *fin de siècle*. Of course, many of these issues are common to the arts throughout history: it is conflict, whether domestic, religious, or political, that captures a spectator's or reader's attention. What does Victorian fiction confront if not the impact of technology on society? Plays as far back as *Oedipus Rex* examine the family in crisis and the effect of strangers on a community.

His Lasting Greatness and Prestige

Linda Hutcheon argues persuasively that "adapters' deeply personal as well as culturally and historically conditioned reason for selecting a certain work to adapt ... should be considered seriously by adaptation theory, even if this means rethinking the role of intentionality" (95). Studios, directors, and actors are all susceptible to the kind of nostalgia I have described Shakespeare as representing. It is their yearning for his poetry, characters, originality, plot, time, and themes that inspires them to take risks and to accept less or no pay to produce or participate in a Shakespeare film. Michael Almereyda, in his DVD commentary on *Cymbeline*, praises Shakespeare for "pre-inventing psychology." But in participating in a Shakespeare play, an adaptation is also a recognition of, and longing for, a label of greatness that only generations of approbation can bestow. It imprints a seal of significance on a director or actor: now they have accomplished something weighty, something important. In *Kenneth Branagh*, Mark White writes, "In *Chasing the Light*, a documentary on the making of *Much Ado About Nothing*, the American actors emphasised, in explaining their interest in the project, both their desire for an artistic challenge and their respect for Branagh. That these Hollywood stars were willing to forsake the astronomical salaries they could usually command for the pittance they would receive for *Much Ado* speaks volumes ... about Shakespeare's enduring appeal to actors of any stripe" (147). Almereyda, in an interview about *Cymbeline* (2015), enthuses: "I am very grateful to actors who will work for low budgets because that shows true commitment. So everyone who was involved in this movie was working because they wanted to collaborate with William Shakespeare" (Emily Rome). A contemporary script has yet to pass the test of time and will likely prove to be ephemeral. Shakespeare has already endured for four hundred years; he is regularly performed in theatres and is on school and university curricula. These directors' adaptations and actors' performances are guaranteed to be shown for longer than films not based on Shakespeare, regardless of their quality.

Shakespeare adaptations, like other heritage films, are also exportable. Emphasis on lavish mise en scène, married to Shakespeare's name, means that foreign markets may take an interest in these films. Often directors add to possible foreign appeal by casting a continental actor in a prominent role: Greenaway cast Isabelle Pasco as Miranda in *Prospero's Books,* Parker selected Irene Jacob as his Desdemona, and Justin Kurzel choose Marion Cotillard for his Lady Macbeth. Inversely, "for non-English speaking stars, heritage ... is key to exportability" (Vincendeau, xxiii). In other words, their audience exposure will be greater with an English heritage film than with a film of another sort made in their own country. Every artist aims for genius – adapting Shakespeare guarantees a brush with genius for the duration of the shooting schedule. Genius is something that few people can claim, and thus the nostalgia for it is closely related to what Plato terms *pothos,* the yearning for what cannot be attained (Illbruck, 140). Whether consciously or not, these filmmakers and actors have a longing to inhabit something as lasting as a Shakespeare play. The nostalgia for Shakespeare displayed by audience members who see the films, however, is likely of a different kind from that experienced by audiences in the 1940s and '50s. Those who went then to see Olivier's films and, to a lesser extent, those of Orson Welles, probably believed they were participating in something inherently respectable and cultivated, British and upper crust. Many spectators now, associating Shakespeare with a more bohemian notion of the artist, see him as a champion of a more subversive kind of culture – he is the bisexual poet who peopled his comedies with cross-dressers and had his mad King Lear deliver an excoriating sermon on the injustices of his hierarchical society (4.6).

Some scholars – among them Gary Taylor, Jonathan Bate, Barbara Hodgdon, and Jonathan Dollimore – view Shakespeare's pre-eminence in our society as at least partly a result of centuries of colonial brainwashing, the success of British cultural propaganda. Bate sees the English defeat of the Spanish Armada as the first step in Shakespeare's preservation. He claims that Lope de Vega, his prolific Spanish contemporary, would hold his place on the cultural pedestal if Spain had won that battle (*Genius of Shakespeare,* 340). Taylor goes further, calling Shakespeare "one of Britain's most reliable commodities in the international cultural marketplace." He writes, "Why do theatre companies in former British colonies perform Shakespeare? They do so because English is the language of their governing classes, and by continually re-performing his works they assert their connection to a cultural legacy that makes them feel superior to other people. Why do theatre companies in Japan and Germany and Brazil perform Shakespeare? They do so in order to demonstrate that they, too, can appropriate the flagship commodity of the world's most powerful culture ... They want to increase their own cultural capital by insuring that consumers associate their brand-name with 'Shakespeare'" (*Guardian*, 4).

Taylor's claims may be partially true. Part of the allure of Shakespeare is his prestige-lending property. However, we should not be wholly seduced by this notion of Shakespeare as a successful product. Most Shakespeare films do not break even. Most Shakespeare theatres and festivals teeter on the brink of bankruptcy, but they keep engaging with Shakespeare, despite the threat of penury. They do so because, as contemporary African-American writer Maya Angelou claims, he speaks to many artists more than any other writer (Prior, 1). Alyque Padamsee, an established director in Mumbai, mounted a production of *Romeo and Juliet* in 2002 because, as he said, "It's so real, we aren't talking about what happened in Verona centuries ago – it happens today, everywhere." He added that he did not anticipate making money from the production; he was producing Shakespeare because he wanted to be in love with theatre again (Haldipur, 1). It has become old-fashioned to admit that an extraordinary artist can speak to us over the centuries – yet, so far, no one wastes time discrediting Mozart as part of an Austro-German plot for cultural hegemony.

CONCLUSION

Despite the adoption of Shakespeare by the young and the hip, it is still tends to be the smaller, independent producers and distributors like Miramax, Fine Line, and Castle Rock and not the major ones in Hollywood that invest in Shakespearean adaptations today. Shakespeare is more popular as a film source than he was in the 1970s and '80s, but he is not blockbuster material.

The future of Shakespearean adaptation into film depends very much on whether the films already made are deemed financially, and to a lesser extent critically, successful by these studios. The financial success of Shakespearean films in the past twenty years has varied hugely. The reasons for this discrepancy are difficult to pinpoint categorically, as so many variables are at work. How much does the relative realism of a project affect its box-office draw? Luhrmann's *Romeo + Juliet* made a remarkable profit for a Shakespearean adaptation, shot for approximately $14.5 million and grossing $135 million worldwide. Loncraine's *Richard III* did not make a profit, grossing US$2.6

million with a shooting budget of £6 million, but even that starts looking respectable compared to the loss suffered by the producers of Nunn's *Twelfth Night*, which grossed only $552,000. Branagh's *As You Like It* has grossed only $443,000 to date also. In contrast, Hoffman's *A Midsummer Night's Dream* has made a fair profit, grossing over $16 million while being made for $2 million.

What can explain this disparity in numbers? My theory is twofold. Firstly, success is partly a question of demographics. The age group that is most likely to see a film in the theatre is 14–30 (with teens still the most important subgroup). The two most profitable feature films using Shakespeare's language, Luhrmann's *Romeo + Juliet* and Zeffirelli's *Hamlet*, featured stars well known to that age span. The directors in each case cast actors who were of the moment when the film premiered. (Even more than Danes and DiCaprio, Gibson was hugely popular, having the year before, 1989, headlined *Lethal Weapon 2*, a blockbuster hit.) The teen movie *Clueless* (1995) makes reference to Gibson's role as Hamlet, obviously trusting it will be an accessible allusion for teens. This is a testament to the fact that Zeffirelli succeeded in his aim to appeal to a young audience (Matheson, 540). Nunn in *Twelfth Night* and Branagh in *Love's Labour's Lost* and *As You Like It* used mostly British actors (with the exception of Kevin Kline in the latter, unfortunately something of a screen has-been now) not known to American film audiences. Parker's *Othello*, which also lost money, made for $11 million and grossing only $2.1 million, still did better than these others because Laurence Fishburne, who played Othello, was recognizable to American audiences (from *What's Love Got to Do with It*, 1993, in which he played another husband who laid violent hands on his wife). In addition, the marketing contributed to box office as it took advantage of the recent O.J. Simpson trial, drawing parallels that made the film seem contemporary.

Secondly, Zeffirelli and Luhrmann both made films of extremely well-known and loved Shakespeare plays. Both feature extreme action and lots of sword-play. Branagh with *As You Like It* and *Love's Labour's Lost* and Nunn with *Twelfth Night* produced plays less frequently taught in North American schools, with dialogue-heavy rather than plot-driven narratives. In fact, Nunn in his preface to his screenplay wryly summarizes the advice given to him when he was shopping his script around: "All in all, then, that seemed to be quite a promising beginning – don't call it *Twelfth Night*, and don't say it is by Shakespeare" (ii). Nunn's *Twelfth Night* exemplifies the opposite extreme of Shakespearean film adaptation to Luhrmann's *Romeo + Juliet*. Where Luhrmann's was a noisy, postmodern, eclectic pastiche, inspired by other films, and a spectacular success in the box office, Nunn's is quiet, literary in its inspiration, and an utter failure at the box office. Neither film uses Shakespeare's settings, but Nunn's pre-Raphaelite setting recalls a finely tuned production of Chekov, while Luhrmann's contemporary Verona Beach suggests the backdrop to a virtuoso rock video. In the Luhrmann, we hear the flat, casual tones of California teens. This mingling of the everyday or lowbrow and the elevated source play may have been the roots of this adaptation's success (French, 27). In Nunn's film, theatrically trained British accents prevail. It is not a hybrid film, in that it does not incorporate other genres as Luhrmann's movie does (the rock video, the opera, the western) and *Shakespeare in Love* (the biopic and the romantic comedy). In *Romeo + Juliet*, some wholesale slashing of the text is in evidence. Nunn believes that you tamper with Shakespeare at your peril. Yet both directors succeed in capturing the essence of their plays. What is it that made *Twelfth Night* such a financial failure? Was it Nunn's relatively conservative approach? Hoffman's *A Midsummer Night's Dream* and Branagh's *Much Ado About Nothing* are fairly conservative in terms of editing and camerawork, whereas Luhrmann's was more cutting edge, using an eclectic score, and breakneck editing. Yet all three of those films were box-office successes. While most film critics found the editing in Luhrmann's film abrasive, it did not prove a barrier to a generation raised on rock videos.

In the end, then, the degree of realism and the style of editing in a film do not seem to be nearly as important as acquaintance with the play adapted and the stars performing in it. Familiarity is an important component of whether or not a film is deemed accessible; it breeds a kind of comfort. Prince Charles, the patron of Branagh's Renaissance Theatre Company, expressed this very idea to Branagh: "The thing he found about *Hamlet* is that it speaks to many people. It is a kind of spiritual comfort-blanket" (Mark White, 55).

2

The Drive to Realism in Shakespearean Adaptation to Film

>There is no such thing as realism. There are only realisms.
>
>Richard Armstrong

Umberto Eco argued effectively that what contemporary people are after in their leisure time, particularly in North America, is a "real" experience; in fact, he claims, the North American "concern with authenticity reaches the point of reconstructive neurosis" (13). This neurosis of seeking an authentic experience is closely related to nostalgia, especially as what is authentic or true is often associated with the past, with what is familiar, recognizable, safe. Advertising, for example, often claims that food is "just like Mom or Grandma made." The experience of eating such food is authentic, not just because the reference to Mom or Grandma suggests the food is made from scratch but also that it is *homemade*. It recalls a familiar, pleasurable experience from childhood, or at least from the images of childhood presented through the media, that the adult wants to revisit. It is not surprising, then, that what filmmakers generally promise us, even when they are adapting Shakespeare to the screen, is an experience that is "real."

The chief obstacle to adapting a Shakespeare play to the screen is the film medium's intense drive towards realism, a drive not shared to the same extent by the original medium – theatre – especially in Shakespeare's day. Today, even in theatre, realism is predominant. Elaine Adams Novak in *Styles of Acting* summarizes the trends on stage of the past two hundred years: "Realism has continued to be the dominant style in our theatre since the nineteenth century, but other styles have been conceived by artists and writers to challenge realism's supremacy ... symbolism, expressionism, epic theatre, and theatre of the absurd" (129). Like these latter forms of theatre in Novak's list, stylization is a feature of some independent art films but almost unheard of in mainstream, successful Hollywood films. Directors of Shakespeare adaptations are all too aware that it is the kiss of death to accuse a film of being "theatrical." In their efforts to secure an audience for their adaptations, then, they often stress what is filmic and, above all, realistic about their films. These adaptors are at pains to tell us how true to life their films are, and not just to Shakespearean life but to life now. Their films are "realistic" (see Kenneth Branagh's screenplay, *Much Ado About Nothing*, vii, viii, ix, x); "accessible" (Branagh's screenplays for *Henry V*, xiv, *Hamlet*, xv, Michael Almereyda's screenplay, *Hamlet*, vii, Trevor Nunn's screenplay, *Twelfth Night*, 8, Richard Loncraine's comments in the Production Notes for *Richard III*); and "relevant" (*Henry V*, xvi, Ian McKellen in *Cineaste*, 47). In other words, they aim to represent life as faithfully as possible on the screen. Franco Zeffirelli, with his neo-realism, makes his "actors' speech as lively and fluent as their physical action," giving his productions "immediacy" (John Russell Brown, qtd by Matheson, 532). Nunn, in the introduction to his screenplay of *Twelfth Night*, expresses his aim "to be as populist and accessible as we could manage short of betraying the text and ... to encourage the audience to believe that what is happening to Viola in disguise is real" (viii, ix).

In their drive for realism, Nunn and the other filmmakers show the influence of the nineteenth century. After Darwin, the striving for scientific truth in art became more and more in vogue, starting with the naturalistic novels of the French, working through Konstantin Stanislavsky's use of psychology in performance and Ibsen's and Strindberg's naturalism, and culminating in the prevailing Hollywood style, which on the whole suggests that we, the audience, are peeping in on the characters' lives – the "fourth wall" idea, borrowed from the now-despised nineteenth-century concept of the Well-Made Play. In *Playing Shakespeare*, Barton observes the same prevalence of realism in theatre acting: "Our tradition is based more than we are usually conscious of on various modern influences like Freud and television and the cinema and, above all, the teachings of the director and actor, Stanislavsky" (8). Later, he adds that he generally wants to evoke a naturalistic style from his actors: "By 'naturalistic' I mean the acting style ... which is the norm in the theatre and film and television today ... a style which deliberately gives an impression of ordinary everyday speech and behavior" (11, 19). Nunn too says that he seeks realism when he directs theatrical productions: "I admit that I do conduct myself, and my rehearsals, according to humanist principles which lead me to uncover every possible imaginable behavioural detail that makes a writer's humanist observations more truthful and recognisable; and therefore that I also search for some 'moral' core that involves the idea of optimism" (NT *Platform Papers*, qtd in Brown, *Routledge Companion*, 285).

Nunn's desire for a "moral core that involves the idea of optimism" is an articulation of a kind of nostalgia for a more hopeful kind of art than is typically produced by the auteurs of contemporary cinema (Tarantino, Coppola, Scorsese, Atom Egoyan, the Coen brothers, David Cronenberg, David Lynch). Certainly this seems to be a contributing factor in Shakespeare's appeal to Branagh also, who was determined "to send out a positive message ... I just got offered a script about a serial killer. And while I don't want to put my head in the sand and pretend awful things don't happen in the world, I do not wish to make a movie about a serial killer" (Mark White, 129–30). For both of these directors, then, realism serves their purpose to counteract the prevailing pessimism in art and entertainment.

There are multiple realisms, not one. As soon as we put a camera in front of a real experience, it becomes mediated reality, shaped by the selection of the lens. Society's notion of what seems realistic is also very specific to time and place. What might have been regarded as a realistic movie in 1930s' Italy can seem theatrical to a contemporary North American audience, for instance. As Timothy Corrigan points out, "The reality of a movie is constructed for a purpose" (45).

In this chapter, I compare and contrast directors of Shakespearean adaptations who predominantly select realistic effects with those who more often choose stylized ones, and then examine their relative success in the box office and what that tells us. Realistic directors of Shakespeare, who take a fairly conservative approach to narrative structure, characterization, setting, and editing – Franco Zeffirelli, Kenneth Branagh, Trevor Nunn, Michael Hoffman, Michael Radford, Richard Loncraine, Joss Whedon, Ralph Fiennes, Justin Kurzel, Christine Edzard, and Oliver Parker among them – outnumber those who take a more eclectic route, in which the impression of reality is often deliberately disrupted by cinematic techniques. In this latter category,

I include Michael Almereyda, Baz Luhrmann, Julie Taymor, Geoffrey Wright, and Peter Greenaway. The contrast between these two sets of directors can be likened to the contrast between mainstream Hollywood films and independent films, or between realistic novels and experimental ones. The differences in directors' approaches emerge in comparing their treatment of Shakespeare's narrative, dialogue, characterization, and setting. Nowhere are they manifested more clearly than in the editing, camerawork, and music.

The distinction between the two groups of directors is really based on what kind of experience they aim to give their audiences. The first group are most concerned with telling Shakespeare's story in the most transparent and effective way they know; the second are providing a filmic essay on the play, a very personal reinterpretation. The way the story is told is as important if not more so than the story itself. Overall, the question we have to ask is: Do the films that furnish us with the illusion that we are watching other people's lives unfold truly create a more truthful impression of reality than those that constantly draw attention to their own art? Catherine Belsey suggests that the answer may lie in the meaning the audience derives from the film – is it pluralistic, or simplistic? "It is possible, however," she says, "to break with illusionism itself, to withhold the 'truth', the coherence which guarantees intelligibility from a single position ... the consequence is a fragmentation of meaning which enhances plurality" (69).

Belsey uses as her example Derek Jarman's *Tempest* (1979), but Luhrmann's *Romeo + Juliet*, Loncraine's *Richard III*, Almereyda's *Hamlet*, and Taymor's *Titus* all suggest multiple meanings to varying degrees. What is intriguing, though, is that the contrasts in the methods of these directors are rarely reflected by a similar contrast in what they say to the media about their films. There, the pressure to please the highest number of spectators prevails, and they all boast of the same features in their works – chiefly realism, accessibility, and relevance.

NARRATIVE STRUCTURE AND GENRE

Richard Armstrong in his excellent book *Understanding Realism* summarizes, "The classical realist narrative forms the essential structure of the nineteenth-century novel, the Hollywood film and the television drama. It is organized around three dramatic shifts: a) the situation is established; b) the situation is disrupted; c) the disruption is resolved and a fresh situation brought into being" (11). While the narrative that Armstrong is describing became commonplace long after Shakespeare's time, his description is general enough that it still fits the Shakespeare play and probably reflects the way in which studio executives regard Shakespeare's plots.

Genre hugely affects the particular shape a film's realism will take. A director approaching one of Shakespeare's comedies may feel better able to take liberties with verisimilitude, particularly of temporal setting, than when tackling a history play. The tradition of realism to focus on ordinary people leading average lives is one that can be accommodated much more easily in a Shakespearean comedy, and to a lesser extent in a tragedy, than in a Shakespearean history, in which the nature of political leadership is always a central theme. Whatever other liberties Loncraine takes, his Richard III is still king and must face a real battle at the end of the film. Yet the aristocratic Montagues and Capulets can easily be translated into twentieth-century business tycoons in Luhrmann's *Romeo + Juliet*, so that their children, instead of being heirs of the leading families in Verona, are merely rich. Similarly, in Almereyda's *Hamlet*, Fortinbras at the end of the film is only taking over a corporation, not a country (although one could argue that the power of today's multinational corporations far exceeds that wielded by any past monarch). In Geoffrey Wright's *Macbeth* and Almereyda's *Cymbeline*, kings are translated into gang chieftains. While tycoons and gang lords are not exactly average people, in that they have achieved great wealth and prominence in their particular society, the same sense of destiny is not attached to them as to monarchs, who are responsible for nations.

The updating of Shakespearean characters in the name of realism is quite successful in Luhrmann's adaptation, but does not really work in Wright's *Macbeth*. By casting Duncan as a gang lord responsible for all kinds of violent and non-violent crimes, Wright has changed the nature of Macbeth's crime. In Wright's film, Duncan is one criminal low-life and Macbeth another. How can the audience feel truly aggrieved at Duncan's annihilation and Macbeth's slight decline into further evil? Similarly, several reviewers complained that the wager over Imogen's fidelity in *Cymbeline* did not work in Almereyda's contemporary setting – in a post-feminist culture, it makes Posthumous look silly, or worse, misogynistic (Sobczynski, 2). Furthermore, the titles of "king" and "queen" sit even more uneasily on a biker gang lord and his wife than on the CEO of Denmark Corporation and his wife in Almereyda's *Hamlet*. Whereas the latter are part of high society in contemporary Manhattan, the former are clearly part of an underworld, which, while moneyed, wears ripped jeans and leather jackets and operates in dreary basements concocting drugs and torturing enemies. That these people, who live a life of crime, should be so concerned about Imogen's chastity, or Guiderius's and Arviragus's hitherto untested honour, is hard to swallow. The heightened eloquence and nobility of their speech contrasts sharply with the brutality they display, as when, for instance, Cymbeline interrogates Pisanio. As with Wright's *Macbeth*, there is a great distinction between enmities that emerge among rivals in drug-trafficking and those that arise as a result of political conflict between nations.

All the directors tend to place huge emphasis on the family relationships in the plays when adapting them for the screen. Family relationships are obviously viewed as an aspect of the story with which contemporary people can still connect. Branagh advised the cast to "view *Much Ado* not as a distant, historical tale but as a story about a family in turmoil that everyone could relate to in some way. As an icebreaker, and to show the play's contemporary resonances, he then asked each actor to reveal something of his or her relationship with a family member" (Mark White, 149).

Annette Bening, who plays Queen Elizabeth in Loncraine's *Richard III*, acknowledges the same strategy at work: "This group of actors ... know how to make the text personal. Even though it's Shakespeare, it's about brothers and wives, and sons and mothers and how those relationships work" (McKellen, website). Bening implies here that normally Shakespeare and realism are mutually exclusive, and that without this particular set of talented actors, nothing about family relations, nothing personal could possibly emerge from Shakespeare's text (as if people did not have families in the Elizabethan period!). Nunn may have initiated this trend to emphasize the domestic over the political, explaining his approach in his 1969 Royal Shakespeare Company *Hamlet*, which underplayed Fortinbras: "I'm much more interested in a very private family affair, and in the working out of Hamlet's final confrontation with Claudius and Horatio" (Martin White, 287). Almereyda chose this same shift of emphasis with his *Cymbeline*: "The play is about the forming of the British Empire. King James had just risen to the throne, and Shakespeare in some ways was reflecting that, even though he's talking about the deep past ... All of that didn't seem relevant to me ... so the script became more focused on the relationships between men and women" (Emily Rome). In his commentary on the DVD, Almereyda is more direct, describing the centrality of family to his adaptation: "Family is important, but broken." The screenplay writer of Fiennes's *Coriolanus*, John Logan, makes a similar point: "Master dramatist that he is, Shakespeare wrote a play about a ferocious warrior whose climax depicts not a battle, but a son weeping in his mother's arms. It is a harrowing family drama as much as anything" (screenplay, ix).

One of the ways in which directors throw added emphasis on family relationships is through the mining of subtext. In Wright's adaptation, our first glimpse of the Macbeths is visiting the grave of their young son. Lady Macbeth weeps bitterly while Macbeth looks on, helpless. Justin Kurzel seems to have been influenced by his fellow Australian in opening his *Macbeth* with the couple at their baby's funeral. Radford in his version of *A Merchant of Venice* also makes more of Shylock's relationship with his daughter, Jessica, than does Shakespeare. Obviously, drawing on family relationships, especially ones with tragic elements, is a foolproof way to engage an audience's emotions, and most of the directors discussed in this book avail themselves of this technique.

ROMANTIC COMEDY

No genre focuses on relationships more directly than comedy. Marrying the beloved is the ultimate purpose of both Shakespearean comedy and Hollywood romantic comedy. Issues between the genders have changed tremendously, of course, in the intervening four-hundred-odd years, particularly because of pressures exerted on the family by both partners trying to balance careers with domestic duties. Regardless, contemporary film directors tend to make Shakespeare's scripts conform to the romantic comedy blueprint.

In romantic comedy, the film's focus is on the relationship between the hero and heroine; consequently, so as not to disrupt this focus, the camerawork and editing, certainly in Hollywood films, have tended to be conservative. In other words, in not drawing attention to themselves, the camerawork and editing in a typical romantic comedy serve the illusion of reality. Armstrong writes, "Unfolding according to the formula 'boy meets girl/boy loses girl/boy gets girl,' Hollywood films adhere to a tradition going all the way back to medieval literature. On the level of reality effect, this formula is made to seem inevitable as one event smoothly follows the last according to the logic of verisimilitude and cause-and-effect. On the level of truth effects, this structure appeals to the romantic notion that there is someone in the world for everyone" (14). This "romantic notion" is at heart nostalgic; it looks back to the Platonic idea (voiced in Plato's *Symposium*) that human beings once had four legs and arms, two heads, and two sets of genitalia. When the gods split them apart, the mortals spent their time questing for their other half, their "soul mate." In postmodern western society, this concept seems to have been largely overthrown, with divorce rife and casual sexual unions commonplace. Yet the romantic comedy still peddles the image of the perfect soulmate.

While Armstrong uses Michael Hoffman's *One Fine Day* as his example of a classic Hollywood romantic comedy, many of his observations hold true for the same director's *A Midsummer Night's Dream*, and for Branagh's *As You Like It* and *Much Ado About Nothing* and even for Luhrmann's *Romeo + Juliet*. Shakespeare's early tragedy follows the comedic structure until the death of Mercutio in act 3, scene 1, and so makes a natural subject for comparison, especially as it is so similar to *A Midsummer Night's Dream* in its language and imagery (indeed, Shakespeare probably wrote it around the same time).

Shakespeare's comedies, and *Romeo + Juliet*, become filmic arenas in which the battle of the sexes is waged by appealing stars in a witty way, often with added "screwball" characterization of one of the leads. A.O. Scott, writing in the *New York Times* about Whedon's *Much Ado About Nothing*, noted this aspect: "For Beatrice and Benedick there is a thin line between hate and love, and a clear line of succession links them to, say, Katharine Hepburn and Cary Grant in 'Bringing Up Baby' and Rock Hudson and Doris Day in 'Lover Come Back.'"

Hoffman's screwball in *Dream* is Helena, played by Calista Flockhart with many a sly reference to Ally MacBeal, the character she played in a popular television series. We watch Helena comically plotting to snag her man while being soaked in a torrential downpour, falling off her bicycle in headlong pursuit of Demetrius, and beating at her own head with her fists in frustration at her amatory ineptness. Similarly, Celia/Aliena (Romola Garai) in Branagh's *As You Like It* falls off tree branches and rolls her eyes at Rosalind and Orlando's mushiness. Even in *Romeo + Juliet,* Luhrmann includes goofy teenage moments. Romeo backs up into the Capulet pool in his efforts to see Juliet on her balcony. At the Capulet ball, he and Juliet exchange amused glances at Paris's nerdy moves on the dance floor. All of this hints at, as Armstrong so acutely expressed it, "some universal idea that sexual frustration manifests itself in clumsy behaviour" (39). In other words, directors add these moments and character details not directly suggested by Shakespeare's scripts to conform to contemporary audiences' notions of psychological realism. Partly because our sense of the way people in love behave is coloured by all the films we have seen, the lovers' maladroit moments have the ring of truth to us. Allardyce Nicoll wrote about the way our sense of reality has been shaped by the movies: "What we have witnessed on the screen becomes the 'real' for us. In moments of sanity, maybe, we confess that of course we do not believe this or that, but, under the spell again, we credit the truth of these pictures even as, for all our professed superiority, we credit the truth of newspaper paragraphs" (35–8). D.R. Shumway further identifies "isolation ... from everyday life" as a feature of the screwball comedy. This we see played out not only in Branagh's *As You Like It,* where much of the action takes place in the forest of Arden, but also in his *Love's Labour's Lost,* set in an academic court that has declared itself cut off from social intercourse. Shumway adds that comedic heroes tend to "scold, lecture, admonish, or preach," also true of Branagh's (and Shakespeare's) Benedick, and to a lesser extent, Biron (404).

Yet another convention of romantic comedy, to which Shakespeare himself contributed, is its sense of timelessness. Despite the shift in power from Duke Senior to his younger brother in *As You Like It,* we derive no definite sense of political period from the play. Politics sets up the situation the lovers find themselves in but then is forgotten. That is why Branagh could (sort of) get away with setting the play in nineteenth-century Japan. Historical background in romantic comedy is not important; the couple's interactions are. Ironically, this lack of historical specificity actually contributes to our sense of the play/film world's realism rather than taking away from it. Instead of miring the key relationship in details that could date it, the mainstream romantic comedy sweeps the spectator up in what seems to be the actual experience of love, in which everything, including the state of the world, is pushed aside in the lover's obsession with the beloved. We have to believe in the characters, and even in their immediate social context, but we do not need to know, for instance, the policies of the current leader or the reasons the nation is at war. This is exactly the way the nostalgic remembers past times – yearning for the happy, social moments while forgetting the political or unpleasant specificities.

ACTION FILMS

In the interests of meeting audience expectations, directors of Shakespeare have not merely drawn on the conventions of romantic comedy but on other popular genres as well. Zeffirelli in his *Hamlet* borrowed from action films and "buddy movies" to make medieval Denmark seem "realistic" to contemporary audiences. As his tragic hero, he cast Mel Gibson, who had played a series of likeable yet antisocial men-of-action in movies like *Mad Max* (D. George Miller, 1979) and its sequels; *Lethal Weapon* (D. Richard Donner, 1987) and its sequels; and *Tequila Sunrise* (D. Robert Towne, 1988). Neil Taylor and Ace Pilkington observe that Zeffirelli works in the traditions of "naturalism" or "*riesumazione*" (Taylor, 187; Pilkington, 30), returning to the detailed, realistic period sets and costumes of the nineteenth century. The director's choice of costumes and mise en scène expresses his yearning for what he viewed as a richer age (see his comment in my concluding chapter); in much of his theatre work and in all three of his Shakespeare films, he draws for inspiration on Renaissance paintings (Matheson, 534). He opens his *Hamlet* not with the watch on the ramparts but with the funeral of Hamlet Senior. This change conforms to the typical Hollywood structure, in which the first ten minutes of the film establish the situation. Shakespeare, in contrast, leaps *in medias res* and later in the scene with Horatio's long speech explains what has preceded the ghost's appearance. Also in keeping with the conventions of the action film, Zeffirelli in this opening scene uses a variety of camera angles and keeps the camera moving. However, one can see how standards of realism in filmmaking have evolved since 1990 when this *Hamlet* was made. The lighting of Paul Scofield's ghost now seems highly artificial, and some of the scenes are obviously shot on sound sets.

Branagh in his *Hamlet* also avails himself of action-film conventions, particularly in the climax with the military coup performed by Fortinbras and his men and Hamlet's swing through the throne room, Errol Flynn style, to skewer Claudius with his sword.

CLOSED CONSERVATIVE ENDINGS
VERSUS OPEN-ENDED AMBIGUOUS ONES

Catherine Belsey argues that "within the terms of the realist cinema, Shakespearean film is predominantly reactionary." In her view, "the standard vocabulary of Hollywood realism transforms Shakespeare's open, interrogative, non-illusionist texts into closed liberal humanist parables" (qtd in Shaughnessy, 11; she cites as examples Joseph L. Mankiewicz's 1953 *Julius Caesar* and Peter Brook's 1970 *King Lear*). This tidying tendency emerges in bold relief at the conclusions to the adaptations. In mainstream Hollywood films, endings tend to be closed, all the loose plot threads neatly tied up, a reflection of the drive of realistic (versus naturalistic) art to shape and select everything carefully. In contrast, Shakespeare's endings often leave elements ambiguous. Whether directors highlight or downplay these ambiguities reveals much about the image of reality they wish to project. In *Hamlet*, for instance, Shakespeare leaves us uncertain as to whether or not Fortinbras will be a good ruler for Denmark, but in the casting and characterization of Fortinbras for film, the open-endedness of the words on the page are necessarily narrowed to one reading (as also happens in a theatrical production). Contemporary films like Branagh's and Almereyda's tend to present a sinister Fortinbras; his assumption of the throne of Denmark is filmed as a military coup. In the wake of the totalitarian regimes we have seen in the twentieth century, a tyrannical Fortinbras is viewed as the more likely and therefore more realistic outcome. However, Zeffirelli in his medieval *Hamlet* cuts the role altogether.

In contradiction of Belsey's assertion, some directors make Shakespeare's conclusions more indeterminate than in his scripts. Luhrmann in his *Romeo + Juliet* leaves it open as to whether or not the feuding families are reconciled by their shared tragedy, as Capulet and Montague stare numbly at the ambulance that bears their dead children away. Shakespeare, however, makes it abundantly clear that the lovers' suicide brings peace to Verona (Capulet addresses Montague as "brother" and offers him his hand; in return, Montague says he will raise a golden statue to Juliet, 5.3). Loncraine too renders the ending of *Richard III* more enigmatic than in Shakespeare's script. Richard's laughing suicide seems to suggest that the new England under Richmond is a place he is happy to escape. Richmond's knowing smile at the camera as Richard falls is not reassuring. Shakespeare's Richmond, on the other hand, clearly plans to restore order to England. Perhaps in deference to Elizabeth I, Shakespeare assigns her grandfather an ideal king's oration to conclude the play. Kurzel's *Macbeth* also ends ambiguously, with Fleance emerging from the forest to wrest the dead Macbeth's sword from the ground and run off with it, his purpose unknown. Is he going to kill Malcolm to fulfill the witches' prophecy? Or will he in time use the sword in the same tyrannical fashion as its previous owner? In contrast, Shakespeare's intention, given that Fleance's descendant was sitting on England's throne, is clear. Quinones observes that Fleance's escape in the original play is "emblematic of the large place that the father-son, augmentative code occupies in Shakespeare's vision" (352). Banquo, unlike Macbeth, has an insurance against "tomorrow, tomorrow, and tomorrow," his son guaranteeing him a place in history, and is therefore less prone to nostalgia.

Nunn and Radford, though falling for the most part into the realistic camp, focus in the last scenes of *Twelfth Night* and *Merchant of Venice* on the characters who have not successfully mated up by the end of the comedy: Malvolio, Antonio, and Feste; and Jessica, Shylock, and Antonio, respectively. In fact, Radford may have been influenced by Nunn's 1997 National Theatre production of *Merchant* in which Jessica ends the play alone, remembering her rejected faith (Martin White, 302). In Radford's film, she stands solitary, overlooking the water, fingering her mother's turquoise ring that gossip claimed she had sold (fig. 1). This moment also confirms the shift in the film to greater emphasis on family relationships. Jessica's sale of the ring is represented in the play as a betrayal of her family, but in the film no such betrayal has taken place. By stressing these isolated characters' inability to fit into the predominant heterosexual couple formula, the directors are subverting the social purpose of comedy and breaking with the tradition of filmed romantic comedy that generally reserves the last few moments for the triumphant union of the hero and heroine. Again, these changes to Shakespeare's emphasis are no doubt made for the sake of realism, as contemporary western society claims to be much more interested in its "marginalized" members than was the case in the more ruthlessly conformist Elizabethan society.

DIALOGUE AND SETTING

Despite the clichés that film is a visual medium and that a picture is worth a thousand words, witty or memorable dialogue is obviously a

Figure 1 Jessica (Zuleikha Robinson) keeps her mother's turquoise ring in Radford's *The Merchant of Venice*, 2004.

production value for a film, one that critics and viewers mention when substantiating their approval. The films discussed in this book all retain most of Shakespeare's dialogue – both an asset and a disadvantage for a film. Shakespeare expressed his ideas brilliantly, but he expressed them mostly in iambic pentameter, often using poetic inversion and always employing a phenomenally huge vocabulary in which words have different meanings and nuances from what they do today. This can obviously be a barrier to immediate understanding of the dialogue, and it can also be seen as an obstacle to verisimilitude. Even in Elizabethan England, people did not talk this way. Like any writer, Shakespeare gives his characters dialogue that is much better than everyday speech – funnier, and more eloquent, with the boring, filler talk excised.

Craig Pearce, co-writer with Luhrmann of the screenplay of *Romeo + Juliet*, explains one solution to this issue: "The trouble is [Shakespeare] writes in this obscure language called Elizabethan, and ninety percent of the world can't understand it. We thought the way to help people was to present these very recognizable characters in the modern world ... Tybalt when he's presented, you know, you get this image of a big, bad gunslinger, so it says to the audience, even if they can't quite tune their ear into the Shakespearean dialogue at that early stage, they'll say, okay, here's a really scary guy and he's good with a gun. Everybody's scared of him. I understand who he is ... They just sort of understand his function in the world and in the story" (DVD commentary). "Recognizable" is the key word in this passage, as it is where nostalgia and realism intersect. We yearn, especially in this era of rapid change, for what is familiar, and deem the familiar "realistic."

At the same time, Shakespeare's *prose* can feel so contemporary that audiences think the director has made it up. Branagh recalled, "The prose wooing scene between Henry and Katherine at the end of *Henry V* prompted many viewers to say that we had made up the dialogue. When we played *Much Ado* in the theatre, this charge was made regularly by backstage visitors. The accusation was not true, but it did say much about the realistic quality of the play" (*Much Ado*, *Screenplay*, viii). Nunn concurs: "Shakespeare's prose scenes have an uncanny contemporary feel of real speech" (Preface, *Screenplay*, x). Part of the audience's reaction to Shakespeare's language in these directors' hands may also reflect their success in drawing realistic performances from the actors, so that it seems as if the words are their own. Dominic West, who played Richmond in Loncraine's *Richard III*, thought that his director also elicited that kind of delivery of the lines: "[He] is constantly bringing you back to a very natural and truthful and modern way of acting and speaking verse that's four hundred years old, and so it sounds like dialogue in a nineties action movie, so that you savour the richness and the colour and the descriptiveness of the words, but it doesn't sound old-fashioned" ("Production Notes"). Ian McKellen, who wrote the screenplay and starred in this same *Richard III*, observes that Shakespeare "frequently captured a conversational tone ... that is ideal for the cinema" (*Screenplay*, 17). Barton, who influenced both Nunn and Branagh and certainly the Richard Eyre stage production on which Loncraine's film of *Richard III* was closely based, shares this approach to directing Shakespeare. The key strategy he recommends to actors is to consider "'What is my intention?' ... to ask that question is the way to act without falseness" (9).

The fact that people in movies always speak better than people in real life, without hesitations and rambling, already stretches credulity (while conforming to dramatic convention). Having them speak blank verse stretches this several steps further (although, as Barton points out, "Blank verse, with its ten syllables, is much closer to the way that we actually talk [than other verse forms – eight syllable lines, or fourteeners]" (27). The most obvious way to minimize this disruption of the illusion of reality is to set the film in Renaissance times, so that the rhetorical flourishes and the vocabulary sit more naturally. Zeffirelli chose a late medieval setting for his *Hamlet*, and Radford, Parker, and Greenaway chose Shakespeare's sixteenth century for their *Merchant*, *Othello*, and *Prospero's Books*, respectively. Branagh with *Henry V* and Justin Kurzel with *Macbeth* set the plays in their original historical periods. However, Greenaway elucidates that he chose both play and period in order to *counteract* the drive to realism: "*The Tempest* is extremely self-referential, and I always tend to feel the most sympathy for those works of art which do have that sort of self-knowledge, that say, basically, 'I am an artifice.' I very much like the idea that when somebody sits in the cinema and watches a film of mine, it's *not* a slice of life, it's *not* a window on the world. It's a constant concern of mine to bring the audience back to this realization" (Rodman, 125).

Choosing the period in which Shakespeare set his play is by no means the most common decision among adaptors of his work to the screen. Generally, more recent settings win out; Luhrmann's *Romeo + Juliet*, Almereyda's *Hamlet* and *Cymbeline*, Loncraine's *Richard III*, Branagh's *Love's Labour's Lost*, Taymor's *Titus*, Whedon's *Much Ado*, and Wright's *Macbeth* are all set in the twentieth century or later. From the point of view of achieving a sense of realism, this decision has advantages and disadvantages. A fairly contemporary setting makes the audience feel a more immediate kinship with the characters and renders their situation visually familiar. On the other hand, the heightened language can sound completely unnatural coming from the mouths of people "just like us."

Some directors have tried to counter this problem by distancing their setting from a specific place and time. Luhrmann sets his tragedy in Verona Beach, a fictional city that shares features with Miami and Los Angeles. His intensely personal cinematic style in conjunction with the fantasy setting contributes to the Shakespearean verse coming across as a sort of new urban slang. To a lesser extent, the same is true of Almereyda's *Hamlet*. The director explains his approach in the introduction to his screenplay: "Given the story's familiarity, it seemed altogether natural to locate a new Hamlet in the immediate present, to translate the Danish kingdom into a multimedia corporation, and to watch the story unfold in penthouse hotel rooms, sky-level office corridors, a coffee shop, an airplane, the Guggenheim museum. The chief thing was to balance respect for the play with respect for contemporary reality – to see how thoroughly Shakespeare can speak to the present moment, how they can speak to each other" (Preface, ix).

In terms of realism, Loncraine's *Richard III* and Branagh's *Love's Labour's Lost* have a slight edge over Luhrmann's *Romeo + Juliet* and Almereyda's *Hamlet*, in that their 1930s courtly settings make formal speech somewhat more believable. Both directors use a high degree of stylization in these films to "mesh the twentieth century imagery and sixteenth century dialogue and make people suspend their disbelief," as Loncraine puts it. "I wanted the acting to be very real and the imagery to be very unreal. I wanted to give it a certain heightened reality, not an unreality" ("Production Notes," 13–14). It is telling that Loncraine seems to correct his own use of the word "unreal," perhaps fearing that his term might turn off potential viewers of his film. It is arguable whether or not McKellen gives a "real" performance. It seemed to me closer to a camp performance (his pirouette on leaving the blood-spattered morgue comes to mind). One could argue that Richard in the play is a larger-than-life character whose addresses to the audience make him naturally theatrical, but McKellen's acting choices seem to magnify rather than diminish the theatricality with which Shakespeare endows Richard.

Production designer Tony Burrough explains the film's setting: "The costumes, for example, were very specific to 1936 ... We're using thirties furniture, thirties architecture [Battersea Power Station, St Pancras Chambers, Senate House, University of London] ... The style of the picture, however, is heightened reality. By that I mean we haven't been slavish to period detail. We haven't been frightened to use something which might not be accurate, but looks perfect in the context ... It's full of anachronisms" ("Production Notes," 15). This mingling of artifacts from different eras is again reflective of a nostalgic as opposed to historical approach. The designer is aiming for an impression of the past rather than a reconstruction. Part of the appeal to viewers derives from this use of "heightened reality" – the 1930s through a designer's eyes. McKellen claims he wanted to "make a Shakespeare film that could be accessible to as wide an audience as possible, and it seems we have achieved that with this film" (*Notes*, 2).

Julie Taymor took an even more eclectic approach in filming Titus's Rome. Hers is a postmodern world in which buildings, armour, and equipment seem to be a collection of other eras' leftovers; the archaic-sounding language is just more evidence of the postmodern mélange in which we exist. Further, in an era in which independent films are typically characterized by excessively quirky and idiosyncratic volubility (witness *Clerks*, 1994 and 2006, or *Juno*, 2007), Shakespearean dialogue does not seem utterly strange. Branagh also chose to mix it up in *Much Ado About Nothing*, in which his women wear a simplified version of an Elizabethan frock, while his men's uniforms seem more nineteenth century. He places these timeless figures in "a realistic background and an evocative landscape" (*Screenplay*, vii). His Messina is a real country estate in Tuscany (not Sicily, the site of Shakespeare's play), the mansion sporting such softened lines that it is hard to pin down its era. Branagh articulated his approach in his screenplay: "We consciously avoided setting this version in a specific time but instead went for a look that worked within itself, where clothes, props, architecture, all belonged to the same world. This imaginary world could have existed almost anytime between 1700 and 1900. It was distant enough to allow the language to work without the clash of period anachronisms and for a certain fairy-tale quality to emerge" (xvi).

Taymor follows the same approach in her *Tempest*, which features eclectic costumes that suggest another time but also include more contemporary touches. The shape of Taymor's costumes for the courtiers is Jacobean, but the zippers used to adorn them channel 1980s punk.

Nineteenth-century settings are popular as well in Nunn's *Twelfth Night*, Branagh's *Hamlet* and *As You Like It*, and Hoffmann's *Dream*. Nunn and Branagh both divulge in their screenplays their reasons for choosing this setting: they feel the period is far enough away from the present that "the heightened language sits comfortably" (*Hamlet, Screenplay*, xv) and the hierarchical society is not anachronistic, yet close enough to our own that we can decipher distinctions in rank from the costumes. Just as Branagh cites as one of his challenges the achievement of a balance between verisimilitude and "a certain fairy-tale quality," so Nunn articulates much the same obstacle. He wanted to find "locations which can serve the fictional or fairy-tale elements of the story but still encourage the audience to believe that ... the social and moral infighting between Malvolio and Sir Toby and Malvolio and Feste is real ... I felt it was immensely important that audiences anywhere should be able to *recognize* the upstairs/downstairs hierarchy of Olivia's household" (*Screenplay*, ix).

Again, *recognition* or familiarity is a great part of what we deem realistic. For us to view something as realistic, it has to mesh with what we have experienced. This suggests that part of the general pleasure in watching a "realistic" film is our nostalgic retreat into the familiar. As Linda Hutcheon puts it, "With adaptations, we seem to desire the repetition as much as the change" (9). A realistic film gives us an experience that is similar to one we have had in the past, if only the previous watching of another realistic film, and therefore is akin to "going home."

CHARACTER/ACTING

Sharon Marie Carnicke describes the prevailing impression that screen acting is more realistic than theatre acting and thus more truthful: "The subtle, facial means of expression demanded by the cinematic close-up has led to pervasive, but deceiving, discourse around issues of sincerity, honesty, and truth in film ... Acting truisms conspire to strengthen and extend this discourse, among them: Laurence Olivier's statement that 'truth [is] demanded by the cinema'" (78). Nunn also acknowledges the drive to realism in film: "It seems to me that the camera requires work of actors that is untheatrical and unstylized. It requires actors to be as truthful as is conceivably possible. The camera is associated with eavesdropping on the real event. Consequently, what is said in front of the camera needs to convey to the cinema audience the sense that it has not been written, that it is being invented by the character in the situation spontaneously" (Knopf, 274). What is valued most highly in a screen performance is realism. The film's endurance as a piece of art rests largely on the quality of the performances. Our assessment of these has become increasingly complicated by the amount of media attention that actors' personal lives receive. Our evaluation of their acting is not only affected by expectations set up by other roles we have seen them play but also by gossip about their personal lives. Johanne Larue makes it clear in her essay "James Dean: The Pose of Reality?" that the actor is the wild card in the director's pursuit of realism and quality. He or she "can be influenced and coached, but ... cannot be programmed ... an unpredictable 'element' set free on the soundstage by the willing director" (296–7). Yet the elusive and hard-to-define truthfulness of the actors' performance is crucial to creating a realistic film.

The filmmakers examined here, even those whose predominant style is surreal, state that the kind of acting they admire is "realistic" and that realism became a key criterion in their selection of actors for their films. Branagh announces his aim in his preface to his screenplay of *Much Ado About Nothing*: "My continued desire in *Much Ado* was for an absolute clarity that would enable a modern audience to respond to Shakespeare on film, in the same way that they would respond to any other movie. Our concern was to do this without losing his unique poetry" (viii).

Luhrmann cast Leonardo DiCaprio as his Romeo because "the words just came out of his mouth as if it was the most natural language possible ... He speaks them as if they really are his words, and that's something you don't always get in a Shakespearean performance" (Pearce and Luhrmann, 1). Almereyda said of Sam Shepherd's performance as Hamlet Senior in his film, "I never saw the ghost played with such an electrifying sense of reality" (*Screenplay*, xii). Nunn remembers a seminal performance he witnessed as a young man: "[David] Waller had already opened my eyes and ears about Shakespeare when, several years earlier, I had been electrified by his astonishingly naturalistic, utterly believable Iago in the minute Ipswich Arts Theatre in my home town. Before that evening, Shakespeare for me had been synonymous with declamation and rhetoric and now suddenly, this turbulent, rule-breaking, unprecedentedly fast-thinking and fast-talking performance was overturning all previously received notions. The text was not being performed or 'spoken,' it was being inhabited" (*Screenplay*, iv). Here Nunn contrasts a realistic Shakespeare performance with the more mannered style he was used to. Branagh makes the same comparison when he writes about the reactions he received to his film of *Henry V*: "Many of those who wrote had enjoyed the apparent 'naturalness' of the acting (which I think is depressing testament to the usual expectation of incomprehensible booming and fruity-voiced declamation)" (*Ado, Screenplay*, viii). Earlier, Branagh pinpointed the inner doubt in his Henry V as key to making a realistic impression: "I wanted to close in with the camera, to see the unsettled inner man, the flickers of uncertainty in his eyes. The medium allowed me to release that bit of performance" (Tomlinson, 60).

Nunn and Branagh continue to emphasize that "realism" was what they were after in their films. Branagh uses words like "real," "naturalistic," "truthful," and "believable" seventeen times in the short prefaces to his three published screenplays (*Henry V, Much Ado,* and *Hamlet*). However, as this chapter's introduction points out, "realistic" is a subjective term, and there are myriad ways in which an actor can attempt to develop a "realistic" performance. One strategy employed by directors is to encourage the actors to create a complex background history for their characters. Branagh in his screenplay of *Much Ado* states that he held both solo sessions and group discussions in which the background of the characters was explored using these kinds of questions: "How long had the soldiers been away? What kind of war had it been? How violent? Which of our men had been killers? How often had they visited Leonato prior to this? How well did they know one another? How old were they? How long did these soldiers expect to live?" (xi). Branagh comments on the usefulness of this process: "This filling in of the 'back story' for each of the characters is one of the most necessary and interesting elements in preparing a characterisation, particularly for the screen ... [It gives] depth to the character beyond what he says and does" (xi).

To viewers, encouraging actors to develop a sense of the background of their character now seems like an obvious tactic for a director, but this may merely prove the extent of Konstantin Stanislavsky's influence. Nunn likewise remarks in his preface to his screenplay that rehearsal time was crucial to him, and that questions like "Feste ... what do we know of him?" (x) were an essential part of the preparation for the film. McKellen goes further: "We have to slightly compensate for Shakespeare by putting into the rise to power the seeds for the fall and the collapse afterwards, so the audience gets genuinely riveted by the quite detailed psychological examination of [Richard's] inner life" ("Interview," r3.org). I would argue, however, that Shakespeare achieves this much more fully in his long playscript than Loncraine does in his film of one hour and forty-four minutes. Furthermore, in Shakespeare's original audience, the educated members would have been acquainted with Richard from history books, the less-educated from two of Shakespeare's three *Henry VI* plays in which he was a character, so "compensation" would not have been required.

Part of the quest for realism as articulated by Branagh and Nunn was to flesh out the minor characters. This technique may be a descendant of Stanislavsky's and Nemirovich-Danchenko's emphasis on ensemble acting and on maintaining a constant sense of the play as a whole. This is in complete contrast to the "realism" of Hollywood romantic comedies in which, according to Richard Armstrong, the supporting roles "are little more than Hollywood occupational traits ... the peripheral characters seeming to provide a feasible background" (19). In other words, their function in the films is not very different from furniture in the mise en scène. To treat Shakespeare's minor characters in this way would be to misrepresent one of the remarkable qualities of his writing: the depth of many of his supporting characters. There are exceptions, of course: Demetrius and Lysander in *Dream* are virtually interchangeable, as are Maria and Katherine and Longueville and Dumaine in *Love's Labour's Lost*. Nunn comments on his interpretation of some of the secondary roles in *Twelfth Night*: "As their names suggest, Sir Toby, Sir Andrew and Mistress Mary are firmly rooted in English rather than fictional, social behaviour. I wanted to stress the naturalism of these scenes, by finding a context wherein Toby can be seen as the overgrown public schoolboy that he is, squandering his life in drink and practical jokes, and Andrew as the lonely second son of a dwindling minor aristocratic family, devoid of qualifications and forlornly needing to make a money marriage to avert his impending bankruptcy ... They seem to me to exemplify a genre of truthful comedy" (*Screenplay*, x). Nunn dramatizes this interpretation by adding sequences not in Shakespeare's play, such as Toby and Andrew's drunken clamber over the Olivia's fence late at night, followed by their hurling pebbles at Maria's window. (I say more about this in chapter 11.)

Branagh also views the fleshing out of supporting characters as essential to a realistic production: "The challenge for a new film of *Much Ado* is not to resist Beatrice and Benedick's dominance but, through the choices made by the camera, to bring to vivid life all the other characters. To take on the play as a whole and realize fully fleshed lives for characters like the Friar, the Watch and Leonato's household" (vii). Branagh achieves this end by adding minor characters to group scenes. For instance, we see the friar enjoying the masqued ball and playing a guitar, moments that add to his realistic role in the community of Messina.

Branagh in his *Much Ado* and *Hamlet* cast high-profile American actors in many of the secondary roles, and Loncraine follows his lead in his casting of *Richard III*. Both directors seem somewhat disingenuous about their motivations. It seems fairly obvious that one factor would be the recognizability and box-office draw of these Hollywood stars, whereas Branagh speaks of the "emotional fearlessness" (*Ado, Screenplay*, x) they bring to the roles. McKellen maintains that he and Loncraine had thematic reasons for casting Americans: "Queen Elizabeth and her brother ... [should] be played as Americans for several reasons. In the original story, they are strangers to the social camp of the King and Richard. A modern equivalent for the 1930s setting seemed to me in contrasting the British royals with a couple of Americans whose manners and voices are different, and of whom the Brits would be suspicious" (McKellen, *Notes*). The film's executive producer, Ellen Little, points to a historical detail lending further credibility to the Americanization of Elizabeth: "In fact, England in the 1930s came within a hairsbreadth of having an American-born Queen" (ibid.). Her statement is an exaggeration, of course; a twice-divorced woman of common descent was never seriously considered as a possible queen of England by anyone but Edward (and Winston Churchill).

Luhrmann, who was less concerned than Branagh and Nunn about achieving realism in his film but more interested in providing an exciting ride for his audience, treats his minor characters very differently from his main ones. His secondary characters are over the top, and, following the tradition of Hollywood romantic comedies Armstrong describes above, have one representative trait each. These traits are taken not from their occupation, as in realistic Hollywood romantic comedies, but rather, in postmodern eclectic style, from the film genre that Luhrmann feels best suits them. Tybalt (John Leguizamo) seems to emerge from a spaghetti western, the cliché of the Latino villain, with his black moustache, twirling guns, and steel-heeled boot grinding out his cigarette. This impression is reinforced by the choice of music, which Pearce describes as "reminiscent of a Sergio Leone type Western" (DVD commentary). Mercutio (Harold Perrineau) is straight out of *La Cage aux Folles* (1978) or *Priscilla, Queen of the Desert* (1994), all camp transvestite. Gloria Capulet (Diane Venora) is a southern belle, equally at home in a Tennessee Williams play/film or the *Dukes of Hazzard* (1979–85). Luhrmann makes comic use of fast motion as we watch her transform herself into an ersatz Cleopatra for the costume party. Benvolio (Dash Mihok) is the frat partier from *American Pie* (1999) or *Porkies* (1982), lug-headed but loyal. By guying the supporting characters, Luhrmann sets his romantic leads apart; they seem natural, composed, level-headed, when all is frenetic and hyped up around them. It is entirely believable that they would be drawn to one another. They are two real human beings who seem to have somehow wandered from their cool, soothing natural habitat of water into a garishly animated world. And when each believes the other dead, they are suddenly isolated again in this alien world, with no one remotely like them to offer solace. By interpreting the setting and secondary cast of characters in this overblown way, Luhrmann, has, surprisingly, made the double suicide more believable and, hence, "realistic."

FORMAL PROPERTIES

Using an older Michael Hoffman film, *One Fine Day*, as his example, Armstrong acutely describes the "realistic" conventions that dictate the typical Hollywood film: "Style must be subordinate to the film's narrative. No aspect of the way in which the film tells its story must get in the way of our ability to follow the story itself. This means that camerawork, editing, lighting and colour must serve the storyline, place you in the most advantageous position to see what is going on and banish any doubt about what you see. There must be no weird angles, choppy cutting or strange lens filters to make you aware of the film as a film, as opposed to real life, for Hollywood realism is designed to make you think that life is how it looks in the movies" (13). This kind of "invisible editing" (also known as continuity editing) and camerawork characterizes many of the Shakespearean adaptations discussed in this book, including Zeffirelli's *Hamlet*, Nunn's *Twelfth Night*, Hoffman's *Dream*, Branagh's *Much Ado* and *Hamlet* (and to a lesser extent, two of his three other Shakespearean adaptations, *Henry V* and *As You Like It*), Parker's *Othello*, Radford's *Merchant of Venice*, and Whedon's *Much Ado About Nothing*. These films are characterized by conventional shot/reaction shot dialogues and unobtrusive cutting. The music fits with the location and period of the setting. The viewer's focus is kept squarely on the performances, so that language, character, and narrative emerge clearly. The absence of fancy camerawork and editing suggests that these directors trust Shakespeare's script to be entertaining enough, and that it is his script that is the real star, not the director's interpretation of that script.

FILMING DIALOGUE

Zeffirelli, in the interest of achieving a sense of realism in his *Hamlet*, typically selects the classic shot/reverse shot format for his dialogues. Armstrong elucidates its advantages: "We seem to hover at the listeners' shoulder, we are never completely shut off from them. In this way we are given privileged access to what's going on, but invited at the same time to share a character's perspective" (16). When Horatio first breaks the news to Hamlet of the ghost, important information for the audience to absorb (1.2), Zeffirelli hardly tampers with the shot/reverse shot format. In earlier dialogue, such as when Gertrude, alone with Hamlet, tries to persuade him to stay at Elsinore and stop grieving for his father (1.2), he uses a modified version, with a greater variety of angles and proximity. In the dialogue between Ophelia and her father in which they discuss Hamlet (1.3), he again breaks up the shot/reverse shot with Ophelia chasing after her father to persuade him that Hamlet's intentions are honourable. Despite the variety, though, all Zeffirelli's editing serves the illusion of reality.

Parker goes even further in privileging the text over the camera in his filming of dialogues in *Othello*. Almost all the dialogues between Iago and Roderigo are filmed as if they were on stage, the two characters sitting side by side, both in the frame. This way we see both characters' reactions to everything that is being said, and an omniscient point of view is maintained. Thus we witness how Iago's words work on Roderigo even as they leave his mouth. Although the effect is less conventionally "filmic," it could be seen as more "realistic": if we were eavesdropping on their conversation, fourth-wall style, we would hardly be jumping from behind one character's shoulder to the other in a matter of seconds. Branagh in *Hamlet* uses a modified version of this technique in significant scenes, such as when Horatio informs the prince of the ghost's appearance (1.2) or when Hamlet challenges Ophelia's sincerity in returning his "remembrances" (3.1). In these scenes, we see the faces of both speakers in profile at the same time, the screen between them filled only with the background.

In contrast, Luhrmann makes the shot/reaction shot format in his *Romeo + Juliet* feel fresh and original by interposing a fish tank between the lovers at their first meeting, although they do not actually speak. The tank magnifies and even slightly distorts their features as they gaze at one another. Luhrmann has thus chosen to stress thematic over narrative content. Romeo and Juliet are like the exotic fish in the tank, rare and vulnerable. Outside the enclosed bubble of their love, they cannot survive. Luhrmann's use of the fish tank is very appropriate, linking his film with Shakespeare's chief source, Arthur Brooke, who also uses fish/water imagery for the couple. Brooke describes Juliet's eyes "floating" until they "anchored" on Romeo (line 224, Appendix II, Arden edition, *Romeo and Juliet*); earlier, he writes about Romeo swallowing "downe loves sweete empoysonde baite" (219). Throughout his film, Luhrmann dresses the pair in watery colours, blue, white, and silver, as opposed to the eye-popping oranges and reds of the other young people, stressing their tranquillity in contrast to the frenzied society around them.

Almereyda in his Manhattan *Hamlet* often steers away from the conventional shot-reaction-shot by using a slow, encircling tracking shot. For example, in Laertes's and Ophelia's first dialogue, Laertes sits facing the camera, while Ophelia sits slightly in front of him, in profile, gazing at a photo of Hamlet, which presumably has initiated her brother's warning. We can see both characters' expressions. The camera very gradually and smoothly moves around them until it is facing Ophelia for her response. Almereyda uses the same technique in the ghost's first interview with Hamlet.

Greenaway is even more radical, doing away with dialogue altogether in a move that backfires for the success of his *Prospero's Books*. Almost the entire script is read by Gielgud in a voice-over. Obviously, this disrupts any illusion of reality, as was Greenaway's intent; it also robs the play of its original dynamism. The characters meander their way through the extraordinarily beautiful set like mutes, never coming to life. Greenaway's background as an artist informs his interpretation. His film is like an art gallery, the spectator equipped with an audio monitor featuring Gielgud's voice. It is visually and sometimes intellectually stimulating, an illustrated talk on Shakespeare's *Tempest*, but never emotionally engaging. At least half of the respondents to a Heritage Audience Survey who had seen the film disliked it (Monk, *Heritage Film Audiences*, 107).

FILMING MONOLOGUES

Monologues, especially soliloquies, obviously pose more of a challenge than dialogues to a film director interested in any degree of realism. In the "real world," only eccentrics speak at length out loud to themselves. The film director has several options available. The soliloquy can be delivered as a voice-over – the character thus appears to be thinking, but we the audience have privileged access to his or her thoughts. This is often deemed the most "realistic" choice, although it is still merely a convention. The other option, one more generally used in the theatre, is to have the character deliver the words aloud. There are two ways to do this. Actors can be filmed speaking to themselves, unaware of the camera. This maintains the illusion of reality – the character is so overwrought that he is unconscious or unconcerned about the fact that he is speaking aloud. Or, the character can be filmed speaking directly to the camera, which acknowledges the artifice of film and the presence of an audience. Loncraine makes extensive use of the direct address to the camera. McKellen, who plays his Richard III, contrasts Loncraine's break with strict "realism" to two other directors' closer adherence to it: "The man turns to the camera and tells you what he's going to do. He includes you in his privacy. He has a personal relationship with the audience. It's a brilliant device in the theatre and I think it's going to be a brilliant device in the cinema. It's one that most filmmakers of Shakespeare dodge. In Branagh's *Much Ado* ... the principal character never talked to the audience. In Olivier's *Hamlet*, he doesn't speak directly to us either. The fact is that Hamlet and Benedict [*sic*] and Richard III need to talk to us" ("Interview," r3.org). In another interview, McKellen summarizes the effect this technique produces: "Richard, the consummate liar, always speaks the truth to the audience, but only to them. This is meant to be disarming for an audience, because they alone are privy to what he intends to do, and they become accomplices [in] his schemes" (Gerber, 1). In the introduction to his screenplay, McKellen adds that this experience "should not be comfortable" (23). His observation about the "disarming" of the audience is significant. Anytime a director disrupts the illusion of reality with a filmic technique that draws attention to the art, he wrests the audience out of their dream-like, vicarious experience of the plot and forces them to puzzle over the moment or scene. It is akin to the Brechtian alienation effect. Although effective in Loncraine's *Richard III*, it definitely conveys a whiff of grease-paint.

Oliver Parker uses this same device to greater effect in his *Othello*. Branagh's tour-de-force Iago invites us into his confidence. The camera allows us to stare into his grim face and deadened eyes as he tonelessly divulges his evil plans. The rapidity with which his face transforms from the open, friendly "honest Iago" the other characters see to the hollow man only the spectator knows is both sinister and comic. While the device is theatrical, almost anti-filmic, Branagh's delivery of his monologues is so deadpan, so devoid of mannered flourishes, his Iago so indifferent to the fates of those he undoes and even to his own fate, that the direct addresses are utterly convincing. We believe we are privy to the machinations of a psychopath. In a total break with realistic illusion, Iago acknowledges the audience's presence, but we are swept along nevertheless.

CHRONOLOGY

Realistic films tend not to share with Shakespeare's plays the sloppiness of the original time frames. Frequently, the playwright cheats, appearing to keep to the unity of time with events taking place in twenty-four hours, or perhaps a few days, but also implying through dialogue that what we see the characters experiencing is of several months' duration. Nunn remarks, "On film such essentially poetic contradictions or vagaries work less well, because scenes are being photographed in a real climate, against real cloudscapes, during a real season, so it becomes much more necessary to be finite about the passage of time" (*Screenplay*, xii). In other words, Nunn judges that a film audience is far less likely than a theatre audience to suspend disbelief. Richard Armstrong concurs, observing that "Hollywood editing is designed to follow the logic of a chronological narrative. In Hollywood 'continuity editing,' as it is called, one plot twist follows on from the last according to the laws of cause and effect. Time and space are logically presented so as to orient you in an apparently natural sequence of events" (16).

Shakespeare's plays are generally organized in this way, events unfolding chronologically – with the exception of the "meanwhile" scenes. These scenes are meant to take place at roughly the same time in different locations, but we see them in sequence because there is no other clear way to present them on stage while maintaining the dialogue in each scene. On film, one could use intercutting (see chapter 11) or even, more confusingly, a split screen. Film directors obviously have more options open to them in terms of presenting time; on Shakespeare's stage, a character's past or memories can only be suggested through references in the dialogue, or shown acted in dumb show on a separate part of the stage, perhaps above the main action; on the screen, it can be shown in flashbacks. Armstrong remarks that "flashbacks and flash-forwards can disrupt the action by introducing past or future events into the present." Yet I think that audiences today are so familiar with these filmic conventions that they barely register them as a disruption. Even the more conservative directors use them: for instance, Branagh's Hamlet remembers bowling in the corridor with his parents and joking with Yorick. His Ophelia remembers making love to Hamlet. In the latter case, Branagh has used the flashback to reinterpret the play in a fairly radical way. If Ophelia has had sex with Hamlet, then she is lying to her brother and father; also, she has taken an incredible risk as a young noblewoman of the time. If Hamlet does not marry her, she is ruined. Of course, her carnal knowledge of Hamlet in this version goes some way to "realistically" explain her bawdy references in her mad songs, which in other productions seem uncharacteristic. Additionally, Branagh reflects predominant social mores – now, in contrast to either Shakespeare's time or the late Victorian era in which the film is set, courting couples generally achieve sexual intimacy before marriage; and in a feminist society, it is viewed as acceptable for women to express their sexual desires. In this flashback, he attempts to guide his audience to read the relationship as passionate, and showing Hamlet and Ophelia as physically intimate is the current shorthand. Is the cumulative effect of the flashback to make Ophelia's character more or less realistic? In my opinion, Branagh's flashback renders her depiction less realistic because it seems anachronistic, even for the late nineteenth century, for a woman of her class and situation to have taken such a risk, especially as Gertrude seems happy with the idea of her marrying Hamlet (5.1.240–2). Ophelia has everything to lose and little to gain by allowing Hamlet to seduce her before wedlock. The stakes are much higher than they would be to a contemporary couple, or even to a nineteenth-century working-class couple; it seems "unrealistic" to ignore this.

Wright, not usually a subtle director, exploits a subtle way of suggesting that the character is remembering. We see Lady Macbeth glance at the swing rocking in the wind, and we know that the sight summons up precious and painful memories of her now-dead son. Yet we the audience have remained outside her head, gleaning her memories only from the sequence of shots from the swing to her face. Perhaps this is more "realistic" than our being suddenly catapulted into Ophelia's memory in Branagh's film. It more closely resembles our relationship to others – we only learn about their memories from what they show us externally through expressions or words. We do, however, enter Macbeth's head. The witches and Banquo's ghost in this film exist only in his imagination. In the interviews on the DVD, Victoria Hill, who adapted the play for the screen and also plays Lady Macbeth, explains that when she and Wright conceived the film, they intended to have the story told from Macbeth's point of view. In contrast, Branagh in *Hamlet* seems to maintain a largely omniscient point of view as we enter several characters' heads at different moments in the film. Wright does not let us infiltrate Lady Macbeth's imagination; we do not, for instance, see her hands covered with blood as *she* must see them in the mad scene.

The visions of Wright's Macbeth are not, strictly speaking, flashbacks but inserts. Macbeth experiences his first vision of the witches in the graveyard; they are a distraction from his grief over his son. His second vision occurs after he imbibes drugs and alcohol. He participates alone in a kind of orgy with the witches on the dance floor of the club, smoke machines and strobe lights creating a neat parallel for fog and lightning. He sees the witches again in his own kitchen, the horrible and exotic ingredients for their cauldron festooning his state-of-the art counter. Another time he seems to have sex with them in an antechamber off the billiard room decorated like something out of *The Arabian Nights*. This scene is highly reminiscent of one in Francis Ford Coppola's *Bram Stoker's Dracula* (1992), in which Harker is seduced by the bloodsucking succubi in a castle chamber similarly adorned with silky throw pillows, the floor covered with sensuous fabric like a satin bed sheet. Armstrong includes such inserts among devices that "tend to disrupt the narrative, recalling mental processes in a character such as memories or visions which, although often explicable, tend to jar with the spectator following a present tense narrative" (18). But Armstrong surely underestimates the mental agility of the average spectator: we have become so film literate that it takes only a second of adjustment before the insert is understood.

Armstrong is not alone in overestimating the potential confusion of his audience. For instance, Carol Chillington Rutter observes that when Parker's Othello imagines Desdemona and Cassio having sex, "nothing keys it as fantasy." Thus, she suggests, we share Othello's distorted point of view and therefore "this sequence raises 'real' doubts about Desdemona" (255–6). However, Othello's vision is discredited by the rest of the film. Othello's imaginings of his wife's infidelity ignite his epileptic seizures and thus become associated with his malady, reminding the audience that these images are in no way accurate.

Similarly, Wright's Macbeth persistently asks other characters to corroborate his sightings of the witches, which they signally fail to do. Banquo's lines (from Shakespeare) even seem to suggest that Macbeth's encounter with the witches was a result of the drugs he took: "You have eaten on the insane root / That takes the reason prisoner" (based on 1.3.82–3).

Taymor breaks up the narrative of *Titus* with the surreal moments that she calls "Penny Arcade Nightmares" in nostalgic homage to the stage production on which the film was based. She also shifts abruptly from one era to another. The film opens in contemporary times, then in an explosion moves back to ancient Rome with the scene in the Coliseum. In the next scene, we are catapulted to World War II, watching Saturninus, sporting a Hitlerian haircut, driving up to the Mussolini-era Palazzo della Civita Italiana to vie with his brother Bassianus for the emperor's throne. At the conclusion, Taymor brings the time frame forward to our own era, again using the device of young Lucius, in black T-shirt, capris, and Doc Martens, exiting the Coliseum holding Aaron's baby. He is both an observer from another (our) time and a participant in the ancient Roman story.

FADES AND CAMERA ANGLES

While Taymor uses an observer character to segue between scenes, Wright in his *Macbeth* employs the retro fade. The fact that the fade is now a relatively rare technique means that we notice it more. Wright often draws extra attention to it by interposing a coloured screen when shifting to the new scene. For instance, he fades the street scene in which Duncan hears of Macbeth's bravery to a red screen and then cuts to the club where Macbeth and Banquo guard the treacherous Thane of Cawdor. Wright uses red as a dominant colour in the film, suggestive, of course, of blood, anger, and violence. Similarly, when Macbeth has his second vision of the witches in the club, the scene is cut up by white flashes of light that fill the screen while a slashing sound is heard. Wright uses this technique to reinforce the otherworldliness of Macbeth's experience, yet these effects emerge "realistically" from the actual setting of the scene, as they are also the lights and sounds produced for the dance floor of the club. In an interview Wright states that he was influenced by Asian cinema, particularly its "use of colour and the kind of restless camera work and the blatant use of lensing. There's a vitality and an innocence about Asian cinema that I find quite refreshing" (interview on *The Movie Show*, replayed on YouTube).

Whedon uses the flare, a technique similar to the fade, in which the screen flashes white to break up two scenes. Whedon distinguishes the two in his DVD commentary by contending that the "White Out ... just felt right ... the Fade Out dissipates energy ... OTT [over the top]." In addition to the flare, shooting his *Much Ado About Nothing* in black and white and framing many of his shots with windows, doors, or banisters are the only effects that draw attention to themselves in an otherwise naturalistically shot film. In his DVD commentary, Whedon says that he aimed for a "feeling of naturalism ... so you feel as if you're there ... it mustn't be studied." With an oblique dig at the techniques Branagh employed in *Much Ado*, he adds that he used "no establishing shots, certainly no crane shots," as he wanted to "be in the head space of the people." He also, of course, wanted to stay within his very modest budget.

Wright exploits the hand-held camera or perhaps the steady-cam to good effect in the scene in which Banquo's ghost appears at the banquet. The camera tilts and wobbles around the table, reflecting Macbeth's sense of being completely knocked off balance by his vision, and echoing the unease felt by the guests as their host breaks down in front of them. Earlier, when Macbeth struggles to kill the die-hard Duncan, Wright uses a canted frame and low-angle camera looking up to Macbeth diagonally, almost suggesting Duncan's point of view from his bed. Wright also uses this diagonal orientation during the opening credits; the words appear in the sky on one side of a stone angel gravestone, which divides the frame. The angel, filmed from a low angle, seems to loom ominously above the viewer.

Almereyda often chooses low-angle shots in his *Hamlet*. The camera looks up at the cold Manhattan skyscrapers as Hamlet explains to his mother that his grief for his dead father is more than show. The low angle renders Claudius (Kyle MacLachlan) more sinister, and Hamlet (played by the physically slighter Ethan Hawke) more overwhelmed by the looming buildings. Later, when Hamlet laments in voice-over his cursed duty "to set it right" and avenge his father, Almereyda employs speeded-up film to show frenzied people and cars on a Manhattan street. He plays with film speed again as Hamlet moves in slow motion, gun in outstretched arm, in his first and unsuccessful attempt to punish his uncle. The director makes good use of the jump cut as well, as a method of showing time passing as Hamlet, sitting in a diner, agonizes over a poem he is composing for Ophelia. All of these techniques disrupt the audience's expectations of being allowed to forget the editing; the intention is no doubt to confuse while throwing off their visual preconceptions.

Wright also speaks about his use of the high-definition camera, necessary as the film was shot in a mere twenty-five days. He waxes lyrical about the "high def's" ability to "pick up the kick of materials and textures ... make very cheap materials look expensive ... it loves jewellery ... loves the gleam in the actor's eye" ("Interview," *Movie Show*). This rich, glistening effect was an important visual reminder in Wright's satirical portrait of the new, ultra-commercial, consumerist Melbourne. In contrast, Almereyda used a pixel camera for many sequences, particularly parts of Hamlet's soliloquies. The grainy, flickering images are a brilliant visual equivalent for Hamlet's inner philosophical turmoil, the thoughts forming themselves even as he speaks them. Almereyda also favours extreme close-ups of eyes and hands, contributing to the claustrophobic effect – characters trapped in their small, Manhattan apartments, hemmed in by walls of skyscrapers. They cannot escape from each other's faces, pressed in too close; so many of the characters, Gertrude, Claudius, Polonius, Rosencrantz and Guildenstern, plague Hamlet with their questions: "Why does he grieve? Is he in love? Why is he sad? Why is he insane?" These techniques, while breaking the "fourth wall," contribute to a kind of psychological realism. We experience vicariously what the main character endures.

MONTAGE AND OTHER CINEMATIC TECHNIQUES

The montage is a form of shorthand for film, summarizing a sequence of events through cutting. As the great teacher of Method acting, Lee Strasberg, pointed out, "It is possible to put strips of film together and create a performance that never was actually given" (Strasberg, 1957, 64, qtd in Carnicke, 76). Montage can be elegiac, as Luhrmann's is at the very conclusion of *Romeo + Juliet*. The director uses it to boost the emotional impact of the lovers' death – we revisit their happy moments together. Or it can serve exposition, as when Nunn effectively uses his credit sequence for a montage in which Viola, with the help of the captain, transforms herself into her twin brother. Luhrmann uses montage in the opening moments of his film as well, to establish the family trees of the Montagues and Capulets, but he immediately sets his viewers on edge with the rapid cutting, which increases in speed as the music intensifies, until he reaches a frenzied crescendo of movement and sound. This rapid cutting breaks the illusion of reality and is often exploited to unsettle the spectator. Luhrmann favours this technique again for the opening feud in *Romeo + Juliet*. This scene was so radically fast for its time that many reviewers (LaSalle, Gleiberman, Howe) were put off – it seemed an onslaught of the senses; yet is this not appropriate for the enactment of a violent feud?

Luhrmann employs other cutting-edge cinematic techniques such as slam zooms and swish pans, particularly in the opening feud and at the masked ball, accentuating the surreal treatment of the secondary characters and the heightened, eclectic imagery and backdrops, a mixture of kitsch and art, antebellum glamour and seedy decrepitude. Again, we experience the party subjectively from Romeo's drugged point of view rather than gazing through a window at the whole scene, fourth-wall style. These techniques serve an experiential kind of realism.

Equally innovative for its time was Greenaway's use of the Graphic Paintbox technology to overlap images on the screen in *Prospero's Books*. The books themselves particularly come alive, their illustrations animated with moving parts – sketched rain actually sweeps over choppy water in *The Book of Water*. Greenaway also exploits slow motion, close-up, and amplified sound for the water-drops that open his film. His use of the water drop is metaphorically resonant, both suggesting the way the sea ebbs and flows into the poetry of *The Tempest*, and also the insistence of creative ideas in Shakespeare's fluid imagination.

Loncraine takes advantage of superimposition much more sparingly, punctuating his film with occasional moments like Lord Stanley's nightmare in which Richard turns on him, his face suddenly morphing into a boar's snarling mug. Loncraine here creates a rich visual equivalent for the animal imagery associated with Richard in the play, while at the same time expressing Lord Stanley's very reasonable fear of Richard and giving the audience a foretaste of his doom at Richard's hands.

DOCUMENTARY TECHNIQUES

Armstrong discusses the irony that using techniques associated with filming real events to shoot fictional ones actually accentuates the fictional aspects: "Employing the conventions of the documentary – voice-over, real locations, interviews, archive footage – but in the service of a false premise, mockumentaries play with that contract between the bona fide documentary and its spectator which stipulates that what they are watching is genuine ... [and] draws attention to both the fabricated nature of all films, documentaries included, and the fallibility of the spectator, wishing to believe in the veracity of films in general and documentaries in particular" (89). Branagh plays with these notions by creating black-and-white newsreel footage to set his *Love's Labour's Lost* in Europe before World War II. For the most part, the nostalgic newsreels are lighthearted, relating royal gossip to the audience in a voice and diction appropriate for the period. Similarly, Wright uses black-and-white video footage, abruptly intercut with the action of his film, to show the police surveillance trained on Duncan's gang. This surveillance footage is more naturalistic than the newsreels in Branagh's film. These newsreels are entirely for our benefit – none of Branagh's characters witness them – whereas the police officer we see in Wright's film behind the camera has the point of view behind the video footage. Later in the film, we see officers at headquarters watching the footage as it is made.

Related to borrowing the techniques of documentaries is the inclusion of a television screen. Luhrmann frames his *Romeo + Juliet* with an old-fashioned TV set showing news reports. The African-American anchorwoman delivers the opening chorus and the final speech of the play. The invitation to the Capulet ball is also delivered on TV by two smarmy talk-show hosts. In Almereyda's *Hamlet*, we see the young prince constantly editing homemade movies on his screen and watching documentaries. *The Mousetrap* is his sophomoric film about his childhood and his mother's remarriage. This *Hamlet* ends with a news report on a television screen delivering the British ambassador's speech. Fiennes uses the same technique in his *Coriolanus* – much of the military and political exposition is delivered from television screens: in Aufidius's headquarters, in the Roman conference room, in Martius's living room, in the bar frequented by the tribunes. This technique reminded me of the early films of Atom Egoyan, especially

Family Viewing. Like Egoyan, these directors provoke us to question our relationship to the media and to popular culture. How much are we victims of mass conformity? Is the significance of Shakespeare's tragedies lessened or magnified by their stories being covered on the evening news? Does it render them ordinary or make them "relevant" and "accessible?"

SOUNDTRACKS

Most of the Shakespearean adaptations discussed here use music in a fairly conventional way to contribute to an overall realistic effect. The music accompanies the action, emerging out of nowhere. Jocelyn Pook's beautiful score composed specifically for Radford's *Merchant of Venice* opens with a song called "Ghetto," sung by Uri Yehuda, full of Eastern beats. Later in the film we hear airy vocal pieces that sound Elizabethan and use lyrics from Shakespeare and Milton. In many adaptations of Shakespeare's plays, directors take the opportunity to have some of the music emerge from the action. A pre-contemporary setting aids with this, as wealthy households of the past would often have a singer or musician in their retinue. In a musical, like Branagh's *Love's Labour's Lost*, all the sung music emerges from the action, but even in *Othello*, Desdemona must sing the "Willow Song." Parker enlivens other moments in his film with its melody.

Luhrmann, Taymor, Almereyda, and Loncraine devised soundtracks that perfectly reflect the visual eclecticism of the films, drawing on classical, jazz, and rock music. Often the music choice is purposefully ironic rather than apt or conventionally "realistic." Loncraine uses jaunty popular tunes for dark moments; for instance, Richard falls to his death to Jolson's ebullient "I'm Sitting on Top of the World."

Often songs or pieces of music can be employed as pauses in the action, or even as shorthand methods of expressing the feelings of one of the characters. For example, in Luhrmann's *Romeo + Juliet*, as Romeo rushes to Friar Laurence in his car after having declared his love for Juliet in the balcony/pool scene, the Wannadies' song blares out: "Because it's just you and me, oh yeah, now and forever." It's a joyous celebration of romantic love. Luhrmann could have made this moment more strictly "realistic" by having the song emerge from the car radio, but it is clearly imposed on the scene from the soundtrack. Similarly, in Branagh's *Much Ado*, when Beatrice and Benedick discover that their love is requited, they are intercut having a jubilant moment, Benedick splashing in the fountain, Beatrice soaring on the swing, Patrick Doyle's music swelling on the score. (For more on the use of music, see the section "Music and Memory.")

DIRECTORIAL INTENTIONS/IDEOLOGY

The ideas that propel a film, or the director's intentions for the film's effect on an audience, appear to be most explicitly exposed in interviews with the director, actors, and producers. However, it must be remembered that such interviews are part of a film's publicity, so it is in the interviewee's best interest to make the film sound as accessible and entertaining as possible. Often the publicity for an adaptation downplays the film's more controversial, challenging, or complex aspects. At the very least, interviews and other publicity material reveal what the creative personnel *want* the audience to believe the film is about. The implicit ideology can only be gleaned by paying careful attention to the choices made in casting, narrative structure, mis en scène, editing, and camerawork.

Armstrong argues that "family values" are "central to the ideological ethos of Hollywood films ... heterosexual closure is the lot of most Hollywood protagonists" (55). This theme may in part explain why Shakespeare's plays are popular sources for adaptations. The comedies progress inexorably towards marriage and family, and the tragedies demonstrate the suffering that awaits members of dysfunctional families. These aspects suggest that Shakespearean adaptations participate in what Duvendak suggests is a nostalgia for past family life, as the North American family is seen to be in crisis. It is entirely possible to wrest contemporary, conservative morals from the outcomes of Shakespeare's tragedies. Othello and Desdemona come to a sticky end because Othello does not trust his wife sufficiently and Desdemona does not communicate openly enough with her husband. Romeo and Juliet's parents are punished for the violent, pointless feud they maintain with a rival family. Claudius brings destruction on his family by killing his brother and marrying his sister-in-law. The Macbeths end badly because Lady Macbeth interferes in Macbeth's career, and he kills the king as a result. If all the characters in these plays had merely attended to their family relationships, none of the suffering would have befallen them.

These morals – gross oversimplifications of complex plays – very much fit with the framework of "realistic" Hollywood films. Adultery is punished severely in most Hollywood films, the instigator often facing death or imprisonment. For instance, in *Fatal Attraction* (1987) the Glenn Close character is drowned in a bathtub for trying (admittedly with psychotic aggression) to woo her married lover away from his family. In *Presumed Innocent* (1990) the Harrison Ford character is almost incarcerated for murder as a result of cheating on his wife, who then kills his mistress. In *Miss Pettigrew Lives for a Day* (2008), Edythe (Shirley Henderson) loses her fiancé as a consequence of her infidelity to him, and the young actress, Delysia, abandons her life of three-timing to settle down to marital bliss with the poorest and most sincere of her suitors. In *Regarding Henry* (1991), the cheating husband and negligent father, Henry, is shot in an armed burglary and suffers brain damage, which results in his becoming a better father and husband. In examples too numerous to mention, the Hollywood film upholds the notion that the ideal family is one in which a husband and wife are faithful to one another and devoted to their children (which means putting the children before their careers, or at least making time to watch their sporting events). Divorce is largely avoided as an explanation for bachelordom; single parents have more often lost their partners through disease or car accident (*Dan in Real Life*, 2007; *Yours, Mine, Ours*, 2005). Couples filing for divorce, or even after divorce, are often reconciled (*Twister*, 1996; *Fool's Gold*, 2008; *Laws of Attraction*, 2004; *The Parent Trap*, 1998; *Sweet Home Alabama*, 2002) – a phenomenon common only to Hollywood romantic comedies. Given these tendencies, it is no wonder that Shakespeare is nostalgically mined for stories: the only divorce in his canon is that of Henry VIII from Catherine of Aragon.

The yearning for a "simpler" past goes deeper still in Hollywood. In comedies, female characters tend to have nurturing careers that display their maternal instincts. They teach school or dance or art or look after dogs or patients (*School of Rock*, 2003; *The Jane Austen Book Club*, 2006; *Crush*, 2001; *Fearless*, 1993; *Meet the Parents*, 2000; *Monster in Law*, 2007; *Tall Guy*, 1989). Again, Shakespeare fits the bill, as most of his women either do not have careers because they are from the idle classes or are ladies-in-waiting, whose job is to serve and take care of others.

Armstrong succinctly summarizes other ideological tendencies of mainstream Hollywood films: "Ideas such as the importance of self-determination combined with teamwork, God, family and country underlie the American economy ... From the earliest age, American children are taught to become high achievers, while team sports are encouraged in preparation for a corporate economy of punishing targets and team spirit. Embodying many of these values, Hollywood films have always been regarded by Washington politicians as the best advertisements for American ideas and products" (57). This concept of self-determination is explored in some detail in *Hamlet* by the prince's soliloquies ("I do not know / Why yet I live to say 'This thing's to do,' / Sith I have cause, and will, and strength, and means / To do't," 4.4.34–7), and by Lady Macbeth in *Macbeth* ("But screw your courage to the sticking place / And we'll not fail," 1.7.60). In the wake of Machiavelli, the notion of forging one's own destiny was much bandied about in Elizabethan drama. Marlowe's heroes are self-made men, much as he, Ben Jonson, and Shakespeare all were. All three playwrights came from fairly humble backgrounds – a blacksmith's son, a bricklayer's (step)son, and a glover's son, respectively – and ended up familiar with court life and courtiers, anticipating the social rise at the heart of the American Dream. It may also be that part of the nostalgia for Shakespeare's time exhibited by his adaptors comes as a result of their admiration for high-achievers, not only Shakespeare himself but many of his characters, and of course, his contemporaries. The Renaissance is viewed in popular culture as a time of remarkable personal achievement; we still use the term "Renaissance man" to suggest a person of wide-ranging accomplishments.

Self-determination is often suggested in the way the films are sold. The publicity for *Henry V* had the tagline "He became king only to prove himself a man"; *Richard III*, "What is worth dying for is worth killing for"; Almereyda's *Hamlet*, "Passion. Betrayal. Revenge. A hostile takeover is underway"; *Prospero's Books*: "A Magician's Spell, the Innocence of Young Love, and a Dream of Revenge Unite to Create a Tempest." The rare quality of the project, its innovation and entertainment value, are also often stressed, as in the following taglines: Zeffirelli's *Hamlet*, "The extraordinary telling of a classic tale"; Branagh's *Love's Labour's Lost*, "A New Spin on the old Song and Dance"; *Titus*: "If you think you know Shakespeare ... Think Again"; Whedon's *Much Ado About Nothing*: "Shakespeare Knew How to Throw a Party." Some advertise their status as romantic comedy, suggesting the trajectory towards heterosexual union: in Hoffman's *Midsummer Night's Dream*, "Love makes fools of us all"; *As You Like It*, "Romance or something like it."

Tackling a Shakespeare script to transform it into film, a director is facing a property that has been acknowledged by the whole world to be "Great Art." This is both an advantage and a disadvantage. Shakespeare's name guarantees that the film project will be taken seriously from an artistic or critical point of view, but it also means that it will be viewed with much scepticism by anyone hoping to make money from the project. There is the fear that audiences will regard the film as something that is good for them, like broccoli – a film they should attend to prove to their social circle that they are cultivated, but one they do not necessarily envisage having a good time watching. This is what Claire Monk might term "an aspirational motivation": obviously, the "broccoli" kind of motivation directors want to avoid. As Branagh joked, "We did not want them [the audience] to feel they were in some cultural church" (*Ado, Screenplay*, ix).

As a consequence of all these fraught expectations, directors of Shakespearean films tend to arm their screenplays with apologia, or auteur's manifestos. Whereas other auteurs stress the originality of their approach, Shakespearean auteurs usually emphasize the realism, currency, and fun of their work. Oliver Parker says of *Othello*, "I was obsessed with the play and realized how exciting it was and how it should really capture an audience in a more physical, visceral way" (Anderson and Sao Pedro, 1). Branagh, in his foreword to his *Hamlet* screenplay, summarizes his approach: "A commitment to international casting; a speaking style that is as realistic as a proper adherence to the structure of the language will allow; a period setting that attempts to set the story in a historical context that is resonant for a modern audience but allows a heightened language to sit comfortably. Above all, we have asked for a full emotional commitment to the characters, springing from the belief that they can be understood in direct, accessible relation to modern life" (xv). Trevor Nunn's aims outlined in the introduction to his *Twelfth Night* screenplay are strikingly similar: "Our intention was to be as populist and accessible as we could manage short of betraying the text" (viii). Loncraine concurs: "I wanted to make an accessible version of Shakespeare, a version that people who are frightened of Shakespeare could go and see without any preconceptions" ("Production Notes," 14).

McKellen maintains that it is not the adaptor's job to resurrect Elizabethan storytelling practices: "I don't think it's ever possible to recreate the past by putting on a production in the way it was first produced ... I don't want to spend my time recreating what Shakespeare was like in the past. I always want to think that my duty, if I am going to serve him at all, is to bring Shakespeare into the present. I think that we should only look at the past to see how it can enlighten the present. And when an actor steps onto a stage to speak Shakespeare, it's not to take the audience back in time but to bring Shakespeare forward" (*Writings*, 3). McKellen's statement meshes with Nunn's and Branagh's aim to be accessible. To the ongoing debate about the best way to serve Shakespeare in our time, Oliver Parker adds the importance of making concessions to the conventions of film: "If you do them [Shakespeare's plays] without making any alteration for the new medium you're working in, then I think you're going to do the piece a disservice ... You have to do something or 'Othello' would be four hours long!" (Anderson and Sao Pedro, 2).

The hybrid nature of the film medium was uppermost in Greenaway's mind when discussing *Prospero's Books*. His intention with the film was to "link the vocabulary of electronic picture-making with the traditions of the artist's pen, palette and brush, permit[ting] a personal signature" (28). He is unusual among the directors considered here in seeming unafraid of revealing his auteur's approach. He does not suggest that his film is "accessible" or even "realistic" but rather views its uniqueness as its selling point. His position may be a consequence of his status in the British film world as a well-respected maverick director. He feels no need to tout his films in the general marketplace.

Wright maintains that he intended to reflect what he sees as the current rampant materialism in Australian culture. He hired set, costume, and make-up designers who all "honed their craft in commercials." Wright valued their ability "to make things seductive and beautiful" so that the audience could share "Macbeth's materialism, and lust, and vaulting ambition" (*Movie Show* interview). Certainly, Dunsinane is glossily and often vulgarly opulent, and the Macbeths have servants to help at their lavish parties. Julie Taymor similarly hoped to reflect current realities in her approach. Of her intentions with *Titus*, she wrote in her screenplay, "I wanted to blend and collide time, to create a singular period that juxtaposed elements of ancient barbaric ritual with familiar, contemporary attitude and style" (172).

Of course, the familiar and the contemporary are also registered by audiences as "realistic" or "accessible"; what is familiar from our own experience of life necessarily seems more "real" than what is unfamiliar or strange. It also feeds our nostalgia. At the same time, Taymor's film is very strange and disturbing, even while elements of it are familiar and contemporary. Sarah Hatchuel notes that the typecasting of Hopkins in a role recognizable to audiences who saw him as Hannibal Lecter in Jonathan Demme's 1992 film *Silence of the Lambs* "embeds a very familiar movie into an unfamiliar play" (116). Taymor saw her approach as bifurcated: "Though I was committed to creating a film whose world would be grounded in a sense of possibility and reality, I was also committed to the ideas I had formulated in the theatre that juxtaposed stylized and naturalistic imagery" (*Titus, Screenplay*, 178). She is referring at the end of the quotation to her Penny Arcade Nightmares, discussed earlier.

In addition to facing the challenges of audience's preconceptions, Shakespearean directors usually have to operate within a constrained financial framework. Michael Almereyda in his preface to his screenplay of *Hamlet* is keen to excuse the low production values of the film: "You don't need lavish production values to make a Shakespeare movie that's accessible and alive" (vii). Wright also confesses that his *Macbeth* was set in the present because "we didn't have the budget to shoot it in a medieval period style (like Polanski). By updating it we could use modern existing locations and costumes, we didn't have to invent everything from the ground up as we would have if we'd gone with a traditional period look" (Loreti). All the directors at some point in the introductions to their screenplays or in interviews have alluded to straitened funds. As Almereyda observes of his *Cymbeline* in the DVD commentary, "It's the nature of these movies [Shakespeare adaptations] to make a virtue of necessity." Studios are still wary of splashing out on a Shakespeare film, which is generally for a coterie audience and dependent on residuals from sales to schools and universities.

CONCLUSION

Branagh's *Henry V* has been credited with some responsibility for ushering in the renaissance in Shakespearean adaptations to the screen. Branagh's Shakespeare films have, on the whole, favoured a realistic approach to the performance of Shakespeare. His style has been echoed and emulated in other Shakespeare films in the past decade, particularly in Nunn's *Twelfth Night*, Parker's *Othello*, and Hoffman's *A Midsummer Night's Dream*. Three of his films are also among the six top-grossing adaptations of Shakespeare to the screen considered here. Other directors have opted for an eclectic approach. Luhrmann directed his Romeo (Leonardo DiCaprio) and Juliet (Claire Danes, trained at the Lee Strasberg Theatre) to act realistically, while secondary characters like Lady Capulet (Diane Venora) and Mercutio (John Leguizimo) deliver stylized performances. Similarly, in Loncraine's *Richard III*, we find an uneasy yoking of realism (Annette Bening's Queen Elizabeth and Kristin Scott Thomas's Lady Anne) with stylization (McKellen's Richard). In the latter two films, the setting is both surreal or anachronistic, and real, and so modern as to set the iambic pentameter into bold relief. Luhrmann's film is the top-grossing Shakespeare adaptation. It is, however, the only one of the more stylized, less realistic treatments of Shakespeare's plays to fare so well in the box office. Three films that fared badly, falling far short of the $1 million mark in profits, took a more experimental approach: Branagh's *Love's Labour's Lost*, Taymor's *Tempest*, and Wright's *Macbeth*. Nunn's *Twelfth Night* is an anomaly, being both generally realistic and financially unsuccessful (IMDB, Box Office Mojo).

Kenneth Rothwell commented in *A History of Shakespeare on Screen* that "a pragmatic Branagh uses whatever film grammar works to his advantage" (248). This summation is equally true of many Shakespearean directors in the fiscally cautious Hollywood of the past twenty-six years. Acting is realistic on the whole, yet often married with stylized sets, music, effects, and camera work to provide visual interest for audiences who are well versed in film but not in Shakespearean dialogue.

The importance of the Shakespearean dialogue in a given adaptation is often revealing of the director's ultimate aim. The directors of Shakespeare who most closely conform to conventional Hollywood norms of "realistic" filmmaking are most interested in telling Shakespeare's story to a new audience, so the Shakespearean dialogue, while reduced, is not obscured by sophisticated production values like self-consciously "arty" editing and camera techniques. The directors of Shakespeare who are most interested in personally reinterpreting Shakespeare's story put their own fiercely unique stamp on it. The first group privilege Shakespeare, the second their ideas about Shakespeare, so that the first comes across as a filmed production of a Shakespeare play and the second a filmed commentary or collage on a Shakespeare play. In the first case, the focus appears to be on Shakespeare's mastery of language and character. Nunn, Parker, Hoffman, Radford, Kurzel, and Branagh, who eschew quicksilver cuts on the whole, depend primarily on the playscript. With their long takes, the focus is very much on the language, the characters, and the performances. In the second case, the audience's focus is centred on the directors' ingenuity, including their original editing. The first approach is better at sweeping us up emotionally, the second better at piquing our intellectual curiosity. It is a rare film that can do both. *Titus* is very successful at appealing both to the emotions and to the intellect; the performances of Anthony Hopkins (Titus) and Laura Fraser (Lavinia) are truthful and touching, while Taymor's frame, sets, and Penny Arcade Nightmares, her music and editing, keep the adaptation fresh and thought-provoking. Greenaway's *Prospero's Books* is less successful. It entirely fails to engage the emotions, as the actors do not actually inhabit their roles. Instead, we are inundated with a collection of arresting, sometimes intellectually stimulating images gathered under the rubric of Shakespeare's *Tempest*.

Luhrmann's *Romeo + Juliet* manages to be both emotionally powerful and stylistically bold and original. Part of its success is that the two leads are treated to much more conservative filmmaking than are the other characters, so that we focus on their feelings while we ponder on the nature of our society, particularly the role of the media, in the scenes in which other characters dominate. Similarly successful in the box office was *Shakespeare in Love*, which shares with Luhrmann's film the realistic performances of the two romantic leads and a marriage of high and low culture, Renaissance and contemporary elements, appealing to a greater variety of tastes and helping to create a bridge between the audience's time and that of Shakespeare.

PART TWO

Remembering Origins

3

Shakespeare's Prologues on Page and Screen

The three chapters in this section, "Remembering Origins," look back at the literary and temporal foundations of these adaptations. This chapter looks at beginnings.

Film directors of Shakespeare almost invariably introduce some kind of frame into their film to help the viewer enter Shakespeare's world and language. When we examine and compare the beginnings of these films, it becomes clear that for the most part Shakespearean adaptors do not think a contemporary audience will enjoy the plays' original openings. More often than not, Shakespeare opens his plays *in medias res*, with several minor characters engaged in discussing the play's hero or heroine or their family. Few film adaptations follow Shakespeare's lead. The issue is not just the challenge of Shakespeare's language, as that would not explain the frequency with which scene order is also altered or extradiagetic scenes created. These directors' innovations suggest that the conventions for performed stories and audience expectations about narrative form have changed hugely since the seventeenth century. In most cases, directors think it necessary to add some sort of explanatory material to smooth the transition to the language and the world of the story.

This explanatory material almost always takes an old-fashioned form – titles appearing on the screen, recalling both the printed play and the silent film, or voice-over, which lends an elegiac tone and reminds the audience of childhood, of being read or told a story. Often these openings acknowledge in some way past adaptations of Shakespeare to the screen. As the subgenre of the Shakespeare film is still small, although growing every year, a director will likely have seen all the films previously based on the particular Shakespeare play he or she is adapting. As it is feasible to view all the film adaptations of *Hamlet*, for instance, the anxiety of influence is acute for Shakespeare adaptors. Consequently, pressures to make the play seem new or their own in some manner, and to justify the innovation, are all the heavier. In the case of previously adapted plays, the opening scene trumpets to the audience what is novel or different about this adaptation.

The prologues provided by the Shakespearean film adaptor are also one of many means to identify the Shakespeare film genre. As Michael Anderegg points out in *Cinematic Shakespeare*, the use of a framing device in a Shakespeare adaptation is a reflection of its status as a subgenre of the literary adaptation (3). For example, the Hollywood literary adaptation is often characterized by opening with text of some kind. *The Lord of the Rings* (2001) DVD menu opens with the inscription on the ring itself, encircling a series of key images from the film. Disney's DVD menu for *Beauty and the Beast* (1991) opens with a book, the pages turning in the wind. Wes Anderson's *Fantastic Mr. Fox* (2009) opens with the image of Roald Dahl's book, while the recent live-action *The Jungle Book* (2016) ends with Kipling's book staged as a magical pop-up. Often a narrator introduces the story. Cate Blanchett launches the *Lord of the Rings* trilogy with her voice-over summarizing the creation of the master ring; we are shown a map with place names. *Sleepy Hollow* (1999) opens with blood-red sealing wax dripping on a last will and testament – text again. These are all indications to the audience that what they are about to watch comes from "Literature" (3–4). Even films not based on literature sometimes make a spurious association with it, as for instance, Wes Anderson's *The Royal Tennenbaums* (2002), which opens with a book, presumably the basis for the film, being borrowed from the library. Such openings suggest the primacy of the printed original over the screen adaptation and imply a nostalgia for a more print-based culture.

The prologues in Shakespearean adaptations can be divided into four general types, reflecting the approach taken by directors to ease their audiences into the Shakespearean world. In each case, by referring back to Shakespeare's own script, it is possible to assess what has been gained and lost in the translation to the screen.

Perhaps the most common technique of introducing a Shakespeare play to a cinema audience is to fall back on explanatory titles. A device common to literary adaptations in general, and to historical epics, it is a way of bridging the gap between past and present, and between two locations – the North American multiplex, for example, and Renaissance Venice. Michael Radford's *Merchant of Venice* (2005), starring Al Pacino as Shylock, opens with titles explaining the status of the Jews in sixteenth-century Venice. The titles provide context for the audience, and they also protect the film from charges of anti-Semitism. They are almost a disclaimer: the views presented by the characters in this film in no way represent those of the filmmaker. An extratextual scene follows, in which we witness an angry mob of Christians denouncing the practice of usury and blaming the Jews. We see a Jewish man thrown into the canal by the irate horde. Antonio, the eponymous hero (played by Jeremy Irons) watches and then strolls through the crowd. He passes Shylock, who greets him by name, and Antonio responds to this friendliness by spitting at his face. At the outset, then, Radford has garnered the audience's sympathy for the Jews in general and Shylock in particular, and the effect is quite different from that of watching Shakespeare's own beginning, which, of course, shows no underlying concern about charges of anti-Semitism.

Shakespeare's play opens with Antonio and his friends Salerio and Solanio discussing Antonio's melancholy, which they attribute to his anxiety regarding his ships at sea. As the scene develops, the audience may surmise that his unease is more likely caused by his unrequited love for the young Bassanio, who enters later. Radford follows his extratextual opening with this scene, but Antonio has already essentially been displaced as the hero by Shylock, not only because his rudeness to Shylock has gained our sympathy for the usurer, but also because Al Pacino outranks Jeremy Irons as a star, and so our assumption is that it is Shylock's story, not Antonio's. This may in fact have been the case even in Shakespeare's time, as the play was given the subtitle "The Jew of Venice." If Richard Burbage played Shylock on Shakespeare's stage, his audience too would have assumed the play was really Shylock's vehicle. Crowl summarizes: "Shylock is one of Shakespeare's most ambiguous characters: is he a comic villain, revenge figure, or tragic hero? Pacino's performance manages to embody many of the character's contradictory elements even as Radford's film wants us to see Shylock almost exclusively as a victim of Christian hypocrisy" (*Shakespeare and Film*, 94).

Michael Almereyda's *Hamlet* (2000) also opens with explanatory titles. While the screenplay starts as Shakespeare's play does with Horatio and Marcellus (here Marcella) seeing the ghost, the film opens instead with the words "New York City, 2000" against a backdrop of shining steel and glass skyscrapers. Then through the back window of moving car, we see these titles: "The King and CEO of Denmark Corporation is dead. The king's widow has hastily remarried his younger brother. The king's son, Hamlet, returns from school, suspecting foul play." The old-fashioned technique of using titles juxtaposes starkly with the modernity of the gleaming cityscape. The titles yield to a night street, with a large billboard ad for Denmark Corp. The camera then focuses on the sign "Hotel Elsinore" carved on a luxurious skyscraper. We cut to a black-and-white image on a camcorder of Hamlet delivering a truncated version of a famous speech: "I have of late, for reasons I know not, lost all my mirth. What a piece of work is a man? How noble in reason, how infinite in faculties, in form how like an angel, in apprehension how like a god, the beauty of the world, the paragon of animals ... And yet to me, what is this quintessence of dust?" (2.2.297–312).

The image of Ethan Hawke delivering this speech in an offhand, melancholy voice is intercut with his own montage illustrating images of the speech with clips of angels, airplanes, and monsters. We cut back to Hamlet in colour, watching his homemade film as he rides an elevator. The word "Hamlet" fills the screen, now a red background, in the same style and font as Hamlet will later use for his own *Mousetrap* film. Then we cut to Hamlet filming a press conference where Claudius makes his inaugural address as CEO of Denmark Corp. Hamlet is filming the media, not his uncle. From these opening moments it is clear that Almereyda is going to use Shakespeare's tragedy to comment on our media-saturated, technology-dominated society. This Denmark is rotten in part because of its solipsistic need to record its every moment on film. In fact, as Almereyda explains in his screenplay, in this film Denmark is a "multi-media corporation" (viii). The opening scene, with its emphasis on Hamlet's camera and those of the press, prepares us for a film in which "every scene ... features a ... recording device of some kind" (x).

The second scene continues much as in the play, only Hamlet's "sullied flesh" soliloquy is said in voice-over as he watches black-and-white footage of his father on his camcorder screen in his room. Meanwhile, Ophelia waits in vain at their appointed rendezvous by the fountain. The scene continues, again as in the play, with Horatio and Marcell*a* and the security guard coming to tell him of his father's ghost. Their account of the sighting is punctuated by flashbacks that use dialogue from act 1, scene 1. This is all very different from Almereyda's script, which maintains Shakespeare's order of events. Almereyda changed the sequence in the editing room as a result of a test audience's reaction: "It became apparent that the Elizabethan language, coming thick and fast at the outset, confused our early audiences. (A test screening organized by Miramax yielded the second worst scores in the company's history.) More to the point, it was troublingly clear that Hamlet's first appearance in the film came too late and felt flat" (*Screenplay*, 135).

Remarkably, many directors alter Shakespeare's unbeatably gripping opening to *Hamlet*. Shakespeare begins his tragedy on dark ramparts with jumpy guards biting out staccato questions, clearly terrified. One would have thought opening a film with the appearance of a ghost in full armour on a castle wall was an opportunity to be seized upon, but it has clearly proved otherwise. Franco Zeffirelli opens his *Hamlet* with Hamlet Senior's funeral and cuts the opening scene altogether. Why?

Almereyda and Zeffirelli change Shakespeare's stunning opening for several good reasons. One reason is that it provides no immediate background. Shakespeare does not reveal anything of young Hamlet until the end of the scene but instead begins with two sentinels, minor characters, one of whom (Francisco) never appears again. Zeffirelli and Almereyda both get their stars on the screen as soon as possible. The background provided in Shakespeare's play is about Danish politics: the recent war with Norway and so on, disclosed in a long speech of Horatio's that a modern film audience might not have the patience or the linguistic skill to understand. Almereyda's test audience had trouble even with his radically reduced dialogue.

The second problem for filmmakers with Shakespeare's opening is that it leaves little room to build suspense. The ghost appears at line 37 in the play. A modern audience is still grappling with the transition to Elizabethan English at this point, and therefore may not fully appreciate the ghostly encounter. Both directors save it for later in the film when Hamlet is directly involved. In fact, the Hollywood convention for mysteries is to avoid the supernatural in the opening sequences; first establish a reassuring mood of normalcy, gradually introduce indications that something is not right, and then rupture the normalcy when the audience is least expecting it. Many Elizabethan and Jacobean plays instead open with a supernatural bang: *Hamlet* with a ghost, *Macbeth* with witches, *Dr. Faustus* with a scholar flagged by good and evil spirits. As people living in the twenty-first century, we tend to think of ourselves as visually quick to catch on, yet it seems that Shakespeare's audience were better at being thrown in the deep end than we are. Of course, some directors have trusted Shakespeare and modern audiences more. Kenneth Branagh opens his *Hamlet* (1996) as Shakespeare does, on the castle ramparts. It is an effective opening, and accessible, even if box-office returns would suggest otherwise.

Almereyda's use of titles is spare and economical, in part because of his choice of setting. He does not need to explain twenty-first century New York to his audience, and he assumes, with good reason, that the cutthroat corporate world makes a close enough parallel with medieval royal politics that his audience will know what to expect. His is not the first corporate *Hamlet*. Japanese director Akira Kurosawa's 1960 *The Bad Sleep Well* was a loose adaptation of Shakespeare's tragedy that exposed corruption in big business. While Almereyda does not cite Kurosawa's influence directly, he describes in his screenplay "watching every version of *Hamlet* available in New York" (x) while preparing to shoot his film.

Almereyda selects the same strategy of introductory titles to introduce his *Cymbeline*. As the plot is much less familiar than that of *Hamlet* and much more convoluted, he includes more titles than in his first Shakespearean adaptation. In this case, eight sets of inter-titles give a brief summary of the entire plot. The first title reads: "For years, Cymbeline, King of the Briton Motorcycle Club, has maintained an uneasy peace with the Roman Police Force." This sentence not only explains the political situation of the film's world but also elucidates the shift to modern times, replacing a king and Roman general with a bike-gang leader, and chief of a group of corrupt police. Almereyda then shows us Ed Harris, who plays Cymbeline, surrounded by three of his henchmen. The second title continues: "The Queen, Cymbeline's second wife, has her own agenda." What follows is a shot of Milla Jovovich at her dressing table, applying red lipstick and then gazing at a photograph of her son, Cloten. The titles elaborate: "But she's losing hope that her son will pair up with the king's only daughter, Imogen." We are then introduced to Dakota Johnson, kneeling at the foot of a four-poster bed, her head drooping in despair. The fifth title reads: "Without consulting her royal parents, Imogen decides to marry Posthumous, Cymbeline's penniless protégé." Almereyda gives us a shot of Penn Badgley walking down a hall, wringing his hands. The sixth title explains: "The marriage triggers the king's rage, setting in motion a series of disastrous events." This is succeeded by a shot of Ed Harris cocking his gun, his henchmen following suit, and heading for the door of the building. The seventh title is merely suggestive: "But fortune brings in some boats that are not steered." We are then treated to a glimpse of Imogen shorn and dressed like a boy, a dazed expression on her face, riding in the back of a car. Almereyda cuts to a shot of Posthumous tied to a table by chains. Bill Pullman, playing his father, looks at him, saying, "My poor boy!" and then disappearing into thin air. The final title reads, "One week earlier." We cut to some bleachers at night. Imogen approaches on a bicycle, and there meets with Posthumous. They share a truncated version of their dialogue in act 1, scene 1, lines 112–2, in which they exchange gifts before Cymbeline appears with an entourage to send Posthumous away.

Almereyda's titles and intercut shots achieve the aim of introducing the characters, but so swiftly and choppily that it is difficult to believe anyone without prior knowledge of the events of the play could follow the snippets of plot. The dependence on so many explanatory titles reveals the inherent challenges in adapting this particular play to the screen – it is simply too crammed with incident to be successfully encapsulated in an hour and a half. The film is all action with little time for characterization or even motivation to be suggested. Dialogue is radically reduced to save time to show all the threads of the plot, and the result is a muddle.

Michael Hoffman's *William Shakespeare's A Midsummer Night's Dream* also opens with explanatory titles. Hoffman uses these in part to justify setting the play not in ancient Athens, under the rule of Theseus and his Amazon queen Hippolyta, but in nineteenth-century Monte Athena, Italy. The tone of the titles, in contrast to those of *The Merchant of Venice* and *Hamlet*, is playful. Hoffman is at pains to suggest that the period setting is going to be fun for the audience, and almost encourages us to laugh at the peculiarities of our forebears. The first title reads, "The village of Monte Athena in Italy at the turn of the 19th century. Necklines are high. Parents are rigid. Marriage is seldom a matter of love." After a short pause, the second title appears: "The good news: the bustle is in its decline allowing for the meteoric rise of that newfangled creation, the bicycle." (The bicycle seems to fascinate Shakespearean directors; Trevor Nunn stuck one into his *Twelfth Night* in 1995 with similar comic intentions. Malvolio anticipated Puck in weaving unsteadily about on a borrowed bike). Hoffman is also careful to include some nostalgic material for those acquainted with Shakespeare's play. He opens with Tinkerbell-style firefly lights, representing the fairies, and Felix Mendelssohn's score. This is what the older generation of cinema-goers has come to expect from Shakespeare's *Dream*, and Hoffman promises them here that they will not be disappointed. In appealing to this same demographic, he moves from the titles to an establishing shot of a grand Italian mansion in a state of bustling preparation. Countless servants set tables on an impeccable lawn, and a profusion of pastel flowers suggests a wedding banquet. The camera then enters a dark, steamy kitchen where a glorious feast is being created.

These establishing shots place the film into its niche (romantic comedy/heritage piece) in cinema history as much as giving the audience the heads-up that a fancy wedding is anticipated. The bel canto music, Tuscan landscape, and aristocratic mansion remind the audience of Merchant/Ivory productions like *A Room with a View* (1986), or *Where Angels Fear to Tread* (1991, dir. Charles Sturridge). The busy kitchen with mounds of game being prepared links the film with sensual delights like *Babette's Feast* (1987). The film seems to share with "heritage cinema" the "aesthetic of display" (Heritage Film Audiences, 18). The promise of a wedding taps into the fad, still continuing, for romantic comedies centred on weddings: *Four Weddings and a Funeral* (1994), *My Best Friend's Wedding* (1997), *The Wedding Singer* (1998), *Polish Wedding* (1998), *The Wedding Planner* (2001), *My Big Fat Greek Wedding* (2002), *American Wedding* (2003), *Wedding Crashers* (2005), *Bride Wars* (2009), *Bridesmaids* (2011), *The Big Wedding* (2013), *The Wedding Ringer* (2015). The entire opening sets up expectations in the audience for visual splendour and romantic sentiment. This mood is in keeping with Shakespeare's own opening, which has Theseus panting for his wedding night and planning to while away the tedious hours till then with entertainments. Hoffman keeps this initial dialogue between Theseus and his fiancée, but by prefacing it with many visual clues, and the explanatory titles, leaves no room for misunderstanding. The titles, with their reference to rigid parents and loveless marriages, prime the audience for the ensuing scene with Egeus and Hermia.

Hoffman cuts the dialogue fairly radically in this scene, being especially ruthless with Hermia's lines, so the titles, in combination with Egeus's stern looks and Hermia's tears, fill the gaps. The cuts do affect the rest of the play, however, as Hermia's character is rendered even more cipher-like. Shakespeare took few pains to distinguish his young lovers with well-developed personalities, but in Hoffman's film, they are reduced further. The women particularly suffer from line cuts. Consequently the sense that their friendship, which has endured since childhood, is threatened by Puck's blundering has none of the impact in the film that it has in the play. In Shakespeare's midsummer night, the lovers experience more of a nightmare than a dream – all of them stand to lose so much love and friendship – but Hoffman has transferred that sense of lost potential to Kevin Kline's henpecked Bottom, and the lovers are merely ridiculous, floundering in the mud. Interestingly, the mud fight between the two young ladies seemed to excite some reviewers more than any other aspect of the film, suggesting that the omission of this scene from the trailers was a missed opportunity (Errico, 110). The substitution of screen business for lines of text is characteristic of the film as a whole. Charles Marowitz explains the consequences of such directorial choices: "The excitement that comes from unbroken dramatic continuity on the stage is fractured and, sometimes lost altogether" (71).

Richard Loncraine's film version of *Richard III* (1995) also opens with titles, blood-red on a black background. Like many pre-twentieth century productions of the play, and Olivier's film, the titles give us material that Shakespeare covered in *Henry VI, Part III*. The use of titles and reference to "sources" are characteristics it shares with the historical film genre. (Interestingly, Branagh's *Henry V* does not start in this way, despite other historical genre features). Where Shakespeare's play starts with Richard alone, wondering what to do now that his occupation as warrior is redundant, the film starts with England still at war. The first set of titles reads, "Civil War divides the nation. The king is under attack from the rebel York family, who are fighting to place their eldest son, Edward, on the throne. Edward's army advances, led by his youngest brother ... Richard of Gloucester." At this point, we see a tickertape emerging from its machine with the words: "Richard Gloucester is at hand. He holds his course toward

Tewkesbury." Then the red titles reappear, announcing that we are at the "Field Headquarters of the King's army at Tewkesbury." We are in a map room bustling with young, uniformed men. One of them takes the tickertape to another, offering it to him with "Your highness?" The prince looks at it with a worried expression, passing it to an older man beside him, who appears even more anxious. The older man heads to the door, the prince following. "Goodnight, your majesty," he says. The king answers, "Good night, sir," and the prince sighs, "Father" – just to solidify the identification in the audience's collective head. Loosening his tie, the prince moves to his private office, where dinner is brought to his desk on a tray. A photo of Lady Anne (Kristin Scott Thomas) is prominently displayed on his desk. As the prince eats, his black Labrador, curled up in front of a lit fire, gnaws on a bone. Suddenly the dog looks up, whimpering, and the prince gestures to his subordinate to stop tapping Morse code. We hear the sound of rumbling, getting closer. A tank bursts through the fireplace and troops enter, shooting. One of the soldiers, in a gas mask, the sounds of his breathing hugely amplified Darth-Vader like (an homage to Branagh's entrance in a swirling dark cloak in his 1989 *Henry V*?) shoots the prince, his blood splattering the painting behind him. Moving to another room where the king kneels, praying, the soldier aims his gun. As he fires, a big red "R" appears, as if from the barrel, followed by the rest of the name: "Richard III." Before the name fills the screen, Ian McKellen rips off his mask to make the identification complete.

This dramatic opening links *Richard III* with two Hollywood genres, the war film and the gangster movie. It anticipates Taymor's *Titus*, which also opens with a domestic scene of eating ruptured by an explosion through the wall. *The Godfather* films too boast many scenes in which the gangsters' victims are surprised in the midst of ordinary tasks – being shaved, eating a meal, not unlike the doomed in Holbein's Dance of Death. The gangster association is continued when we cut to Richard, in full military regalia, sitting in the back of a limousine while jazz plays. We catch glimpses of the City of Westminster, London, as the credits roll. Loncraine introduces us to each member of the York family in turn as they prepare for, or arrive at, the celebratory party. For extra clarity, he groups the family together for a photograph, freeze-framing them and superimposing more red titles: "Edward is King. The York family celebrates their victory. Now, they hope, begins their lasting joy." We cut to a jazz singer on a stage singing a version of Marlowe's "Come Live with Me and Be My Love," as Edward and Elizabeth dance. They later sit on thrones, making their status clear. The camera focuses in turn on all the players, with the notable exception of Queen Margaret, whom Loncraine and McKellen have cut from the cast, transferring a few of her lines to the Duchess of York. Then Richard takes the microphone from the jazz singer and starts to speak the words of Shakespeare's opening soliloquy: "Now is the winter of our discontent / Made glorious summer by this son of York." The whole credit sequence takes only ten minutes but economically manages to fill in the political background and introduce all the main characters, revealing some of their idiosyncrasies to the film audience.

A history play demands more explanation for a modern audience than a comedy or tragedy, which is why Loncraine can justify an extended set of titles. The modern cinema audience is likely ignorant of the events of the War of the Roses and will also have difficulties with the huge cast of characters in a play like *Richard III*. Richard's opening soliloquy, phrased as it is in metaphors, is insufficient to provide background. The literate members of Shakespeare's audience were, in contrast, generally well versed in recent English history; his own plays, the *Henry VI* trilogy, would have served to remind the illiterate members of the crucial events that led up to Richard's accession. Loncraine is wise to intersperse his many titles with action and dramatic images. The information is thus apportioned in digestible chunks with visual reinforcement.

Loncraine provides an excess of period details to link the War of the Roses with his 1930s setting. The wealth of details also connects the film with popular mini-series on British aristocratic families (such as *Upstairs, Downstairs*, 1971–75; *Edward and Mrs. Simpson*, 1978; *Churchill: The Wilderness Years*, 1981; *Downton Abbey*, 2010–15) in which we are made acquainted with their estates, dogs, and menus. Nothing is lost by this opening, as Richard still delivers the better part of his soliloquy alone, in the men's room. His conspiratorial sotto voce guarantees that, as in the play, we are party to his secrets and chiefly interested in *his* progress. Loncraine's titles, unlike Hoffman's and Radford's, do not give details about the setting, as 1930s London is familiar enough to most of the audience, but they are crucial for audience comprehension nonetheless.

Controversial British filmmaker Peter Greenaway was one of the first to profit from Branagh's success with *Henry V*, making *Prospero's Books* in 1991. The film opens with titles that explain the background of Prospero and Miranda's presence on the island but also emphasize what distinguishes Greenaway's film from Shakespeare's play *The Tempest*. Greenaway takes up the well-known critical conceit that *The Tempest* represents Shakespeare's farewell to his art, so Prospero is imagined as a playwright. It is worth quoting the titles:

> Prospero, once Duke of Milan, now reigns over a faraway island, living there with his only daughter, Miranda.
> Twelve years earlier, Prospero's brother, in league with the King of Naples, had exiled Prospero and his daughter from their home.
> One evening, Prospero imagines creating a storm powerful enough to bring his old enemies to his island. He begins to write a play about this tempest, speaking aloud the lines of each of his characters. It is the story of Prospero's past, and his revenge.

As the titles indicate, Greenaway wants his film to be as much about the writing of *The Tempest* as about the events in it. His second preoccupation is given away by the film's title. One of Greenaway's chief interests in adapting Shakespeare's romance was to speculate on the nature of the books Gonzalo stowed away on Prospero's boat. Greenaway creates twenty-four books, using Paintbox computer technology (designed for visual artists), and interlaces descriptions of these books with the text of Shakespeare's play.

Shakespeare begins his play with sailors (minor characters) dealing with a storm. His opening scene is dominated by visual and sound effects, while his second scene is focused on verbal narrative, "with the verbal ultimately triumphing as Prospero assures Miranda that all the elaborate effects she has just seen have been merely so much illusion" (Lisa Hopkins, 107). In contrast, in Greenaway's opening, words and images hold equal sway. He starts his film with the main character, Prospero. First we see water slowly dripping, the sound many times amplified. Then we hear Gielgud's voice-over of lines from scene 2: "Knowing I loved my books, he furnished me / From mine own library with volumes that / I prize above my dukedom" (lines 167–9). Meanwhile, a quill writes these words in calligraphy on parchment – yet another literary adaptation that opens with text. These lines are central to Greenaway's interpretation, and so he takes them out of context, as Almereyda did with Hamlet's admission of melancholy, to guide the audience.

Then, Greenaway introduces the first book, *The Book of Water*, and another voice-over, not Gielgud's, describes it. In the next shot, we see Gielgud in a huge bath or pool. Water drops into his outstretched palm. Propped before him, out of the water, are *The Book of Water*, and the blank book into which he is writing the words of *The Tempest*. Standing by the pool is a little cherubic boy in a red silk loincloth: Ariel. We see a hand write the word "Boatswain" on parchment, and Gielgud repeats this, Shakespeare's first word in *The Tempest*, over and over. Ariel joins him, and he begins to laugh as they shout it joyfully together. Then Gielgud delivers other lines from the first scene, their order jumbled, and his voice is echoed, deepened, and distorted to convey the voice of the boatswain and Sebastian and Gonzalo; these lines appear on the parchment. Gielgud and the audience look into *The Book of Water* at a moving image of a large sailing vessel tossed by a storm. Then we see Gielgud, dressed like a Venetian doge, writing at a desk. Back in the pool, Ariel starts a prodigious pee on a toy ship that Gielgud has set floating there. Then Prospero at the desk looks into the second book, *The Book of Mirrors*, which is also described in voice-over. The significance of *The Book of Mirrors* soon becomes apparent, as there are double images everywhere. Prospero is simultaneously in the pool and dressed at his desk. The model galleon is both perched on his desk and floating in the pool. Ariel is represented by four actors (see chapter 13). Then Michael Nyman's music starts up and naked servants aid Prospero out of the pool and on with his garments, signalling the start of the movie proper; the credits begin to roll. Prospero's careful investiture provides the opening bookend. The film closes with him (very Lear-like) divesting himself of his clothes.

The Book of Mirrors not only reflects but also can allow parallel time periods to exist. The reader can, as the voice-over explains, see himself as a child in one mirror, and an old person in another – see the past and the future. The play is, of course, very much concerned with Prospero's past and future. Greenaway divides his screenplay, which is very different from the finished film, into three sections: Prospero's past, covered in his long speech to Miranda (1.2); his present, in which he manipulates the Neapolitan and Milanese courtiers; and the future, in which he ensures his dynasty through the union of Ferdinand and Miranda.

Greenaway's method of introducing his audience to his singular approach cannot compete for entertainment value with Shakespeare's own opening to *The Tempest*. Shakespeare begins in the middle of a storm, the mariners desperately trying to save their ship and crew while the aristocrats get in the way. Greenaway's explanatory titles and complex images are intriguing and visually stunning, but provide no real entry to the narrative of the play. Having one actor read all the lines from the play also saps its energy. However, Greenaway's real interest is not in the story, characters, or even the themes of Shakespeare's *The Tempest*; it is in the process of creating a play or a book. What he presents is a web of images such as might have inspired Shakespeare's own language and verbal imagery in the play. Right away this separates Greenaway from the other directors hitherto discussed. He is not trying to make Shakespeare's story accessible and entertaining to a modern film audience; he instead has created a visual essay on the imagery of *The Tempest*. His explanatory titles are misleading, for they suggest there will be a narrative, a story of revenge. Instead, we are shown the inside of a clock – that clock is Shakespeare's mind (as imagined by Greenaway) when he was in the process of writing his last solo play. The whole film manifests an obsession with the creation of art. We are given tableaux that could have served as models for high Renaissance painters like Veronese and Rembrandt. Throughout, snippets of Shakespeare's text in beautiful calligraphy appear across the screen, reminding us of the artistry and craftsmanship that went into penning a "fair copy" manuscript at the time of Shakespeare. Greenaway's film is full of nostalgia for the art, beauty, and creativity of the past, or as he terms it, "my taste for historic paintings" (Ciment, 164).

As we can see from these five films, directors use explanatory titles for two main reasons. First, they provide context for period setting and help to justify a shift in time frame or emphasis; second, they supply expository background that Shakespeare's original audience would have gleaned from the speeches of the opening scene (which modern audiences may have difficulty following), and from their own prior knowledge of the story from popular sources. In addition to creating titles, three of the five directors considered above chose to highlight the main character from the opening moments of the film (Radford, Almereyda, and Greenaway), while Shakespeare saved his character's introduction for a later scene.

Another technique that, like the explanatory titles, privileges text over image is to open the film with Shakespeare's own words written on screen. Branagh's *Much Ado About Nothing* (1993) begins with the words of Shakespeare's song "Sigh No More Ladies," and Baz Luhrmann's *William Shakespeare's Romeo + Juliet* (1996) starts with the words of Shakespeare's own prologue. In both cases, this device allows the audience to become accustomed to Shakespeare's language before being plunged into having to assimilate information from quick-moving dialogue that is only *heard*. In each case, the words up on screen convey crucial information: *Much Ado* is going to be about the war of the sexes, and the main issue will be fidelity in love, while *Romeo and Juliet* is about a pair of star-crossed lovers whose union is doomed by their parents' feud. The best way to open your screenplay, Syd Field advises, is to "know your ending" (qtd in Platinga, 43).

In each case, the director is not confident that the printed words are enough and has them repeated orally, by Beatrice (Emma Thompson) in *Much Ado* and by Father Laurence (*sic*; Pete Postlethwaite) in *Romeo + Juliet*. In fact, the words of the chorus are related to us in three different ways in Luhrmann's film: first, by an anchorwoman on a small, old-fashioned TV screen – evidence of the hip regard for old technology that is so prevalent in the steam-punk novels that target the same demographic. Then, the words of the initial chorus appear simultaneously in print and in Postlethwaite's voice-over, and are flashed in print on the screen again. The second and third delivery of the prologue is intercut with a choppy montage that gives us establishing shots of Verona Beach, especially the colossal religious statues, with nostalgic homage to Fellini's *La Dolce Vita* (1960). Perhaps too this visual allusion to Fellini is a hint to the audience that this will not be a conventional Shakespeare adaptation but something altogether more avant-garde. This montage introduces us to the chief characters and gives us glimpses of the tragic action to follow in an aggressively edited style not unlike a rock video. The montage gives way to Shakespeare's opening brawl scene, here transported to a gas station.

Luhrmann is indebted to Branagh's *Much Ado* for the structure of his opening, although he does not follow Branagh's exact order. Branagh opens with the text of the song and follows with an establishing shot of Leonato's estate in Messina, while Emma Thompson's voice-over of the song continues. Then he starts Shakespeare's act 1, scene 1 to interrupt it with a montage of the men arriving on horseback (with homage to John Sturges's *The Magnificent Seven*, 1960, and Akira Kurosawa's *Seven Samurai*, 1954) and the men and women bathing in preparation for their reunion. Here again the montage is a departure from Shakespeare's script but is useful in setting the mood. Branagh's montage is joyous and sensual, Luhrmann's staccato and frenzied.

The third major device employed by filmmakers to accustom their audience to the Shakespearean world is to create a new or extratextual scene, most often completely non-verbal, which introduces key themes or provides background in an economical, visual fashion. Ralph Fiennes opens his *Coriolanus* (2011) with a close-up on a knife being sharpened. The knife bears symbols etched on the blade, and the flickering light suggests a fire. The low-tech nature of the first few seconds suggests the original setting of the play: ancient Rome. Fiennes in the DVD commentary explains that he wanted the opening to have "some mystery about it." Then the camera pulls away and we see that the flickering light emanates from a television screen, not a bonfire. On the screen is a newscast featuring a protesting crowd and the isolated figure of Coriolanus at the front of a tank. (Opening with a TV newscast shows the influence of the hugely successful Luhrmann *Romeo + Juliet*.) A caption reads that Coriolanus has imposed martial law, suspending civil liberties until the war with the Volscians is over. We are in the Volscian headquarters as Aufidius tortures a captured Roman soldier for more information in a scene not in Shakespeare's play but cleverly made up of lines from various other scenes in the play. The material on the TV screen is the closest element in the film's opening to that of the play's, but by introducing Aufidius in person first, rather than the nameless citizens as Shakespeare does, and Coriolanus on the television in the same scene, Fiennes throws extra emphasis on their rivalry and then friendship. The blade that opens the film is "important," according to Fiennes, and certainly it reappears when Caius Martius and Aufidius fight each other, and then again when Aufidius deals the death jab to the eponymous hero.

Julie Taymor's *The Tempest* (2010) opens with a close-up of a black sandcastle sparkling in the sun and the sounds of the tide and a gentle rain. The rain starts to erode the sandcastle, as ominous music builds. The camera pulls back to reveal that the sandcastle is on a young hand. Pulling back further, the camera shows us a teenage Miranda (Felicity Jones) standing in the driving rain, looking dismayed at the wreck of her creation. The crumbling sandcastle is a perfect metaphor for much of what Shakespeare has to say in the play about the impermanence of magic, art, and human life. Prospero famously remarks,

> The cloud-capped towers, the gorgeous palaces,
> The solemn temples, the great globe itself,
> Yea, all which it inherit, shall dissolve,
> And, like this insubstantial pageant faded,
> Leave not a rack behind: we are such stuff
> As dreams are made on; and our little life
> Is rounded with a sleep (4.1.152–6).

Like the fragile sandcastle, Prospero's magic visions, the performances in Shakespeare's own Globe Theatre, and human life itself sparkle for a moment in the light and then fade from view, kept alive only in memories. Taymor's medium, however, is not quite like that. Films can be preserved for a long time and watched again and again, so the performances are not as evanescent and transitory as those on stage. Shakespeare also had no guarantee that print would keep his works alive for so long (although he boasts about this possibility in some of his sonnets) and in so many manifestations all over the world. Perhaps to a filmmaker like Taymor, the sandcastle represents the ideal concept behind the film that never quite made it to fruition after all the collaborating and editing. Certainly, her *Tempest* has none of the conceptual brilliance of her *Titus*, the passion of her *Frida* (2002), or the charm of her *Across the Universe* (2007). This initial metaphor, so promising in the way it provides a visual image for some of the play's central themes (death, transformation, impermanence), is a fairly isolated example in the film, which lacks a strong directorial interpretation. This is not a postcolonial *Tempest*, or an art and nature *Tempest*, or a Prospero-as-Shakespeare saying farewell to his art *Tempest*; it is a strangely hollow *Tempest*, in which none of the play's profundities resound.

The first few moments are in my opinion the most exhilarating in the film. We follow Miranda's gaze from the sandy puddle in her hand to a lightning spear striking a sailing vessel on the horizon. Taymor then powerfully intercuts between the people on the ship in a frenzy of activity to save themselves, to a close-up on Miranda's bare feet and legs pounding the black sand in slow motion as she runs to stop Prospera from drowning the passengers and crew. The storm is so realistically filmed that it is difficult to hear the dialogue onboard.

As with her previous Shakespeare adaptation on screen, Taymor has opened her film with a child at play, and in each case, a child creating a pretend world. Miranda creates a fairy-tale castle out of sand and passively watches it fall from exposure to the elements, whereas the boy at the opening of *Titus* has created a war scene on his kitchen table and is himself the agent of destruction, felling the toy troops and pouring ketchup on them. Once again, these two images of children at play suggest very strongly the act of creation – the playwright composing fictional worlds from his imagination, the director making a filmed narrative. Both openings, by using traditional children's activities, acknowledge the playfulness of the grown-up work of playwriting and film directing. These openings remind us that those adult jobs are to entertain; at the same time they suggest that these games, and their adult equivalents, also represent what is most wonderful and terrible in human endeavour – our capacity to create and destroy.

Of course, whenever an adult film shows a child or childhood activity, nostalgia rears its head. The sandcastle conjures up pictures of the ideal childhood summer, long sunny days spent idling on a beach. Again, this is an appropriate image for Shakespeare's *Tempest*, influenced as it was by accounts of the Virginia Company's shipwreck on Bermuda and the descriptions of the paradise of ease and pleasure the Englishmen discovered. The sandcastle also anticipates the sea imagery so dominant in the play, of which Taymor makes too little. It suggests the theme of lost innocence, which applies to so many of the characters in various ways: Prospero's trust in his brother, shown to be fatally misguided; Prospero's trust in Caliban, teaching him and lodging him in his cell until Caliban betrayed him by trying to rape Miranda; Caliban's trust in Prospero, showing him all the riches of the isle, only to have them stolen from him and be forced into slavery; Alonso and Gonzalo's trust in Antonio and Sebastian to guard them as they sleep, when their sole intention is to murder them.

Branagh employed the same technique, opening with extradiagetic material in his 2000 *Love's Labour's Lost*. After the credit sequence in which curlicue white script on a red satin background introduces the four ladies and lords with character names, photographs, and actors' names, we are treated to a retro black-and-white newsreel. Branagh delivers a 1930s-style narration as a newspaper headline appears that reads, "War Imminent," followed by footage of the four lords divesting themselves of their aviator jackets to don scholars' robes instead. The cheery voice relates the King of Navarre's plan to devote himself and his fellows to a rigorous course of study, celibacy, and fasting until the war drags them away from court. In addition to the obviously "yesteryear" feel of bichromatic newsreel, any voice-over employed in a film tends to bestow an elegiac tone; it is reminiscent of being a child again, listening to someone tell a story. The newsreel serves the practical purpose of conveying important exposition in modern rather than Early Modern English, so that when the material of the play proper begins with Navarre's opening speech (of which the first fifteen lines are cut), the audience is merely reviewing information they have already heard in a more accessible form. Branagh returns to the same method of opening a Shakespeare adaptation with an additional pre-credit action sequence in his 2006 *As You Like It*, but that is considered in chapter 4.

Australian director Geoffrey Wright opens his 2006 *Macbeth* with an extradiagetic scene in a graveyard. As the opening credits roll, white on a black background, we hear a group whispering, then see a grey stone angel at a canted angle against a pale sky. The frame is suddenly filled with a hissing, redheaded young woman desecrating the statue. She is joined by two other nubile women dressed as schoolgirls with berets, kilts, and backpacks, all with red hair and lots of black eyeliner. They gleefully race around the cemetery, gouging out stone angels' eyes with a screwdriver (a nod to Gloucester in *King Lear*?) and then spraying the eyeholes red with cans of graffiti paint. Are they suggesting that the action that follows must not be seen by angelic eyes to prevent their intervention? The three come together in an impromptu circle to utter the first few lines of the play:

> When shall we three meet again
> In thunder, lightning, or in rain?
> When the hurlyburly's done,
> When the battle's lost and won
> That will be ere the set of sun
> Where the place?
> Upon the heath
> There to meet with ...

The screen then fills with red letters spelling MACBETH in a way that recalls the title of Loncraine's *Richard III*. We cut to a small moon in a dark, cloudy sky, and the strange group-whispering sound. Then, a close-up on Sam Worthington's face. He watches the witches leave the cemetery, and turns to look at a sobbing woman (Lady Macbeth) placing white roses on a gravestone inscribed with the words "Beloved son" (fig. 2). Lady Macbeth seems unconscious of the desecrating teens, but later in the film we realize that this is because only Macbeth sees them – in Wright's version, they are his fantasy. The dead child introduced in this extradiagetic material not only makes sense of Lady Macbeth's references to "giving suck" but also provides a reason for her drug-numbed despair in the film, which in turn motivates Macbeth to do her will and murder Duncan. Once again, we see the trend in Shakespeare adaptations to place family dynamics at the centre of the interpretations, tapping into the "universal" experience of being a member of a family, which an audience would find more familiar than that of removing obstacles to attain a throne.

These credits are another example of the trend of opening a Shakespeare film with children – not only the naughty schoolgirl witches but the dead son of the Macbeths. Does Geoffrey Wright open with schoolgirls as a wry comment on his audience's most probable experience of the play – as a school text, a copy of which might even be found in the witches' backpacks? It pairs nicely with the moment late in the film in which Worthington's Macbeth dons a kilt, like the schoolgirl witches, and does an impromptu jig – hybrid gestures of both reverence and irreverence that acknowledge high-school study of the Scottish play and cheekily announce or reinforce that this film is something else entirely. It is once again an invitation to the audience to play, like the wicked schoolgirls, for the duration of the film, which was marketed as an exciting boys' night out – all guns and heaving bosoms, violence and sex. The whole little scene in the graveyard is tinged with nostalgia – for the youth and beauty of the Twilight-esque witches (the first book of Stephanie Meyer's *Twilight* series was published in 2005) whom Macbeth clearly admires, for the child buried under his feet whom he can never retrieve, and for his wife in her pre-mourning phase, loving and alive.

Justin Kurzel's opening for his *Macbeth* (2015) owes much to his fellow Australian's. We hear the wind, then see the name "Macbeth" in red type. Music begins to play as we are confronted with the misty

Figure 2 Macbeth (Sam Worthington) watches his wife (Victoria Hill) arrange roses on their son's grave in Wright's *Macbeth*, 2007.

mountains of Skye. Our first encounter with Macbeth is, as in Wright's film, as a grieving father. The hand-held camera zooms in on him placing stones on the eyelids of his dead baby. For a contemporary audience, this is a humanizing opening. In interviews, Kurzel reveals that this death was to be the motivation for the Macbeths' ruthless ascent to the throne, their ambition a distraction from their terrible loss (Leigh, 15; Barnes, 13). Macbeth (Michael Fassbender) takes a few steps back from the child's body to join his wife (Marion Cotillard) (fig. 3). At some remove from the rest of the mourners, we see three mysterious women with a little girl, all pale, with strange, deliberate scars carved on their faces, watching the funeral. These are the witches.

Kurzel's intertitles then announce that the greatly outnumbered royal army, under the generalship of Macbeth, faces a decisive battle against the rebels in which the king has deployed his last reserve. This reserve army, we see, is made up of young boys so untested as to need their daggers strapped to their wrists. In the play Macbeth shares the captaincy with Banquo, and there is no mention of the king's followers being outnumbered, but in the film Macbeth is clearly leading the last campaign to save a beleaguered king. Kurzel thus raises the stakes, making the salvation of Duncan's dynasty rest on Macbeth's shoul-

Figure 3 Macbeth (Michael Fassbender) and Lady Macbeth (Marion Cotillard) grieve at their baby's pyre in Kurzel's *Macbeth*, 2015.

ders against insuperable odds. Shakespeare's Macbeth is a military hero; Kurzel's is the sole saviour of Scotland. Once again, as with many other openings of Shakespeare adaptations, a new stress on children has been added to the original, not only the dead Macbeth baby but also the pubescent soldiers facing their death on the battlefield. The emphasis has thus altered from political intrigue to family emotions. The family in crisis is again at the centre, as Duyvendak observes of many Hollywood films, seeing in this filmic trend a yearning for the conventional family set-up of the past, in which the father worked, the mother cared for the children full-time, and the family spent leisure hours together.

Taymor in *Titus* (1999), like Luhrmann and Almereyda, uses an opening, extratextual scene to set in motion a commentary on modern society (see chapter 7 for a detailed description). Similar to Luhrmann and Almereyda, she seems to be criticizing the media's role in recording and thus anaesthetizing us to violence. The child has become jaded about violence through the omnipresent television, turned on even when he is "multi-tasking" – eating lunch and playing a game. Luhrmann's anchorwoman presents the tragic feud as just another piece of news. Almereyda's Hamlet includes a military plane taken from TV footage of the bombing in Bosnia (*Screenplay*, 135) in his initial montage of the "the paragon of the world." Unlike the other two directors, however, Taymor does not develop the media presence in her film. The television in the opening scene is its only manifestation. However, she does continue to use the boy as a voyeur figure, a modern witness to some of the more horrific violent acts. This choice may show the influence of Jane Howell's 1985 BBC television production of *Titus* in which young Lucius plays a similar role.

Shakespeare's *Titus Andronicus* opens with Saturninus and Bassianus vying for political power; Taymor saves this scene for the third one in her film, after Titus has sacrificed Tamora's son Alarbus. Her choice to add the modern scene and tamper with Shakespeare's order throws emphasis on the themes of war and violence and minimizes the tragic import of Titus's foolish support of Saturninus. In Shakespeare's opening scene, Titus is like Lear, setting up his own downfall through his lack of good judgment in favouring the craven Saturninus above the noble Bassianus. Taymor's decision robs Titus of some of his agency. In her film, he seems more the victim of a society devoted to martial codes than a man who *chooses* blind adherence to Roman rules over common sense. The decision to make Titus more of a victim may be revealing of the dominant Hollywood conventions – on the whole, ambiguity in the protagonist is eschewed for a clear, linear "character arc." We see this same smoothing-away of ambiguities in Branagh's Benedick (see chapter 10).

Oliver Parker creates an opening scene for his erotic thriller version of *Othello* (1995) that is both effective and confusing. The film begins at night on a canal in Venice, with somber Italian strings playing as a gondola approaches. A white woman rests her head on a black man's shoulder. As the gondola nears the audience, the black man covers his face with a white mask of tragedy, a tear painted on the cheek. We never see this couple again. As the first gondola glides away, a second appears in which a veiled woman (Desdemona) pushes the curtains back to look at the shore. A gentleman helps her from the gondola and she runs through a covered market, the ground strewn with dead flowers (is it Carnival?), passing two well-dressed couples. She turns down a littered alley with wicker baskets piled high. Iago and Roderigo see her approach and they steal from sight. She ducks inside a building, perhaps a chapel, and removes her veil. Parker then cuts to dignitaries heading purposefully through lighted streets to San Marco. Inside the palace, the Doge silently reads a scroll as serious senators look on. Parker selects a line of dialogue from act 1, scene 3 – the Doge says, "Tis certain then for Cyprus" – and then transposes and alters from other parts of the play some plausible dialogue to follow: "But who shall lead our business against the Turkish fleet?" A senator answers, "Othello. Another of his fathom we have none." Lodovico concurs: "The fortitude of the place is best known to him." Then we cut to a black hand placing a ring on the wedding finger of a white hand. The camera rises, taking in a crucifix and a priest.

Our first glimpse of Othello has him kissing Desdemona and wearing a close black hood, looking slightly sinister. Roderigo, peering through a gap in a barred window, gasps in pain at the sight of the kiss and begins with Shakespeare's first lines, "I take it much unkindly." Iago does not answer him as he does in Shakespeare, for he is nursing his own grievance, expressed in lines cobbled together from his first long speech:

By the faith of man,
I know my price, I am worth no worse a place.
One Michael Cassio, a Florentine
Must his Lieutenant be
And I, of whom his eyes had seen the proof
God bless the mark – his Moorship's Ancient.

When Iago mentions Cassio, we are given another glimpse into the chapel where, in ceremonial fashion, Othello gives Cassio his dagger and then embraces him.

In the play, Cassio is ignorant of the marriage until Iago lets him know of it in act 1, scene 2. In Parker's film, he is witness and best man. Parker tries to give the friendship between Othello and Cassio more visual manifestations. We see in flashback that they attended functions at Brabantio's house together, and at the film's end Cassio secretly passes Othello the same dagger to kill himself rather than face humiliation and imprisonment in Venice.

Parker's opening is effective in that it establishes an air of tragic foreboding with the darkness and mist on the canal and the melancholy music. It also conveys in visual form information about Othello and Desdemona's secret wedding, which the audience might have missed in the initial dialogue between Roderigo and Iago. It labels Othello, with his unconventional garb, as a foreigner. It economically establishes his friendship with Cassio, and Roderigo and Iago's resentments, again all visual reinforcements of the expository material in the opening dialogue. But as Samuel Crowl notes, it promises more than it delivers in suggesting, with the couple in the first gondola and the white mask, that the racial theme will be key (*Shakespeare and Film*, 93). In fact, apart from Shakespeare's own allusions to Othello's status as an alien in Venice, not much is made of his race in the film. Similarly, the mask and the dead flowers seem to suggest a time of Carnival in Venice, which would have worked nicely with the Venetian attitude (expressed by Brabantio, Iago, and Emilia) that Desdemona's choice of spouse is a sign of a mad, topsy-turvy world; yet we are given no other indications of Carnival through the rest of the film. Nor, as Crowl points out, does Fishburne's Othello ever seem to assume the mask of a white man's identity (93). However, the masks, acting as second faces, do anticipate the interpretation of Iago as a Janus-faced character. Carolyn Jess-Cooke notes that Janus was the guardian of doorways and thresholds, and Parker composes many of his shots in a way that frames his characters using what Patricia Dorval termed "threshold aesthetics" (qtd in Jess-Cooke, *Shakespeare on Film*, 80). The framing, in the case of Othello, often makes him appear trapped, confined.

Parker, like many of the other directors discussed, introduces his main characters earlier than Shakespeare does. Desdemona is the first of the *dramatis personae* we see, followed by Iago. This order of appearance reflects Parker's focus in the film. Othello is less central to his interpretation than Iago, and Desdemona's beauty garners more attention from the camera than Othello's anguish. Shakespeare opens his play with Roderigo, a secondary character, and the initial emphasis is on Iago's cynical world-view, whereas the glimpse we catch in Parker's film of the bi-racial couple in the gondola, and of Othello and Desdemona's wedding, suggests that the romantic and sexual aspects of the tragedy will be equally emphasized. This is true up to a point, as Parker creates scenes in which Desdemona dances for Othello, the two consummate their marriage, and Othello imagines Desdemona committing adultery with Cassio.

Like Parker, Zeffirelli in his opening scene for *Hamlet* (1990) throws attention on the object of the men's desire, in this case, Gertrude. Zeffirelli's establishing shots of Elsinore give way to a crypt and the sound of weeping. The first close-up is of Gertrude (Glenn Close) looking girlish with two golden plaits framing her crying visage. Crowl cites this as one of many instances of Zeffirelli's passion for the "opera diva," which Close becomes in this adaptation. Gertrude takes from her hair a gold ornament in the shape of a rose and places it on her dead husband before swooning into Polonius's embrace. Hamlet (Mel Gibson) is seen next, throwing earth on his father's corpse. This image is a true indication of what is to follow, as Zeffirelli makes the Oedipal reading of Gertrude and Hamlet's relationship key to his interpretation of the play. Not only is the opening scene with the ghost cut, but also Scofield's ghost is an ineffectual presence in the film. We see him dead in this initial scene, and he fails to come alive in his subsequent appearances – a sharp contrast to Brian Blessed's powerful soldier in Branagh's version (with memories of Exeter from *Henry V*) and Shepherd's menacing father in Almereyda's film. All the men fail to command the screen, overshadowed by Close's luminous Gertrude, as Crowl argues persuasively in his article "The Golden Girl and a Fistful of Dust" (Cineaste, 57).

The advantage of opening the film with the funeral is that it clearly establishes for the uninitiated the transference of power from Hamlet Senior to Claudius. This gain in clarity is outweighed, in my opinion, by the loss in scrapping Shakespeare's tremendous opening scene. From its first line, Shakespeare's *Hamlet* is in the interrogative mood, and the questions that the play asks are chiefly metaphysical. Why are we here? What does our human life mean, straddled as it is between the existence of beasts and angels? What happens after death? Is there any way to escape suffering, or must we merely endure it? What does our life signify if those who love us forget us after our death? Modern directors of *Hamlet* lose sight of this important aspect of the play by grounding it so realistically in specific locations and period details, and make it chiefly a drama of family dynamics, no director more so than Zeffirelli. His *Hamlet* is a story of a son in love with his mother. Almereyda's is a tale of a boy in love with his camera and himself. Branagh's is a story of a prince in competition with his uncle for power over Denmark and his family. Shakespeare's *Hamlet* is beyond summary, but certainly, metaphysical considerations loom very large.

Joss Whedon's *Much Ado About Nothing* (2013) yet again opens with an extradiagetic scene. The camera ushers us into what appears to be an undergraduate's studio apartment – beer bottles and small heaps of clothes on the floor, scanty, cheap furnishings. A young man is dressing quietly, while a naked young woman, back turned to him, apparently asleep, lies in the rumpled bed. The man leaves the room without saying goodbye, an uncertain expression on his face. The camera zooms in on the woman's face, awake. She sighs, rubbing her forehead with her hand.

This scene economically establishes for the audience that Benedick and Beatrice have had an unsuccessful relationship prior to the beginning of the play's events. By using this concept as the key to his interpretation, Whedon shows the influence of Branagh's *Much Ado* (1993) in which this exchange from Shakespeare's act 2, scene 1, became central to the characterization of the play's witty duo:

> DON PEDRO: Come, lady, come; you have lost the heart of Signior Benedick.
> BEATRICE: Indeed, my lord, he lent it me awhile, and I gave him use for it, a double heart for his single one. Marry, once before he won it of me, with false dice, therefore your grace may well say I have lost it (258–3).

Branagh writes in the introduction to his screenplay of the film, "Emma Thompson and I both wanted to suggest former lovers who had been genuinely hurt by their first encounter, which perhaps occurred at the tender age of Hero and Claudio in the play" (xi). Whedon keeps these lines of Beatrice's, and, following Branagh, has her deliver them in close-up, but, unlike Branagh, he seems to have found them insufficient to make this backstory clear to the audience, and so provides this initial visual reinforcement. The decision may have been based on conventional Hollywood structure – crucial information about the central couple is not generally left until a third of the way through the film (page 33 in Branagh's eighty-three-page screenplay). Shakespeare could get away with this because, technically, Beatrice and Benedick are not the central characters of the play – Hero and Claudio are. Their story is well under way before Beatrice and Benedick's asserts itself.

Whedon's extradiagetic material continues with shots of cars parking on a prosperous street, reminiscent of the wedding scene in Coppola's *The Godfather* (1972). Then, we watch as food is prepared in a kitchen, recalling, although on a smaller scale, the anticipation of the party that opened Hoffman's *A Midsummer Night's Dream*. The consumption of wine and cocktails is a strong visual component throughout Whedon's adaptation, reinforcing the impression that he (or the publicity division) wanted to make with the film's original tagline on the poster: "Shakespeare knew how to throw a party."

The fourth method of opening a Shakespeare film is the most obvious: start as the original text does. Branagh's *Henry V* and *Hamlet* both do this. (For a description of the opening of Branagh's *Hamlet*, see chapter 6.) Screenwriting guru Robert McKee writes that a mature artist "never calls attention to himself," yet the opening of Branagh's *Henry V* does just that, and it is one of the masterly strokes of the film (qtd in Stam and Raengo, 2–3). It begins with a black screen. We hear a match struck and a glow grows on the face of the Chorus, played by Derek Jacobi. We hear him descending what sound like metal stairs until he flicks the switch of an industrial light, and we find ourselves in a film studio, with all the accoutrements of the filmmaking process around us, many of them marked HV, in readiness for the next day's shoot. Jacobi quickens his pace as Doyle's lush score builds, heading to great oak doors appropriate to a medieval castle – part of the set.

Many critics have seen in this metacinematic opening Branagh's challenge to Laurence Olivier, whose 1944 *Henry V* opened metatheatrically in the Globe Theatre. It is as if Branagh is saying, "My adaptation is for today's audience, whose medium is film, and film is not a poor substitute for theatre!" Branagh cuts eleven of the opening speech's lines (1.1.15,16,19–26) describing the synecdochical nature of the theatrical illusion ("a crooked figure may / Attest in little place a million," for example), because those lines would not apply to film in which many extras present a fairly realistic army and real horses print their proud hoofs in the receiving earth. By setting this speech in a sound studio, Branagh acknowledges the ties between theatre and cinema, and the complicit part the audience still plays in an artistic illusion, even if that illusion is much more realistic. For the duration of the film, we enter into a contract with the filmmaker to accept that his set and fields are actually locations in the real Middle Ages, that his actors are real historical figures, and that we are somehow watching the events of a reign as they unfold, rather than two-dimensional images flickering on a screen. The film *Anonymous* (2011), which attempts to debunk Shakespeare, the man from Stratford, as the author of the plays, and replace him with the Earl of Oxford, oddly enough pays direct homage to both openings, with Derek Jacobi, clad much like Branagh's Chorus in a long coat and scarf, rushing through the debris back stage in a large New York theatre to be on time for the opening curtain of a show about the "real" author of Shakespeare's plays. The stage on which he stands segues into a stage under which Ben Jonson hides himself and "secret" manuscripts in Jacobean London. Branagh himself seems to remember his acclaimed opening for *Henry V* when he ends his *As You Like It* with Rosalind walking in between actors' trailers, delivering the epilogue, until we hear Branagh off screen yell, "And cut."

After looking at many films from the past twenty-eight years, we can identify four different approaches used by directors to guide their cinema audiences into Shakespeare's worlds. The first, and most common, is to use explanatory titles. The more radical the interpretation of the play, the more titles and preamble are necessary. Loncraine and Greenaway both use pre-credit sequences at least ten minutes long. Loncraine needed this time to clarify the historical background, the large cast, and the shift in period setting to his audience. Greenaway required the space to introduce his unconventional and disjointed narrative style and to distinguish the aims of his *Prospero's Books* from Shakespeare's *The Tempest*. The second approach taken by directors is to open with Shakespeare's own words on screen. The two directors who use this method both had the easier task of adapting plays that were more immediately accessible to their audiences (who would be familiar with the story of *Romeo and Juliet*, and the romantic comedy format of *Much Ado*). They also chose settings that were less alienating – Branagh's Messina and Luhrmann's Verona Beach are timeless, fantasy locations. The third technique seized on by directors was to create a new, mostly non-verbal scene to establish theme and character. Of the eight directors who opted for this approach, six were adapting tragedies or tragicomedies: *Titus*, *Macbeth* (both 2005 and 2015), *Hamlet*, *Coriolanus*, *Othello*, and *The Tempest*. Perhaps this choice reflects the fact that action is less ambiguous in tragedy. Death defies explanation. The fourth method is to maintain Shakespeare's own beginning.

The explanatory titles of the first method and the use of Shakespeare's own words up on screen of the second method both demonstrate a yearning for the printed form. The third approach, creating an extratextual, mostly wordless scene, is also essentially nostalgic, recalling the dumb show used by Shakespeare and his contemporaries, and used for the same reason – to make abundantly clear to the audience something about the action of the narrative proper that follows. The fourth method is again nostalgic because it maintains something from England's past literature, and from an older art form, theatre, mostly unchanged.

4

Nostalgia for the Stage in Shakespearean Films

This chapter examines moments in Shakespearean films in which the director has chosen to *add* a representation of the theatre; that is, one that is not implied by Shakespeare's script. For example, Olivier's representation of the Globe Theatre at the opening of his *Henry V* (1944) could be considered, but the performance of the Murder of Gonzago in his screen version of *Hamlet* (1948) would not.

Many screen directors have, as one might expect, made metacinematic allusions in their films. Branagh opens his *Henry V* (1989) in a sound studio, reflecting the influence of Olivier's version but differentiating himself from it. However, even today, when the audience for Shakespearean movies is so much more *film* literate than *theatre* literate, directors still choose to bridge the gap between film and theatre by including visual reminders of the script's origins. This tendency appears to be one of the defining characteristics of a film adaptation of a famous play, and another symptom of Shakespearean directors' nostalgia for the past.

Theatrical images, in addition to clarifying and heightening key moments for audience members unaccustomed to Shakespeare, also contribute to a film's status as prestige cinema. They flatter the audience with their association with theatre literacy and the appreciation of aristocratic interiors. Theatrical images can also suggest a yearning for the freedom to play of childhood, and for past eras before mass media largely replaced literary and theatrical culture. Each time we as audience are reminded of the play's origins through theatrical images, we are obliged to interrogate the whole process of transforming a play into a film. In recent cinema, the act of adaptation has wider implications: we are forced to consider not only the shift from theatre to film but also the translation of culture, from Elizabethan to contemporary times, English to American, monocultural to multicultural, national to global. These theatrical moments encourage us to think about what has been gained and lost by each translation.

Thus, the presence of a theatrical image in a Shakespeare film speaks volumes. Even though filmmakers have compelling reasons to *avoid* connecting their film with the theatre, they persist in so doing. Consequently, they risk their films being marginalized as derivative hybrids or recorded plays, or relegated to the classroom as pedagogical aids. The survival of the Shakespeare film is based on the assumption that the stories, characters, and even the language can be transferred to the screen without reference to or reminders of theatre, a medium that is now often considered elitist, and is economically threatened. Yet how can Shakespeare film directors reasonably avoid acknowledging the origins of their project? No audience would be deceived. Shakespeare's first association in most people's minds is still with the older media of theatre and writing, not with film and DVDs. Does this mean that a Shakespeare film will always be a hopelessly indirect experience – a kind of spectre of the original play, at many removes from its true purpose? If so, why do directors further remove the experience by reminding us with their inclusion of theatrical images that we are watching an artifice? Perhaps an answer to these questions is that the Shakespeare film is the perfect expression of the postmodern age – it is a hybrid, a collage of old and new that smacks of nostalgia. These films display yearning for our cultural past, and even for our childhood, for our freedom to "play." According to Brian Boyd in *On the Origin of Stories*, our drive as a species to create performances and to watch the performances of others comes from our evolutionary heritage of play. We play, he argues, to hone our survival skills: "The amount of play in a species correlates with its flexibility of action" (11). In other words, our wistfulness for game-playing is more important than it sounds. It is a longing for a phase of life when there was time to acquire and improve necessary skills.

The images of theatre in film encourage the audience to consider the differences between the two art forms, and they remind us of the artificiality of both in a way that can approach Brechtian alienation. For example, Luhrmann in his *William Shakespeare's Romeo + Juliet* (1996) introduces Romeo sitting on the stage of an old, ruined cinema, the proscenium arch towering above him. While Luhrmann's script pointedly refers to the ruin as a film palace (17), nevertheless, the architectural remains could easily be those of an Edwardian theatre. The proximity of a building proclaiming itself "the Globe Theatre and Pool Hall" only adds to the strength of the connection. The first time we see the ruined Sycamore Grove Theatre, Romeo is alone, suggesting the solitary nature of watching a film, especially today when we more often view movies on our televisions or computers than with other people in a cinema. The original Globe, recalled here by the Pool Hall, provided a very different sort of entertainment – a communal sort. Spectators were constantly aware of each other's reactions to the play, as they sat opposite one another in broad daylight. A degree of Brechtian alienation was thus necessarily achieved as the spectators could not forget that they were participating in an artifice. Luhrmann seems cognizant that something has been lost by our solitary screenings. As Richard Burt observes, in the special DVD of *Romeo + Juliet*, the menu trailer presents the Sycamore Grove Theatre in its pre-ruined state. The curtains open, showing us credits followed by clips from the film, changed to appear as if they were taken from silent movies. The inclusion of this kind of menu on the DVD is fascinating. First, it recalls the theatrical origins of *Romeo + Juliet*, as the proscenium arch cinema could easily be a theatre. Second, by making the clips look like silent film excerpts, Luhrmann is also reminding the audience of film history, particularly Shakespearean film history. (Shakespeare was a favourite hunting ground for early filmmakers.) Third, Luhrmann seems to be attempting to give the television audience a simulated experience of watching a film in a cinema (Burt, 4). In each of these three options, nostalgia for some other time or art form prevails.

The fact that this same proscenium arch in its ruined state frames some of the most important moments of the plot – the introduction of the tragic hero, the Montague boys' preparation for the ball, Tybalt and Mercutio's duel, and Mercutio's death – means that these moments become infused with a self-consciousness they would not otherwise own. The proscenium arch reminds us that this is Shakespeare, this was theatre, and these are actors performing. As Katherine Rowe observes, the gaping hole where the screen of Sycamore Grove cinema would once have been recalls "Shakespeare's 'wooden O,' stood up vertically, on end" (45). Here as in many other instances,

Luhrmann seems to be acknowledging the composite nature of his project, and indeed, of all postmodern art. He has borrowed from theatre, from film history, from English Renaissance culture, and contemporary American urban culture.

The other prominent stage in Luhrmann's film is the platform between the two staircases at the Capulet mansion. This platform becomes the site of various operatic mini-performances. Before we meet Juliet, it is the place from where both the nurse and Gloria Capulet shout her name, summoning her for her tête-à-tête with her mother. Later, at the ball, it becomes the stage for Mercutio's cross-dressed performance of the song "Young Hearts Run Free."

Luhrmann's operatic background is clearly evident at the Capulets' ball, as Mercutio and Capulet both perform. Capulet sings a mini-aria, "Amore, amore, amore," then does a comic, suggestive dance on the stage, coyly lifting the skirt of his sequined Caesar tunic (a further allusion to Shakespeare's other works?). This stage bears classical columns, recalling the inception of theatre, and even a painted Greek backdrop. It is in front of this that the hired singer sings, "I'm Kissing You."

So many sets in the film recall a theatrical past for the script. The carousel at Sycamore Grove where Benvolio first approaches Romeo is another platform. The balconies from which Gloria Capulet, the nurse, and Juliet look out remind us not only of the traditional staging of the "balcony scene," which Luhrmann transfers to the Capulet pool, but of other public performances, from the Pope's audience at the Vatican to the balcony of any stage, used to extend the acting space. The cathedral becomes another source of representations of the stage. The boys' choir sings from the church balcony overlooking the rest of the pews, both when Father Laurence says mass after agreeing to marry Romeo and Juliet and at the wedding itself. Later, the altar on which Juliet lies will be another stage, lit, as Shakespeare's Blackfriars stage was, by candles, and approached by steps. The large circular fountain, topped by a colossal statue of the Sacred Heart of Jesus, is another platform, again equipped with steps, on which Tybalt enacts his final scene when Romeo shoots him. The captain of police gives his final speech on the steps of the cathedral, encircled by the grieving families and onlookers.

Michael Almereyda similarly selects theatrical settings for some of the most significant scenes in his *Cymbeline*. Imogen and Posthumous are first shown together under the bleachers in a park or stadium, kiss-

Figure 4 Imogen (Dakota Johnson) and Posthumous (Penn Badgley) kiss goodbye under the bleachers in Almereyda's *Cymbeline*, 2014.

ing and saying their farewells (fig. 4). This is the film's first scene from the Shakespeare play, following the titles and a montage that do not use Shakespearean language. In other words, the first time the audience hears Shakespeare, it is in a space associated with performance, if of the athletic persuasion. In his running commentary on the DVD, Almereyda also explains that he chose the bleachers because it "evokes a prison," metal bars framing the star-crossed couple.

Later in the film, we see Cymbeline in a bar, among a small audience, watching his queen sing Bob Dylan's "Dark Eyes" on stage with a microphone. Almereyda in the DVD commentary notes the appropriateness of the lyrics, as the men of the play all hold "misconceptions about the women they love." The opening line of the song goes, "Oh, the gentlemen are talking." The penultimate line is "Passion rules the arrow that flies." The director actually describes the male characters as "deranged" in their response to women. The king (Ed Harris) wears a besotted expression as he watches his wife perform. Intercut with the bar song is the business of Iachimo being transported in his chest to Imogen's bedroom. In this highly theatrical device, Iachimo pops out of the chest like a puppet in a puppet theatre. The scenes in the film most expressive of sexual desire, and in the two above, the male gaze, are associated with the art of performance. Almereyda makes an important distinction between them, however. Imogen and Posthumous kiss under the bleachers and are thus associated with the audience rather than the performers of a spectacle. The site is also one associated with forbidden teenage embraces, implicitly signifying the couple as the film's Romeo and Juliet. Iachimo is both spectator, watching the sleeping Imogen, and actor, performing his Tarquin-like role. The queen performs for Cymbeline – appropriately, as he discovers at the conclusion that everything she has said and done in his presence has been an act – utterly false. At the same time, Almereyda chose the Dylan song, according to the DVD commentary, to express the queen's residual "resistance to a world she wants to become a part of," the violent bike-gang realm she intends to rule through Cloten.

Such self-consciously theatrical moments in Shakespearean films abound. In Kenneth Branagh's *Hamlet* (1996), loosely based on the Royal Shakespeare Company Adrian Noble production (1993) in which he starred, theatrical images are used to help characterize Hamlet for the viewer. When we first see Hamlet's apartments, the object initially offered to the view is an eighteenth-century model theatre. Then we take in his extensive library. Its handsome mahogany shelves and leather-bound volumes, its collection of masks and puppets, indicate to the audience that Hamlet is learned and cultivated and prepare them for his keen interest in the theatre later in the play. The elaborately recreated mise en scène and the choice of the stately home Bleinheim Palace for the main set also qualify Branagh's *Hamlet* for inclusion in the genre of heritage film. One could easily apply to this film Andrew Higson's observation that by "celebrating and legitimating the spectacle of one class and one cultural tradition and identity at the expense of others through the discourse of authenticity, and the obsession with the visual splendors of period detail," an essentially nostalgic and conservative message is conveyed to the audience (119).

Branagh's Hamlet employs a mask from his collection of antic faces when he feigns madness. In act 2, scene 2, he surprises Polonius by jumping out from behind a pillar wearing a *"grotesque commedia dell' arte"* (*Screenplay*, 56) skull mask. Sarah Hatchuel in *Shakespeare, from Stage to Screen* notes the theatricality of Branagh's throne room "with its side tiers, its upper galleries and its suspended balconies." The flimsiness of the walls, made obvious when Hamlet runs through the rooms after the murder of Polonius, and the sense of back-stage activity created by the spying behind the mirrored doors, further contribute to the metatheatre of the film (98). The stage is never far away in this film, and each time its images appear, the naturalistic, Hollywoodian, David Leanesque style of telling the story is disrupted.

The most striking extratextual theatre image in the film occurs when Hamlet plays with the model theatre as he delivers the "O what a rogue" soliloquy (2.2.538). We see his face framed by the proscenium arch of the toy stage, a visual reminder of the prince's earlier metaphor for his own head: "while memory holds a seat / In this distracted *globe* [italics added]." Hamlet punctuates the line "the play's the thing / Wherein I'll catch the conscience of the King" (2.2.593–4) by sending a king puppet to Hell through the little trapdoor. Trapdoors were, of course, also an important feature of Shakespeare's stage, especially useful for the ghost's entrances and exits. These metatheatrical interruptions in the narrative flow flatter the audience by assuming that they are in the know; and this flattery is a part of the work's status as a "heritage film."

The mise en scène of Hamlet's apartments confirms this status. The audience can vicariously enjoy the aristocratic ambience of the room and bask in the reflected glory of its sophistication. Even if we are watching it on television, the theatrical paraphernalia in the room links us to the privileged theatre audience. As Linda Boose astutely observes, "the insistent theatricality of Shakespeare's play ... becomes bound up with nostalgia for some utopian – or at least preferable – cultural past with which Shakespeare is metonymically linked" (Burt and Boose, 10). This yearning is visually reinforced as we identify with Prince Hamlet, gazing with him and at him through the frame of the model theatre. Boose's "utopian cultural past" in the case of Branagh's *Hamlet* is one inhabited by the nineteenth-century British aristocracy invoked by the costumes, and the eighteenth-century society suggested by setting the film at Bleinheim Palace.

Adrian Noble, director of the film *A Midsummer Night's Dream* (1996), a play that, like *Hamlet*, alludes to the theatre perhaps more than any other in the canon, presents through metatheatre a yearning for a traditional English childhood, a childhood that incorporates Mendelssohn-filled productions of *A Midsummer Night's Dream*, and children's classics on page, stage, and screen. Sprengler comments on the popularity among nostalgia narratives of protagonists "returning to the site of their childhood home ... Whether accessed physically by visiting the childhood home or mentally through flashbacks ... the past envisioned today functions as the blueprint for a better tomorrow" (74). Noble's film is directly based on his successful 1994 RSC stage production. Like Branagh's mise en scène, which provides us with the "house porn" of mahogany shelves and tastefully framed engravings, Noble's opening mise en scène gives the audience relief from contemporary childhoods filled with garish plastic and shiny metal from Fisher-Price and Nintendo, by immersing them in the details of a cozy Edwardian nursery. His camera lingers on the handcrafted wooden theatre, puppets, and furniture. Noble is here tapping into a widespread nostalgia; we can see it in the success of companies like Pottery Barn Kids, which essentially market a "quality," old-fashioned childhood. Noble's film (inadvertently?) comments on the way we stage-manage our lives, setting the scene for our children's youth with tasteful decor and playthings that appeal not to children but to parents, who are wistful for a simpler, more innocent past that likely never existed.

Noble's mise en scène immediately suggests to a contemporary audience sets from "classic" plays and illustrations from "classic" books, and thus "worthwhile pursuits" for adults and children alike: reading and theatre-going, particularly Shakespeare. Films like this one are a balanced part of an upwardly mobile diet. As Douglas Lanier expresses it, "The Shakespeare films of the 1990s might be understood in retrospect as participating in a much larger fin de siècle project, the recuperation of traditional literary culture for an age of mass media" ("Nostalgia and Theatricality," 154).

Noble, like Branagh a theatre director turned cineaste, employs in his *Dream* metatheatrical techniques strikingly similar to Branagh's in *Hamlet*, which came out the same year. (This similarity is not surprising, since Branagh's film was based on Noble's production of *Hamlet*.) Noble creates in his film a frame in which a boy dreams the events of the play after falling asleep reading an Arthur Rackham illustrated edition of it. As with Hamlet's apartment, the first objects we see as we zoom Peter Pan–like into the Edwardian nursery are the boy's marionettes hanging from the ceiling, and his model theatre. Later, the boy summons fairies by blowing bubbles into his toy theatre. Gazing into this little theatre, Oberon and Puck plan to trick Titania. They crouch so that the stage, as in Branagh's *Hamlet*, is at eye level, while the boy looks at them through the other side. Just as Hamlet contrived his next move by manipulating the king puppet, so Oberon,

Puck, and the boy devise the potion antics, with little puppets representing the Athenian lovers. At the end of this scene, we see the boy working all the fairies by marionette strings. This staging animates puns that Shakespeare incorporates in his dialogue, like Oberon's lines, "We the *globe* can compass soon / Swifter than the wandering moon" (italics added) (4.1.98–9).

Noble's toy theatre sequence is similar to Branagh's, yet it achieves different effects. Branagh's film, subscribing to Hollywood demands of naturalism, tries to suggest that the toy theatre is just something that happens to be in Hamlet's room and gives him his idea to trap the king. Noble's approach continually acknowledges artifice. The boy's toy theatre in this scene stands in a kind of limbo, on a dark stage hung with many light bulbs to suggest stars. Behind him are *Alice in Wonderland*-style doors in primary colours, leading nowhere. We are in the land of the surreal. The alien landscape and the actors' address to the camera keep the audience at a remove from the events of the story. To what purpose?

Noble seems to have wanted the audience to get in touch with a childlike sense of wonder, yet surely this would have been more successfully brought about by a naturalistic approach. The film does achieve a kind of wonder, but it is at the nifty contrivances of theatre, and at the dreamlike mise en scène rather than at the magical nature of the story. Because no actor in the film (except for the boy) conveys much emotional reality, the audience remains detached. Does Noble want us to interrogate our own nostalgia as well as to feel wonder? Interestingly, it may be Trevor Nunn who started the trend to use children's toys symbolically in Shakespeare. In his 1970 RSC stage production of *The Winter's Tale*, he used a mirrored box, life-sized, in which Leontes, Time, and Hermione's statue appeared in turn, and Mamilius had a toy version that rotated by clockwork.

Noble's fairies, also wearing primary colours, and bouncing on bright umbrellas, recall Peter Brook's seminal Stratford-on-Avon production of *A Midsummer Night's Dream* (1970). Nor is this the only allusion to a theatrical image. The *Peter Pan* opening and the furnishings of the nursery recall past productions of J.M. Barrie's stage classic, in which Pan and fairies, attached to wires, also fly about. The boy, falling down a hole in the next scene, Alice-like (another children's classic with a stage history), pops his head out of a stove in the mechanicals' meeting place like a character from Beckett or Stoppard.

Both Branagh and Noble, by prominently using model theatres, are exploring several themes. The theatres not only reinforce our awareness of the artificiality of the medium but also remind us of the plays' origins and afterlife. We remember Shakespeare, and, because neither model theatre is Renaissance in style, we remember the theatre that followed, especially the Edwardian and Victorian. As Lanier points out, these were eras in which the theatre was the most successful form of entertainment, before the popularization of cinema ("Nostalgia and Theatricality," 161). The model theatres make us aware of theatre history while commenting on or feeding into our nostalgia for the past. This past includes "play" in all senses of the word, whether child's play – manipulating toys and imagining worlds the way Hamlet and Oberon do when they move their representational puppets around the little stage – or its more adult version of creating plays filled with child-like wonder, like *A Midsummer Night's Dream* and *Peter Pan*.

Julie Taymor with her film *Titus* (1999) straddles the gap between the dominant realism of Branagh's *Hamlet* and the artifice of Noble's *A Midsummer Night's Dream*. Her motion picture was closely based on her stage production for the Theatre for a New Audience in New York. She follows Noble in creating a frame for the film using a little boy. As Lanier notes of Noble's film in his essay "Nostalgia and Theatricality" on filmed versions of *Dream*, the use of a child actor immediately draws attention to the artifice (162–3). Taymor's opening and closing scenes, both involving the child, are set in the Coliseum, the large open-air theatre where Romans enacted violent games much like the boy in the frame, only using humans instead of toys. Thus, in the first ten minutes of her film, Taymor establishes that war is an elaborate performance played by males of all ages and eras.

Taymor uses many platforms and stage-like raised daises throughout the film. Most do not draw attention to themselves, as the play's cast of characters are politicians, their lives carried out in the public eye. Thus Taymor's metaphor, along with Shakespeare's before her, is enlarged. War is merely a constructed performance, but so is the ruling of nations. The exercise of power in the film is continually linked with theatre, even when this link is not explicit in Shakespeare's play script. The most obvious example of this is when Aaron sends messengers to return the dismembered Andronici heads and hand to Titus. The body parts arrive concealed in a little vaudeville van, reminiscent of Franco's propaganda vans in the Spanish Civil War, in that it pumps out music. It also boasts audience chairs, and red and black curtains. Lanier observes, "With many other stage directors of the late twentieth century, [Taymor] shares a self-conscious celebration of theatricality" ("Julie Taymor," 458). The moment, unbearably cruel in Shakespeare's text, is even more painful here. When the vaudeville van arrives, young Lucius (also the boy from the frame) is delighted. Theatre is equated with play – an escape from reality. But in this play, and in this film, all theatre is harnessed for revenge, from Tamara enacting Vengeance herself, to Titus assuming the role of chef; the actors' traditional toying with their audience becomes a torture.

Richard III is another play that naturally lends itself to representing the stage, as the eponymous hero is a consummate actor. The part is itself a theatrical image – the king with the hump (in the 1989 film *The Tall Guy*, plans are laid for a musical adaptation with a hit song, "I've a Hunch I'll Be King"). The role can thus be compared to another iconic part, that of Hamlet, the black-clad prince holding a skull. Richard Loncraine's film of the play (1995) exploits more contemporary theatrical images. Ian McKellen, knighted for his contributions to British theatre, plays the title role, and the film borrows heavily from an acclaimed stage production that was famous on both sides of the Atlantic: Richard Eyre's World War II production for the National Theatre in 1990, which also starred McKellen (Rothwell, *Shakespeare on Screen*, 231). Loncraine is obviously not the first director to transfer a theatrical legend to the screen. Olivier transferred himself, and Peter Greenaway in his film *Prospero's Books* (1991) preserved John Gielgud as both a theatrical image and a Shakespearean icon.

Loncraine chooses to translate what is usually a private moment, the play's opening soliloquy, into a performance. Ian McKellen delivers the first half of the monologue through a microphone on a stage previously occupied by a jazz soloist. His audience is a large gathering of Yorkist family and friends. In this way, by turning this part of the famous soliloquy into a public speech, Loncraine can economically suggest each character's allegiances with reaction shots. McKellen performs the rest of the speech standing alone in front of a mirror, like an actor reciting his lines before getting his last call (something Branagh may have borrowed for his "To be" soliloquy in his film *Hamlet*).

Loncraine takes another overtly theatrical scene in the play (3.7) and renders it even more obviously stagey in his film. Before Richard meets the mayor and people of London, he is led to a theatrical dressing room fitted out with a strip of lights around the mirror. There he is treated like a starlet about to go on stage and meet her public; he even has flowers on his dressing table. Two women tend to his appearance, one about to shave him or make up his face, the other buffing his fingernails. Jazz plays on the radio. When Catesby announces that Richard is "with two right reverend fathers," he can barely keep a straight face. Instead of appearing between two bishops as he does in Shakespeare, Richard appears alone holding a black-bound book; the film audience know it is a novel, but the mayor and people of London must assume it is a prayer-book or Bible. Through the device of the dressing room, Loncraine heightens the humour and clarifies the scene for the audience, most of whom are unfamiliar with the play, making it obvious that Richard's reluctance to take the throne is entirely feigned.

Oliver Parker's *Othello* (1996) gives Iago a chessboard as a powerful (if somewhat overused) metaphor for his manipulation of the other characters. As he confides in the audience, announcing his plan to undermine Othello by suggesting that Desdemona has played him false with Cassio, he steers a black king, a white knight, and a white queen around the board. Branagh in the role of Iago recalls the moment in *Hamlet* in which Branagh sent the king pawn in his toy theatre to hell through the trap door. Parker cleverly returns to this chess image later in the film when we see the pieces representing Othello and Desdemona (black king, white queen) plunge into the ocean and sink. The chessboard is like a model stage, and the pieces like puppets that Iago operates. This metaphor is especially rich in the Elizabethan setting used by Parker as it remembers allusions to the game in Jacobean and Elizabethan theatre (Middleton's *A Game at Chess* and Ferdinand and Miranda "discovered" engaged in the game at the conclusion of *The Tempest* are instances). It also summons to mind the dominant sixteenth-century comparison of life on stage to life on earth, with God assigning our parts and arranging our entrances and exits, as suggested by both Jacques in *As You Like It* ("All the world's a stage," 2.7.139) and Macbeth at the end of his tragedy ("Life's but a walking shadow, a poor player," 5.5.23).

Christine Edzard's *A Children's Midsummer Night's Dream* (2001) also opens metatheatrically, with a uniformed school group attending a puppet performance of *Dream*. The puppets' wooden forms are a visual synecdoche for the exaggeratedly "posh" voice performers

(Derek Jacobi and Samantha Bond) who deliver their lines. Edzard seems to be animating on screen the dull image that Shakespeare had at many schools in the past. With the literally wooden show on stage, Edzard triggers older audience members' memories of teachers in the classroom playing scratchy LPs featuring the excellent elocution and sonorous voices of Laurence Olivier and John Gielgud. Shakespeare critics Hindle and Burnett see a kind of political and generational challenge in the way Edzard has her young inner-city students commandeer the performance, ditching the puppets. The implicit message seems to be that these children, with their youth and passion and natural, unadulterated urban accents, can infuse the old script with new life (Hindle, *Studying Shakespeare on Film*, 62–3; Burnett, "Fancy's Images," 167). Yet, the presence of children in this film, as in the others discussed here, can also strike a nostalgic note. As Stanley Wells has observed, "For many people [*A Midsummer Night's Dream*] forms their first introduction to Shakespeare" (Penguin Shakespeare's *A Midsummer Night's Dream*, 7). This introduction often takes place in the classroom where the schoolchildren are encouraged to read parts aloud, or in some cases, perform in a school production of the play. Still the Shakespearean play most often performed at schools, this play, among all those of Shakespeare's canon, is particularly associated with children. Not only is it one of the few that does not dwell on adult themes like adultery, murder, or revenge but also the parts of the fairies lend themselves especially to performance by children. Certainly, the secondary fairies in Shakespeare's day must have been played by boy apprentices, and, as Wells remarks, this play would have required more young actors than most of Shakespeare's canon (13).

As most members of Edzard's audience would be adults, childhood is naturally a subject that encourages yearning. A child's perspective is emphasized from the opening of the film, as Burnett points out, with the over-the-shoulder shots showing the puppet show from the child-audience's point of view. Thus, the film becomes another invitation to the cinema audience to "play." This invitation becomes even more obvious when the children take over the performance, and then, at the conclusion, drown out the adult voices. For the duration of the film at least, the cinema audience is encouraged to empathize with the children and their need to overthrow adult authority manifested by their interruption of the puppet show, and their shedding of their uniforms in favour of costumes that glow and glisten (dress-up clothes).

Even though the adults are the repressive figures in the film's universe, the cinema audience is encouraged to forget for a couple of hours their grown-up status and to side with the subversive children and their desire to "play." As in her *As You Like It*, Edzard is again attempting to open up the parameters of Shakespeare, reminding us that he belongs not just to the privileged playgoer, the educated, and the prosperous, but is entertainment for everyone, from the powerless child outwards. It is not surprising that the adaptor of Dickens's *Little Dorrit* should, just as with her *As You Like It*, make something of a social protest out of the film, placing underprivileged children at the heart of the play, as Dickens did in many of his novels. Despite this earnest intention, Edzard's film is bound to appeal to the adults in the audience who, burdened with responsibilities, enjoy a vicarious couple of hours reliving their childhood, particularly the raging hormones and silliness of adolescence, represented in Shakespeare's play by the four lovers, Hermia and Lysander, Helena and Demetrius. When these roles are taken on by thirteen- and fourteen-year-olds, the mercurial emotions seem more natural and less ridiculous than in Shakespeare. What we lose in hilarity, we gain in pathos.

In Branagh's film adaptation of *As You Like It* (2006), the natures (and regimes) of Duke Senior and Duke Junior (Frederick) are contrasted by showing which aspects of their adopted culture they admire. Duke Senior is introduced watching a gentle, beautiful Kabuki actor waving a branch of purple flowers about the stage to soothing zither music. As Sarah Brown observes of *Twelfth Night*, "Kabuki theatre, with its all-male cast, emphasis on cross-dressing and disguise, and reliance on music and ringing, is an appropriate medium for a revisioning" (9). It is similarly appropriate for *As You Like It*. The usurping duke, in contrast to his brother, commands a performance of Sumo wrestling.

Branagh's "dream of Japan" is a space to play and escape. His film is framed by acknowledgments of the artificiality of art – paint-brushed haiku and Kabuki theatre before the credits, and movie trailers and lights during the epilogue. Branagh's Forest of Arden, defined by close-ups of plants and spiderwebs (with homage to Kurosawa's and Brook's filmed Shakespeare), is a place of spiritual and physical recreation, in which the outcasts consult a Buddhist monk, practice tai chi, listen to songs and music, and meditate in the gravel Zen garden. The Kabuki dancer waving his/her floral branch in front of a natural scene

Figure 5 Duke Senior (Brian Blessed) and his court watch a Kabuki performer (Takuya Shimada) in Branagh's *As You Like It*, 2006.

painted on the stage flat anticipates this world of harmonious nature, the one with which Duke Senior is associated throughout (fig. 5).

Branagh shows the influence of Trevor Nunn's *Twelfth Night* in the way he provides the background material before the opening credits, thereby keeping the non-Shakespearean part of the film (the Kabuki performance, interrupted by a ninja coup in which Duke Senior is supplanted by his martial younger brother) strictly apart from Shakespeare's dialogue. The film opens with a haiku slowly appearing on a curtain, which is then parted to reveal a Kabuki actor's face, painted white like a geisha. His slow, graceful dance is intercut with shots of ninjas stealthily emerging from the lake outside the Duke's palace or lowering themselves down from the roof on ropes. Branagh focuses as much on the audience's delight in the Kabuki performance as on the performance itself. We witness Duke Senior, Rosalind, and Celia, sitting side by side with expressions of transport on their faces (perhaps a somewhat exaggerated response to the quiet little scene on stage). Touchstone seems a little less entranced, as he tickles Celia's ear with an origami animal. Suddenly, the Kabuki actor seems distracted, eyes fixed on a blade's point poking through the ceiling of the stage. The audience registers a slight unease at the performer's lapse, and then ninjas burst through the windows at the back of the hall and the backdrop to the stage. Art, beauty, and culture are destroyed in seconds by military might. Also (inadvertently, I'm sure) Japanese theatre is swept definitively aside by English; Shakespeare's dialogue starts after the Kabuki performance is destroyed, and the poor actor is deprived of his wig in an oddly out-of-sync moment of comic humiliation.

While the stage graced by the Kabuki dancer is the most obvious example of nostalgia for the theatre in Branagh's *As You Like It*, it is by no means the only one. The same stage, shorn of its painted flat, becomes the dais on which the new duke sits, surrounded by sinister ninja guards all clad in black armour. Later this same hall is transformed into the sumo wrestling arena, the round space in which Orlando and Charles fight, framed to distinguish it from the spectators' space. In between these two scenes, the camera discovers Rosalind in her chamber prostrate on the floor weeping as Celia tries to comfort her. The dramatic pose of the pair, and the bare floor that they lie on, in combination with the painted natural scene on the bedroom wall behind them, again creates the impression of a stage peopled by actors. This effect contributes to that of the whole movie, that the cast of characters is *playing* at being Japanese in much the same way as children play "house." Apart from the western style of their garments, the characters in the film seem to live like the inhabitants of their adopted country. There is little to no furniture in the rooms; the characters sit and lie on the floor when they converse, and in the opening scene, during the Kabuki performance, Audrey appears to be offering sushi to the duke. Perhaps Branagh based this depiction of the expatriates' lifestyle on research, but it would seem to me that in a British enclave, the denizens, likely homesick for their native land, would cling more fiercely to their own habits and cuisine than they would at home. Would not British merchants in Japan, like those in India, insist on importing their own furniture and teaching their cooks at least some of the familiar dishes they liked to eat at home? But Branagh has covered his bases by announcing his film as a "dream of Japan."

The Zen garden in the Forest of Arden also forms a sort of stage as it is set apart by the low fence that surrounds it. This theatrical impression is strengthened by the way in which only one character at a time seems to take advantage of the garden, so that each appears to be centre stage, the focus of attention. Jacques meditates in the middle of it, demanding songs. Celia idles her time in it, until Oliver appears and she is smitten. Many of the characters practice tai chi – and each time it is a mini-performance. Jacques, as played by Kevin Kline, is always performing. During his rants, the other characters stop what they are doing and encircle him, creating an impromptu stage or arena. All of these elements are visual reinforcements of the theatrical motif that runs so strongly through the play. Lines like the duke's "This wide and universal theatre / Presents more woeful pageants that the scene / Wherein we play" prompt in turn the Seven Ages of Man speech, which Branagh highlights by quoting it in the last line in the opening haiku, "All the world's a stage."

Geoffrey Wright's *Macbeth* (2006), set in contemporary Melbourne, also makes recourse to theatrical images. Macbeth first speaks to the witches on the dance floor of a club, disco lights swirling around the three as they determine Macbeth's destiny. There is no audience to their dance, Banquo having retired to the bathroom to vomit. When he returns, Macbeth tells him of the apparition. Banquo laughs it off as the effects of the drugs the two thugs imbibed earlier. No one in this production other than Macbeth ever sees the witches; the fact that they appear to him on the dance floor, with dry ice and coloured lights, adds to their insubstantiality. They are a performance of his fantasy only. Wright thus maintains the realism of his film, excluding any element of Jacobean folklore that might remind the audience of the play's age and Christian framework. In a more self-consciously theatrical moment, Macbeth, learning of the imminent attack on his estate, appears in a black leather kilt and does an impromptu jig for his astonished bodyguard. One of film's more intelligent moments, this cheeky acknowledgment of a more traditional production of the Scottish play on which the film is based comes just as the film draws to a close.

Justin Kurzel in his adaptation of *Macbeth* (2015) adds a coronation scene to Shakespeare's script. This sequence is highly metatheatrical, as Macbeth and his lady stand elevated on the altar of a gothic cathedral to receive their crowns and be anointed with holy chrism as courtiers watch. The camera alternates between focusing on the solemn face of Macbeth (Michael Fassbender) and on the faces of his audience, many of whom look wary of him, especially the Macduffs. When the courtiers approach to kiss his hand after the ceremony, it is clear from their conflicted expressions that many are performing a role, as they suspect he has achieved the kingship through foul play.

Despite the gorgeous costumes and the light sifting through the gothic windows, Kurzel achieves a sinister mood for the coronation. When the courtiers chant "Hail Macbeth" repeatedly, there is no joy or enthusiasm in the sound. The actors all convey a vivid sense of going through the motions out of a grim sense of duty; even the king looks weary.

Ralph Fiennes's *Coriolanus* is a nostalgic project for the director, as he acted it to some acclaim on stage in London in 2000, directed by Jonathan Kent. As well, Gerard Butler, Fiennes's Aufidius, had his acting debut in a production of *Coriolanus* at the Mermaid Theatre in 1996, directed by and starring Stephen Berkoff. Traces of theatre abound in the film. The subtitle near the beginning of the film reads, "A Place Calling Itself Rome," in homage to John Osborne's 1970 version of the play. Fiennes comments in the DVD supplementary material that he had to seek legal permission to do so. Towards the end of this commentary, Fiennes explores the complicated relationship between film and theatre: "The scary word in all of this is theatre. Cinema and theatre are arguably miles apart but also extremely close. The term 'theatrical release' acknowledges that cinema is also essentially an act of theatre ... Film likes that which is completely unforced behaviour."

Fiennes includes in his film use of a stage not explicitly in Shakespeare's text. When the tribunes challenge Coriolanus to defend himself against accusations of tyrannical intent in act 3, scene 3 of Shakespeare's play, the scene is presumably meant to take place in a public square or street, although there is no specific stage direction. Fiennes cleverly transposes the scene to a television studio. Coriolanus is placed on a stage with a live audience of the Roman people watching and participating, cameras rolling. His obvious discomfort with the situation reinforces the character's inability to perform on any other stage than a battlefield. The scene in turn underlines his mother's unreasonableness in expecting a man she has raised exclusively as Rome's sword suddenly to become an adept politician and crowd-pleaser. (As Coriolanus asserts, "Would you have me / False to my nature? Rather say I play / The man I am" [3.2.14–16]. It is not as if the other patricians in the play really feel more concern for the plebeians' lot – they are just better at hiding their contempt.) Fiennes also seems to be commenting on the way politicians today must behave like television personalities to succeed on election day. Service to the nation is not enough – a smooth presence on stage and television is required in order to triumph.

Joss Whedon adds to the existing theatricality of the masked revel in his *Much Ado About Nothing* by including two extratextual performances. As the guests mill around the garden, twin female trapeze artists, borrowed from Canada's Cirque de Soleil, writhe in a tree. In the dining room, a man at the piano and a female guest perform a few bars of the song playing on the sound system, Whedon's own version of "Sigh No More, Ladies." These two additional performances serve two purposes. The trapeze artists, described in Whedon's script as performing "an intricate, sensuous *act*" (italics added), contribute to the charged sexual atmosphere at the party (74). Their performance in a scene in which the prince secures Hero on Claudio's behalf reinforces the message that even a romantic proposal can be mere lines delivered by the participant, as Benedick implies in act 1, scene 1, when he quizzes Claudio about the sincerity of his feelings for Hero: "Do you play the flouting Jack to tell us Cupid is a good hare-finder?" (1.1.164) – a line left out of both Whedon's and Branagh's adaptations. The two guests jamming in the dining room furnish another detail to the setting Whedon describes in his DVD commentary as "a wild party nobody can leave." Guests are dancing, singing, swimming, and finding quiet places for amorous encounters.

The extraordinary aspect of these metatheatrical scenes is that in all these films they made the final cut. If, as Fiennes jokes, "the scary word in all this is theatre," why do screen adaptors of Shakespeare persist in drawing attention to the origins of their projects? The answer is prestige. No studio executives green-light a Shakespeare film thinking that they have a blockbuster in the offing. The most they can hope for is a modest profit and critical acclaim, with some recuperation of funds through sales to schools, libraries, and universities. The wished-for prestige is garnered through Shakespeare's name and his continued association with high culture. The metatheatrical moments are a reminder to the audience that they are participating in a significant cultural event. In addition, these metatheatrical moments are a (perhaps inadvertent) revelation of the directors' longing to be involved with an artistic work that is lasting. A Shakespeare film will continue to be viewed for many years on YouTube and at educational institutions, in spite of failure at the box office, because it is an adaptation of a Shakespeare play, a work acknowledged to be of great literary importance. In this way the Shakespeare film is unique. Any other kind of film that flopped in the cinema would die a quick death. As long as Shakespeare continues to be studied in schools and universities, celebrated at festivals, and performed in theatres, the endurance of the screen adaptation of his work is secure.

5

Death Rituals in Shakespeare, Almereyda, and Luhrmann

During Shakespeare's own lifetime, rituals surrounding death were radically altered. The Catholic practices of which he may have seen vestiges in his childhood or as a young man in Lancashire were being systematically eradicated by the new Protestant regime. Whereas Catholics had in place a complex system to cope with grief, including ways of affecting their afterlife through prayers, masses, and good works, Protestants were efficiently forbidding such traditions without replacing them with full, rich alternatives. Stephen Greenblatt, in his biography of Shakespeare, *Will in the World*, argues that this new absence of death rites left many English people bereft of an adequate way to cope with grief (312).

Taking this cultural moment as my point of departure, I examine two film adaptations of Shakespearean plays that focus on death and grief. I have selected Baz Luhrmann's *William Shakespeare's Romeo + Juliet* (1996) and Michael Almereyda's *Hamlet* (2000), as they have so many elements in common. Both films are set in present-day metropolises and play extensively with twenty-first-century technology to comment on our society.

Almereyda's New York is a city devoid of any external signs of religion. Further, Almereyda cuts the gravedigger scene entirely and severely curtails Ophelia's funeral. Yet he maintains many of the religious allusions in the play's dialogue, and of course the ghost attests to the presence of an afterlife (even if his portal to Purgatory is a Pepsi dispensing machine). Hamlet, played by Ethan Hawke, indeed seems to reflect the loss that Greenblatt attributes to the English people after the Reformation. The only true consolation this bewildered Hamlet receives for his grief over his father's death comes from a Buddhist monk on television who urges his listeners "to interbe" rather than merely "to be." Ophelia has even less in the way of ceremony in the film than in Shakespeare's text, granted nothing but the mechanical platform on which her coffin rests and the flowers tossed onto it by Gertrude.

In contrast, Luhrmann's Verona Beach is a city overflowing with religious iconography, although the examples of Catholic kitsch that appear in every scene are generally treated by the characters as little more than accessories. At the same time, in this Catholic city, the characters still have rituals surrounding death that lend a kind of beauty and even meaning to their grief. Juliet lies on a bier in the church heaped with flowers and surrounded by candles, displaying some thought, care, and remnants of tradition with which the family can busy themselves during their most despairing hours.

Even if the two directors knew little about Protestant Wittenberg and Elsinore and Roman Catholic Verona when they made their decisions, they obviously responded to elements in the texts that prompted them to select very different approaches to treating the themes of religion and death so important to both tragedies.

The Italianate passion of the earlier play, and the cooler, more rational tone of the later one, have clear reflections in these contemporary film interpretations. The reference to period sources detailing the church rituals under the Catholics and the Protestants, and the comparison between Shakespeare's scripts and the two screenplays, suggest that more of the conflicted views on religion typical of Shakespeare's period emerge in these films than might at first be supposed. What might this say about the place of religion in the societies in which these films were made? Has the pluralism of western society given us more ways and opportunities to express our grief, or has it merely left us bewildered and uncertain? Is the continued popularity of *Romeo and Juliet* on stage and screen (witness Carlo Carlei's 2013 *Romeo and Juliet*) in some small measure the consequence of a nostalgia for a culture that had set protocols for every major event in a person's life: baptism, marriage, and even death, thus giving those involved the security of knowing what was expected?

First, some historical background. Shakespeare's knowledge of Catholic Verona was likely limited to the reading he had done, but his acquaintance with the vestiges of Catholic England may have been considerable. Most of the Shakespeare biographies that have emerged in the past fifteen years or so (those of Park Honan, Stephen Greenblatt, Peter Ackroyd, and Anthony Holden) contend that Shakespeare was brought up Catholic and spent his so-called "lost years" as a tutor in a recusant Lancashire household. Even if this were not the case, he was likely acquainted with the old Catholic funeral practices. Historians concur that in rural areas, despite the reforms of Edward and Elizabeth, the practice of the faith varied a good deal from minister to minister, and, in the case of death rites, in accordance with family wishes. James V. Holleran summarizes the situation in "Maimed Funeral Rites in *Hamlet*": "In general, church ritual moved away from the old, elaborate Roman rites to the new, simplified forms of Continental Protestantism. But even these gradual changes were diversified, resisted, and often ignored. The particular form of funeral rites in late sixteenth-century England depended on such considerations as religious preference, social standing, the College of Heralds, local customs, civil and canon laws, directions in a will, and the clergyman" (68).

The old Catholic ritual started with a visit to the dying person's house, where the priest would administer the last rites in the presence of friends and family. These rites included a confession (private), reception of the Eucharist, many prayers and psalms, and often a reading from scripture. A similar visit took place right after the death. Then the priest and friends and relatives participated in the preparation of the body for burial. The body was not left alone after this point; friends and relatives took turns sitting by it, praying and singing. Food was offered to the mourners. The morning after the wake, there was a procession to the church. The body was carried on a bier if the deceased was poor or lower middle class, in a coffin if more well-to-do. A white pall cloth was draped over the body or the coffin, often large enough to half-conceal the pallbearers, usually close relatives or friends, who carried the corpse through the town to the church. As the procession wended its way, the assembled mourners chanted psalms and the church bells tolled, reminding those unaware to come to the requiem mass, or at least to say prayers for the dead. Once the bier or coffin was placed in the church, it was surrounded by lit votive candles (Litten, 148). The office of the dead was then said, with Matins and lessons from Job, then the Lord's Prayer and a series of responses, followed by another prayer. The liturgy might contain a homily on the significance of death in a Christian life, but never a eulogy. Then the funeral mass would be celebrated. At the end, the bier was sprinkled with holy water and a concluding prayer was recited. The assembled then proceeded to the graveyard, accompanied by the anthem "In Paradisium." Sprigs of rosemary were distributed (144). The priest blessed the grave, and the closest relatives lowered the body or the coffin into the open grave, with many prayers following. These prayers often addressed the dead person directly: "I commend thy soul to God the Father Almighty, and thy body to the ground." All the mourners threw their rosemary onto the corpse (ibid.). Then they returned to the church for more prayers ("De profundis" and the antiphon) and finally retired to the closest relation's house for a banquet. The poor were often invited, and alms distributed. Prayers and masses were said for the repose of the soul on monthly anniversaries of the death (Rowell, 71–2).

From this summary, it is obvious that mourning the dead took about three full days out of grieving friends' and relatives' lives. The forms were elaborate, involved the whole community, and required time and effort to achieve. Most importantly, they provided a sense of continuity for the grieving. Their beloved had started on a journey to the afterlife and was probably waiting in Purgatory. With prayers, alms, and masses, the mourners could still affect the beloved's fate, who was not yet taken entirely beyond their reach.

Shakespeare gives us some of this traditional Catholic ritual in *Romeo and Juliet*. The nurse, Lord and Lady Capulet, Paris, and Friar Laurence gather about Juliet's bed on the morning she is discovered in a death-like torpor. They mourn her loudly, crying and wringing their hands according to the stage directions in the first quarto (Arden, 211). Friar Laurence delivers an impromptu sermon on the place of death in a Christian life, reminding them all of Juliet's happiness in heaven. Then he directs them to strew her corpse with rosemary and dress her in her best array, preparing her for burial. Capulet summarizes the rites that are to follow: black funeral, melancholy bells, sad burial feast, sullen dirges, and flowers. The first quarto stage directions tell us that the mourners strew Juliet with rosemary and then close the curtains about her bed (213). The next we hear, Balthasar has seen her "laid low in her kindred's vault" (4.4.20), the Capulets' monument. He speaks of her in the present tense, paralleling the direct address to the deceased in the Catholic burial (the Reformed rite referred only to the body).

Luhrmann, out of economy, cuts much of the mourning scene. After Juliet takes the potion, the following shot focuses on the white curtains above her bed, suggesting a shroud or pall. We next see Father Laurence removing the empty vial from her bed, his Bible and rosary beside him. He nods to two men in black who roll down the bedclothes and place her on a stretcher as the priest stands at her window, wiping his eyes. Then we cut back to her room, now empty, her bed made, and little angel candles lit at its foot. The scene moves to the church full of mourners in black. The camera pans across the sad faces of the nurse, Capulet, and his wife wearing a black mantilla. Funeral music plays, and we hear a bell tolling. There are flowers and candles everywhere. Father Laurence stands at the back of the church, presumably waiting to start the requiem mass. It is this scene that Balthasar sees and rushes off to report to Romeo.

Of course, it is not the first time in the play we have witnessed the Capulet family grieving. In act 3, scene 4, Capulet explains to Paris that his household is in mourning for Tybalt, and thus he has not broached the subject of marriage with his daughter. Shakespeare gives us no stage directions to suggest how this mourning state might have outwardly been manifested on stage, but Luhrmann conveys it in his film with the darkened house lit only with candles, and a pale, subdued Gloria Capulet, who appears to be wearing no make-up. The scene is a high contrast to the ball scene, when the Capulet mansion was overflowing with light, sound, and people, and Gloria Capulet was highly painted as Cleopatra.

The scene that reveals most about Luhrmann's approach to the death rituals in the play is the last, where Romeo enters the church to join Juliet. Shakespeare gives us few details about the Capulet monument. It is clear that it is underground as Romeo brings a mattock and a crowbar to enter the sealed tomb. Juliet and Tybalt lie shrouded on biers; there are no coffins. Paris brings holy water and flowers with which to strew Juliet's body. Luhrmann in his film draws on all the Catholic traditions for this scene. Juliet is elevated at the front of the church on a bier covered with a white silk pall and many little cushions bearing her initials. She is dressed in her wedding gown ("her best array"), a bouquet of flowers in her hand. Votive candles not only surround her bier but fill the church. Angel statues remind us of the altar in her bedroom. There are white flowers everywhere, and blue neon crosses at each pew. The central aisle leading to Juliet's bier is strewn with a carpet of rose petals.

Luhrmann lavishes time and attention on this scene. He uses one long take as Romeo slowly walks towards the bier, washed with blue aquatic light that reminds the audience of all the watery baptismal moments in the film. Wagner's "Liebestod" from *Tristan und Isolde* plays during the scene. Despite the kitschy neon crosses, the set is very beautiful. Many critics writing about Luhrmann's *Romeo + Juliet* spend much of their ink on the double suicide at the end; strangely, the scene has provoked contradictory responses. Some, like Rothwell (*Shakespeare on Screen*, 244), see it as a continuation of Luhrmann's parodic treatment of the play, whereas others see it as lushly romantic (Lehmann, "Strictly Shakespeare?," 218; Hodgdon, "*William Shakespeare's Romeo + Juliet*," 97). Most are fascinated by it, judging by the amount of space it garners in both reviews and scholarly articles. I think this reveals a nostalgia in reviewers and scholars echoing Luhrmann's own.

Luhrmann is drawn to the operatic drama of a traditional Catholic funeral. Death rituals are no longer part of most of our lives; funerals now tend to be cursory affairs from which people outside the immediate circle of family and close friends often excuse themselves. They are generally brisk and business-like events that take as little time as possible from our busy days. Creating a beautiful funeral service is rarely a consideration. The attention lavished in Luhrmann's film on Juliet's corpse and the aesthetics of death are foreign to contemporary English-speaking society. The scene not only comments on the director's taste in composition but also suggests something about his reading of the Latino Capulets. The Capulets are shown not to have understood their daughter during her life (her father is physically abusive at one point); and have inadvertently thwarted her deepest desires, but they wish at least to give her the prettiest send-off manageable. Luhrmann suggests this gives them some comfort, judging by the actors' calm faces at the funeral, even if it is of the basest, most material kind.

Luhrmann may have drawn his funerary images from current Catholic practice, which is not so very different from the elaborate Tudor rites summarized earlier. As in Tudor times, there are four parts to the rite. First, the priest visits the dying or dead at home (or in hospital); then there is a wake or viewing (often now taking place at a funeral home, where one assumes the two black-clad men in Luhrmann's film were taking Juliet). This is followed by a procession (now in cars) to church where there is a mass. The coffin is still covered with a white pall, symbolic of the robe of baptism. A paschal candle is lit near the coffin at the beginning of the church ritual. After mass, the procession goes to the cemetery; there is a blessing of the grave, a reading of scripture, and prayers, and then everyone returns to the home of the family or to a restaurant for a lunch or dinner. Some of the details Luhrmann includes seem to have come from the Mexican location of the shoot. Alfredo Michel Modenessi sees in the elaborate decoration of Capulet monument "allusions to our religious tradition of Dia de Muertos [All Souls Day]. This rich cultural event is re-elaborated ... with the strictly fin-de-siècle touch of the neon light crosses, a somewhat recent addition to our religious paraphernalia. The flower carpet therein is also a fine artisanal tradition linked to religious fervor that extends from Spain to, among other places, Mexico, Guatemala and El Salvador" (112).

One of the reasons Luhrmann chose Mexico as his location was because "he felt it provided a landscape where corporate values had not yet absorbed or destroyed the ties of traditional religious piety." The film's designer, Catherine Martin, said of the location: "Religion still has a very strong presence there, culturally and visually" (Litson, 46). Of course, the name of the city in the film, Verona Beach, recalling Miami Beach, and the large presence of Anglo-Americans in the cast, suggest that the film takes place in a southern American city with a sizable Latino minority. Juliet's elaborate funerary ritual thus suggests that, in Luhrmann's conception, Fulgencio Capulet has maintained customs from his own homeland, though it is unclear from which Hispanic tradition he derives. This is another instance of the prevalence of nostalgia in these films and in our culture. Those who have moved to a new country characteristically cling to the traditions they associate with their homeland, even while those traditions are rapidly changing in the nation they left behind. This experience is well documented, as Susan Matt in her study of homesickness attests: "Migrants who returned after years away discovered that home was no longer what they had imagined it to be. Their homes had changed and so had they. As a result, [they] began to yearn not just for a lost home ... but for a lost time as well. As they journeyed between old homes and new, many began to wonder if they had any home whatsoever. A sense of homelessness began to emerge that would become endemic to modern life" (6). This yearning for a lost time and place, which seems expressed in Juliet's funeral rituals, is akin to the sense of loss Greenblatt describes many English men and women experiencing with the Protestant eradication of their beloved funerary rituals.

For both Shakespeare and Luhrmann, enriching their versions of *Romeo and Juliet* with Roman Catholic allusions was a choice. The source poem by Arthur Brooke does not provide this kind of Italian local colour, yet Shakespeare made it central to his play. This is evident from the number of Catholic oaths and references he includes, which Brooke assiduously avoids. Here are a few examples: "By'r lady" (1.5.33), "O God's lady dear" (2.4.62), "marry" (used as an oath meaning "by Mary," 16 instances, two of them at 1.1.37; 1.5.11), "St. Francis" (2.3, 5.3), "benefice" (1.4.81), "ghostly confessor" (2.5.21), "shrift" (2.4.65, 4.2.15), "confession" (4.1.23), "evening mass" (4.1.38), "St. Peter's Church" (3.5.114, 116). The sonnet shared by Romeo and Juliet at their first meeting is also redolent with Catholic terms like "shrine," "palmers," "pilgrims," and "saints" (1.5.92–109). Luhrmann, who keeps this whole sonnet in his film, follows Shakespeare in foregrounding Catholic imagery, especially in the costumes and accessories. Both Luhrmann and Shakespeare were creating their respective works in times of virulent change, and in both works the attitude toward religion is a key symptom of that change. Luhrmann lives in a western culture that is fast eradicating religion. His native land, Australia, in a decade saw a decrease in those professing Christianity from 68 per cent in 2001 to 61 per cent in 2011 (according to the Australian Bureau of Statistics Census, 2011; no more recent census is available yet online). Shakespeare lived in a society that radically altered its religion with each new monarch: "Within a comparatively short period, 1549 to 1559, England had experienced four prayer books. To the common man it must have been confusing" (Litten, 153).

Both playwright and filmmaker look with some longing at times and places that maintained some continuity in their religious traditions – fifteenth-century Verona, Italy, and twentieth-century Mexico City. Shakespeare's interest in Catholic traditions is evidenced by the fact that he added so many allusions to the faith that were not in his source; most importantly, his rendering of Friar Laurence is largely sympathetic. Arthur Brooke, in contrast, is insulting of his order: "For he of Frauncis order was, a fryer as I reede, / Not as the most was he, a grosse unlearned foole" (lines 66–7, appendix 2, Arden *Romeo and Juliet*, 251). Luhrmann maintains Shakespeare's sympathetic treatment of Laurence, cutting from the final film (in contrast to the published screenplay) the scene in which the priest is shown in the least flattering light – when he abandons Juliet beside the dead Romeo to investigate a sound.

Luhrmann's nostalgia is obvious in the high romantic treatment he gives the tragic couple. He surrounds them with purifying water throughout the film: bathtubs, sinks, aquaria, swimming pools, and that final aquatic blue light. He hearkens back to times of chivalry by costuming Romeo at the ball as a knight in shining armour and Juliet as a medieval angel. Then, he has them die to the strains of Isolde singing to her dead lover, Tristan, bathing them in the light of a thousand candles. His camera pulls away and up from the dead lovers; they are seen on their bier, elevated, seemingly levitating, suspended by the light, like the patron saints of true love ascending into heaven. Visually, the last shot of the two bodies on the white, floating bier is closer to an assumption or apotheosis painting (like Correggio's *Assumption of the Virgin*, 1526–30) from Shakespeare's time than, as some disparaging critics have said, a Sting or Madonna video (Gleibermann, "Wherefore Art?," 46; Buhler, 91).

Shakespeare's *Hamlet*, even more than his *Romeo and Juliet*, manifests the conflicted views about religion in his society. One would think that Shakespeare would make the world of the play – set in Denmark, with a hero recently returned from Wittenberg – at least nominally Protestant, but it is a mix, much like rural England, including, probably, Stratford-on-Avon. As Theo Brown writes, "People do not forget the ancient reverences ... in times of emergency they will resort to them as best they may. We may expect that henceforward [from the Reformation on] there will be two levels of belief: the one held officially – and sometimes with an excessive and even persecuting fervour – and the other not publicly acknowledged but actually relied on in private" (8).

Greenblatt observes that Horatio and Marcellus adopt "the official Protestant line ... there were no ghosts at all ... apparitions ... were mere delusions, or, still worse, they were devils in disguise, some to tempt their victims to sin" (*Will in the World*, 320). The two men warn Hamlet against the ghost, viewing it as an evil agent that might trick him into committing suicide (1.5.5–55). The ghost himself, though, is definitely pre-Reformation. He has come from Purgatory, a Catholic concept rejected by the Reformers (Livingstone, 144). He tells Hamlet he is "Doomed for a certain term to walk the night / And for the day confined to fast in fires / Till the foul crimes done in my days of nature / Are burnt and purged away" (1.5.10–13). He also laments that his brother killed him before he received the last rites, "unhouseled, disappointed, unaneled, / No reck'ning made, but sent to my account / With all my imperfections on my head" (1.5.77–9).

Claudius's fratricide is merely the first act of many rupturing traditional rites and ceremonies. Hamlet Senior, despite being buried according to tradition, has not been properly mourned, especially by his widow. During Claudius's reign, all burials are handled badly, from Polonius's "hugger-mugger" interment, to Ophelia's "maimed rites," to the black requiem mass that Claudius sets up to send Hamlet to his death (the transformed wine sitting on a kind of altar, offered to Hamlet to change his state, and shared by Gertrude and Claudius). Not until Fortinbras accedes the throne is due ceremony again observed. Hamlet is given a soldier's burial, perhaps not entirely appropriate for him, but at least he is accorded full funeral rites. Shakespeare often uses ruptured rituals to make a point in his plays: observe the number of broken nuptials in the canon. Usually the lapse is a symptom of political corruption – something rotten in the state.

Michael Almereyda's film is set in secular, contemporary New York, but he maintains many of the religious allusions of the Elizabethan playscript. Horatio's warnings against the ghost are edited out, as Hamlet encounters his father alone in his room. Horatio merely alerts him to his presence on the security camera by calling him from the guard's desk in the lobby. Given the unabashedly technological approach to the sighting of the ghost, it is surprising then to hear Sam Shepherd speak with searing conviction of his torments in Purgatory, his unconfessed sins, and his deprivation of the last sacraments (*Screenplay*, 30–2). Unlike Luhrmann's Capulets and Montagues, the Hamlet family and the Polonius family in this film are not given religious accoutrements of any kind, yet their language is studded with references to religion. In Hamlet's first conversation with Gertrude, mother and son are striding along in a New York City canyon, gleaming skyscrapers on either side, Gertrude sporting a pair of trendy sunglasses. Strangely, she still says, "Let not thy mother lose her prayers, Hamlet" (15). Her prayers are for her son to make his homecoming from Wittenberg permanent. Yet Hamlet is mourning for the home he has lost with the death of his father. Once again, this yearning connects Hamlet with a contemporary audience; Peter Berger describes the modern state as "the homeless mind" (82). Claudius, in a slick dark suit, reproaches Hamlet for a will "most incorrect to heaven" (*Screenplay*, 15), seeing his stepson's pining for the recent past as a weakness, a maladjustment. In contemporary times, when change is ubiquitous and flexibility constantly required, many people might sympathize with this anti-nostalgic point of view, but not with the way it is expressed. This is not how corporate New York speaks, and Almereyda, unlike Luhrmann, has made no effort to render his setting distinct from his locale. Luhrmann's Verona Beach is a constructed fantasy metropolis in which the Elizabethan verse comes across as a kind of local slang, a cool accessory to match the guns and T-shirts emblazoned with pictures of the Virgin Mary and the Sacred Heart. Almereyda wants it both ways: an accessible setting, with Shakespeare's language censored only for economy, not for content.

Polonius's burial happens off-stage in Shakespeare's play. We are merely told about it by Claudius, who worries about the hasty nature of the interment (4.5.82), and by Laertes, who complains about his father's "obscure burial – / No trophy, sword, nor hatchment o'er his bones, / No noble rite nor formal ostentation." This neglect cries "to be heard, as twere from heaven to earth / That I must call't in question" (4.5.211–14). Why Claudius did not give Polonius a proper burial is never explained. He is the king, so he could have arranged everything as he wished. Politically, an official funeral would have been a more astute choice, assuaging the natural outrage of Polonius's offspring. Claudius himself admits he has acted "greenly" (4.5.81). His irreligious neglect of sacred rites is, however, consistent with Shakespeare's characterization of him and would have confirmed in the original audience's minds that he was fundamentally corrupt and unworthy of his office.

What function, however, can Claudius's neglect of ceremony fulfill in a contemporary adaptation of the play? In Almereyda's film, since it is set in present-day New York, we are not aware of Claudius's lack of ceremony, because our society is one that has largely reduced and removed ceremony – a process that started with the Reformation. Accordingly, Almereyda cuts both Claudius's and Laertes's references to Polonius's burial. Instead, we are shown – revolving in a coin-operated washing machine – the bloody sheet in which Hamlet shrouded the counsellor. Almereyda has here substituted for allusions to Elizabethan ritual a cliché of crime film: Hamlet is trying to erase the evidence of his murder.

The absence of references to Claudius's neglect of ceremony makes his characterization as a villain more challenging and entirely dependent on our belief in the ghost – problematic in a secular, corporate setting. We only have the ghost's word for it, and Claudius's own behaviour at Hamlet's film, to confirm that Claudius is a fratricide, and therefore unworthy to be king (or CEO in this case).

In Shakespeare's script, Ophelia in her deranged way attempts to make up for the lack of ritual surrounding her father's burial. In her first mad appearance, she chants a song that she asks her hearers twice to "mark." The song fulfills the function of the psalms sung in a funeral procession:

> He is dead and gone, lady,
> He is dead and gone.
> At his head a grass-green turf,
> At his heels a stone ...
> White his shroud as the mountain snow –
> Larded with sweet flowers,
> Which bewept to the grave did – not – go
> With true-love showers (4.5.29–39).

Like a true mourner, Ophelia also cries over the deceased: "I cannot choose but weep to think they should lay him i'th'cold ground. My brother shall know of it" (4.5.67–8). At her next entrance, she continues the death rites, once again referring to details of the burial, real or imagined: "They bore him barefaced on the bier, / ... And on his grave rained many a tear" (4.5.165–7). She then distributes flowers, including the rosemary traditionally passed out to the mourners to strew the corpse with during the interment. The people who witness her song are those who would have attended the funeral, had there been a proper one. Ophelia ends her own rites much as the Roman Catholic priest would have completed the funeral, with a prayer for the deceased (Reformers denounced prayer for the dead; see Livingstone, 144) and for all present: "God a mercy on his soul. And of all Christian souls, I pray God. God b' wi' ye" (197–8). Her funeral obsequies finished, she exits. Truly, there is method to her madness. All of this is a tremendous reproach to Claudius. This insane young girl still knows what is due her father; she is overwhelmed with outrage at the compromise of her family honour, while the sane king does nothing.

Almereyda's Ophelia sings the same lament, but in his film the motivation seems forced. Why, unless she was unusually traditional, would a twenty-first-century New York teen be disturbed by the lack of ceremony attending her father's burial? Is it another sign of the director's unconscious nostalgia for a period when people made time to mourn? Almereyda has established nothing to suggest that this Ophelia was brought up in any faith or tradition. Her father's apartment is modern and streamlined, with little in it to suggest his personality except for the quantity of books. Once her brother arrives, Ophelia distributes Polaroid photos of flowers and plants to her audience, including rosemary, but her final prayer is cut. The choice of Polaroid photos fits with Ophelia's characterization in the film, as she is shown to be a keen photographer with her own darkroom. This pursuit links her to Hamlet, who experiments with a camcorder in the same obsessive way that she takes photos. It also fits into Almereyda's theme that the world of the play is one in which media saturation has left the characters alienated. All their experiences are indirect, mediated. Shakespeare's Ophelia gave real flowers; the twenty-first-century Ophelia hands out photos of them. The photos also link Ophelia's dirges to twenty-first-century death rituals. Almereyda sets this scene at the Guggenheim Museum. Gertrude and Claudius are hosting some kind of function, but both are dressed in black and the scene suggests a secular memorial for the dead, which often takes place in museums and art galleries – today's hushed temples of worship – and features photographs of the deceased, or in some cases, by the deceased (in a posthumous retrospective) displayed to those present. The next death ritual in the play is, of course, Ophelia's own. This one is complicated because she is seen as having committed suicide, a fact Gertrude seems at pains to conceal, at least initially, from Ophelia's brother (see Scolnicov, "Gertrude's Willow Speech"). The suicidal nature of the death means that even a king dedicated to proper ceremony might have felt obliged to curtail the rites.

It is worth briefly summarizing the practices surrounding the burial of suicides in Shakespeare's time before examining the scene in both play and film. As Michael MacDonald in "Ophelia's Maimed Rites" explains, "Canon law took little notice of the burial of suicides. After the canons of 967, the English church ignored the matter until 1661, when a rubric forbidding ministers to read the burial service over those who 'have laid violent hands upon themselves' was belatedly inserted in the Book of Common Prayer" (314). The burial of suicides was therefore guided by custom, MacDonald says. The custom at the time was to bury a suicide at a crossroads or highway at night with a stake through the heart to save the community from spiritual pollution and even a haunting (ibid.). Of course, to be considered a self-murderer, and therefore diabolical, the deceased had to be judged *compos mentis* and the act itself determined premeditated. Records reveal, however, that most local juries erred on the cautious side, and only raving lunatics were spared the label of *"felo de se"* – killer of self (MacDonald, 310) – and permitted some Christian rites. Shakespeare's second gravedigger is accurately reflecting the current status quo when he observes, "If this had not been a gentlewoman, she should have been buried out a Christian burial" (4.7.23–5). What is surprising is that Claudius did not go further in exerting his royal influence to procure more ceremony for Ophelia. One would think he and Gertrude would be at pains to show their sorrow for the tragedy that has befallen the Polonius family through their nephew/son's agency, especially as Laertes is so ready to take revenge and as Claudius regrets Polonius's botched burial. Indeed, during Shakespeare's time, monarchs and dukes had the power often to persuade the priest to treat a suicide as an ordinary death. So why does Claudius not exert his royal prerogative? (MacDonald, 312). Perhaps it is because Shakespeare needs the distorted rites to make two important points. First, ceremony has disintegrated under Claudius's corrupt reign, and second, Elizabeth and James I were not so different in this regard, both depriving their populace of the comforting rites they had enjoyed under previous monarchs.

Additionally, Shakespeare seems to have been interested in airing the current debate on the burial of suicides. Certainly he presents many facets of the question. The priest and gravediggers hold the most common view of the time, that suicide of any kind was diabolical and therefore unworthy of Christian burial rites. Laertes, Hamlet, and Horatio ("I am more an antique Roman," 5.2.294), however, seem to represent the emergence of more liberal views, influenced, no doubt, by classical literature, in which suicide is often portrayed as an honourable exit. Ophelia's suicide reminds the audience of Hamlet's own temptation to escape, with which he wrestles in all his soliloquies.

Ophelia's burial is the only one shown on stage in this play so preoccupied with last rites. Hamlet understands at once that the burial must be for someone of noble birth who has taken her own life: "This doth betoken / The corpse they follow did with desp'rate hand / Fordo it own life. 'Twas of some estate" (5.1.214–16). This recognition signals the chasm between our culture and Shakespeare's. Medieval and Renaissance princes would have been taught which protocol accompanied which corpse and likely would have attended several state funerals by the age of thirty-three. A man of the same years today might never have been to a funeral and could have only a vague idea of the order of ceremony, culled from films and books.

The rites the priest describes as having been accorded Ophelia, and even the ones she has not been permitted, seem to be of Catholic rather than Reformed origin:

> Her obsequies have been as far enlarged
> As we have warranties. Her death was doubtful,
> And but that great command o'ersways the order
> She should in ground unsanctified have lodged
> Till the last trumpet. For charitable prayers,
> Shards, flints, and pebbles should be thrown on her,
> Yet here she is allowed her virgin rites,
> Her maiden strewments, and the bringing home
> Of bell and burial ...
> We should profane the service of the dead
> To sing sage requiem and such rest to her
> As to peace-parted souls. (5.1.220–33)

The character speaking is referred to as a "priest" (Reformers rejected the term as being too closely associated with the idea of performing a mass; see Livingstone, 414). His designation, and his allusions to "charitable prayers," "bell," and "requiem," seem to suggest he is performing a curtailed Roman Catholic rite. Furthermore, he speaks of Ophelia in the present tense, as the Catholic ceremony does, and does not refer to her merely as "the body." Like Juliet, Ophelia is to have virginal flowers strewn upon her. A bell will be tolled to remind others not at the service to pray for her soul. The stage directions in the second quarto and the First Folio specify a coffin, but the first quarto mentions only "the corse." This is interesting, because the difference would have been significant to the audience: a lady of Ophelia's standing would have normally been given a coffin. But Roland Mushat Frye suggests in *The Renaissance Hamlet* that the action in the scene of Laertes trying to take her in his arms indicates that there is no coffin, and that this omission is what marks her rites as "maimed." He also notes that it would have been traditional in a lower-class burial for the closest relatives to lay the corpse in the ground, so Laertes's action of leaping into the grave would not seem so outrageous a breach of etiquette to Shakespeare's audience as to our own. Also, Frye contends that Laertes's embrace of the actual body would have been dramatic and intimate; obviously something would be lost if he were merely grappling to open the coffin, as he does in Almereyda's film (245).

Laertes tries to improve what he views as inadequate rites for his sister, just as, in a sense, Hamlet and Ophelia did for their fathers. He asks the priest "What ceremony else?" (5.1.219) as many relatives of suicides must have done in Shakespeare's day. When the priest refuses to embellish the rites, Laertes takes matters into his own hands. He provides a kind of eulogy – a Protestant practice – speaking of Ophelia's unpolluted flesh, but then also envisions her transformed into a "minist'ring angel," which is not orthodox Christian belief. In no Christian doctrine during Shakespeare's time were human beings thought to metamorphose into angels. The two were considered separate species. The same concept is maintained today in the Catholic doctrine.

Almereyda must be the only director in the history of *Hamlet* who does not allow his leading actor to embody the iconic image of the prince holding a skull (although we see a clip of Gielgud in that pose on Hamlet's television). He cuts the gravedigger scene entirely because "in the editing room it became clear that I'd failed to get it right. The tone and timing were off, and the whole episode seemed to sidetrack Hamlet's response to Ophelia's death. The movie worked better with the prized scene cut out" (*Screenplay*, 106). It is almost a cliché of adaptation to assert that what adaptors leave out is as revealing as what they leave in, but nonetheless it is true. Almereyda's choice to excise the gravedigger scene reflects our contemporary attitude to death – we think of it only as it affects us emotionally and individually. In other words, the focus should be on Hamlet's grief for Ophelia. But the Elizabethans and Jacobeans thought that contemplation of death in general terms, as manifested by Hamlet and Horatio's discussion with the gravedigger, was beneficial to the soul. Shakespeare's audience would have thought that Hamlet was making himself wiser and more stoical by mulling over death, whereas now his deliberations might be seen as unhealthily morbid (Frye, 207). Shakespeare was likely far more interested in what Hamlet thought about death, and the way in which he could air the philosophical musings of his time in this scene, than in the degree to which Hamlet was sad that his girlfriend had died.

One might argue that contemporary western society is almost uniquely uninterested in death. Certainly ancient Egyptians, sixteenth-century Europeans, and Victorian British could be said to have had a cult of death. What is at the root of our present-day avoidance of the subject? Fear? Are we more afraid of death than our forebears because so many now do not believe in an afterlife? Or is it because we have more successfully postponed death than previous eras, so that it has become mainly the provenance of the old, an embarrassing failure in our fit and prosperous lifestyle? The old in our society are shunted away into seniors homes so that they cannot remind us of our mortality.

Almereyda includes a visual allusion to one of the few Christian rituals that still thrives in our secular society and also reminds us of death and the afterlife: Halloween. Our Halloween corresponds closely in the calendar year and in its significance with the Dia de Muertos drawn on by Luhrmann in his film. When Almereyda's Horatio and Hamlet arrive on a motorcycle at the cemetery (shot on Halloween Day), they see four costumed children running through the gravestones – two witches, a bear, and a masked, cloaked boy in black. Earlier in the film, costumed children were seen in the lobby of Hotel Elsinore. These visual reminders of death replace the verbal ones in the original script – namely the long discussion on the subject with the gravedigger. Asked during an interview why he set both *Hamlet* and *Cymbeline* around Halloween, Almereyda responded, "It's a kind of pagan ritual that persists to this day, and it also allows a way of thinking about the presence of death and the proximity of death to daily life ... We tend to both acknowledge death and deflect it, and Halloween is part of that" (Emily Rome).

Almereyda's gravedigger is seen digging and singing. A small group of mourners clad in black appear (fig. 6): Claudius, Gertrude, Laertes, a young woman (Ophelia's friend?), some bodyguards. With them is the priest, who is given a single sentence: "And but that great command o'ersways the order / She should in ground unsanctified have lodged / Till the last trumpet" (*Screenplay*, 109). These lines again seem anachronistic in the setting. Current practice in the Catholic Church makes no distinction between the funeral rites accorded suicides and

Figure 6 Gertrude (Diane Venora) and the court attend Ophelia's funeral in Almereyda's *Hamlet*, 2000.

those given to other deceased. The pluralism of Protestant sects means that there is no set liturgy or form of ritual for the dead, but again, suicides are treated in the same way as other deaths.

In contrast to the lavish bier that Luhrmann's Juliet is given, Almereyda's Ophelia has little but a bare mechanical platform on which her coffin rests, and on which Gertrude tosses a couple of pink flowers. Behind the mourners stand two tacky, multicoloured wreaths, garish against the autumnal landscape. Almereyda allows Laertes most of his lines in this scene. For a twenty-first-century young man, his concern for ceremony is unusual, but then, so is his protectiveness of his sister's chastity, since as Martha Nochimson writes in her *Cineaste* review of the film, "The original impetus for the brother and sister to trim their passions to suit traditional rules is inoperative" (37). Is this another revelation of Almereyda's nostalgia for more traditional times? Or, rather, is it his admiration for Shakespeare's language, which he is loath to cut, even though it jars with his setting?

Luhrmann seems to have recognized better than Almereyda the need to create a setting in which a palpable presence of religious faith makes the religious language and the traditional values natural. In present-day Los Angeles, why would Juliet be so eager to ascertain whether Romeo's "bent in love be honourable?" In Verona Beach society, however, as in the Mexican society that film designer Catherine Martin describes, "Sex before marriage is frowned on" (Litson, 46). Almereyda needed at least to establish that the Hamlet and Polonius families were unusually religious or conservative to justify both the language used by the characters and their concern for traditional virtues like chastity and family honour. Instead, as Nochimson astutely observes, "This Hamlet is a part of an individualist society where nothing supersedes private wishes. Almereyda's audacious attempt to adapt the play to the screen for a modern culture characterized by fragmentation, alienation, and discontinuity is not just a change of scene, but a change of ethos that kicks the supports out from under all the motivations in his source of inspiration" (37).

By cutting most of the gravedigger scene, Almereyda loses much of the audience's sense of Hamlet's development. By the fifth act, he has become much more serene and accepting. Still, despite the fact that this Hamlet's society is not one that regularly prepares itself stoically to accept God's will, even if that will includes immediate death, Almereyda keeps Hamlet's lines, "There's a divinity that shapes our ends, / Rough-hew them how we will" (5.2.10–11) and "We defy augury. There's a special providence in the fall of a sparrow. If it be now, 'tis not to come. If it be not to come, it will be now. If it be not now, yet it will come. The readiness is all. Since no man has aught of what he leaves, what is't to leave betimes?" (5.2.166–70).

In Shakespeare's play, when Hamlet dies, Horatio gives him a brief but memorable epitaph: "Now cracks a noble heart. Good night sweet prince/ And flights of angels sing thee to thy rest" (312–13). Zeffirelli and Branagh maintain these lines – unsurprisingly, as Branagh keeps every line and Zeffirelli sets his play in medieval times where the sentiment is appropriate. In the Almereyda film, despite the fact that Hamlet, bloody from Laertes's gunshot, dies against the metal railing of a Manhattan balcony, the lines still ring out, and as in Zeffirelli's case, end the film proper. The newscast reporting Fortinbras's accession in Almereyda's film acts a kind of addendum. Harry Morris, in his *Last Things in Shakespeare*, sees these lines as an absolution for Hamlet, reminding us that they are a paraphrase of *In paradisum*, "the antiphon sung at Roman Catholic burials while the body is carried in procession to the grave: '*In paradisum deducat te angeli*'" (57). In his note on the same page, Morris adds, "The modern Gradual indicates that a second antiphon was added directly onto the last word of the *In paradisum* and had been a part of the *Rituale Romanum* since at least 1614." J.G. Davies, in *A Dictionary of Liturgy and Worship* (98–9), claims that this second antiphon was traditional by the time the 1614 rite was authorized. The words of the antiphon, if available to Shakespeare, are perhaps closer still to Horatio's words: "Chorus angelorum te suscipiat et ... aeternum habeas requiem" (*Graduale Romanae Ecclesiae, Ordinarium Missae*, Tournai, 109). The procession with the corpse at which these antiphons are sung seems to have suggested to Shakespeare the procession Fortinbras arranges to have Hamlet's body carried "to the stage" (5.2.397–8).

Why, with his corporate setting, does Almereyda choose to keep this religious reference as the last line of the action? Perhaps it is because on that cold, industrial balcony, Shakespeare's original words lend to the carnage a grandeur, and a continuity between the desperate struggles of human beings in the past and in the present that the tragedy's conclusion cannot do without. Shakespeare's tragedies generally end with a glimmer of hope, an emotion often distrusted by twenty-first-century stage directors, who, taking their cue from Jan Kott's *Shakespeare Our Contemporary*, end the play with a dreary sense that Denmark's corruption will only be perpetuated by Fortinbras. Yet, with Horatio's hope that Hamlet is about to enter an eternity of bliss, his short life does not seem entirely in vain.

The last lines of Shakespeare's *Hamlet* are apt for a play obsessed with death rites. Fortinbras's final speech is the arrangement of Hamlet's funeral. This speech, in which Fortinbras takes care of a eulogy ("For he was likely, had he been put on, / To have proved most royally"), the music, ("Soldiers' music"), and pall bearers ("four captains"), as well as the extra drama of the "rites of war" and an ordinance, must have suggested to the original audience that here at least was a leader who understood the importance of ceremony and sacred ritual. This reading contrasts with the typically cynical one of Fortinbras as an incoming despot. Almereyda originally planned to have Fortinbras arrive by helicopter to devastation on the corporate rooftop, but the scene was an unqualified disaster. "Everyone's confidence was jolted by an awareness that this was pretty surely not the best way to end the movie ... The last-ditch solution ... involved transposing Fortinbras's lines to another corporate mouthpiece, a newscaster, making Hamlet's replacement more cruelly anonymous. Robert MacNeil ... was lured out of retirement ... and additional lines were lifted from the Player King's speech: 'Our wills and fates do so contrary run / That our devices still are overthrown; / Our thoughts are ours; their ends none of our own'" (143).

Once again, Almereyda's choice to replace Fortinbras's plans for Hamlet's funeral with these lines shows a desire to have his cake and eat it too. Gone is the attention to ritual so out of whack with our streamlined age, yet the lines replacing it suggest that we are not masters of our own destiny, that some force other than human is in charge of our ends. The Player King seems to be anticipating Hamlet's lines "there's a divinity that shapes our ends, / Rough-hew them how we will" (5.2.10–11). Once again, this point of view seems at odds with the hyper-contemporary, secular corporate setting that Almereyda has been at pains to establish. It is almost inconceivable that a newscaster would start to philosophize about our place in the universe at the end of his report, especially as he is reading his musings from a teleprompter.

Both Luhrmann and Almereyda exhibit a kind of longing for Shakespeare's time in their interpretative choices. Even though they set their adaptations in contemporary settings where the watchful eye of the security camera has all but replaced the omniscient God, both compromise the recognizability of these locales through directorial decisions. Luhrmann creates a hybrid metropolis, in which a version of Catholicism prevails among the majority of the citizens. This hybridization allows him to maintain the religious allusions with which the play is studded, and the elaborate death rites that dominate the last act. Almereyda, while slashing the script of *Hamlet*, yet makes no consistent effort to render the language as secular as the setting. It is Shakespeare's language that he feels nostalgic for, as is evidenced by the final words of his screenplay, a comment on the Player King's lines: "Safe to say they'll survive a deluge of further adaptations, images and ideas, until silence swallows us all" (143). The religious language sits uneasily at times with the gleaming, modern interiors and pared-down death rites, but it nonetheless appears to have been integral to Almereyda's overall sense of the play.

His Hamlet's only real consolation for the grief he feels for his father's murder comes from the television broadcast of the documentary *Peace Is Every Step: Meditation in Action: The Life and Work of Thich Nhat Hanh*. In it Hanh suggests that we should not be alone; we need other people; we need a new verb "interbe" instead of just "be." Almereyda also includes stills of a Botticelli angel (Hamlet's camcorder footage at the beginning of the film) and a Buddha statue postcard that is part of Hamlet's collection. Like Luhrmann's New-Age Catholicism, these visual religious allusions seem random, more like accessories than true faith, but they nonetheless influence and motivate the characters. Both Romeo and Juliet seek out Father Laurence as the only adult in their society they can trust, and this is the same in Verona Beach as it was in Shakespeare's Verona. Richard Burt notes that "Hamlet takes his cue from ... Hanh's comments, and touched by his memories of Ophelia, is next seen composing and recomposing his poem to her late at night in a coffee shop" (*Shakespeare, the Movie, II*, 293).

This yearning for a time when people knew what they believed is a more exaggerated version of what Greenblatt sees as Shakespeare's own state, especially after his own father and his son Hamnet died. Shakespeare lived in a time of religious upheaval; he witnessed the dawning of the secularization of western society that we see today in its maturity. His own ambiguity about the changes taking place seems to be registered in the number of Catholic details he added to his source for *Romeo and Juliet*, and in the extended debate on the issues of death, suicide, and the afterlife in *Hamlet*. Greenblatt sees in the latter a "broader sense of doubt and disorientation in a play where the whole ritual structure that helped men and women deal with loss has been fatally damaged." He sees the play as Shakespeare's way of working out his own complex grief: "Shakespeare would have experienced the consequences of this damage as he stood by the grave of his son or tried to cope with his father's pleas for help in the afterlife ... He was ... part of a very large group, probably the bulk of the population, who found themselves still grappling with longings and fears that the old resources of the Catholic Church had served to address" (*Will in the World*, 320–1).

The conclusions of these two Shakespearean tragedies see a restitution of the ritual structure. In *Romeo and Juliet*, the feud has ended, and the parents intend to ritualize their children's love by erecting golden statues; they have become like patron saints of young love. Fortinbras's arrangement for Hamlet's funeral replaces the "hugger mugger interments" that characterized Claudius's reign with "the rites of war" – not ideal, but something. Both Luhrmann's and Almereyda's films, however, end with television screens, and a newsreader has the final word on the tragedies. This shared element seems to comment on our western society's replacement of religion with technology and the media. All our experiences, even that of death, are at one remove, filtered through a screen; thus, we are riddled with nostalgia for authenticity even in our grief.

PART THREE

Disguise, Genre, and Play

6

Gothic Aspects of Kenneth Branagh's *Hamlet*

This section, "Disguise, Genre, and Play," considers the way Shakespeare and his adaptors engage with material that falls outside the province of social norms. Kenneth Branagh's fascination with gothic subjects in his adaptation of *Hamlet* provides the theme of this chapter. Chapter 7 considers how rivalry for power in both *Titus* and *Prospero's Books* leads to the "othering" of the opponent through employment of the grotesque. Chapter 8 looks at the way cross-dressing complicates our assumptions about male and female attributes in versions of *As You Like It* and *Twelfth Night*, and chapter 9 examines two politicians' attempts to disguise the true state of affairs from their people with the sweet smoke of rhetoric in Branagh's *Henry V* and Ralph Fiennes's *Coriolanus*.

The gothicism of Branagh's *Hamlet*, highlighting elements in Shakespeare's tragedy such as the setting, the ghost, and the themes of death, decay, and madness, labels it as falling not only outside social norms but also outside the norms for adaptation of Shakespeare. Mainstream critics were not kind to his 1996 film. The consensus, especially among British reviewers at the time of its release, was that it was grossly overblown. Yet rather than being viewed as a ham-fisted director, Branagh can be seen as one with naturally gothic sensibilities. I am deploying the term here in both its main denotations, as referring to the medieval art movement and to the revival of that movement in the late eighteenth and early nineteenth centuries, when architecture and novels imitated certain medieval forms.

John Collick in his book *Shakespeare, Cinema and Society* observes that gothic writers used Shakespeare to create "a new form of literature through which they tried to address the overwhelming and, at times, terrifying social change of the era" (22). Collick later adds that these authors "tried to tackle the horrors of industrial society" using Shakespeare as one of their mechanisms, viewing his characters as "motivated by extremes of emotion and threatened by the supernatural agents of dynastic tyranny" (193). Thus, Collick sees the gothic authors' tendency to look back to an Elizabethan writer for inspiration as a way of coping with the rapid change in their society – a nostalgic tendency that they share with current film directors. In times of extreme change, artists return to traditional models for reassurance. Arguably, no society has faced change as radical and speedy as our own; the mechanization of the Industrial Revolution had nothing on the digitization of our own era, with people communicating far more through personal devices and avatars than face to face. Linda Bayer-Berenbaum in her seminal work *The Gothic Imagination* (1982) asserts that technology, and gene and clone work, bring us "closer than ever before to a fulfillment of the Gothic fear of monstrous devastation, of the violation of nature, or of an altered, maimed existence" (16). Branagh's film turns to the inherent gothic elements in *Hamlet* to express our cultural moment, in which environmental Armageddon is an ever-present threat.

At first glance, Branagh's *Hamlet* might seem the least gothic of the screen versions of the play. Its setting is atypical both for *Hamlet* films and for gothic novels. Branagh's Elsinore is the heavily baroque Blenheim Palace, which, with its Corinthian porticos and pediments (Yarwood, 253), owes more to classical tradition than to gothic. The interior of the palace is brightly lit, quite unlike the sepulchral, medieval-looking spaces chosen by Laurence Olivier (1948), Franco Zeffirelli (1990), and Grigori Kozintsev (1964) in their filmed adaptations of the play, or by Horace Walpole, Ann Radcliffe, and others in their novels.

Liam Lacey, film critic for Toronto's *Globe and Mail*, explicitly separates Branagh's interpretation from the gothic: "Perhaps it's a reflection of Branagh's determined normalcy that he has resisted the Gothic, morbid atmosphere often associated with *Hamlet*. His setting – with England's stately Blenheim Palace filling in for Elsinore – is almost glaringly bright. The 19th century setting, suggestive of the last days of

Russia's Romanov dynasty, emphasizes the intrigues and public politics of the royals. The atmosphere in the opening scene [*sic*], set in the opulent court, is festive" (C1). Strangely, it is exactly this normalcy, this glaring brightness, that makes Branagh's Elsinore the perfect backdrop for murder, ghostly visitations, and madness. The macabre is only magnified by being contrasted to the quotidian. Branagh is simply giving his audience a more modern version of gothic horror than did Olivier, Zeffirelli, and Kozintsev. As Bayer-Berenbaum observes, "In the modern horror stories where ancient castles have disappeared, the gothic writer clothes his tale in the fabric of the familiar" (33). Branagh makes huge efforts to render the Danish royal family familiar to us. We are treated to flashbacks in which the family curl together (*Screenplay*, 36) and Hamlet as a young boy plays with Yorick (149).

As Donald Beecher points out, "Nostalgia is a form of flight from the distastefulness or danger of the present, and perhaps in proportional ways: that the more the current circumstances displease, the more focused and intense the fantasies will become" (7). Branagh's flashbacks, his own interpolations onto Shakespeare's text, emphasize Hamlet's misery in the present and his longing for the past – a past when his family was intact and he was blissfully unaware of his mother's sensuality and disloyalty. His present, however, tinctures his memories with a sinister aspect that fits the gothic nature of the film. When he remembers curling with his family in the hall, the adult Hamlet imposes a cynical interpretation of his uncle's exchanges with his mother, the camera lingering on their laughing faces, on Claudius's embrace. The brightness of the corridor thus exposes to Hamlet that his yearning is for a happy family that perhaps is only the fantasy of his younger self. Owen Gleiberman notes in his perceptive *Entertainment Weekly* review:

> It's like an Elizabethan version of *The Shining*. Shot on huge, bold, dazzlingly well-lit sets (the royal court is a hall of mirrors dominated by a hypnotic chessboard floor), it too is about a man led to dementia – and murder – by a ghost preying on his demons. What links the film memorably to Stanley Kubrick's is the way that Hamlet's battle with his incipient savagery takes place not in the usual murky catacombs but right out in the open, in the "objective" glare of what could almost be a surgeon's operating theater. The illumination is visual, and metaphysical, too: Even when he's

sputtering with rage, this Hamlet remains tortuously rational, a man pinned down under the white-hot klieg lights of his own consciousness. (35)

The Shining also zeroes in on the relationship between an evil father-figure, a weak mother, and their only son. The Caligari floor and the fun-house-like hall of mirrors create, as Branagh hoped, "an atmosphere of incipient paranoia" (Andrews, 62), a modern version of the traditional shadows and fog. Branagh is unstinting with these as well, particularly in Hamlet's first encounter with his father's ghost.

As a director, Branagh has always been drawn to gothic subject matter. According to his biography, *Beginning*, he grew up watching a fair amount of television, especially films, which likely included some of the classic horror pictures. He chose to direct and star in *Mary Shelley's Frankenstein* (1994). He directed and starred in *Dead Again* (1991), a film about "the avenging past ... the past that is dead or thought to be" (Kendrick, 75), a typical gothic plot concept. Even his comedies have gothic aspects: for example, the grotesque masks at the ball, and the extended mourning scene in *Much Ado about Nothing* (1993). Moreover, his initial attraction to *Hamlet* was to its gothic features. Seeing it on television for the first time at eleven years of age, he was chiefly struck by the ghost of Hamlet's father (*Screenplay*, xi). At fifteen, he was thrilled by its suspense, by Ophelia's madness, and by the duel, all of which would be at home in a gothic novel (xi). By his thirties, the play's theme of death was "a subject of constant fascination and curiosity. The whole notion of mortality is what we are all obsessed with from the moment we arrive here. My intense enthusiasm for the play springs out of what light it sheds on all that" (Mark White, 137).

In his introduction to his screenplay, Branagh describes a nostalgia for his initial reactions to which he is "still connected" and which he would like "to pass on" to his audiences (xv). One critic has noted perceptively that many of Branagh's directorial choices in *Hamlet* transform Shakespeare's play into a dramatized romantic novel (Willson, 7). Others complain that he is "in your face" (Andrews, 66), "over the top and lacking in 'nuance'" (Coe, 41), but these are exactly the qualities that make him the ideal director for gothic subjects: the gothic is the art-form of the extreme. Gothic writers like Walpole and Radcliffe are interested in violent emotions brought about by extraordinary situations. One opinion shared by most film directors of Shakespeare is that the performance of his scripts requires heightened intensity of emotion. As Almereyda said of *Cymbeline*, "The characters get unhinged and go in dark directions and get submerged in jealousy and bitter crazy feelings. I wanted to respect the urgency of those emotions and get actors who could handle them" (Emily Rome). Bayer-Berenbaum sees the desire to magnify and intensify consciousness as a chief characteristic of gothicism (14–15). Can one think of a dramatic character more intensely conscious than Hamlet? She also notes the gothic writers' tendency to present an "orgy of emotion" (20).

Hamlet contains a surprising number of traditional gothic ingredients, which is why it had such a strong influence on the gothic writers, who seem to quote the play, directly and indirectly, more than any other (Varma, 125, 30; Collick, 22, 138; Miles, 107). In fact, the cross-fertilization between Shakespeare and the gothic is remarkable. Shakespeare drew on indigenous medieval (gothic) art forms, the morality and mystery plays. Then, the early gothic writers looked back to Shakespeare to provide them with an artistic model that was freer, more natural and various than the rigid Classical paradigms imposed on them. In turn, it is the eighteenth-century and particularly the nineteenth-century views of Shakespeare's genius that have come down to us and to directors like Branagh (Bate, ch. 6).

Indeed, gothic writers have influenced Shakespeare almost as much as he influenced them – that is to say, the modern image of Shakespeare is gothicized. This is particularly evident in theatrical and cinematic history. The melodramas that dominated the stage prior to and concurrent with the invention of film were influenced by Shakespeare: "Half-hour versions of *Macbeth* and *Hamlet* were shown in which most of the text was excised, leaving the ghosts, battles and murders" (Collick, 15). The melodramas "evolved in tandem with the pseudo-Jacobean narratives of the Gothic novels" (15), which themselves were full of pseudo-Shakespearean rhetoric (Kendrick, 76, 115). Silent films of *Hamlet* were gothic in style too, focusing on duels and graveyards – the extreme actions and emotions of the plays (Manvell, 17–18). Olivier, with his Freudian chiaroscuro castle, was not immune from gothic influences. Kozintsev's sensibilities too in his *Hamlet* closely parallel those of eighteenth-century British gothic writers, as John Collick argues persuasively (137–8). The definitive characteristics of gothicism reveal a surprising number of parallels with Shakespeare's *Hamlet*. The settings, themes, and even the characterization found in many gothic novels seem to be offspring of Shakespeare's famous revenge tragedy. Branagh has seized on these elements and heightened them, resulting in a particularly gothic reading of the play, which is just as legitimate as Olivier's Freudian or Kozintsev's sociopolitical interpretations.

Shakespeare's brilliant opening scene of *Hamlet* establishes a tense atmosphere with the watchmen's clipped exchange about the cold weather (1.1). In this, Shakespeare echoes the Wakefield master, a medieval (gothic) playwright, who opens *The Second Shepherd's Pageant* with complaints about unusually severe conditions. In both cases, the uncommon weather is an augury of something extraordinary about to happen. Gothic novelists use natural conditions in a similar way. Bayer-Berenbaum observes that they prefer an unsettled sky, a howling wind, and preferably a storm to prevent the victim from escaping the castle or convent (23). Exceptional contrasts and conditions, both geographic and climatic, "magnify reality; between the greatest extremes lies the greatest breadth" (Bayer-Berenbaum, 22–3). Radcliffe's *The Mysteries of Udolpho* includes a Hamlet-like encounter between an eerie vision and some frightened palace watchmen, one of whom claims that it "was so still, you might have heard a mouse stir" (273), an echo of Francisco's "Not a mouse stirring" (1.1.11).

Branagh intensifies the gothicism by adding to the bitter cold of the opening scene "a mystical and disturbing night sky ... the wind picking up speed" (*Screenplay*, 4). In his script, the wind becomes closely associated with the apparition: "A fierce wind still blasts them each time they turn to look at ... the great mass" (5). The pathetic fallacy continues, with many of the scenes taking place in "misty," therefore mysterious, conditions (119, 120, 154). Of course, the natural Oxfordshire climate may have generated some of the mist, but not all the snow. John Mullan in the *Times Literary Supplement* is sarcastic about the lavish quantities of artificial snow, pointing out the incongruity with Ophelia's floral suicide (19). Once again, Branagh can be defended by an appeal to gothicism – he is presenting sharp contrasts in the climate. His use of snow certainly suggests a hostile external world, especially when it joins forces with Norway's "dark, wild ... ferocious" (i.e., Byronic) Prince Fortinbras, and is so "vicious" that it "engulfs the battered Palace" (*Screenplay*, 8, 133). Branagh thus insists on the Northern European setting – comparisons to Russia and Sweden appear in several articles (Crowl, "Interview," 7; Lacey, C1; Wilson,

7) – and links the film to the Bergmanesque Adrian Noble production I attended in which Branagh starred a few years before.

All of Fortinbras's part is maintained in this four-hour screen *Hamlet*. Branagh was here influenced by Noble, who also used an uncut text for the 1992 RSC production. Branagh enlarges the impression made by the Norwegian prince by cutting from Elsinore to Fortinbras at various points in the film. Clearly Branagh is setting up Fortinbras as a rival to Hamlet, leading the audience to compare the two princes much more than in the usual stage or screen productions, where Fortinbras's role is radically reduced or cut altogether. (In both Olivier's and Zeffirelli's films of *Hamlet*, Fortinbras is excised; in Almereyda's, he is a photograph shown on the final newscast.) This comparison is reinforced by Branagh's inclusion of Hamlet's "How all occasions do inform against me" soliloquy, also often cut in performance (Zeffirelli and Olivier both cut it), in which Hamlet unfavourably contrasts himself to Fortinbras.

What both links and separates the two princes is nostalgia. Fortinbras, the man of action, is obsessed with avenging a past event, his father's murder and defeat, but he seems unconcerned by ethical considerations regarding the act of revenge. Hamlet, who has been assigned the same task – avenging a father's murder – reflects on the past and on the dead and considers his action with such thoroughness that he is delayed from executing it. He philosophizes about memory, seeing in his mother's and the court's forgetfulness a nihilistic lack of meaning in human existence. If even a great king can be so quickly forgotten, what is a mere man's life worth? The task that Hamlet has set himself is to remember his father and so to learn from the past. For instance, by remembering that his own father told him he died unshriven, he does not kill Claudius at prayer. In fact, he only kills Claudius after a series of proofs that his uncle is murderous: the evidence of the ghost, his uncle's collapse at the Mousetrap, his command that England execute Hamlet, and finally, his inadvertent murder of Gertrude and Laertes. The anti-nostalgics might claim Hamlet waited too long to wreak revenge, that he could have saved the lives of Polonius, Ophelia, Gertrude, and Laertes had he killed his uncle earlier. But if the alternative is Fortinbras, who cheerfully leads two thousand souls to their death "even for an eggshell," then Hamlet's thoughtful delay begins to seem reasonable, a process of gathering evidence. In Branagh's film, the thinker who delays is more virtuous than the active man who does harm, as is made clear with the final image of soldiers knocking Hamlet Senior's statue to the ground, leaving it a pile of rubble. The close-up of the pieces recalls the prevalence of architectural ruins as a feature of the gothic (Beyer-Berenbaum, 27). Moreover, Fortinbras is erasing history in a way that seems both sinister and vengeful. In his grey uniform, marching across vast expanses of snow, he evokes a Soviet general, or even the KGB, rewriting history to maintain absolute control over citizens' image of their nation.

The winter setting contributes not only to a Soviet-style Fortinbras but also to the general gothic-style pathetic fallacy, explicitly articulated in the script. After Polonius's murder and Hamlet's exile, a "windswept Elsinore looks bleak in the winter light. A huge shadow is cast across its face" (*Screenplay*, 123). Yet the weather at Elsinore is not unrelievedly bad. Gothic contrast is provided when Hamlet "looks out to a glorious blue sky" before exclaiming, "This most excellent canopy the air, look you, this brave o'erhanging firmament" (62).

The epic setting of the film is highlighted by the use of 70mm film stock. This larger-than-life quality is both apt for the gothic nature of the project (a quest for the "sublime") and suggestive of Branagh's homage to David Lean and the sense of spectacle in *Doctor Zhivago* and *Lawrence of Arabia*. Branagh sought out Lean's cinematographer Alex Thomson to achieve the desired scope (Mark White, 200). It is no coincidence, either, that Julie Christie, Lean's Lara, was recruited to play Gertrude.

Shakespeare's firmament hangs over the castle of Elsinore; and the castle is a typical locale in gothic novels (Bayer-Berenbaum, 21). Elsinore is a castle of "indirections." Polonius and Claudius conceal themselves on several occasions to spy on Hamlet (3.1, 3.4). Jan Kott in *Shakespeare Our Contemporary* is eloquent about the air of espionage and paranoia that surrounds the castle (48-9). Perhaps it was this atmosphere that led Walpole, who claimed Shakespeare "was the model I copied" (Walpole, ii), to fill Otranto with the secret passageways and hidden doorways (25, 28) that have become some of the most recognizable features of gothicism. Branagh gets carried away with trapdoors in his Elsinore. He uses secret apertures no less than sixteen times (*Screenplay*, 23, 44, 46, 53, 76, 81, 85, 99, 103, 116, 124, 125, 133, 169). He even makes wry allusions to his penchant for this gothic cliché in little asides in the exposition: "OPHELIA enters through *yet another* hidden door" (46, my italics) and "entering from, *yes, another* hidden door" (85, my italics). The convent and the chapel, invariably Roman Catholic, are other favourite settings for gothic novelists (Bayer-Berenbaum, 23). Walter Kendrick writes in *The Thrill of Fear*, "Gothicism and Catholicism made a natural pair, because most of the surviving gothic structures in England had been built in the service of pre-Anglican Christianity, and because decor and religion alike exuded an air of slightly spooky mystery" (41).

Walpole sets part of the climax of *The Castle of Otranto* in the church where Alphonso's tomb lies (109). Shakespeare, working in a theatre that favoured flexibility over elaborate sets, is not specific about where Polonius bids adieu to Laertes, or where Claudius attempts a prayer. Branagh chooses to film both these scenes in a chapel, responding to the focus on morals in both and also referring to the underlying finality. This is the last time Polonius will see his son, the last time Claudius will consider repentance. Chapels are associated too with weddings and funerals – Ophelia's wedding, which never happens, and the funeral of Claudius's victim, old Hamlet.

In the farewell scene, Branagh has "organ music playing in the background" (*Screenplay*, 26), typical of modern horror movies. What Dracula film would be complete without the dismal strains of Bach's Toccata and Fugue in D Minor? Branagh further darkens the tone of the scene after Laertes's departure when Polonius interrogates Ophelia in the confessional. Branagh describes Polonius as "menacing" and speaking with "quiet threat"; Ophelia as "frightened," "alarmed," and "utterly panicked" (27–8). Ophelia here has reason to fear her father's questions, as memories of her lovemaking with the prince flash through her head. This alteration to Shakespeare's original, in which we are evidently meant to think Ophelia honest when she claims that Hamlet has wooed her in "honourable fashion," is an example of Branagh's efforts to make the play more contemporary. (For more detail on this, see chapter 2's section on chronology.) The whole timbre of the scene, sexual flashbacks excepted, is reminiscent of many gothic episodes in which a beautiful young woman attempts to escape the threat presented by an older man, possibly her guardian, in a church or a chapel. Isabella in *The Castle of Otranto*, for example, seeks haven from her guardian, Manfred, in the Church of St Nicholas after he has tried to coerce her to become his wife and possibly attempted to rape her (Walpole, 25). While Polonius is not a sexual threat to his daughter, sex is the issue that creates the tension in the scene. Bayer-Berenbaum includes in her list of typical cast members of the gothic novel "the interfering, brutal fathers" and the "innocent virgins" (23), a fairly accurate summary of Polonius and Ophelia in Shakespeare's script. In Branagh's, however, Polonius also shows himself to be tender (*Screenplay*, 82), and Ophelia is no virgin. Kermode writes, "It's worth remembering that in some sources she [Ophelia] was his [Hamlet's] mistress" (116).

The sexual deviancy (particularly incest) that is an underlying part of gothic novels does rear its ugly head in many interpretations of *Hamlet*. Claudius's marriage to his sister-in-law is referred to as "incestuous"; Hamlet's obsession with his mother's sex life is famously perceived as unhealthy. Some productions, including Almereyda's film, even suggest that Laertes's feelings for his sister are not entirely brotherly. While I agree with Lisa S. Starks and Courtney Lehmann's conviction that Branagh's film is ostentatiously non-Oedipal, especially in contrast to Zeffirelli's, my undergraduates persist in seeing an undercurrent of sexual frisson between Branagh's Hamlet and Julie Christie's Gertrude in the closet scene. This is suggested to them by the close-ups on their eyes and lips, by Hamlet's rough ripping open of her bodice at the beginning of the closet scene, provoking her to call for help, and by his tossing her onto her bed more than once. The fact that my students saw an Oedipal reading in an interpretation that has generally been viewed as assiduously "hetereonormative" shows the prevalence of the play's association with the Oedipus complex. The Oedipal interpretation contributes to Hamlet's portrayal as a man lost in reminiscence. Sprengler observes that "'fixation' and 'regression' share with nostalgia the attempt to return to a place of origin and the inability of recollection alone to facilitate this return. In the Oedipal trajectory, the male child's longing for unity with its mother and to return to its first home (the womb) is a desire for an ideal and irretrievable past stage of childhood ... a key feature of the nostalgic experience [is] a desire to return to the time that immediately preceded significant change. Nostalgia has been theorized as a sentiment that attaches itself to periods on the verge of transformation and to the moments marked by the availability of choice" (16).

With his flashbacks of the young Hamlet laughing with Yorick and curling with his parents, Branagh has added to the sense created in Shakespeare's script that Hamlet wishes he could turn back the clock to the days when his father was alive and the family happy. The director expresses in his autobiography *Beginning* the "sense of belonging nowhere" (81), which scholars of nostalgia would recognize as a common feature of millennial angst in recent western culture. Of course, obsessive reminiscence and sexual deviancy have traditionally been included as symptoms of mental disorder. Andreea Ritivoi notes nostalgia was described by a physician named R.A. Vogel in 1764 "as a kind of paranoia characterized by melancholy and mental aberrations. Four years later, French doctors included the disease among the *morositates*, in the class *vesaniae*. These early classifications indicate that nostalgia was largely deemed a nervous disorder" (21). Hamlet's melancholy is thus perfectly suited for a gothic treatment of the play.

The gothic genre was fascinated by disease and aberration, and this aspect of Shakespeare's tragedy contributed to the particular popularity of *Hamlet* with gothic writers. Bayer-Berenbaum writes, "The Gothic hero ... has refined or augmented one aspect of himself to the point of inner tyranny. The intensity of the psychotic and the power of his psychosis to devour all other parts of the self fascinates the Gothic mind" (39-40). This description suits both Hamlet, who, by his own admission has cleared his mind of all else but his ghost-set task of vengeance (1.5.95-104), and Ophelia, who has given herself over entirely to grief (4.5.71-2). Their circumstances are similar – both mourn murdered fathers, and long for the simpler days of their youth, cut short by the tragedies that have befallen them.

Before he has even seen the ghost, Hamlet, with rose-tinted spectacles, remembers his parents' marriage as perfect. Hamlet Senior was

> ... so loving to my mother
> That he might not beteem the winds of heaven
> Visit her face too roughly! Heaven and earth,
> Must I remember? Why, she would hang on him
> As if increase of appetite had grown
> By what it fed on ... (*Screenplay*, 17)

The ideal of eternal fidelity, a bulwark against the encroachment of time, is something to which Hamlet too subscribes as a lover: "Never doubt I love," he writes to Ophelia. He also must prove his enduring love to his father by righting his wrong, but he does not have an eternity to achieve this quest. His father, like Henry IV with Hal, as Ricardo Quinones (326) has observed, acts as a watchguard of the time for Hamlet, chiding him with tardiness, whetting his almost blunted purpose (3.4.97–101).

Hamlet self-diagnoses this passivity as melancholia – "I have of late ... lost all my mirth" (*Screenplay*, 62) – at least to his classmates, whom admittedly he trusts like adders fanged. Robert Burton, who must have been collecting data for his great opus, *An Anatomy of Melancholy*, while Shakespeare's company was performing *Hamlet*, defines melancholy in his poetical "Author's Abstract" in a way that would also suit the later diagnosis of nostalgia:

> When I go musing all alone
> Thinking of divers things fore-known.
> When I build castles in the air
> Void of sorrow and void of fear,
> Pleasing myself with phantasms sweet,
> Methinks the time runs very fleet.
> All my joys to this are folly
> Naught so sweet as melancholy.

Hamlet's case seems almost a literalization of what Burton describes in metaphor: he is alone at Elsinore thinking on the past, dwelling on his father while everyone else seems to have forgotten him. Hamlet too is visited by "phantasms sweet" – his father appears to him when he misses him most. His mother and uncle seem to accuse him of wallowing in grief, suggesting he takes a kind of pleasure in it (1.2.68–108), as does the subject of Burton's poem.

Ophelia's first set of mad songs (4.5.46–65) harp on the warnings her father and brother gave her earlier in act 1, scene 3:

> Let in the maid, that out a maid
> Never departed more ...
> Young men will do't if they come to't
> By Cock they are to blame.
> Quoth she "Before you tumbled me,
> You promised me to wed."

In Branagh's film, Ophelia's mad songs seem redolent with regret that she did not heed her relatives' advice, as now, unchaste and unmarriageable, she is left without a protector – her father dead, her brother in France, her lover on his way to England. These two characters have seen their immediate worlds rapidly and irrevocably altered, their assumptions about their own futures overturned; nostalgia, a living in the past, is one way they deal with the trauma.

Claudius too tries to return to a more innocent past in an effort to save himself: "Bow, stubborn knees; and hearts with strings of steel, / Be soft as sinews of the new born babe. / All may be well" (3.3.70–2). Branagh uses the same confessional as earlier in the film for this prayer scene. Hamlet hides behind the grille, his dagger's point poking through the filigree, aimed at his uncle's ear (101–2). Roman Catholic imagery seems a surprising choice for Branagh, given his own admission that he hates "organized religion" (Mark White, 80), in addition to the Protestant character of Denmark, and the prince's study at the seat of the Protestant Reformation, Wittenberg. The selection of a Catholic chapel as the venue could be dismissed by lumping Branagh in with all the other Hollywood directors who find Catholic imagery – the colourful stained glass, the gaudy statues and candles, the incense – impossible to resist. It is naturally more dramatic than the austere reformed alternatives with which Branagh, a Protestant native of Belfast (*Beginning*, 2), must have been raised. Yet Shakespeare's play does have scattered Catholic allusions that may have suggested themselves to Branagh's gothic sensibilities (for details, see the previous chapter). As Frank Kermode points out in *Shakespeare's Language*, the ghost regrets that he died without last rites (1.5.77), which he distinguishes, and Kermode translates as "without the Eucharist, without absolution, without the anointing" (108).

Branagh gives us glimpses of the Purgatory to which the ghost claims he is doomed (1.5.10–13) as he leads Hamlet into the forest – the "wild forest" being one of the typical gothic settings that Bayer-Berenbaum includes in her list (23). Shakespeare is not specific about where father and son reunite. Marcellus observes that the Ghost "waves" Hamlet "to a more removèd ground" (1.4.61). Horatio is worried that the ghost will lead his friend "toward the flood ... / Or to the dreadful summit of the cliff / That beetles o'er his base into the sea" (1.4.69–71). There is no mention of a wood. Nevertheless, what these locations have in common is their savagery: Ruskin noted "savageness" as one of the "moral elements of Gothic," here speaking of the medieval art movement (4). Radcliffe, in *The Mysteries of Udolpho*, describes the chateau of St Aubert as surrounded by the Pyrenees, which "sometimes frowned with forests of gloomy pine" (119). Without the mountains, this could be an apt description of Branagh's forest, the backdrop for the most obviously gothic scene in the film. In pseudo-gothic language, Branagh describes Hamlet's pursuit of the ghost "through woods exploding with terror ... Explosions through the trees, cracks in the ground, the very earth itself shaking" (*Screenplay*, 33). Later, the earth "cracks open to reveal an ominous gateway to hell. Agonized voices from beyond pierce the night's dull ear" (34). And finally: "The trees around them are starting to move ... The trees still shaking. The earth smouldering ... The ground moving under their feet, the trees aquiver. Smoke spurting out behind them as they run through the woods" (42).

Branagh's reviewers took particular exception to these gothic excesses. Brian Johnson in *Maclean's* observed, "During Hamlet's midnight encounter with his father's ghost, as cheesy effects show the earth cracking open and erupting with fireballs, it looks as if Branagh is suddenly remaking his *Frankenstein* movie" (101). Gary Crowdus wrote in *Cineaste*, "Branagh also reveals a predilection for showy, sensational effects; notably in the initial ghost scene, which assumes Hammer horror-film dimensions" (17). Terence Rafferty in the *New Yorker* commented, "Branagh's direction rarely passes up an opportunity for a big visual effect: when the ghost of Hamlet's murdered father appears to him, the smoke and flames of Hell erupt from beneath the ground" (80). I would challenge these easy dismissals with Horatio's speech in act 1, scene 1, in which he compares the prodigies in nature that Denmark has been experiencing to those of Caesar's Rome just before the leader's assassination. Horatio claims that "heaven and earth together" have acted as harbingers of doom to his countrymen (127–8). Prodigies in nature were accepted by many Elizabethans, if not by twentieth-century film critics.

Perhaps if Branagh had chosen a traditional medieval or Renaissance setting rather than a late nineteenth-century one for his film, reviewers would have been better prepared to accept gothic effects. Gothic writers copied their Elizabethan and Jacobean masters in using prodigies in nature to create an aura of catastrophe. Bayer-Berenbaum writes, "At the same time that the gothic writer penetrates the world of the twisted mind, he enlarges the outer world to include abnormal, bizarre occurrences, simultaneously plunging inward and outward, into the perceiver and beyond the perception, thereby developing the dimensions of reality in both possible directions" (39). While she does not mention either *Hamlet* or Shakespeare in her book, this passage could be speaking specifically of *Hamlet*. What she describes parallels the Renaissance notions of macrocosm and microcosm. The disturbance in Denmark's rule is reflected in the prodigies noted by Horatio and, more directly, in the appearance of the ghost, which sets off a chain of events resulting in Hamlet's mental disturbance (feigned and real) and Ophelia's madness. Kenneth Rothwell also defends Branagh's special effects (*History*, 256), explaining that they "derive from Hamlet's expletive, 'a worthy pioneer!'" (1.5.163). Robert Jephson in his play *The Count of Narbonne* (1781) provides us with an example of the gothic writer's use of prodigies: "The owl mistakes his season, in broad day / Screaming his hideous omens; spectres glide, / Gibbering and pointing as we pass along" (in Kendrick, 115). The last line and a half are a poor paraphrase of Horatio's "the sheeted dead / Did squeak and gibber in the Roman streets" (1.1.118–19).

The ghost who causes all this trouble is fully described in Shakespeare's dialogue. Armed, "cap-à-pie," he wears "his beaver up," has a black beard streaked with silver, and looks sorrowful and pale (1.2.200–42). Walpole, who in the preface to his second edition of *The Castle of Otranto* spends many words defending Shakespeare, also has a spectre in armour, likewise come to chastise a usurper, Manfred. Collick concludes from the similarities, "There is little doubt that the giant ghost in *The Castle of Otranto* is derived from Walpole's reading of *Hamlet*" (138).

Walpole enlarges his ghost and presents him using synecdoche: a mammoth helmet, arm, or leg at a time. Branagh's ghost resembles Walpole's armoured giant almost more than it does Shakespeare's. The ghost is an animated statue, described as "immense" (*Screenplay*, 1), erected in honour of the recently dead king. The ghost painted on glass in the Russian half-hour *Hamlet* (*Shakespeare: The Animated Tales*) is also immense: he appears to tower two hundred feet over Hamlet (I am indebted to Thomas Pendleton for pointing this out to me). Like Walpole, Branagh gives us only fragments at a time: "We glimpse only part of the sculpture as the camera climbs higher ... the stone countenance of OLD HAMLET" (1). And later: "The last stroke of midnight hits as we settle on the huge hand, which holds a sword hilt, and just as he would seem to cut, a great rasping noise like fingernails on a blackboard sears through the night and we see the statue's hand pull the sword from the scabbard with a savage rip!" (2). Walpole's and Branagh's synecdoches not only build suspense but also create a sense of the grotesque, crucial to the gothic aura. They may have been inspired by Shakespeare's own use of synecdoche for the other king, Claudius, whom Hamlet describes as "a mildewed ear / Blasting his wholesome brother" – an image that cannot but recall the manner of King Hamlet's death (3.4.65–6). A ghost is central to both works because "the supernatural ... represents the ultimate expansion of consciousness" (Bayer-Berenbaum, 32). Both Hamlet and Manfred learn the truth about their dynasty and themselves through the agency of a ghost.

Branagh may not have been directly inspired by Walpole's giant; more likely he was influenced by Kozintsev's film *Hamlet* (1964), where the ghost is shot from low angles to suggest enormous height (Collick, 139). Branagh's technique of maintaining a high point of view for the ghost throughout the first scene (*Screenplay*, 5, 6, 9) creates the same effect. Horatio and the guards "throw back their heads" to take in "the size and height of this ... thing" (5). If it was indeed Kozintsev's ghost that made Branagh inflate his own, Branagh was once again responding to gothicism. Collick makes a strong case for the parallels between Kozintsev's work and that of the British gothic writers, focusing particularly on the similarities between Walpole's and Kozintsev's ghosts and castles (137–8).

Ghosts and castles are by no means the only elements shared by Shakespeare and gothic writers. Three motifs that are central to Shakespeare's *Hamlet* – death, decay, and madness – are favourite tropes in gothic novels. Bayer-Berenbaum writes about the gothic awe of the powerful (27) and desire for "the partial, the drastic, the extraordinary" (39). Death, decay, and madness have power over strength, beauty, and reason; they imply an "absence of limitation" that appealed to the iconoclastic gothic mind (31). The conversation about death and decay in Shakespeare's gravediggers' scene, the images of disease and rotting vegetation, and the preoccupation with insanity, assumed or real, would not be out of place in any gothic work, except that gothic characters might treat these things with more horror or reverence than their Renaissance predecessors (Kendrick, 29). Beyer-Berenbaum notes that "a fascination with diseases and decomposition represents a liberation from the confines of beauty" (28). Shakespeare himself must have felt this sense of liberation, testing the extraordi-

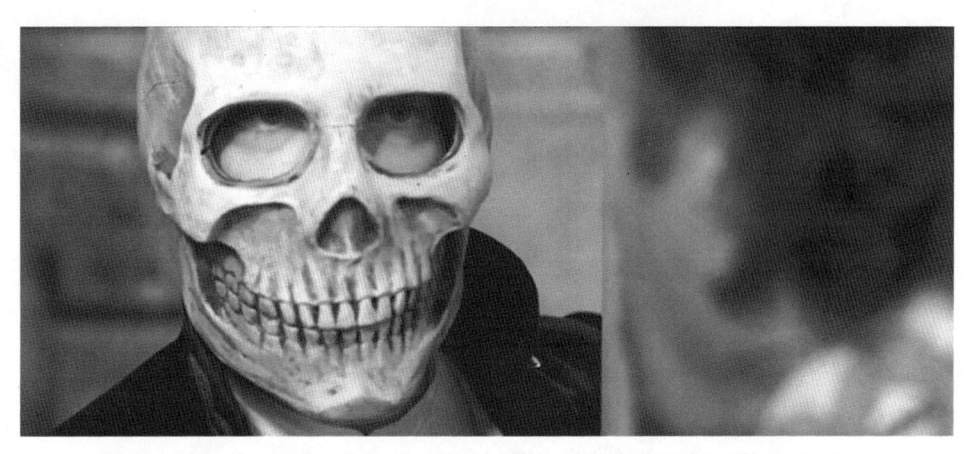

Figure 7 Hamlet (Kenneth Branagh), wearing a skull mask, surprises Polonius (Richard Briers) in Branagh's *Hamlet*, 1996.

nary powers of his art with what is repellent as a change from what is picturesque. He juxtaposes, for instance, Gertrude's pretty aria describing Ophelia's floral end with the gravedigger scene where decomposition is considered at length.

Branagh magnifies these gothic themes in several ways: first, he films the fullest possible text (a combination of the Folio and Quarto texts that would have been strange to Shakespeare's audience) so the spectators finally hear the extended version of Hamlet's disquisition on death over Yorick's skull, entertaining every image of sickness and decay and every manifestation of madness. Second, Branagh's direction intensifies whatever is macabre or grotesque in the play. When Polonius is killed, a crane shot shows us a huge pool of blood spreading across the floor. Ophelia's mad scenes are stripped of their usual prettiness. She throws herself at her father's body and howls like an animal. She is strait-jacketed and confined to a padded cell, brutally hosed down with icy water as "therapy." She plucks at her own raw fingers instead of doling out real flowers. She does a demented dance worthy of *The Changeling* or *The Duchess of Malfi*. After the intermission, we are again shown in flashbacks Polonius's death and Ophelia's "primal yell" of "ugly grief" (*Screenplay*, 119).

Furthermore, Branagh is generous with skulls. The First Gravedigger uncovers a surprising number of bones, and in an earlier scene, Hamlet frightens Polonius with a skull mask (fig. 7) (56). We see in this once again Branagh's spiritual kinship to Walpole. In *The Castle of Otranto*, Frederic is surprised by a figure in a hermit's cowl who turns around to reveal "the fleshless jaws and empty sockets of a skeleton." Frederic's reaction suggests Walpole's nostalgia for Shakespeare's *Hamlet*: Frederic's "Angels of grace protect me!" (107) recalls the prince's "Angels and ministers of grace defend us" (1.3.20). Earlier, Branagh's Hamlet consults an "ancient tome ... on demons and demonology," and the camera focuses on "a grotesque illustration of skeletons" (*Screenplay*, 23).

All these examples intimate that Branagh is not hamming up *Hamlet*, as many of his reviewers imply, but rather is responding to gothic features of Shakespearean tragedy recognized by Romantic novelists in the eighteenth and nineteenth centuries and by filmmakers from the silent era onwards. These qualities of Shakespeare's *Hamlet* go beyond settings and apparitions to many aspects of the whole gothic philosophy. John Ruskin likens the ambition and veracity of the medieval gothic art movement to the Christian injunction "Do what you can. And confess freely what you are unable to do; neither let your effort be shortened for fear of failure, nor your confession silenced for fear of shame" (10). Ruskin is here comparing the gothic tendency to attempt complex designs, even if imperfectly rendered, with the Classical preference for simplicity perfectly executed. He thinks the latter led to repetition and a lack of originality, independence, and dignity on the part of the artist. He associates gothic proclivities with Christian aims for heavenly perfection or transcendence. Transcendence is central to gothicism (12) and to *Hamlet*: "There are more things in heaven and earth, Horatio, / Than are dreamt of in your philosophy" (l.5.174–5); "There is a special providence in the fall of a sparrow" (5.2.167). Branagh explained that his whole performance of the role "would be directed towards that moment [articulated by the second quotation] when Hamlet achieves the peace he craves by simply accepting whatever fate has in store for him" (Mark White, 199). Hamlet as a character attempts much: he talks with a ghost, tests its truth, converts a queen, and brings a king to justice. He is also adept at admitting failure, at least to himself – all his soliloquies harp on this. Moreover, he asks huge questions about human nature, about our place in the universe, about mortality.

Shakespeare's effort in writing the play and Branagh's in filming it in its entirety both meet Ruskin's gothic standard, opting for richness, inclusiveness, variety (what Erasmus termed *copia*) rather than simplicity, selection, and perfection. Many critics have taken issue with both Shakespeare and Branagh for the unwieldiness of their projects, the flawed nature of the results (T.S. Eliot saw *Hamlet* as "an artistic failure"). But both have aimed high, like the architects of the great gothic cathedrals. We can sympathize with Ruskin's exhortation to be like the noble gothic artists and attempt more and fail, rather than attempt less and succeed. Existential progress is based on this notion.

Branagh was ahead of the trend in gothicizing *Hamlet*. From Anne Rice's vampire novels through the phenomenal successes of the Harry Potter and Twilight series and the many derivative novels they spawned to the zombie obsession, the gothic has been revived like an undead corpse, and shows no signs of flagging. Another director of *Hamlet*, Michael Almereyda, commented on this trend in an interview about his new film, *Cymbeline*: "America is more and more in its craziness turning into a perpetual Halloween celebration ... Pop culture is more and more about skulls and skeletons and zombies and vampires, and that's not just on Halloween. [By setting both Shakespeare adaptations at Halloween] I was just trying to make a little bit of a statement ... without being too didactic" (Emily Rome). The century has turned, but millennial angst lives on, and artists still seek solace from the spectre of death in works from a society better at making sense of it: Shakespeare's.

7

Art and the Grotesque in Julie Taymor's *Titus* and Peter Greenaway's *Prospero's Books*

Like the gothic, the grotesque is a kind of subgenre in which the author plays with a subversive conjunction of contradictory elements. In the gothic, the creepy and the sublime are explored in the same work. In the grotesque, two elements usually kept separate are yoked together. Both Julie Taymor's *Titus* (2000) and Peter Greenaway's *Prospero's Books* (1991) are painterly films that revel in the grotesque. While Shakespeare's *The Tempest* and particularly his *Titus Andronicus* lend themselves naturally to this approach because of the presence of hybrid creatures, flesh indulged and abused, and a mixture of horror and fun in the plots and the poetry, Taymor and Greenaway build on what they find in the playscripts to emphasize the grotesque. Both directors respond to grotesque aspects in the plays that express our own society's uncomfortable sense that violence and entertainment are inextricably linked. Thus, their films are characterized as products of the postmodern cultural moment. As Anthony R. Guneratne puts it, "An alert critic might well recognize in this obsession with hybridity a central tenet of post colonial theory, that the resistance to the notion of cultural plurality (and hence the presupposition of a pure and potentially superior culture) is part of nationalist and imperialist discourse" (237). It is no coincidence that these two films that celebrate plurality in their artistic expression also focus on figures who resist plurality: Titus and Prospero. Taymor and Greenaway are not just responding to the *copia* integral to Shakespeare but are also distancing themselves (not necessarily consciously) from forms of art that appear characterized by generic wholeness and a strict adherence to the Classical unities (such as in French Classical drama) often avoided by English Elizabethan and Jacobean dramatists and alien to postmodern film audiences.

At first glance, Shakespeare's brutal early tragedy *Titus Andronicus* (1594) seems to have little in common with his elegant late romance *The Tempest* (1611). On closer examination, both centre around powerful, aging male protagonists – the general Titus and the magician-duke Prospero – and both treat the subjects of empire-building, leadership struggles, rape, revenge, and retribution. They are also shot through with nostalgia. Titus shows himself homesick for a time when Roman values of martial self-sacrifice were uppermost in his society; Prospero and Caliban both pine for the era before their first encounter with one another when they held sway over their kingdoms. These themes lend themselves to a grotesque treatment, as hostile races view each other as barely human, rival leaders attempt to humiliate each other by revealing weaknesses, and the violence of rape, revenge, and retribution throws attention on the human body in all its absurd vulnerability. Nostalgia is inherently grotesque, as those afflicted with it sigh for a time and place that is lost forever and may never have existed in the form imagined; it is therefore a hybrid of truth and fantasy. Prospero himself admits that his return to his dukedom will be a very different experience from his last of ruling Milan, as he is now twelve years older: "And thence retire me to my Milan, where / Every third thought shall be my grave" (5.1.314–15).

The translation of verbal poetry into screen images is often a grotesque process. Shakespeare writes largely in metaphor, and a literalized metaphor is in essence grotesque. The poet himself points out the grotesquerie of taking metaphors literally in his sonnet "My Mistress's Eyes Are Nothing Like the Sun." Taymor particularly has a talent for taking an image in Shakespeare's verse and using it as a concrete, visual cue for her costumes, set, and choreography. The results are striking and usually grotesque. As Douglas Lanier astutely observes, "Thematically, Taymor is strongly attracted to material that explores the relationship between civilisation and the darker impulses – especially monstrosity and violence – that underlie or threaten it, issues that surface with particular force in her productions of *The Tempest* and *Titus Andronicus*" (*Routledge Companion*, 458).

The term "grotesque" is, strictly speaking, a definition of a type of visual art, first used in the early sixteenth century to describe the wall decorations on ancient Roman chambers, that, sunken over time, were found underground, much like crypts or "grottoes." These decorations were extraordinary combinations of human, animal, and vegetable matter. Giorgio Vasari writes about them in *Lives of the Most Eminent Painters, Sculptors and Architects* (1550) with fascination and disdainful amusement: "Grotesques are an irregular and highly ridiculous sort of painting, done by the ancients to adorn vacant spaces, where in certain places only things set up high were suitable. For this purpose they created all kinds of absurd monsters, formed by a freak of nature or by the whims and fancies of the workmen, who in this kind of picture are subject to no rule, but paint a heavy weight attached to the finest thread which could not possibly bear it, a horse with legs of leaves, a man with crane's legs, and any number of bumblebees and sparrows; so that the one who was able to dream up the strangest things was held to be the most able" (8).

Grotteschi celebrated hybrid creatures; the marriage of two separate entities in one body throws emphasis on the physical fact of the body and the balance of its parts. Montaigne, according to Neil Rhodes in his *Elizabethan Grotesque*, was among the first to apply the term to writing, comparing grotesque art to his own literary efforts (in his essay "On Friendship"), which share with it their "variety and strangeness" (Montaigne, 1). It is not mere coincidence that the early sixteenth century also saw in France the emergence of François Rabelais's chapbooks on Gargantua and Pantagruel, the heroes of which are monstrously large beings (1534). Rabelais's emphasis on the body, with his detailed descriptions of all its functions, was influential in the development of what we now term the grotesque in writing. Thomas Nashe most exemplified the art in English, although he was by no means the only proponent of the new species of satirical journalism, both celebratory and cautionary. (Other writers who might be described as contributing to the grotesque include Gabriel Harvey, Thomas Lodge, Thomas Dekker, and Thomas Middleton). Rhodes comments on the hybridity of this new art form: "The comic prose pamphlet develops directly from the didactic material which had aimed to produce that garish mixture of sensational news (plagues, civil wars, monstrous births), accounts of urban 'vice' (plays, fashions in dress) and good counsel, which the middle-class Elizabethan found so palatable" (50).

Both *Titus Andronicus* and *The Tempest* present this potent blend, especially in their filmmakers' hands. *Titus* opens at the end of one war, with the Goths, and concludes with another, against Rome.

Aaron's half-black, half-white bastard is considered a monstrous birth by his half-brothers and the nurse. Tamora and Aaron concoct a vile pantomime in which they "find" the culprits of Bassanio's murder and the stolen gold. Taymor clads her cast in an eclectic and over-the-top set of costumes that would have given the Puritan pamphleteer Philip Stubbes a heart attack. In Greenaway's version of *The Tempest*, Caliban is tormented by plagues – agues and cramps that rack the near-naked body of the dancer who plays him (Michael Clark). A bloody insurrection seems to have been the precursor to Antonio's usurpation of Prospero's dukedom – his courtiers lie in bloody baths, surrounded by torn pages of their books. Greenaway gives us not one but two monstrous births: those of Caliban and Miranda's sibling. Prospero prepares a play with the help of Ceres to entertain the newly betrothed Ferdinand and Miranda. The Europeans arrive on the island attired in absurd excesses.

Shakespeare's *Titus Andronicus* was probably written in the early 1590s, when the grotesque flourished in England. Oxford editor Eugene M. Waith links Shakespeare's *Titus* with Nashe's *The Unfortunate Traveller*, although he states that it is impossible to ascertain who was indebted to whom. Nashe and his previously mentioned fellow pamphleteers employ images of heterogeneous composition, such as a description of a disease using culinary vocabulary, creating in the reader a mixed reaction of humour and revulsion. This disturbing combination of emotions is exactly what is felt by many spectators of Shakespeare's *Titus Andronicus*, and, even more, of Taymor's filmed version, *Titus*. It is also an accurate description of many spectators' reactions to Greenaway's *Prospero's Books*. "Grotesque" seems a particularly useful term to apply to film, as it is a hybrid art. It begins with words, then resembles something like theatre in that actors say the words and pretend to be the characters created by those words. Finally, it uses the art of photography to record the performances and the art of editing to shape them into a narrative. As Guneratne has memorably expressed it, "Shakespeare films are innately hybrid texts: the smell of greasepaint and the taste of popcorn, no less than the residues of printers' ink, can be felt in them" (212). In fact, "grotesque" is a term that more appropriately applies to film than to written works, as film, like the grotto decorations, is predominantly visual. Even the written grotesque is often compared to the cinema; Rhodes writes that "the grotesque images in Nashe's writing seem to flash cinematically past the eye" (21).

Shakespeare's *Tempest* does not necessarily spring to mind in conjunction with the "grotesque." However, Greenaway's film *Prospero's Books* brings into sharp relief the many grotesque elements in Shakespeare's late romance. Caliban is the most obvious example of the grotesque, himself a hybrid creature, spawn of a mortal witch, Sycorax, and the devil and described by other characters as a "monster" (2.2.30), a "mooncalf" (3.2.21), and "a strange fish" (2.2.27). Indeed, Trinculo is not sure if Caliban is a man or a fish when he first encounters him. Ariel too is a hybrid creature, an airy sprite who can transform into fire or a harpy – a part-woman, part-bird creature. The setting of the play also lends itself to the grotesque. Shakespeare, in creating his magical island – part Mediterranean, part Caribbean – drew upon the remarkable accounts of travellers, filled with tales of wonders like "men whose heads / Do grow beneath their shoulders" (*Othello* 1.3.143–4) and the unicorns (3.3.22) mentioned by Sebastian in the play.

Taymor and Greenaway can count among their antecedents Giuseppe Arcimboldo's painted heads made up of animal and vegetable matter, Tobias Stimmer's weird portraits, Hieronymous Bosch's and Pieter Bruegel the Elder's nightmarish scenes, and even Leonardo da Vinci's grotesque heads. Moreover, Rhodes's definition of the Elizabethan grotesque is particularly useful to apply to these two films: it "derives from the unstable coalescence of contrary images of the flesh: indulged, abused, purged and damned" (4). This description could serve as a summary of the events of *Titus Andronicus*, in which feasting, sex, rape, and dismemberment play huge roles. While it does not seem so appropriate to Shakespeare's *Tempest* (although even there, bodies are rewarded with feasts and punished with cramps and agues), it is certainly apt for *Prospero's Books*. This film parades before its viewers the naked body in all its variety of age and type. Greenaway comments on his stress on the body in his films: "Cinema doesn't connect with the body as artists have in two thousand years of painting, using the nude as the central figure which the ideas seem to circulate around. I think it is important to somehow push or stretch or emphasize, in as many ways as I can, the sheer bulk, shape, heaviness, the juices, the actual structure of the body. Cinema basically examines a personality first and the body afterward" (IMDB).

In addition to the use of the grotesque, the two films here share many other elements. Both treat the theme of revenge. The plot of

Titus revolves around Tamora avenging her son's death and mutilation at Titus's hands, and then Titus retaliating for the rape and dismemberment of his daughter, the loss of his hand, and the death of his two sons. *Prospero's Books* focuses on the revenge wrought by the magician on his usurping brother and his accomplice, and on Caliban's attempt to avenge himself against Prospero's theft of his island. Greenaway – not surprisingly, as he made his film in a postcolonial England – adds a physical literalness to the subversive voice that Shakespeare gives Caliban. Michael Clark's dance, which owes something to Nijinsky, is rebellious, incorporating crude pelvic and bottom thrusts and impudent hand gestures, virtually giving the audience the finger. Caliban also defecates on Prospero's books. As Robert Stam put it, Greenaway "retroactively liberates the oppressed colonial characters of the original" (42), at least in Caliban's movements.

Both films have been described as "painterly" – their directors overtly alluding in their films to works of art, and aestheticizing violence in a way that is grotesque; what is brutal is also beautifully filmed. Greenaway in fact trained as a painter. Adam Barker gleans in an interview that the British director's "heroes include modernists such as the painter R.B. Kitaj and the composer John Cage, but also Jacobean dramatists such as Ford and Webster. He is especially drawn to the masque form – the courtly entertainment – where it was not unknown for the king himself to participate in elaborate stage allegories representing the power of the monarch" (112).

Greenaway's engagement with the masque is overtly nostalgic, as it is an artistic form with little cultural relevance today; Renaissance masques are almost never performed. On the few occasions when they have been resurrected, it has been largely in academic settings (like Case Western Reserve University's production of Jonson's *Oberon, The Faery Prince*, 1993).

HYBRIDITY

Hybridity is probably the defining characteristic of the grotesque. The hybrid creature is seen as unnatural, monstrous, even comical in the way it marries incongruous body parts from different animals. In the tradition of theatre, the hybrid creature invites comparison between the two things it combines and often draws attention to its unique gait. Samuel Beckett's plays reflect this tradition, again suggesting the spiritual kinship between our own age and the Early Modern age. His characters' bodies are always compromised – they can only crawl or only sit; they are permanently confined to barrels or chairs or hills of sand. The psychological maiming of World War II is suggested by the physical incapacity of his characters. His intention was to emphasize also the alienation effected by industrialization – that human beings have become more like mass-produced machines. We perform only a narrow range of activities; locked in our mindless routines, we have become automatons (as Charlie Chaplin so comically animates in the *Modern Times* sequence when he emerges from his first day on an assembly line).

Taymor suggests all of this in the opening scenes of *Titus*. In the initial scene, we are presented with a hybrid creature – a boy with a paper bag for a head, a crude version of a helmet. Like a malfunctioning machine, he wreaks mindless carnage on his toy soldiers (an eclectic mix representing different eras of war and violence) and on his dinner with his bottle of ketchup and his utensils. After a cataclysmic explosion, the boy is carried by a clown figure, both comic and terrifying, to the Coliseum, where Titus and his soldiers return from war, half mud, half men. They are bristling with metal, wearing armour and carrying weapons. Taymor directs the Roman army to enter the Coliseum with a stiff automated march that recalls the boy's wind-up soldiers. These men are killing machines, grotesque hybrids, half terracotta soldier, half rusty machinery. Their stately progress around the arena is strangely beautiful.

Shakespearean film scholar Samuel Crowl suggests that Taymor's visuals in this first scene, the mud and the slow pace, remind us that Titus is "encased in ancient ideas about Rome and the patriarchy that Shakespeare's play is challenging" ("Julie Taymor's Film," 46). In other words, Titus is suffering from nostalgia for the old Rome. Taymor is also making a similar comment to Beckett, that war dehumanizes men, turning them into machines, weapons, mere clay and metal. One of Taymor's characteristic techniques when making the film was to flesh out lines from Shakespeare's text – a key to successful adaptation, in my opinion. Titus remarks to his brother:

Marcus, we are but shrubs, no cedars we
No big-boned men framed of the Cyclops' size

> But metal, Marcus. Steel to the very back,
> Yet wrung with wrongs more than our backs can bear. (4.3.46–9)

The lines suggest that the Andronici are bionic men with steel backbones, and, if humble like low-growing shrubs, they are tough like them too.

Hybridity in the film almost always articulates this same message. Tamora and her sons are first depicted wearing mangy animal skins – they are half human, half beast. Is Taymor suggesting that Rome's more sophisticated technology has taken the dehumanization one step further than that of the Goths? The Roman soldiers are only half alive; their military system has taken the predatory, bestial part of them and transformed it into a more efficient killing engine. The transforming power of the Roman system is all-encompassing. We later see Saturninus throned in a huge, roaring wolf chair, but the wolf is sharp and stylized and studded with rivets like armour, and Saturninus looks small and absorbed by it. The system has swallowed him whole.

Tamora, after being assured by Saturninus of compassionate treatment, appears in a gold dress with a rigid bodice, again resembling armour (or an Oscar statue). Her hair is braided close to her head and wrapped in gold ribbon. She wears gold eye shadow in a band about her eyes and gold lipstick. She has been transformed by Rome from animal to metal in a very short time. Now she is Saturninus's possession, his jewel given by Titus. For the wedding reception she exchanges her gold breastplate for a gold lamé dress, with a stiff gold hairpiece shaped like a crown – still a hybrid, half metal, half woman. Again, Taymor seems to have made Shakespeare's verbal images visual. Aaron describes his Goth lover as a sun-woman, touched by Midas, all gilded, hot metal:

> Now climbeth Tamora Olympus' top ...
> As when the glorious sun salutes the morn
> And having gilt the ocean with his beams,
> Gallops the zodiac in his glistering coach. (2.1.1–7)

Saturninus's palace reception chamber boasts a pool, and in the pool drifts a huge mermaid floatation device, part woman, part fish.

The mermaid is grotesque with outsized breasts, nipples painted black like targets. The mouth is black also. The effect is both titillating, the erogenous zones darkened to emphasize them, and frightening, the unnatural colour suggestive of disease and death. Demetrius avails himself of the mermaid's ample backside while receiving sexual favours from a woman similarly tattooed with black paint. The mermaid's breasts are later comically deflated by Titus's arrows.

More importantly, Lavinia's rape scene transforms all those involved into hybrids. Taymor literalizes the image Shakespeare gives to Marcus when he first discovers his raped and mutilated niece:

Speak, gentle niece, what stern ungentle hands
Have lopped and hewed and made thy body bare
Of her two branches, those sweet ornaments,
Whose circling shadows kings have sought to sleep in. (3.1.16–19)

Taymor places Lavinia on a tree stump and replaces her cut-off hands with sprays of broken twigs. She is half woman, half tree, like Daphne escaping Apollo. Later, young Lucius gives her wooden hands, purchased at a bizarre and grotesque shop that sells body parts for dolls and statues. Lavinia, played by Laura Fraser, with her porcelain skin and wooden hands, becomes yet another hybrid, half doll, half woman.

When Lavinia writes her rapists' names in the sand using her mouth, memories of her trauma flood her mind, and she sees herself as a doe with a deer head and hooves vainly holding down her billowing skirts, like a grotesque Marilyn Monroe (*Seven Year Itch*, 1955). Chiron and Demetrius are remembered as ravening tigers. Taymor acknowledges the hybridity in the words of her screenplay: "Demetrius and Chiron, half human and half ferocious tiger, attack and ravish the doe/woman" (117). Again, she wisely takes her cue from Shakespeare's dialogue. Just before the rape, Lavinia entreats Demetrius to show her pity: "When did the tiger's young ones teach the dam? / O, do not learn her wrath, she taught it thee" (81). Taymor prepares this imagery carefully, as the brothers appear at the wedding reception in animal-print suits. She also recalls in this imagery Titus's line, "Rome is but a wilderness of tigers" (3.1.54).

This image of Lavinia on a column base as Monroe attacked by tigers memorably conveys Taymor's point about our society's voracious appetite for celebrity. The icon is shown to be consumed here, even while, ironically, it is Taymor who is cannibalizing the famous image of Monroe for her purposes. The image is a tremendously rich one, also suggesting that when the male gaze rests on Monroe, coyly holding down her skirts, it is a form of rape. Our society puts female beauty on a pedestal but ultimately destroys it, as Monroe's fame eventually destroyed her.

Another example of Taymor's use of hybrids is the vision that troubles Titus, lying prostrate at the crossroads as his sons are spirited away for execution (Penny Arcade Nightmare #2). In it, his son Mutius appears as a sacrificial lamb on an altar with his own human head. Angels blare their trumpets. The simile of a man as a lamb to the slaughter is common to Judeo-Christian imagery, but when Taymor literalizes it, sticking a human head on a sheep's body, it seems comic and strange. In her screenplay she explains that she was thinking of Abraham and Isaac for this scene. She does not elaborate to point out that this comparison highlights Titus's distorted values. Abraham was only willing to sacrifice his son because his Creator told him to, whereas Titus takes it upon himself out of slavish devotion to an unworthy new emperor to kill his son for defending his sister's honour.

The most obvious instance of hybridity is when Tamora and her two sons appear as Revenge, Rape, and Murder. Taymor calls this scene her Penny Arcade Nightmare #4. Even its title suggests the presence of the grotesque – both fun and funny, like a penny arcade, and terrifying, like a nightmare. Tamora's armour with its sagging breasts is comical, yet it also suggests decay and disease, and her brutal headdress and coned gauntlet arms are frightening. She is half weapon, half woman. Revenge's costume is reminiscent of both the Statue of Liberty and images of Blind Justice – ironic allusions, as Tamora's plans in this scene have little to do with liberty or justice. Chiron's girl's underwear is silly on him, yet also suggests that he may have stolen it from his victim, and the owl headdress is menacing. He sits in a dead tree, a branch thrust phallic-like between his legs, part bird of prey, part tree, part man. Demetrius's sadomasochistic underwear is ridiculous, while his ferocious tiger headdress and snapping mouth hands are scary.

The last hybrid monster in the film is Aaron, buried up to his armpits in sand. He is half man, half sand. Shakespeare must have influenced Beckett's depiction of Winnie in *Happy Days*, an absurd image. That absurdity, mixed with despair, is part of the grotesque. These hybrid creatures are tragic because they have lost touch with their humanity. Crowl notes that Aaron is also associated in the film with cages – in the family game room and when his son is shown in a tiny cage at the end of the film ("Julie Taymor's Film," 46). Once again, this imagery links the Goths with animals.

Greenaway's *Prospero's Books* too abounds in hybrid creatures. Ariel is depicted in the opening scenes as half boy, half Italian fountain as he pees an unceasing powerful stream of urine on a toy boat in a pool – the ship in the tempest in miniature. Greenaway stresses Ariel's likeness to a fountain by dressing him as Cupid. The effect is comical, yet because we know that those on the ship believe they are facing death, there is menace in the child's play too. As the film progresses, we see Ariel in four stages of maturity – young child, pubescent, teenager, adult. Often we see at least three Ariels together, as when they urge Prospero to have mercy on his victims.

Greenaway also illustrates Prospero's account of Ariel trapped in a pine tree, bits of twig spilling from his mouth. Here he is half boy, half tree. It is another grotesque image, recalling Giuseppe Arcimboldo's Autumn, the head and neck made up of wood and leaves (anticipating Greenaway's Allegory of Autumn towards the end of the film?). At the fake banquet prepared for the Neapolitans, Ariel, as in Shakespeare's play, appears as a harpy, part woman, part bird, accompanied by Greenaway's own inventive hybrids of "seven black reptilian fauns – all horns and feathers and sexual parts" (Greenaway, 128). Hybridity here is used to terrify the usurpers, confronting them with what is unnatural and monstrous, a reflection of their own unhallowed souls.

The fascinating books that intercut Shakespeare's dialogue in the film are themselves hybrids. As Guneratne observes, "At every opportunity Greenaway makes the contents of books mutate and the books themselves move" (236). They are small living worlds, as objects and creatures come in and out of the pages, which shift and transform before our eyes. Miranda's mother, Susannah, is depicted as the inverse of this. When describing the volume *The Anatomy of Birth*, Greenaway shows us Susanna pregnant with Miranda's younger sibling. Her womb is covered with a flap of flesh, which she pulls down to exhibit her unborn baby. It is fascinating and gruesome at the same time. We want both to look and to turn away – a reaction that is at the heart of the grotesque. There is peril involved also, as Susanna dies in childbirth, and, with the discussion of *The Book of the Dead*, we learn that her name was the last inscribed. In the world of the grotesque, nothing is simple – new life and death, youth and decay are inextricably and nightmarishly linked. This aspect of the grotesque links it with nostalgia; the act of looking back inevitably reminds us of the passage of time, and thus, indirectly, aging and mortality.

Caliban is a hybrid in Shakespeare's text: half man, half devil ("not honoured with / A human shape," 1.2.283–4) or, if Trinculo is to be trusted, half man, half fish. In the film, Caliban's (Michael Clark's) hybridity is suggested by his baldness, his corseted naked body, his movements, and his red, bound genitalia. He is a man, but he moves in a unique way, like an acrobat, a dancer. He is associated in the film with water, mud, urine, and excrement and lives in a cave that resembles a Hell's Mouth from a cycle play. He is all nature and no art – apart from his dance, but that seems integral to him, not learned but innate. In the scene of his birth, which Prospero describes to Ariel in the play and Greenaway illustrates, his grotesque bald witch-mother Sycorax, tongue thrust out in the effort of labour, produces something that does not resemble a human baby.

Comparable to Taymor's soldiers at the beginning of *Titus*, Greenaway's dancers, nude and half nude, male and female, move through space like wind-up toys, repeatedly performing the same staccato steps like automatons. Their movements are mechanical, unnatural, but this art is offset by their bodies, which exhibit the full range of human possibilities, thin and plump, young and old, firm and sagging. This range of types rather than ideal bodies suggests an element of satire: this is not Deadly Theatre, not safe and reverential Shakespeare with decorous doublet and hose, but the human experiment in all its flawed wonder, filtered through Shakespeare's lens. We are made acutely aware of body parts as penises, breasts, buttocks, and rolls of fat jostle and jiggle, even while the movements are exactly repeated like clockwork. The immobile faces, fixed in neutral expressions, coupled with repeated, jerky movements, are at once eerie and comical. The dancers are like lunatics, making compulsive, meaningless gestures. This impression of insanity is reinforced by the sound of hysterical laughter that fills the gap between passages of Michael Nyman's precise score. At one point we see an assembly line of naked people passing the same book along, rapidly glancing at the same double-page spread before giving it to the next person. This image again seems to underline Beckett's point about the dehumanizing effects of industrialization. Without books, there could be no industrialization, no colonization. The written word gives one man the authority over another – the king's signature, the lawyer's document, even the inventor's instructions on how to make his weapon are the talismans of power. The natives on Prospero's island merely glance at the book they pass along, because they are illiterate. Prospero's literacy, his ability to read his magic spells, gives him power over them.

Greenaway's island waters teem with sea nereids; in contrast to Taymor's mermaid raft, his aquatic women are beautiful pale creatures who save Ferdinand and the other mariners from drowning. Greenaway also creates creatures that are one with the air – eight people who represent the winds of the four corners of the earth, or the four points of the compass. Each couple has a male and a female, and to suggest the winds blowing from everywhere, Greenaway has an Asian couple, an African couple, and two white couples (America and Europe, perhaps?). They are like incarnations of an elaborate compass rose, cheeks absurdly puffed out in the effort to blow a stormy wind around Prospero's library, sending papers flying. Greenaway tells us in his screenplay that they are "a quotation from Botticelli's Birth of Venus" (60) – another instance of his nostalgia for the great art of the Renaissance. These hybrids pick up on lines from the text which play with the four elements. Ariel is associated with air, fire and water – "I come / To answer thy best pleasure, be't to fly, / To swim, to dive into the fire, to ride / On the curled clouds" (1.2.189–92) – and Caliban with earth – "Thou earth ... thou tortoise" (1.2.316, 319).

Hybridity is so much a part of *Prospero's Books* not only because the film is peopled with hybrid creatures but because Greenaway's techniques are redolent with hybridity. James Tweedie focuses on the "hybrid text" in his article on the film, examining the way the director intercuts Shakespeare's dialogue with his own descriptions of Prospero's twenty-four books. But he also notes the hybridity of sound and visual images, incongruous and cacophonous: "The film uses digital pyrotechnics to reaffirm the potential hybridity of those arts [theatre, literature] and the cinema" (113).

The film does boast a strange and wonderful mix of sounds – Nyman's repetitive, mechanical score and the wild mélange of bird and animal cries, the dripping and sloshing of water (for more on this, see chapter 13). Greenaway also deploys visual metonymy: a dripping faucet to convey the slow and repetitive drip, drip, drip of time; or slow motion, or the dilation of a shot by editing (whereby the same gesture is repeated ad infinitum), or a well-chosen synecdochic gesture (e.g., distracted doodling). Each approach has advantages and drawbacks (Walker, 33). Taymor's composer for *Titus*, Eliot Goldenthal, also uses an eclectic mix of musical styles. As Elsie Walker notes, solemn mass music is associated with Titus, jazz with Saturninus, and heavy metal and chaotic rock with Chiron and Demetrius.

FLESH INDULGED AND ABUSED

Another crucial dimension of the grotesque is its emphasis on flesh indulged and flesh abused, flesh purged and flesh damned – a preoccupation that demonstrates the literary grotesque's indebtedness to sermons. Shakespeare gives us Caliban, his flesh tormented and punished by Prospero with cramps and agues, when what Caliban wants is for his flesh to be indulged by Miranda ("O ho, O ho! Would't have been done! Thou didst prevent me – I had peopled else / This isle with Calibans," 1.2.344–9). Is it for his attempted rape of Miranda that Caliban's genitalia are bound in the film? Caliban's release is to curse, to urinate and excrete on Prospero's books, and to express his forbidden sexuality in dance. Prospero also abuses Ferdinand's flesh, enslaving it to render Miranda a harder-won "prize." Stephano and Trinculo indulge their flesh with too much wine, then have it abused with Ariel's torments, which ultimately punish and purge them for the sin of premeditating usurpation and murder. The film is full of images of bathing and drowning, flip sides of the same coin. Bathing represents the flesh indulged, drowning the flesh abused.

Women's flesh is particularly seen to be abused. Women are as subjugated to the men in the film as Ariel and Caliban are to Prospero. We first hear Miranda moaning piteously in her sleep, and then we see her wracked with a nightmare – a vision of the tempest her father has set in motion. Sleep, which should "knit up the raveled sleeve of care," is here tormenting, not restoring, her. We see her strain away from Prospero as he drags her, with a vice-like grip on her arm, to visit Caliban, who tried to rape her. We see Susannah sadly opening her womb like an anatomy demonstration. Claribel, the princess of Naples, lies naked on her African bed, holding her bleeding genitalia. It is unclear whether the blood issues from her deflowering or from genital mutilation, but whatever the cause, she looks deeply miserable. James Tweedie observes, "This violation of boundaries [in hybridity] also bears the burden of castration, disfiguration, and what [Michael] Fried calls a 'wounding of seeing': the depicted assault on the body is both 'painful to look at … and all but impossible, hence painful, *to look away from*'" (113). Greenaway is, after all, the director of *The Cook, the Thief, His Wife and Her Lover* (1989), which produces a catalogue of horrors, including cannibalism, to rival those in *Titus Andronicus*. *Titus* is all about flesh abused: hands and tongues cut off, bodies raped, caged, mutilated, buried alive, and eaten. When flesh is indulged, it is at worst wholly decadent, at best tinged with melancholy, never simple, always a grotesque hybrid of pleasure and guilt. After Titus gives the initial speech in the film, the Roman soldiers stand or sit like statues, caked in mud, under steaming showers. The bodily relief and pleasure after the exhausting struggle of war is palpable but tinged with sadness – some are missing limbs, others their dead comrades.

At the wedding feast, Saturninus is drunk and groping his new wife like a clumsy teenager. Later in the film, he lies naked like a baby on Tamora's bare breasts. His indulgence of his flesh comes across as ridiculous, pathetic; he is infantilized as the younger, less-experienced partner and ruler of the couple. Taymor's added scenes of their lovemaking merely exacerbate the impression Saturnine gives in Shakespeare's play of inept leadership. The trio of Goths in the palace seems particularly depraved. Their physical deportment to one another often carries tinges of incestuous intent. Chiron and Demetrius in both play and film most notably indulge their flesh by satisfying their lust for Lavinia in rape and dismemberment, while Tamora and Aaron sate their adulterous libidos secretly. For their indulgence, all are punished with torment and death. In the film, Demetrius and Chiron are hung upside down on meat hooks in Titus's kitchen until they are slaughtered like calves and baked in a pie. Tamora is fed this pie, then told about its contents, then stabbed by Titus with a carving knife. Aaron is buried in the sand, a dish for the vultures.

Following the grotesque tradition, Taymor emphasizes the body even beyond what is given her by Shakespeare's text. At the beginning of the play, Tamora and Titus confront each other over Alarbus's flaming entrails. Later, the scene in which Saturninus accosts the Andronici over their supposed "treachery" of stealing Lavinia away is filmed in a piazza adorned with a colossal dismembered marble hand and foot. The presence of these huge body parts is absurd yet disturbing, reminding us again of the cost of war and empire. It is also reminiscent of Hugh Walpole's *The Castle of Otranto*, in which a mammoth helmet, arm, or leg appears to haunt Manfred. Taymor may also have been influenced here by Branagh's *Hamlet* (1996), which opens with an immense statue of the dead King Hamlet coming to life, the camera focusing on one huge limb at a time (see chapter 6). Taymor's limb-strewn piazza anticipates Penny Arcade Nightmare #1 later in the scene, in which the torso and limbs of a Classical sculpture fly towards the camera, flames in the background. A bloody line appears on the torso – the line Titus cut into Alarbus – and the torso begins to breathe more and more rapidly. This vision hangs in the air between Titus and Tamora. Another example of Taymor's grotesque emphasis on the body is her addition of the statue-parts shop where young Lucius purchases his aunt a set of wooden hands.

In a stroke of genius, Taymor has Aaron throw Titus's severed hand casually into a Ziploc bag and fix it to the rear-view mirror in his sporty car as he roars off. There it swings instead of fuzzy dice. It's a Quentin Tarantino moment, horror and comedy mixed. Another striking incidence of the grotesque revelling in flesh abused is the sideshow wagon that arrives at Titus's courtyard. The wagon's side is lifted to display to him his sons' heads and his own cut-off hand on a Victorian pedestal table in a kind of velvet-lined puppet theatre while carnival music plays. This cruel use of his misery for cheap entertainment finally tips Titus over the edge. He can no longer cry, so he bursts out laughing. Jonathan Bate writes astutely about this moment in the introduction to the screenplay:

> Critics in the eighteenth and nineteenth centuries could not cope with such incongruity. Its affront to stylistic decorum was thought

to be on a par with the play's shocking lack of respect for the principle of poetic justice, in which the evil are punished and the good are duly rewarded ...

Modern movies have made us familiar with characters like Aaron the Moor, who delivers a verbal pun one moment and a stab in the guts the next. Titus' unexpected laugh helps us to comprehend the way in which human beings deal with inexpressible anguish, rather as Brian Keenan, one of the Western hostages in Lebanon, describes in his memoir, *An Evil Cradling*, his discovery of the saving grace of humour: "In the most inhuman of circumstances men grow and deepen in humanity. In the face of death but not because of it, they explode with passionate life, conquering despair with insane humour." (10)

"Insane humour" is a good description of much of the grotesque. In addition, the theatrical display of cut-off body parts underlines another of Taymor's themes – the celebrity treatment of violence in our society: "The play was ripe for adaptation to film, speaking directly to our times, a time whose audience feeds daily on tabloid sex scandals, teenage gang rape, high school gun sprees and the private details of a celebrity murder trial" (*Screenplay*, 174). We watch news of war and murder on TV alongside police dramas and hospital soap operas until we are jaded. Taymor satirizes our society's tendency to treat violent news stories as just more entertainment. Can we still distinguish between real violence and fictionalized violence? Why do we seek out violence in our entertainment? This film cannot help but prompt these questions when it is framed by scenes in the Coliseum, the arena in which life-death struggles were displayed to amuse Roman spectators. How different are we from the ancient Romans? Taymor often comments in her screenplay on the appropriateness of a Croatian coliseum standing in for the one in Rome, as Croatia was about to be torn apart by war and violence.

FOOD AND HORROR

Food in both films becomes a source of flesh indulged and abused at the same time. In *Prospero's Books*, the Neapolitans are presented with a sumptuous feast that recalls, as Greenaway intended, a Veronese tableau (128). Just as they are about to partake, they are punished by the appearance of Ariel as a harpy, and the seven reptilian fauns added by Greenaway. In *Titus*, the striking initial scene in which the young boy eats his meal while watching television and wreaking carnage on his toy soldiers with ketchup is an excellent example of food being linked to violence and pain. It also once again links violence with entertainment and celebrity as represented by the blaring television set. This scene anticipates the two dinner scenes in Shakespeare's play, which Taymor beautifully directs, finding the perfect grotesque balance between horror and comedy. The absurd dinner-table scene in which young Lucius kills a fly again associates food with death and sorrow, but Titus and Lucius make brave attempts to be merry, imagining the black fly as Aaron the Moor, who lately deprived Titus of his hand.

Neil Rhodes writes about two Renaissance authors who traded in the grotesque, "Sharply aware of the body's capacity for mutation, both Nashe and Rabelais use grotesque food imagery to remind us of the essential similarity between our own flesh and the flesh we feed it with: the devourer is devoured" (42). This observation is hugely apt for *Titus*. The glee with which Anthony Hopkins as Titus prepares the final cannibalistic feast is accentuated by the details of the chef's costume (the detail of Titus entering as a cook is actually Shakespeare's) and the flesh pies cooling by a window with billowing chiffon curtains (à la Betty Crocker, Taymor wryly notes in her screenplay), accompanied by a cheerful 1930s Italian tune. The director is channelling nostalgia for pre-war and 1950s domestic life, both real and imagined, with ironic intent. She prepares her audience for the idealized family life of television shows like *Leave It to Beaver* or *Happy Days* and then inverts it with the horror and cannibalism of Shakespeare's play. By casting Anthony Hopkins as Titus, she is once again recycling popular iconography as the actor was best known at the time for his role as Hannibal the Cannibal in *Silence of the Lambs* (1991). Hopkins gives Jessica Lange's Tamora encouraging nods as she partakes of the human-flesh pie, seeming to say, "Eat up now, it's good for you." It is in this final banquet that we see all the elements of the grotesque uniting. Flesh is indulged at the feast with the luxury of eating a rare delicacy – human flesh. It is also abused – Tamora's sons are reduced to meat on a plate; her flesh revolts and her soul is damned by eating what is unlawful. In contrast, Titus and Lavinia are purged by the ritual of revenge and suicide (although these same rituals that bestowed honour upon them in ancient Rome damn their bodies and souls, according to their Elizabethan Christian audience).

The final slew of murders is made more explicitly grotesque by Taymor's direction. Shakespeare's stage directions note that Titus kills Lavinia and stabs the empress; in the dialogue, Saturnine kills Titus and Lucius kills Saturnine. Taymor's cast employ the tools furnished by the dining table – the consumers have their lives consumed: Titus stabs Tamora with a carving knife; Saturninus kills Titus with a candelabra; and Lucius retaliates with a serving spoon shoved down the emperor's throat. It is both horrible and comic, a dinner party gone terribly wrong. The accoutrements of a civilized evening out – the elegant clothes, the soft candlelight, the silver goblets, the waiters pouring wine – are the backdrop for the most brutal and bestial acts imaginable: cannibalism, suicide, and murder. Taymor wanted this banquet scene, which concludes the play, to recall her added one that opened the film – the boy watching war, and making toy war at the table until real war destroys his kitchen. We consume violence in our entertainment and then violence consumes us, Taymor's film declares.

GAMES AND HORROR

Contemporary entertainment-seekers are accustomed to linking games and horror in their minds. In high culture, Beckett and Stoppard have their characters play games in which the stakes are nightmarishly high; in *Waiting for Godot* and *Rosencrantz and Guildenstern Are Dead*, the hapless central duos are forced to play for their ultimate destiny. In low culture, horror films abound in possessed dolls and creepy hide-and-seek games in which the outcome for the losers is death. Again, the grotesque is not strange to twenty-first-century spectators.

Horror and fun are linked in both *Prospero's Books* and *Titus*. In a surreal game of tag, young Lucius runs away terrified from his Aunt Lavinia, who, handless and tongueless, tries to catch him so she can use his book of Ovid to reveal her rapists' identities. Ovid, probably Shakespeare's favourite author, was a master of nostalgia himself. Both his *Tristia* and his *Espistulae ex Ponto* are works entirely devoted to homesickness and the use of art to cure it. Monica Matei-Chesnoiu in

Geoparsing Early Modern English Drama claims that Shakespeare's works show the influence of these two Ovidian pieces (184n12). While Lavinia is not demonstrating longing in any way for the painful recent past, she is inaugurating a grotesque version of a childhood game summoning up in the audience a yearning for childhood linked with a frankly nostalgic poet. In the initial scene of the film, in which young Lucius plays with his food and his toy soldiers, Taymor writes in her screenplay: "The horror. The fun." Boys will be boys and play with death, she seems wryly to imply. The addition of the clown figure, who carries Lucius from the contemporary world to ancient Rome, presents Titus with his decapitated sons, and holds Aaron's baby aloft in a cage for all the aghast spectators in the coliseum to witness, is again an amalgam of horror and fun. His manner is jolly, playful, and ridiculous, but he admonishes us to look freshly at the violence in the play and hence in our society.

Prospero's Books uses the same mixture of horror and fun, notably in its treatment of drowning. (Let us not forget that Greenaway directed the playful and menacing *Drowning by Numbers*, 1988.) The Nereids saving the Italians from the sea seem serene and smiling. The tableau of the mariners, clumsy in their waterproof gear, being soaked by a torrential rain that only falls on them while Prospero looks on, dry and comfortable, is both fun and sad. Ariel plays various voice games with the gormless trio of Trinculo, Stephano, and Caliban, setting them against each other and confusing them. Then, Ariel chases them with ghostly hounds in a game of tag or an inverted hunt in which the animals pursue the people.

ART AND HORROR

Both Taymor and Greenaway use an artistic vocabulary to describe what they are doing on screen. In her director's notes, under the heading "Envisioning the Violence," Taymor writes, "My cue came from Shakespeare himself. The genius of his drama is that he juxtaposes very direct, simple and visceral actions with immense poetic verbal imagery" (*Screenplay*, 183). In another part of the screenplay she writes, "In adapting *Titus* to a screenplay, the challenge was to maintain the contrasts and scopes in Shakespeare's vision: his story and language are at once poetic and very direct, shifting between graphic, base emotions and ephemeral, mythic revelations" (178). These descriptions of Shakespeare's art could be a description of the grotesque. Rhodes writes, "In the case of imagery, the dragging together of incongruous verbal elements is a major feature of the grotesque" (25). Shakespeare brings together the sublime and ridiculous, or at least the quotidian and base, together with high art. Taymor envisions Lavinia as "a sculptured goddess on a pedestal" in her flashback to the rape (184). She is "the Venus de Milo, soon to be completed with truncated limbs and all" (184). Titus is figured as Marat in his bath, the painting by David, as he uses his own blood for ink (185). As with Greenaway, Taymor's artistic models and inspirations are mostly pre-twentieth century, suggesting the director's yearning for older forms.

This blend of high art and low action is even truer for *The Tempest* than for *Titus*, as it benefits from the outpourings of Shakespeare's mature quill. For instance, Caliban, the swamp thing who tried to rape the fifteen-year-old Miranda, is also given some of the most beautiful poetry in the play ("The isle is full of noises..."). Greenaway's subject matter is, of course, not as replete with horrors as Taymor's, but the plot of *The Tempest* centres on revenge, and it is unclear in the play what Prospero would have done to his enemies had Ariel not urged him to be merciful. Furthermore, there is the attempted rape, as well as several plans to commit murder. Greenaway expresses his nostalgia for early seventeenth-century plays: "The other aspect of Jacobean drama I like is its extraordinary relish for risk-taking. It's very visceral, very corporeal and often plays with extremely taboo subjects" (Barker, 113). For his Prospero, Greenaway drew on two famous Renaissance images of St Jerome (those of Antonello da Messina and Georges de la Tour), but once again the distinction between the original subject and its descendant only serves to emphasize the violence in *The Tempest* (screenplay, 39, 50). St Jerome's self-imposed hermitage parallels the magician's exile on the island; both are imagined as devoted to their books. But while Jerome used his isolation to grow in holiness, Prospero uses it to wreak revenge. Greenaway asks in his screenplay, "Are we truly the product of what we read?" (12), just as Taymor seems to ask if we are truly what we watch. Greenaway also sees Prospero as Blake's Chronos with his set of compasses "preparing his geomancy to ensnare his enemies" (152). Both Chronos and Prospero are jealous old rulers unwilling to concede to younger contenders. Greenaway makes much of John Gielgud's aging flesh; he bookends the film with its nakedness, suggesting its vulnerability, its imminent death and decay. Taymor too suggests this grotesque aspect of old age with Titus stripped of his armour, smaller and frailer as he sits naked in his bath. Both men occupy their last days setting things straight for their heirs, so that the power now denied them will be given their children.

Greenaway's Prospero uses his magic to recreate the architecture of home on the island. A replica of Michelangelo's Laurentian Library staircase adorns his palace. In each case, art is used to beautify revenge, control, and imperialism. Miranda is clad like Botticelli's Primavera to captivate Ferdinand and restore Prospero to his kingdom; the flashback in which Antonio plans his coup d'état is staged, in Greenaway's words, as a "Veronese seen through Dutch eyes" (68).

To suggest the "effeteness" of the shipwrecked Neapolitans, Greenaway used as his model a young man painted by Rembrandt (108). The decadence of the new arrivals to Prospero's isle, with their monstrously huge hats and ruffs, absurd pompoms on their shoes, and lace masks across their eyes, recalls Philip Stubbes's censures of the excesses of fashion in *The Anatomie of Abuses* (1583). Stubbes's tone betrays a certain fascination – the usual mixture of attraction and repulsion we find with the grotesque, which is why, no doubt, Thomas Nashe copies it in several of his works. James Tweedie summarizes: "Others identify Greenaway as a participant in the gradual, scattered but undeniable emergence of what might be described as 'mannerist cinema,' whose characteristics include a concern with theatrical mise-en-scene, the use of tableaux, hyperbolic lighting effects, [and] quotation from painting" (114).

What interests me about Tweedie's comment is that it recognizes not only Greenaway's nostalgia for the art of the past but also that Mannerist art in the High Renaissance partook of the grotesque. Mannerist art indulged in the urbane and odd with its strangely attenuated limbs, stylized features, small heads, and artificial poses. The unnatural proportions contribute to a sense of anxiety or unease in the viewer closely resembling the effect induced by much modern and contemporary art. Art historians consider that Mannerism eventually deteriorated into what was merely grotesque. This all connects with what Jonathan Bate wrote in his introduction to *Titus*, that in many ways the plays of the Early Modern period in England reveal far closer sensibilities to our own time than does the drama of the intervening periods. As contemporary people, we respond to the exploration of the bizarre, to the underlying anxiety that the grotesque expresses better than the generations so concerned with order, decorum, and genre rules. Shakespeare typically "mixes it up" – his plays are perfect examples of *copia*; tragedies and comedies alike have strong elements of humour and suffering, of beauty and horror. This variety and juxtaposition is familiar to us, everywhere in our own entertainments. At fairgrounds and playdiums, we pay to be turned upside down, frightened to the point of shrieking, nauseated from dizziness and bad food, lurched at by oversized, stylized animals like Mickey Mouse and Pluto. (Greenaway in an interview expressed admiration for the inventiveness of Disney.) In our cinemas, we pay to watch horror films and "art films" from Quentin Tarantino, David Lynch, and David Cronenberg. At home, we consume beautifully shot hospital and crime television dramas. We twenty-first-century spectators are no strangers to the grotesque. It is a form we have made our own. This is why we yearly adapt Shakespeare for the big screen rather than Corneille or Racine, Dryden or Davenant. We don't believe in poetic justice, things neatly squared away, sorrow relegated solely to tragedy, and laughs confined to comedy. Life in the twenty-first century seems stranger and more complicated than that.

Both *Titus Andronicus* and *The Tempest* are essentially stories of revenge. Taymor alludes to the examples of revenge and violence in our world today in her director's notes, particularly to Kosovo, where part of the film was shot shortly before war broke out there. Taymor claims that she stylizes Lavinia's rape and dismemberment because she did not want it to take over the film, stealing the power of the final banquet scene, which must be the climax. This sounds plausible enough, but after my first viewing of the film, what stayed in my mind was the image of the stunning Laura Fraser on top of her tree stump like a Degas ballerina, twigs for hands, blood spilling out of her mouth in a stream. The visual contrasts of Fraser's pale skin and white dress against the backdrop of the stark, black, burnt remnants of trees, the black twigs attached to her arms, her black hair blowing in the wind, and the red blood were gorgeous. But should they be? This character has been raped and dismembered, her life destroyed. As Elsie Walker writes about *Titus*, "The message about violent dangers is in danger of being supplanted by the loving attention to painterly, aesthetically pleasing detail" (198).

But Taymor is not alone to blame for this glorification of violence: Shakespeare too makes the aftermath of the rape beautiful in Marcus's mouth. Marcus describes his niece when he first encounters her wrecked body in full, poetic rhetoric:

> Alas, a crimson river of warm blood,
> Like to a bubbling fountain stirred with wind,
> Doth rise and fall between thy rosèd lips
> Coming and going with thy honey breath. (2.4.22–5)

Clearly, Shakespeare here is in a different artistic phase from the later, raw realism of Lear's "Howl, howl, howl, howl." By then he had experienced the loss of a child and knew what he was writing about. And in addition to his personal anguish, Shakespeare could draw on the collective anguish of his society. Just as our society is constantly reminded of impeding ecological and political disasters, Shakespeare's world too was apocalyptic, beset by plagues and wars, failing crops and shifting belief systems. Rhodes, with typical astuteness, writes, "Given the constant emphasis upon analogy in Elizabethan thought, grotesque imagery must often imply a warping of the natural order which in turn has connotations of vast social destruction" (47).

We look back to Shakespeare's time for an apt expression of the grotesque mix of beauty and destruction we see in our society. Other eras in English drama shied away from the stark juxtaposition of terrible agony and high art, but in our era, an era in America and Europe of both unprecedented prosperity and casual violence, this juxtaposition seems all too familiar. While this coexistence of beauty and violence, anguish and humour, has been an eternal feature of human life, not every era is bold or foolish enough to expose its reality.

These two directors look to Shakespeare to express their sense of the grotesque instead of writing new scripts in our contemporary version of English because they have a nostalgia for his rhetoric and poetry, for his irreplaceable talent. If our lives are grotesque, at least we want that grotesquerie expressed in the grand style. Our postmodern, jaded age would not tolerate high poetry in our contemporary English on screen; it would seem pretentious, overly formal. So we let Shakespeare speak for us in iambic pentameter. His poetry expresses the ugly realities of life, rape, revenge, murder, disease, and death, with a mixture of elegiac glory and gallows humour that reveals the resilience of our humanity, in spite of the odds against us.

8

Five English Screen Directors' Approaches to Cross-Dressing in *As You Like It* and *Twelfth Night*

In this chapter, transvestism joins the grotesque and the gothic as another way in which the marginal and the subversive are explored in adaptations of Shakespeare to the screen. While the gothic highlights extreme and even unhealthy states of mind, and the grotesque investigates the peculiarity of hybridity, cross-dressing interrogates behaviour that falls outside conventional gender expectations.

Why did Shakespeare cross-dress eight of his female characters? Joan in *Henry VI, Part 1*, Julia in *Two Gentleman of Verona*, Jessica, Portia, and Nerissa in *Merchant of Venice*, Rosalind in *As You Like It*, Viola in *Twelfth Night*, and Imogen in *Cymbeline* all don male garb for part of the play. An obvious practical reason for this is that Shakespeare was working with boys, not young women. Highly talented though they must have been to assume huge, dominating roles like Rosalind and Cleopatra, performance must have been easier for them, and more credible for the audience, when these boys reassumed their male attire in huge sections of his plays. Rosalind and Viola spend more stage time cross-dressed than any of Shakespeare's other women, so they are the obvious ones on whom to focus.

In addition to this practical reason for using transvestism in his plays, Shakespeare asserts several significant points with it through sly asides that draw attention to what lies beneath the costumes (for example, "OLIVER: You lack a man's heart. ROSALIND: I do so, I confess it" *AYLI*, 4.3.165–7; "FESTE: Now Jove in his next commodity of hair send thee a beard. VIOLA: By my troth I'll tell thee, I am almost sick for one" *TN*, 3.1.44–7.) At a time when male and female roles in society were rigid and proscribed, these cross-dressed characters stimulate important questions about gender and identity. Gender and class are closely linked as indicators of identity both largely recognizable from externals – clothes, posture, gestures, gait, and (though not exactly an external) voice. And while my focus in this chapter is on gender, some discussion of class is unavoidable. Certainly, with respect to both gender and class, Shakespeare seems to have been fully aware of what Marjorie Garber called "the power of the transvestite to unsettle assumptions, structures, and hierarchies" (37).

Twelfth Night, or What You Will and *As You Like It* appear, even from their titles, to ask radical questions. In Shakespeare's script, Orsino and Olivia fall for the same person, although Orsino is in denial because he thinks Cesario is male – or a male eunuch, for that is how Viola asks the captain to present her (1.2.52, 58) – and Olivia is trying to resist because she thinks Cesario is beneath her in status. Yet Viola is worthy of their love, and Shakespeare shows Orsino and Olivia as foolish when they fight their sincere feelings. Both ultimately satisfy their wills. Olivia marries Viola's kindred spirit, Sebastian, who, as a twin obviously devoted to his sister, must be presented as sharing many of her inner as well as outer qualities. Orsino marries Viola, who has performed all the duties of a best friend to him, and this makes her an ideal life companion. As she happens to be a woman, heir-production is not a problem. Orlando is thus marrying his confidante in the socially and morally acceptable package of a female body. Platonic love with a twist. Who can blame Phoebe for wanting Ganymede instead of Silvius? Are class divisions enough to make her choice erroneous, or was she wise to aim high, and try for the best partner she could get – beautiful, passionate, and witty?

It is no wonder that anti-theatricalist sermonizers like William Perkins and Philip Stubbes were particularly exercised about the cross-dressing aspect of Shakespeare's theatre (Callaghan, 33). Shakespeare seems to be suggesting to his audience that a change of clothes transforms the destiny of the wearer and those responding to him/her. The anti-theatricalists recognized this but, unlike Shakespeare, found it deeply threatening (Levine, 23–4). Their anxiety came from their belief that clothes were an outward sign of a person's essence, and an extension of that essence. If it were allowable to change the gender of these clothes, then men might be read as women and women as men, and all manner of sin might result. In a society ruled by absolutes, how could one be at peace when the outward sign of God-given gender and identity could be altered at will, deceiving all those one encountered? These Puritans were not exercised over nothing, over a mere costume change: they wished to maintain the strictest rules about clothing because they knew how much meaning was attributed to attire. Like Polonius, they recognized that in their society "the apparel oft proclaims the man" (1.3.72). They perceived in the cross-dressing of the theatre, albeit unconsciously, a radical inversion of the way people had thought about gender and identity for centuries.

Ironically, the very object of the wayward desires in the plays, the cross-dressed heroine responsible for setting in motion all these radical questions, also redirects all the desire and passion in the plays to their appropriate places (Crewe, 107). Rosalind as Ganymede essentially tricks Phoebe into a marriage that is socially acceptable – to a man of her own class rather than to a woman of a much higher class. Viola as Cesario, though not as proactive in neatly pairing everyone off, clearly tells Olivia that she will be wed to "no woman" and feels it necessary to retrieve her "woman's weeds" before Orsino formalizes their engagement. Shakespeare, as always, is asking sweeping questions: how much can we control our feelings for others? How much of who we are and what we believe has been determined by our social milieu? To what degree are we free agents in creating our identity? Is its essence made for us by a higher power, or is it put together piecemeal by our experiences, or both? Our anatomies make it clear that the sexes are fundamentally different. Yet, in Sonnet 20, among others, and in his plays, Shakespeare acknowledges that each of us has qualities traditionally associated with the opposite sex. Queen Margaret, Joan of Arc, and Lady Macbeth are all compared to men in their "undaunted mettle," and Romeo and Lear are compared to women when they cry. Shakespeare questions the extent to which our biological differences must affect every aspect of our life other than the act of procreation and, particularly, affect our attraction to other people. Emilia in *Othello*, for instance, speaks of this issue in a remarkably contemporary, proto-feminist manner:

Let husbands know
Their wives have sense like them. They see, and smell
And have their palates both for sweet and sour,
As husbands have ... And have not we affections,
Desires for sport, and frailty, as men have? (4.3.92–100)

Here Emilia contends that women have the same sexual appetites as men, including a desire for novelty. This position would have been seen as a radical one in western society as recently as the 1950s, if not later.

What chiefly interests me is the way in which five film and television productions – three of *As You Like It* and two of *Twelfth Night* – dramatize the moments of transformation from one gender to another and the homoerotic tension that results. By choosing to adapt a Shakespeare play, these directors to varying degrees express an anxiety about rapid social changes from which Shakespeare represents a kind of escape. Underlying the BBC's and Branagh's adaptations of *As You Like It* is a nostalgia for the heteronormative values ultimately supported by the conclusion of the comedy. Edzard's *As You Like It* expresses a yearning for a pre-Thatcher, Labour-governed Britain, or even for Shakespeare's own society, which was not yet fully given over to the capitalist system that permitted the greed of the 1980s. Supple's *Twelfth Night* confronts anxiety regarding multiculturalism, the contrast with monoculturalism implied by the fact that his colour-blind casting is still a fairly new practice. The audience, not expecting an Asian Viola and an Orsino of African descent, is bound to compare this production with more conventional past productions, inducing in some spectators a wistfulness for the familiar, monocultural *Twelfth Night* of their youth. Supple's own indebtedness to this kind of production is exposed in his obvious homages to Nunn's *Twelfth Night*. Nunn also shows a nostalgia for the heteronormative society of the past in his extradiegetic ending, which reasserts Viola's femininity in a way that Shakespeare's text does not.

What is fascinating about Shakespeare's scripts for the two plays is that no great fuss is made by the female characters who pretend to be boys – their gender switch seems to them no more than a matter of changing their clothes. This is very different from the gravity with which the Puritan writers endow appearance. Rosalind and Viola decide in a mere few lines that they will assume male disguises (*AYLI*, 1.3.113–21; *TN*, 1.2.49–55). The next time they appear in the scripts, the transformation has already been accomplished offstage. This lack of attention in the script to the moments of transformation may also be a result of Shakespeare's confidence in the theatrical conventions of his day. Additionally, he may have found that a sudden, *fait accompli* transformation was essentially more dramatic, more comic, than one witnessed on stage (not to mention simpler and more decorous to effect). Certainly prominent films have taken this approach. In *Some Like It Hot* (1959), we see Jack Lemmon and Tony Curtis as men, dressed in suits, with Curtis aping a woman's voice on the phone to secure their positions with the all-female band. The next shot is a close-up of two pairs of what appear to be female legs in black-seamed stockings and high heels, teetering down a train platform. This close-up is important, because as Lemmon will soon admit, walking on heels is a big challenge for men. The abrupt change is comic, and as the camera pans up the new costumes to the men's prissy, lipsticked mouths, verging on hilarity. Of course, Shakespeare did not have quite the same comic material available to him. The sharp contrast provided by the transformation from big, muscular, hairy man to woman is inherently funnier than the change from girl to boy, boys being still young enough to be androgynous. Furthermore, Shakespeare's audience were aware that their heroines were played by boys anyway, so the humour derives more from the layering of gender than the gender switch. It is the potential for clever lines and situations that the boy-acting-a-girl-acting-a-boy plot toys with more than the actual moment of transformation.

We could go further than Garber and say that not only are "all theatrical gender assignments ... ungrounded and contingent" (39) but so are all stage identities. The lack of fanfare over transgendering reveals perhaps more about Shakespeare's society than about his theatre – his society read a person through his clothes, her appearance. Was it psychologically plausible of Shakespeare to suggest that a girl who is dressed as a boy and presented to society as a boy will be unquestioningly accepted as a boy? I think it was. Could we be assured of the same reality today? I think, despite, or because of, markedly increased androgyny in clothing, hair styles, and gestures, we could. One only has to think of the lyrics of the Killers' pop hit "Somebody Told Me" in which the singer learns that the girl he is after has "a boyfriend who looks like a girlfriend." The phenomenon of the "metrosexual" would seem to support the plausibility of Shakespeare's use of the cross-dressing device even in productions with contemporary settings. Set *Twelfth Night* or *As You Like It* in current, urban settings, and the actresses playing the leads need not trouble themselves too much about slips in their performance (in or out of character) from traditional images of masculinity. Corin actually raises something akin to this point in *As You Like It*, pointing out that the courtly habits of perfuming and kissing hands (habits with which a contemporary metrosexual might feel comfortable) would be ridiculous in the country even while they are accounted good manners in court (3.2.44–62). There are countless examples in film of convincing cross-dressing: *Some Like It Hot* (1959), *Jules et Jim* (1961), *Tootsie* (1982), *Victor/Victoria* (1982), *Yentl* (1983), *Mrs Doubtfire* (1993), *The Crying Game* (1993), and *She's the Man* (2006, based on *Twelfth Night*). What all these films suggest is that society reads gender based on external signs, not on some unchanging essence that exudes from each person determined by their genitals. In contemporary film, a change of clothes is presented as enough, as it was in Elizabethan English drama, to convince the world that a girl is a boy. These films, like Shakespeare's plays, rely to a certain degree on the fact that human beings are wonderfully various in their gestures, postures, and gaits and on the whole also lamentably unobservant of details. We make assumptions based on what is most probable; for example, Duke Orsino's courtiers seem to work on the assumption that it is more likely that the new favourite, Cesario, is a rather effeminate young man (as Orsino does: "all is semblative of a woman's part," 1.4.31–4), or even a eunuch, than that he is actually a shipwrecked female in disguise. Similarly, the people surrounding Mrs Doubtfire dismiss as her personal eccentricities the behaviour that the cinema audience recognizes as emerging from the character's prior life as a man.

The five contemporary productions I have selected span two media and a couple of generations. The first is the 1978 BBC television production of *As You Like It* starring Helen Mirren as Rosalind (described by Rothwell as "somewhat sullen," *History of Shakespeare*, 112). Produced by Cedric Messina, directed by Basil Coleman, and filmed at Glamis Castle in Scotland, it was targeted at the American educational market. I have included it despite its being made for television and earlier than my 1989 start date in order to contrast an earlier treatment of cross-dressing in Shakespeare with the treatments of it in my chosen period.

The second is the 1992 feature film of *As You Like It* directed by Christine Edzard (who also directed *Little Dorrit*, 1988, and *The Children's Midsummer Night's Dream*, 2001). This is an independent film, which Rothwell calls "a labour of love." Edward Fox plays Jacques, and a young unknown, Emma Croft, plays Rosalind. Edzard attempts an allegory between the world of the play and Thatcher's Britain. The court is depicted as the centre of the corporate world; the Forest of Arden is the Docklands, where the dispossessed gather, those rendered homeless by corporate greed. Edzard's choice of setting seems an implicit criticism of Thatcher's National Heritage Acts (1980, 1983), which promoted the preservation of beautiful landscapes and stately homes. These acts were criticized as being motivated by nostalgia for the privileged existence of the upper classes in former days. The thematic focus is on the disparity in the two groups' lifestyles in a way that recalls the Dickensian social protest of *Little Dorrit* and his other works.

The third selection is the 1996 feature film of *Twelfth Night* directed by Trevor Nunn with Helena Bonham Carter and Imogen Stubbs. The two estates, Olivia's and Orsino's, are sharply contrasted. Olivia's is a pre-Raphaelite fantasia, with russet leaves and velvet abounding. Orsino's court is a stagnant military academy. One trailer promoted the film as a gender-bending comedy: "Before Priscilla crossed the desert, Wong Foo met Julie Newmar, and the Birdcage was unlocked, there was *Twelfth Night*." Emma French, in her useful book *Selling Shakespeare to Hollywood*, comments that this tagline situates "the film in the genre of transvestite comedy rather than filmed Shakespeare adaptation" (58). In contrast, *Shakespeare in Love* (1999), a much more financially successful film, conspicuously left the cross-dressing of its heroine out of the advertising material, both poster and theatrical trailer (48). French comments: "The only scene in the trailer in which Paltrow still retains part of her male disguise comes in a love scene where Will Shakespeare unwinds her from the cloth she has used to flatten her breasts. Hollywood's conservatism regarding both the representation of homoeroticism in mainstream films, and genre conservatism in terms of emphasis on the film as a romantic comedy, is evident in both poster and trailer for *Shakespeare in Love*" (49).

My fourth choice is Britain's Channel 4 production of *Twelfth Night* (2003) directed by Tim Supple with Parminder Nagra (of *Bend It Like Beckham* and ER fame) playing Viola. This version, with a contemporary setting, focuses on multiculturalism and political asylum. Richard Armstrong summarizes the mandate of Channel 4's formation in 1982 as "a crucial attempt to find and cultivate a cinema audience for British realism. Channel 4's remit was to appeal to minority groups and the unrepresented in British society" (95). This adaptation reveals heavy influence from Nunn's version in certain cuts and choices, which is why it is included despite not being a feature film.

The fifth production is Kenneth Branagh's film *As You Like It* (2006), set in a British community in nineteenth-century Japan. The tagline, "Romance, or something like it," is an apt hint of the rather vague directorial vision underpinning the film. Many film critics noted, accurately in my view, that the Japanese setting "doesn't amount to much" and is poorly sustained once the action moves to the Forest of Arden (*Variety, Times, Daily Mail*). However, as the haiku opening the film declares, it seems that Branagh intended only "a dream of Japan," and *that* he has, in a way, achieved.

POLITICAL BACKGROUND TO THE FILMS

Shakespeare's theatre was associated with transgression in a way that separates it from cinema today, which is on the whole a socially sanctioned form of entertainment. His theatre was built in Southwark, or "the Liberties," lands outside the City's jurisdiction. Stephen Buhler sums up what that meant for Elizabethan Londoners: "The theatres invited citizens to leave off productive work, visit the precincts where other questionable activities occurred, and witness actors defying the norms of behavior. Depending on the roles they assumed, the players would violate rules of conduct proper to status, class, gender, age, religion, or occupation" (125).

Mainstream Hollywood studios and, to a lesser extent, television stations protect the current status quo rather than challenging it at every turn. As Robert Stam observes, "Contemporary Hollywood films tend to be phobic toward any ideology regarded as 'extreme,' whether coming from left or right" (Stam and Raengo, 43). This pressure to conform translates into different ways of performing transvestite roles. At the same time that Shakespeare's theatre violates certain rules of conduct, his comedies also promote the ideal of companionate marriage, using cross-dressing as an aid in achieving this end rather than as an invitation to "an alternative lifestyle."

Jonathan Crewe, comparing the play *Twelfth Night* to the 1993 film *The Crying Game*, sees in the latter film the same underlying promotion of the norm, even though that norm no longer has marriage at its centre. He sees the film reflecting the "whipsawing oscillation between misogyny and homophobia" he views as characteristic of "the dominant political culture of the present." Crewe was writing in 1995 about a film from 1993, one year after Edzard's *As You Like It* premiered, and three years before Nunn's *Twelfth Night*. "In effect," Crewe continues, *The Crying Game*'s "exemplary negotiation of sexuality, race and gender risks succumbing to a cultural misogyny and homophobia within which the figure of the male transvestite performs a powerful negative function, anticipated in *Twelfth Night*" (107).

If by negative function Crewe means a drive towards heterosexual union, then the figure of the transvestite in the five productions considered here also performs a powerful negative function for those films. That drive exists in the playscripts provided by Shakespeare. The performances colour or alter that drive in three out of five cases. Even if the central couples in these productions end up married, as they do in the Elizabethan scripts, along the way other possibilities have been suggested, and even seriously entertained, in the interstices between lines, where actors and directors can especially leave their stamp on the plays. One aspect of the disguises that should not be forgotten is that, initially at least, Shakespeare envisioned Viola disguising herself not as a young boy but as a eunuch. This is a very different matter from Rosalind's disguise as a "man." The word "eunuch" would seem almost to preclude the possibility of homoeroticism in Orsino's growing attachment to his page.

While the place of feature films in our society may be fundamentally less transgressive than the role of theatre in Shakespeare's society, the film genre to which the Shakespeare adaptation is connected, "heritage cinema," is seen by some scholars as playing a progressive role "by representing the lives of women, lesbians and gay men, ethnic minorities and the disabled in the national past" (Richard Dyer and Ginette Vincendeau, European Heritage Film Conference leaflet, qtd in Monk, *Heritage Film Audiences*, 19). The very fact that the protagonists of both these plays are women, and cross-dressed women at that, is transgressive when compared to the bulk of mainstream films in which heterosexual male heroes predominate. Rosalind especially goes against the norm in that she is the character who drives much of the plot and changes the lives of the other characters. Even in 2015, it is rare to see a feature film with an actress cast as the active protagonist rather than as a sidekick/girlfriend. Nostalgia for comedies that include such powerful heroines may partially explain the immense popularity of loose adaptations of *Twelfth Night* (*She's the Man*) and

The Taming of the Shrew (*10 Things I Hate About You*), which both boast strong female leads.

As You Like It, BBC *Production* (*1978*)

Cedric Messina and Basil Coleman were aiming in their BBC production of *As You Like It* for what one might (with trepidation) term a "straight" production of the play. They wanted to win over a wide television audience and were hoping for video sales to schools afterwards. The style was described by costume designer Robin Fraser-Paye as "vaguely medieval," shot against the bold, romantic backdrop of Glamis Castle and its gardens. Anticipating Emma Croft in the Edzard film and Bryce Dallas Howard in the Branagh film, Mirren's Rosalind makes no real attempt to act like a man once cross-dressed. Her voice, gestures, and walk are still redolently, evenly archly, feminine. The effect is to render the scenes between Rosalind and Orlando (Brian Stirner) in Arden unambiguous. It is hard to believe that Orlando thinks Ganymede is male, since the audience remains unconvinced. Stage conventions are harder to swallow in the real forest of Glamis than in a magical stage Arden. It is as if the two lovers are playing a self-conscious game of pretending that Rosalind is Ganymede (Bulman, 177). There is little of the homoeroticism here that abounds in the two productions of *Twelfth Night* in which, once cross-dressed, Imogen Stubbs and Parminder Nagra respectively are credible as young men. The greater degree of sexual ambiguity in these later productions reflects the radical change in social attitudes towards homosexuality since the 1970s. It also demonstrates two facts: first, that educational entertainment is essentially conservative, and second, that the BBC sought assiduously to avoid any overt politicism that would date its production, intended as it was to live in school and university libraries for some time to come. We cannot know for certain whether or not Shakespeare intended to arouse a frisson in his audience by having love scenes played out between characters who were read as being of the same gender by the other characters. The playful epilogue of *As You Like It* suggests that indeed he did. The BBC production seems to be at pains to suppress this tendency, if it existed in the script, perhaps because of the projected high-school audience. *As You Like It* was made at the end of one of the most tumultuous decades for social change in history. The 1970s saw the Equal Pay Acts (1970, 1973) and the Sexual

Discrimination Act (1975), the election of an outed lesbian MP, Maureen Colquhoun (1977) in Britain, the assassination of Harvey Milk in the United States (1978), and the galvanization of the gay rights movement that resulted. The BBC in 1979 seems not to have felt the same pressure to allude to current socio-political realities in their production as Edzard, Nunn, or Channel 4 did in theirs.

As You Like It, *Christine Edzard's Film*

Edzard attempts a critical commentary on Thatcherism in her *As You Like It*, which failed both in the box office and with critics. *The New Statesman* uses the film as an example of disastrous modernization, finding "its joyless characters wandering through a blasted Docklands in forlorn pursuit of contemporary parallels" (1). This harsh criticism is typical of the 1980s and early '90s in British media. The political polarization of the period resulted in a vitriolic style of debate, even in the realm of culture, as witnessed by the binary extremes in the journalistic disputes over "heritage cinema" and over the talents of director/actor Kenneth Branagh.

Edzard tries to make the contrast between the corridors of corporate power (the Court) and the poverty-stricken Docklands (Arden) more obvious by shifting the structure of Shakespeare's script so that scenes in the different locations follow one another. In the first scene between Celia (Celia Bannerman) and Rosalind (Emma Croft), Edzard pans tables laden with patisseries, and we watch Rosalind, plate heaped, wolf down cream cakes at a steady rate, only pausing to speak. Edzard uses this tea party as a symbol of excess. In her attention to detail in clothes, the director expresses herself both as a woman of the theatre and a director in sync with Shakespeare's own time when clothes indeed made the man. From the writings of Perkins and Stubbes, we can assume that for many Elizabethans, "essence resides in the apparel rather than what lies beneath it" (Callaghan, 33). So it is significant that Edzard dresses all the women in the scene in big designer hats and powerful shoulder pads. The corporate clique, with their luxury cakes and haute 1980s couture, contrast sharply with the shivering outcasts huddled round a rusted garbage-can fire and eating scraps thrown into a pot.

Once Rosalind and Celia plan to escape the court together, Edzard again focuses on conspicuous consumption. The location this time is

Celia's burgeoning walk-in closet. Celia rapidly selects clothes as she hurls rejects to the floor to join others in an increasingly obscene pile. She rams her selections carelessly into a suitcase, showing either her contempt for the consumerism of her father's court, or, more darkly, her spoilt sense of entitlement regarding her expensive clothes. Or, more simply, merely her anger at her father and her need for haste, and perhaps Edzard's wry note that even when heading for a forest, high-society women bring an unnecessary number of clothes.

In the concluding wedding scene, the whole cast gather in the same corporate foyer where all the other scenes at court were shot, only now the foyer is hung with construction cellophane. This construction seems to herald a new era in which outcasts and corporate climbers will work together for a more equitable society (especially as the cellophane recalls the building material of the shelters erected by the homeless in Arden). The old regime has ended and the new regime is beginning.

Edzard, it would seem, is suggesting that Rosalind and her banished father are trying to cure England of its Thatcherism in their solidarity with the homeless. They are healing political ills – the rich and poor are together in final scene, with little distinction in clothing. Alan Walworth notes the healing motif in Shakespeare's script: "Rosalind offers to cure Orlando's love 'madness' by becoming at once both the beloved disguised as a healer and a healer impersonating the beloved" (62), but it is England's madness that Edzard seems most interested in exploring in her production.

Twelfth Night, *Trevor Nunn's Film*

Nunn too creates a kind of upstairs/downstairs political scene, with added shots of Malvolio (Nigel Hawthorne) inspecting the kitchen and the cleanliness of the maids' hands, while Olivia (Helena Bonham Carter) lolls on her sofa, idly glancing at sketches she has done. Nunn deliberately contrasts the two courts: Orsino's estate, run like a military academy, is a traditionally male environment that would be extremely challenging for Viola, a late Victorian lady reared to be delicate and decorative. We can see here the influence of *Some Like It Hot*, which Nunn in his wonderful introduction to his screenplay refers to as "a perfect work of art" (iv). In it Lemmon and Curtis are thrown into several traditionally female situations, like the midnight feast on the train (really a sort of sleepover party), the heart-to-heart in the ladies room, and the swimming and cavorting on the beach, which test their costumes and their self-control to the utmost. In the first scene, for example, Marilyn Monroe, attired only in a sexy black negligee, comments on Lemmon's hot and trembling body as she snuggles up to him in his berth. As "Daphne," he quickly invents an illness that accounts for what is really his state of arousal. Similarly, Imogen Stubbs's Viola rises to the challenge of Orsino's male court, galloping across the countryside, smoking cigars, and playing billiards with great aplomb. Nunn seems to be suggesting that even Victorian men and women, given the chance, could fulfill each other's roles, and therefore the difference between the sexes is cultural as well as anatomical.

Unlike the directors of the other versions of *As You Like It* considered here, Nunn clearly wanted a convincing young man from his heroine. Imogen Stubbs as Cesario is "Chaplinesque," as Samuel Crowl aptly put it (*Shakespeare Bulletin* 15, 37). The *New York Times* once described Chaplin as conveying "an obscure nostalgia ... for liberty, simplicity, poetry, leisureliness, dreams" among not only American audiences but also French, German, and Chinese ones (1 April 1931, 23). That makes Chaplin a perfect model for Stubbs, as Viola is the heroine of what is arguably Shakespeare's most bittersweet play, in Nunn's frankly wistful adaptation. One of the most compelling aspects of Stubbs's performance is her lowering her voice, something not attempted, or at least not sustained, by any of the Rosalinds considered here. This distinction should not be underestimated in its impact on the audience. Robert Stam in *A Guide to the Theory and Practice of Film Adaptation* summarizes: "Ever since the advent of sound, the cinema has been 'vococentric' (Chion), oriented toward the human voice. Voices in the cinema both provide information and provide a focus for spectatorial identification" (Stam and Raengo, 36). In addition to her husky voice, Stubbs strides about with her hands thrust in her pockets, punching Orsino (Toby Stephens) when he teases her about her "rubious" lips. She later pushes Sir Andrew (Richard E. Grant) quite aggressively when he accuses her of breaking his head, and performs quite credibly in their duel. Nunn has Orsino and Viola almost kiss in a highly charged scene in the stable as Feste (Ben Kingsley) sings "Come Away." Furthermore, Antonio (Nicholas Farrell) is clearly in love with Sebastian (Stephen Mackintosh) in this production, embracing him with an expression of great passion on his face as

Sebastian weeps over his drowned sister, and following him with longing eyes as Sebastian leaves for the Duke's court. The *frisson* of transvestite comedy was clearly seen by those marketing Nunn's film as a selling point, as it was marketed with the slogan "Never send a boy to do a man's job, especially if he's a girl."

Twelfth Night, *Channel 4 Production*

Director Tim Supple, while clearly influenced by Nunn's production, adds a whole new dimension to *Twelfth Night* by creating a backstory explaining Sebastian's (Ronny Jhutti) and Viola's (Parminder Nagra) flight from their home. The opening scenes juxtapose Orsino (Chiwetel Ejiofor) listening to an aria from Mozart's *Magic Flute* and Sebastian waking Viola in the middle of the night so that they can escape from their burning house through a window. Some kind of brutal military coup is taking place, and they see their mother beaten and arrested by armed thugs. When they embark with many other hapless citizens, it is as refugees – boat people. Perhaps this emphasis on multiculturalism reflects changes made to immigration policy by the Labour government under Prime Minister Tony Blair after eighteen years of conservative reign in Britain; in particular, the abolition of the Primary Purpose rule in June 1997 allowed foreign spouses of British citizens easier entry.

Supple clearly wanted to create a multicultural society in Illyria. The Channel 4 website notes on the production describe Orsino, played by an actor of African descent, thus: "His dress is plain – though around his neck is a chain of gold and jewels suggesting ideas of exotic lands and great wealth. He wears a plain black shirt and a sarong – a kind of wraparound dress worn by men and women in the Far East. Again this choice of costume is revealing. It hints at the faraway nature of Illyria and introduces clothing that is sexually undetermined. It is a hint of the unreliability of dress as a clue to a person's identity that is central to Viola's disguise" (21). Clearly, the director is also exploring racial stereotypes, adding another dimension to Shakespeare's original questioning of gender and class norms. Illyria displays a postmodern mishmash of cultures; the signifiers attached to each character, especially Orsino as described here, are so conflicted that the director has made it impossible to pigeonhole anyone as specifically adhering to a single culture. Thus, his *Twelfth Night* speaks to our own multicultural time, in which African-American music, Japanese pop art, Korean rock videos ("Gangnam Style"), and international food are part of every western student's experience in a way that would astonish their largely monocultural grandparents. Supple thus bridges the generational divide with his adaptation. To the older generation, he gives the nostalgic pleasure of a beloved Shakespeare comedy; to the young students, he provides a recognizable cultural mélange.

In a scene that echoes the bathtub episode in Nunn's production, Viola massages Orsino's back with oil. The Channel 4 website's promptings about this moment are also elucidating about Supple's conception of the film: "What do you feel is going through Viola's mind at this point? She is likely to be experiencing a mix of emotions. To what extent do you think that these emotions might be intensified by her ethnic origin? Why do you feel the director might have chosen to include only a very brief sequence from Viola's point of view at this point? How might this express her mixed emotions?" (32). The students reading these notes are encouraged to consider the way in which a traditionally reared East Indian woman (probably Hindu or Muslim) would feel about seeing a naked man and being obliged to touch this man in an intimate way. Interestingly, Viola's cultural upbringing in this production makes an excellent modern parallel for the way in which the Elizabethan Viola in Shakespeare's script and the Victorian Viola in Nunn's influential production were also imagined to be reared. Both Nagra and Stubbs initially register shock and embarrassment at the idea of intimacy before marriage and avert their eyes, but their discomfort is replaced by sensual enjoyment as they caress the men they love. Nagra acknowledges this same taboo associated with her ethnic origin in her life today, anticipating the reaction to her first nude scene in the TV show *Compulsion* (2008): "I always said I'd never do a nude scene but now I have. I know there will be a huge fuss when *Compulsion* comes out. It's partly because of the fact I'm Asian. People don't expect me to do that. I never expected myself to do that" (Parminder Nagra Online).

As You Like It, *Branagh's Film (2006)*

Branagh set his *As You Like It* in a European community near a treaty port in Japan in the nineteenth century. Duke Senior's and then Duke Frederick's court is peopled by British merchants and their families who have adopted some aspects of Japanese lifestyle. Curiously, though, once Duke Senior's court is exiled to the Forest of Arden, the countryside is also inhabited by Europeans. In fact, Branagh seems to have employed only two Japanese actors, both in extremely minor roles: as Charles, the bested wrestler (in this case, sumo), and William, the bested lover. This casting decision seems particularly insensitive given the colonial nature of the English-speaking presence in Japan in the nineteenth century (witness Puccini's *Madama Butterfly*). One would think that in his repeated visits to Japan, Branagh could have rustled up a few more native-born actors for his film. In this respect, as in some others I discuss below, the film leaves a curiously old-fashioned impression. It is hard to believe that it emerges from a director who has lived much of his adult life in central London, one of the most multi-cultural cities in the world, and who has a stated policy of blind casting. Thus his nineteenth-century Japan is diversified only with two main characters of African descent and no chief characters of Japanese origin.

Like the Channel 4 *Twelfth Night*, Branagh's film was created during the Blair years of so-called "liberal interventionism." Blair himself was seen by the media as a "new man," sensitive, and sharing domestic duties with his "career woman" wife, Cheri. With a "new man" at the helm of his nation, it was an appropriate time for Branagh to adapt Shakespeare's comedy exploring gender definitions. Given Blair's mistakes in siding with Bush over the non-existent "weapons of mass destruction," perhaps the rather insensitive use of the Japanese setting is merely another expression of the zeitgeist. It might not be unfair to accuse Branagh of a certain nostalgia for the British Empire. His *Henry V*, while it never romanticizes war, exposing all its mud, blood, and suffering, is nevertheless a patriotic film. His *Love's Labour's Lost* shows British men redeeming themselves in the women's eyes with heroic acts during World War II. The class system that exists in Shakespeare's scripts is clearly presented, never blurred. In Branagh's *Hamlet*, the camera enjoys the lavish lifestyle of the aristocracy. In choosing colonial pockets of Japan to set his scene, Branagh is doing more than appropriating Eastern aesthetics: he is (inadvertently) making the Japanese themselves extraneous to the events in the film set in their country. The focus is squarely on, in the words of the introductory titles, "Merchant adventurers [who] brought their families and their followers and created mini-empires."

The same nostalgia for a "simpler" time is evident in the way that Branagh removes any subversive challenge inherent in Rosalind's cross-dressing by having her completely unbelievable as a young man. Of all the cross-dressed actresses here described, Bryce Dallas Howard makes the most negligible attempts to seem boyish. Her voice is unchanged from her female scenes, and her costume does little to conceal her femininity. This has the effect of making everyone who is taken in by her disguise seem half-witted. Orlando, it is true, has only seen Rosalind's face once, and it was mostly hidden by a fan, but even if he does not recognize her as Duke Senior's daughter, it seems incredible that he could believe her to be a boy. The film critics from *TV Guide* and the *Daily Mail* also found her masquerade unconvincing and unsatisfying. Film demands more realism than theatre, and a successful adaptation keeps this fact always in mind.

GENDER TRANSFORMATIONS

As You Like It, BBC *Production*

When Rosalind (Helen Mirren) first appears, she wears a white and gold gown with bell sleeves and a princess waist. Her headdress is elaborate, almost absurd, with curved horn-like protuberances and a white veil. Her cousin Celia (Angharad Rees) is dressed almost identically. What makes the costume even more ridiculous is that the two women are shown playing a form of tennis on the castle grounds wearing yards of flowing fabric with décolletage and detail. The dramatic impracticality of the garments states very clearly that ladies of this class are meant to be decorative only.

When Celia and Rosalind discuss their flight from the court, Rosalind dramatizes with gestures her plans to don a "curtle-axe" and "boar spear." Mirren acts this out with satirical verve. As Christina Luckyj observes about Rosalind in Shakespeare's script, "Her imitation of masculinity promises to expose its artificial construction through parody" (223). Unlike the Violas here considered, Rosalind is given no extra-textual transformation scene. When we next see her in Arden, she wears doublet and hose, with a hat like a fez atop a mass of blond curls. She still looks quite feminine, with obvious eyeliner and mascara, her shapely legs revealed in skin-tight hose. As with all the other productions under scrutiny, when her disguise is threatened, she reasserts her "masculinity" by hitting her interlocutor. Mirren strikes Oliver (Clive Francis) casually on the chest after he remarks on her fainting.

At the conclusion, the transformation back to womanhood is again achieved off-screen. Rosalind and Celia appear with Hymen (John Moulder-Brown) in flowing white Grecian robes, white flowers in their long, loose hair. Mirren's Rosalind has not enjoyed her stint as a man, and throughout her performance gives the impression of barely containing her femininity, which bursts out at the seams in almost parodic feminine gestures, giggles, and squeals.

Coleman retains the epilogue. Speaking straight to the camera, as Mirren delivers the line "If I were a woman," she raises one eyebrow slightly in acknowledgment of the undeniable facts. On television, this is bound to have a bigger overall impact than the same gesture in theatre, depending on the size of the venue. In a big space, the actor coming to the edge of the stage to deliver the epilogue is certainly foregrounded, but not in the intense and utterly revealing way of a close-up in which every flicker and shade of expression can been seen. The lift of Mirren's eyebrow is something only those spectators sitting closest to the stage could witness in a theatre. As Robert Stam remarks, "Unlike literary [or dramatic] point of view, filmic point of view is usually quite precise and literal. We can look 'with' a character, for example, or the director or actor can look directly at us, in a way unavailable to the literary author or character" (Stam and Raengo, 39). While an actor on the stage can look directly at the audience, only some members will be able to see the expression clearly.

As You Like It, Edzard's Film

Edzard makes Rosalind (Emma Croft) as feminine as possible when she is first introduced. She is wearing a long burgundy floral-print dress, a necklace (also a necessary prop – she needs to give it to Orlando, played by Andrew Tiernan, after the wrestling match), and flowing blond locks. The next time we see her, she is in another ultra-feminine ensemble, a long black skirt, pink cardigan, and a white blouse tied with an extravagant bow at the neck.

Unlike Viola in the two *Twelfth Night* productions examined here, Rosalind has no extended transformation scene. As her cousin Celia (Celia Bannerman) packs her suitcase in the walk-in closet, Rosalind briefly tries on a boyish cap while planning her disguise. The next time we see her, in Docklands, she is fully transformed. Her long hair is hidden except for a few waifish wisps. She wears jeans, a work jacket, black wool toque, and construction boots, which, Rothwell remarks, is a "modern unisex style" that "blends nicely with the play's androgynous politics" (*Shakespeare on Screen*, 217). Her costume is, of course, also a show of solidarity with the labouring class.

Edzard makes an interesting and significant decision in act 2, scene 2, as Aliena reveals the author of the verses to Rosalind. Inside a rustic cottage, observed by no one but Aliena, Rosalind removes her cap and ostentatiously shakes out her blond mane. Her gesture changes the whole tenor of the scene, making it even harder for the audience to forget that Rosalind is a girl. It is an action that Shakespeare's boy actor would almost certainly have avoided.

Throughout her scenes in Arden, Croft hardly bothers to seem "masculine." She skips and pirouettes around Orlando, movements few straight male teenagers today would be caught making in front of their straight male peers. In a half-hearted attempt to seem masculine, she punches Orlando on the arm when teasing him about his point-device accoutrements, a gesture she then repeats at the concluding wedding scene. The actor playing Orlando registers no clear discomfort or tension when Ganymede quickly kisses him when Celia "marries" them, although he sweeps his fingers across his lips directly afterwards. What message is Edzard trying to convey with this action? Is Orlando discreetly wiping away the kiss? Or is he savouring it in disbelieving delight? Is he secure enough in his heterosexuality to allow a kiss from a boy pretending to be and closely resembling his true love? Did he enjoy the homoeroticism? Or, finally, does he suspect that Ganymede is a girl?

One of the crucial differences between the transvestism of *As You Like It* and that of *Twelfth Night* is that Rosalind, unlike Viola, concludes the play dressed once again as a woman. Greenblatt points out that "in returning dressed as a woman she also allows for the possibility of a recuperative interpretation"; she is "reabsorbed" into the community as a wife having completed her task of educating Orlando and herself (91). Of course, in Edzard's interpretation, the education Rosalind provides is also a political one for the audience.

Rosalind's final costume is a wedding dress and veil made from construction cellophane. It is highly feminine, with a full ruched skirt, but it also makes a statement. She has not had recourse to the designers, who, we are meant to think, clothed all the women at court in the opening scenes. She has made her gown herself from found materials, the same materials used by foraging Docklanders. This cellophane, which suggests the corporate building being renovated (a word greatly associated with the greedy 1980s and early '90s) is also the same material that Orlando (and the other homeless) use to construct a shelter against the wind and rain. Her dress represents a unifying gesture: the corporate/court world under the old Duke's care will include the dispossessed of Docklands/Arden.

However, the movement towards unification seems to rest mostly with Rosalind. Unlike Shakespeare's Oliver, Edzard's does not offer all his goods to his brother Orlando after he meets and falls for Aliena. Perhaps Edzard was not prepared to recoup Thatcherist consumerism's primary representative in the film to such an extent. Following through with her conception of foregrounding national politics and economics, Edzard cuts the epilogue, in which Rosalind self-consciously plays with the liminal space between genders and between life and theatre.

Twelfth Night, *Nunn's Film*

Anticipating Supple, Nunn opens the film with extratextual material. Martin White observes that opening his productions with a striking image is a tactic Nunn "has frequently used throughout his career" (286). The first time we see Viola (Stubbs), she is wearing an Eastern costume, a yashmak covering her nose and mouth. Long dark hair is visible. Her eyes are made up with Cleopatra-like eyeliner. Her brother (Stephen Mackintosh) is dressed identically. They perform "O Mistress Mine" at a kind of fancy-dress party on board ship. As the song progresses, they reveal that each is wearing a moustache. Nunn thus suggests from the start that appearances are deceptive and that gender and identity are more slippery than we tend to believe. When a storm hits the vessel, Sebastian and Viola rush to their cabin and change into their normal clothes. Viola's clothes are demure and feminine: a long grey skirt, and a white blouse. She has long, wavy blond hair that fans romantically about her in the wind and the sea waves. Her brother dons a dark military uniform with brass buttons.

Figure 8 Viola (Imogen Stubbs) surveys her transformation into a man in Nunn's *Twelfth Night*, 1996.

After the shipwreck, when Viola persuades the captain (Sid Livingstone) to help her with her disguise, Nunn shows the transformation at length (over five minutes of screen time) as the opening credits roll. Nunn is careful to alter Viola's request that she be presented as a "eunuch" to a "boy." There are several possible reasons for his change. Eunuchs were much rarer in the Edwardian period of Nunn's film than in Elizabethan times. The contemporary film audience would be either confused or put off by the idea and disappointed by the lack of homoerotic frisson. Finally, Nunn could simply be following Shakespeare's lead, as the playwright seems to have forgotten about this later in the play. Certainly there are no more references to Cesario's supposed mutilated state after act 1, scene 2. In any case, Nunn's captain picks up scissors and begins to cut Viola's hair, at which she looks distraught and covers her face with her hands. The captain undoes her corset at the back and it falls on the floor. But, as if to suggest that becoming a man will not be the unadulterated, liberating experience one might expect, the constraint of the corset is replaced by the binding of her breasts. Viola puts on her brother's military trousers (from a trunk washed ashore) and stuffs the front with a rolled handkerchief, giving the captain a wry look as she does so. As he helps her bind her breasts, she sighs repeatedly with discomfort. Then she buttons her brother's shirt and jacket (fig. 8) and exchanges her little boots for her brother's bigger ones. The captain looks her up and down, nods his approval, and then teaches her how to walk like a man, striding along the rocks by the sea. Viola also roughens her voice by shouting, something that would have been unnecessary had Nunn chosen to maintain Viola's plan of presenting herself as a eunuch, a castrato prized for his singing voice (1.2.52, 58). The final touch is the application of the same moustache we saw in the opening scene, as Viola looks at a photo of her twin brother, whom she has, to the world, become through this transformation.

The next moment in the film when we are made aware of Viola's disguise is when the fencing master at Orsino's court adjusts her position by clasping her chest. Viola looks alarmed. In the next scene, Orsino teases Cesario about his/her feminine appearance and is pushed roughly away. Then, with Olivia, Viola strokes down her moustache nervously after she utters the word "profanation" in the countess's ear. But the most dramatic reminder of the disguise is during the "I left no ring with her" speech, which Nunn breaks into two parts. The second half is said in front of her bedroom mirror. Viola removes the binding, squeezes her breasts together to relieve their discomfort, and rips off her moustache. This unbinding moment will be recycled to great effect in *Shakespeare in Love* (1999) when Will undresses his muse Viola de Lesseps, who has been pretending to be a boy actor.

We next see Nunn's Viola cry out in alarm as she must follow her master in jumping over a low hedge on her horse. After the ride, Orsino calls Cesario into the room where he is having his bath, and Cesario shields her eyes as she walks past his naked body. Sitting behind him, Cesario is given a sponge to wash his back, something both seem to enjoy hugely. Orsino seems almost disappointed when Cesario abruptly breaks off with "Shall I to this lady?"

Nunn effects a several-staged transformation back to womanhood for Viola. When she and Sebastian compare evidence of kinship, Sebastian, in the same gesture he used on board ship before the opening credits, removes her moustache. Then Orsino proposes to her, and she kisses him passionately on the mouth. He then removes her hat. Later in the same scene, Feste fastens her necklace, found on the beach, around her neck. Finally, as the concluding credits roll, we see Viola in a peach ball gown, her hair cleverly arranged with white roses to hide its shortness. She dances with her brother, Orsino, and Olivia in celebration of the nuptials, and the couples kiss. Nunn, as he did at the opening, keeps the extratextual material distinct from Shakespeare's script with use of the credits. Still, seeing Viola in her "woman's weeds" again has a huge effect on the conclusion of the comedy. With this extradiegetic scene, Nunn reasserts the heterosexual norm. The inserted sequence lessens the ambiguity of Orsino's attraction to Cesario/Viola, making it seem as though the homoeroticism was merely a passing phase or that Orsino somehow sensed Viola's femininity all along, despite her disguise.

Twelfth Night, *Channel 4 Production*

When we first see Viola (Nagra), she is asleep, wearing a feminine nightgown. Later, in the ship's hold on the fishing vessel that rescues her, and in the tailor's shop, she wears a long pink silk dress and a satin shawl in silver and blue with a floral design. Her hair is long and curly. She has a collection of traditional, thin gold bangles on her wrist. The camera lingers in a tilt shot over her female attire before she exchanges it for a male disguise. The richness and utter femininity of her clothes remind us of her high status in her own country, and thus the challenges she will face in becoming not only a man but a lackey to the duke. Of course, if she were really presented as "an eunuch" as in Shakespeare's script, the pressure to speak in a deep voice would at least have been alleviated. But, as in the Nunn film, this line is cut. It is clear that Viola is presenting herself as her own twin brother (without his name, of course) rather than a castrato. In a scene that owes much to Nunn's version, we see her remove her female accoutrements and replace them with masculine ones. As she sits in a tailor's shop, hemmed in by dark rows of suits that surround and tower over her, she looks lost in this male world. In the mirror she sees her brother's image overlapping her own. Then her hair is cut, her breasts are bound, her shirt buttoned, her trousers belted, and her hair gelled back, all in quick close-ups. The sequence concludes with a tilt shot of Viola fully dressed as a man. In contrast to Nunn's treatment, the transformation takes place in the body of Shakespeare's script, occupies little screen time, and is accompanied by aggressive rock instead of Nunn's poignant, lyrical music.

Again taking his cue from Nunn, Supple has Viola deliver her soliloquy "I left no ring with her" alone in her bedroom at night. Whereas Nunn split the speech, having Viola deliver the first half directly after Malvolio leaves her, and the second in solitude in her room, Supple's Viola delivers the whole soliloquy in her bedroom, clad only in her white shirt. She unbuttons her shirt, lies on her bed, and then looks in a three-way mirror, while we the audience are treated to flashbacks of her caressing Olivia's lips and oiling Orsino's naked back – the latter a scene that owes much to Nunn's film.

Nagra's performance of the scene suggests much about Viola's state of mind. Her dwelling on the moments of intimate contact with both Orsino and Olivia suggests that Viola is generally aroused by being in love and in close proximity to Orsino. Her examining her breasts in the mirror seems almost like self-reassurance. She needs to assure herself, after Olivia's obvious conviction that she is a man, of her potential to charm Orsino with her femininity at some future date, and perhaps to ascertain that the binding has done no damage.

Supple sticks to Shakespeare's script and departs from Nunn's example by keeping Viola in male attire at the end. In the script, Orsino demands that she change into her "woman's weeds." Viola herself seems to feel that her identity will be in question, even with her twin brother, until she is dressed in her own clothes again:

> Do not embrace me till each circumstance
> Of place, time, fortune do cohere and jump
> That I am Viola, which to confirm
> I'll bring you to a captain in this town
> Where lie my maiden weeds. (5.1.249–53)

In this final scene Nagra seems strangely subdued, as if the speed of all the couplings has overwhelmed her.

As You Like It, *Branagh's Film*

Branagh dresses his Rosalind in a Victorian white silk dress with a red and white Japanese print on the collar, cuffs, and bustle. Her long russet ringlets are adorned with a red flower pinned over one ear. When she first proposes the idea of disguising herself as a man, the moment is doubly artificial. For one thing, the idea occurs to her because she is "more than common tall," but Bryce Dallas Howard is not particularly tall and is certainly shorter than Celia (Romola Garai). Then, Howard says the word "man" as if it were a foreign term, and Celia echoes this pronunciation, making for a stagey instant on the screen. Branagh cuts Rosalind's subversive lines about her disguise, which mock the fact that even men themselves are posing as men, or self-fashioning themselves in a macho way:

> A gallant curtle-axe upon my thigh,
> A boar-spear in my hand; and in my heart
> Lie there what hidden women's fear there will,
> We'll have a swashing and a martial outside,
> As many other mannish cowards have
> That do outface it with their semblances. (1.3.114–20)

None of the Rosalinds discussed here are costumed according to these lines, and Branagh's Rosalind does not even utter them. In a period setting, having her bear arms would seem to be an obvious way to make her seem more masculine, yet none of the directors have followed Shakespeare's cue. In Branagh's case, the decision to forgo weapons seems to fit with the sharp contrast he has achieved between Duke Frederick's martial court, established by ninjas, ruled by a samurai lord, and entertained by sumo wrestlers, and Duke Senior's rural idyll, in which philosophy is preached and starving courtiers hesitate to kill deer for food. Branagh has clothed the denizens of the Forest of Arden in soft, earthy browns and mossy greens, in striking contrast with the shiny black armour of Duke Frederick (Brian Blessed looking much in this role as he did as Exeter in Branagh's *Henry V*), and the clear primary colours (blue and red) of his daughter and niece's gowns. Perhaps the earth-toned costuming of Duke Senior and his retinue reflects the influence of environmentalism on Branagh's conception of Arden. Environmentalism and Asian philosophy are today's answer to Shakespeare's pastoralism. A Zen garden is the trendy conception of escape from urban bustle.

If Shakespeare did equip his Rosalind as Ganymede with weaponry, he would have incurred the ire of the stiffer elements in his society and perhaps titillated his usual spectators. The idea of a girl wearing male attire and carrying weapons was considered shocking by many in that era and earlier, as is witnessed by the stern pronouncement made by one of Shakespeare's sources, Raphael Holinshed, regarding Joan of Arc's "shamefullie reiecting hir sex abonminablie in acts and apparel, to haue counterfeit mankind" (604–5). Philip Stubbes in 1583 was even more damning of women who wore men's clothes: "Our Apparell was given us as a signe distinctive to discern betwixt sex and sex, and therefore one to weare the Apparel of another sex is to ... adulterate the veritie of his owne kinde. Wherefore these Women may not improperly be called *Hermaphroditi*, that is, Monsters of bothe kindes, half women, half men." Audiences today would likely have the opposite reaction, viewing the adoption of weaponry as a sign that Rosalind was a proto-feminist character, taking charge and well able to defend herself, admirably strong and powerful. (Witness the female role models created for children by Disney: the cross-dressing warrior Mulan, the arrow-shooting Merida in *Brave*.) Other spectators might find weaponry regrettable in either sex.

Rosalind, Celia, and Touchstone leave Duke Frederick's court in their usual garb, but when we see them next, the two women are walking in the forest transformed by their attire into country folk. The camera lingers for a moment on Rosalind's buff-coloured suede boots and then pans up her body, taking in her warm brown pantaloons, light tan jacket, and chocolate cap, charmingly set over her reddish curls. While the costume is very different from her frilly Victorian gown, it nevertheless reveals her slim shape. To the modern audience, the outfit would not be at all odd on a girl. This is one of many aspects of the cross-dressing scenes that is radically altered since Shakespeare's day. Women in Shakespeare's day did not wear doublet, hose, and weaponry (Moll Frith, the Roaring Girl, excepted). The distinctions between male and female dress were dramatic. Now, when men and women's clothes are largely interchangeable, Rosalind's cross-dressing does not seem like a male disguise, and therefore her act is even more unbelievable. It appears that Branagh did not want to dim the glamour of his young star or render the wooing scenes with Orlando sexually ambiguous by having Howard deepen her voice or disguise her face with facial hair, as Stubbs did in *Twelfth Night*. In fact, as Hatchuel observes in her review of the film, "Branagh revels in the reality of the female body to add touches of comedy as when a naked Rosalind bathes in the river only to hide rapidly under a tree to avoid Orlando's scrutinizing look" (367). (The scene is reminiscent of one in Disney's 1998 animated feature *Mulan*.) The consequence of Rosalind's obvious femininity, however, is a slackening of tension. If Rosalind makes so little effort to conceal her gender, the audience cannot help feeling it is not really necessary for her to be disguised, and furthermore, that her disguise seems to have no motivation other than to give her the freedom to test Orlando's love. Certainly, after Rosalind meets her father, she no longer needs the disguise for her own and Celia's protection.

It seems that there is more at stake with Viola's disguise than Rosalind's, as, until her brother's revelation, Viola is an unprotected young woman in a foreign and hostile court. Rosalind always has both Celia and Touchstone to act as chaperones, and then later, recourse to her father if she needs him. The fact that she is never isolated in the same way as Viola means that she is free to refer to her femininity without obfuscation with Celia and Touchstone, a kind of pressure valve. Viola only hints at her femaleness in double entendres, mostly with Feste but occasionally with other characters. Her only release from the tension of maintaining her disguise is when she is alone, soliloquizing. Furthermore, the differences in their characters also affect their need for male disguise. Viola is a more passive character, one who reacts to others and is open to experience; she "goes with the flow," while Rosalind seems more in control. By the conclusion of the play, Rosalind is almost a Svengali, manipulating the other characters in a way that appears, through her own intention, almost magical. The male disguise thus seems largely a whim on her part, in order to become more intimately acquainted with Orlando until she deems him ready for her female self. Perhaps her stance is a result of being a duke's sole heir: she has been prepared for a life of power and responsibility.

In contrast, Viola's revelation of her femaleness is completely outside her control. It happens because of her brother's chance encounter with Olivia's household. Without his arrival like a *deus ex machina*, Viola would be in a tight spot indeed, hopelessly in love with a man who believes her also to be a man and wants to kill her for her supposed betrayal. Rosalind, in contrast, seems not only aware of most of the events in the play but actually behind them. She is also unique among Shakespeare's cross-dressed heroines in spending most of her time as a boy, pretending to be a girl, to "cure" Orlando of his love-sickness.

CONCLUSION

These two comedies, both with cross-dressed heroines at their centre, created by Shakespeare with only one other play (*Hamlet*) intervening, have much in common. In both, as Crewe sums up, "the attractive young ... transvestite turns out to be what 'everyone' really wants, or wants to be identified with, hence his 'timeless', 'universal', and unique appeal. All things to all men and all women, he is posited as the universal object of desire, or, as *The Crying Game* puts it, 'anybody's type'" (107).

What is it that makes Rosalind and Viola so universally desired? They have in common the ability to articulate passion. In Nunn's version, Viola captures Orsino's heart when she responds to his question about the quality of the love song: "It gives a very echo to the seat / Where love is throned" (*Screenplay*, 43). Orsino, impressed, replies, "Thou dost speak masterly" (44). Crewe's description of Viola as what "everyone wants to be identified with" is therefore acute. Orsino wishes he had made Cesario's remark. He admires Cesario for expressing feelings so enviably well. Similarly, in many productions, Olivia truly falls for Viola when she delivers the "Make me a willow cabin at your gate" speech (1.5.257f). Viola is able to articulate Orsino's passion, unlike his other, older, more conventional *nuncios*, because she feels the same passion (but for Orsino) herself. Again, Phoebe falls for Rosalind when she is passionately and wittily defending the rejected suitor, Silvius. Rosalind knows what it is to have one's love threatened, as hers is for Orlando by her disguise. The sincere and gifted articulation of passion is what makes these cross-dressed heroines lovable to everyone.

It is also probable that nostalgia for this kind of rhetoric is in part what attracted these directors to adaptation of these plays. Not only are these characters caught in the throes of grand passions, such as contemporary literature rarely explores, substituting more tentative, cynical, or dysfunctional feelings, but they are also able to give eloquent voice to these profound feelings.

Despite their many common features, Shakespeare alters his second major transvestite comedy in an important way. In his *Twelfth Night*, Viola remains dressed as a man at the end, and her reinstatement as a female is to be indefinitely delayed, as Stephen Orgel points out, by the fact that the captain who is taking care of her clothes is in the vengeful Malvolio's custody ("Nobody's Perfect," 27). Rosalind, on the other hand, ends the play "in a sign and shape so unmistakably female as to give joy to Orlando and consternation to Phoebe" (Garber, 76). Yet the clarity of this outward femininity is deliberately confused by the epilogue, in which Rosalind "deliberately breaks the frame to acknowledge the 'real' gender of the actor ('If I were a woman, I would kiss as many of you as had beards that pleased me, complexions that liked me, and breaths that I defied not' [5.4.214–17]) and [calls] attention to her underlying male 'identity' as an actor ('If I were a woman'). [By these means,] Rosalind opens up the possibility of a male/male homoeroticism between male audience member and male actor that is the counterpart of the male/male homoeroticism animating Orlando's conversations with Ganymede, as well as the converse of the female/female homoeroticism figured in the play by Phebe's infatuation" (Garber, 76).

The layers of gender possibilities are therefore more complex in *As You Like It* than in the more streamlined *Twelfth Night* in which we see Viola as a girl only in one short scene. Rosalind has, in contrast, three scenes dressed as a woman. It is tempting to speculate about the boy actors who originally played these roles. Did the same actor who played Rosalind play Viola a year or so later when his voice had begun to break, and so might Shakespeare have accommodated his increasingly obvious maleness by cutting scenes in which he had to be female? If that were the case, why did Shakespeare initially envision Cesario as a eunuch? Certainly, the anomalies around the lines about who should sing the songs in the play seem to suggest the actor playing Viola, while originally intended as the singer, was unable to fulfill that task.

In the five productions examined here, the pressures on the actors playing Viola and Rosalind were quite different. Three out of four of the directors felt it necessary to show the cross-dressed heroine relieving herself of her disguise away from prying eyes. The BBC version, which adheres most faithfully to Shakespeare's script, is the only production that does not show the transvestite character removing part of her costume. At the same time, Mirren's and Howard's costumes and approaches to the role are the least "masculine" of the five actresses, so it is unnecessary to remind the audience of their femininity. Both productions of *Twelfth Night* insert a transformation scene. Contrastingly, in all three productions of *As You Like It*, the transformation of gender, both at beginning and end of the play, takes place, as in the playscript, offscreen. Both productions of *Twelfth Night* take the disguise seriously, and the actresses are convincing as young men, resulting in scenes charged with homoeroticism. In all the productions of

As You Like It, the actresses barely conceal their femininity, and therefore any transgressive suggestiveness with Orlando is minimized, although accordingly maximized with Phoebe. Is homoeroticism between women somehow deemed more palatable for audiences than homoeroticism between men? Channel 4's *Twelfth Night* is the boldest in suggesting homoerotic attraction between Olivia and Viola, and also Orsino and Cesario, reflecting contemporary British society's greater degree of comfort with sexual ambiguity. In addition, Supple's use of a backstory "has the effect of disrupting Shakespeare's authority," according to Sarah Brown et al.: "Even though the production at first seems comparatively faithful, subtle adjustments allow the adaptor's 'voice' to displace that of Shakespeare" (9). Branagh's *As You Like It* shies away from such homoerotic frisson, even though it is the most recent filmed version of either play. Does this fact, coupled with the nineteenth-century colonialist setting, suggest a nostalgia on the director's part for a time when gender identities seemed simpler, more clear-cut? The earliest production, the BBC's *As You Like It*, is, more predictably, equally uncomfortable with sexual ambiguity, emphasizing Rosalind's femininity in all her scenes with Orlando.

These productions, unsurprisingly, show as much about the particular time and circumstance in which they were created as they do about Shakespeare. What Robert Stam writes about adaptation from novel to film applies equally well to adaptation from play to film: "The question becomes whether an adaptation pushes the [original work] to the 'right' by naturalizing and justifying social hierarchies based on class, race, sexuality, gender, region, and national belonging, or to the 'left' by interrogating or leveling hierarchies in an egalitarian manner" (Stam and Raengo, 42).

Two out of five of the adaptations discussed here, the BBC's (1978), which intended to deliver the worshipped bard's collected works to audiences in schoolrooms and living rooms everywhere, and Branagh's (2006), which attempted to give *As You Like It* a fresh, trendy look (a Japanese aesthetic) for a new generation, seem to uphold a conservative status quo, or at least express some form of nostalgia for it. On the other hand, as Stephen Buhler writes, "The cultural significance invested in Shakespeare lends additional authorization for all manner of transgressive enterprises" (126). Three of the productions discussed travel more in this direction. In 1992, Edzard used Shakespeare to criticize Thatcherism. In 1996, Nunn employed him to explore sexual ambiguity, and in 2004, Channel 4 enlisted him to depict the causes and results of multicultural societies. Thus, these three could be viewed as nudging the plays towards the "left" in the political or social arenas. However, none of them tamper with Shakespeare's conclusions, which, true to traditional comic form, uphold the heterosexual norm of men marrying women.

9

Propaganda and the Other in Branagh's *Henry V* and Fiennes's *Coriolanus*

While in *Hamlet*, *Titus*, and *Prospero's Books* the characters are cloaked in the Gothic or grotesque guise of extreme emotions and even madness born of grief and lust for vengeance, and in *As You Like It* and *Twelfth Night* the heroines adopt male roles to interrogate their future mates, in the political plays discussed in this chapter, rhetoric is the disguise that hides the truth. In Shakespeare's *Henry V* and *Coriolanus*, the themes of war and class conflict are as volatile as in the dramas of our own day. As Shakespeare obviously wrote during specific political moments, he must have soaked up the atmosphere of the time and reflected on its dominant issues. He would have had a honed feel for the censor's knife – how much he could get away with. The tension between Shakespeare's articulation of the status quo – what I term here propaganda – and his own criticism of it is what makes these two plays especially fascinating. Just as riveting is what two contemporary film directors make of this tension, and how they too respond to the political pressures of their own time in their art.

Propagandizing is a narrowing process: by winning converts to a particular view, it necessarily closes them off to other views. In both the plays and films examined here, propaganda works to divide people into smaller groups, groups that are antagonistic to one another – English against French, patrician against plebeian – by emphasizing what binds one group together and separates them from others. In this way, propaganda is analogous to what Jan Willem Duyvendak terms "the politics of home," so much a part of western leaders' rhetoric today. Apparently, what we truly want from our leaders is that they reflect, and protect, our own sense of home: "What is felt as home

... develops out of a dialectic between what belongs to the place and what does not; what is mentally near and what is far; what feels like 'inside' and what does not; who are considered 'we' and who are labeled 'others' ... feeling at home is a highly selective emotion: we don't feel at home everywhere or with everybody. Feeling at home seems to entail including some and excluding many" (31, 39).

When Henry V mounts his military campaign to regain the French lands won by his ancestor Edward, he must also carry out a program to unify his English soldiers against the enemy. When the Roman state calls itself a republic, its leaders must be seen to be approved of by the people, even while those leaders deny the people their daily food. The Roman authorities give rights with one hand while taking away with the other. In each case, propaganda operates so that the citizens will internalize the state's message: war against France is good – they have taken our land and now we will retrieve what is ours; patrician generals like Coriolanus are good – they keep the people safe from invaders. Shakespeare presents these authoritarian views, but he also leaves plenty of room in his plays for dissenting voices. Henry's English are not at all the band of brothers he pretends they are – they are divided amongst themselves into Welsh, Irish, Scottish, and English sub-groups, into aristocrat, yeoman, and common classes, and, perhaps most importantly, into pro-Henry and anti-Henry factions. Even messages promulgated by the pro-Henry faction, the Chorus and Hal's Eastcheap tavern friends, Shakespeare renders ambiguous by the juxtaposition of their scenes. The Chorus's glorification of Henry is often undercut by the ridiculous aping of it by the lowlife characters, whose hearts may be in the trim but whose diction is ludicrous, and whose behaviour is slothful. In *Coriolanus*, Menenius with his belly parable may convince the plebeians around him of the patricians' service to them, but they are still without corn. Shakespeare weighs the pros and cons of absolutism through his presentation of Coriolanus, who, despite his role in vanquishing the dictator Tarquin, is no republican; and thus, the playwright safely presents a consideration of the absolute monarch on England's throne, James I.

People are far more likely to recognize propaganda in news reports, advertising, and political speeches than to acknowledge its presence in their visual entertainment. This is especially true with the medium of film, which is so powerful and all-consuming that it is extremely hard to maintain a critical distance when watching. This task becomes even more difficult when the narrative has been constructed by a master like Shakespeare, who was a highly experienced playwright when he composed *Henry V*, and especially *Coriolanus*. He knew exactly how to build suspense and manipulate the emotions of his viewers. He himself built in checks that Brecht would have admired, however. The Chorus in *Henry V*, by its constant exhortations to help with the dramatic illusion, reminds us that it is just that: an illusion. The moral ambiguity of all the characters in *Coriolanus* and of the title character in *Henry V* also stops the audience from completely submitting to our emotions, although Shakespeare lets us forget these aspects when it suits him (in the Agincourt pre-battle oration, for example). However, contemporary film directors are acutely aware that the language and setting can be alienating even while the narrative and characters are powerful. Thus, they make special efforts to overcompensate, giving the audience as much to enjoy visually as possible and stripping down the dialogue so as to speed the plot along. The Shakespeare adaptor's anxiety to make the material entertaining means that there is even less chance that the audience can retain a critical distance and thereby spy out the propaganda underlying the projects. Furthermore, the film medium's drive towards realism and clearly understood motivation means that its directors and actors are tempted to flatten out ambiguities that the theatre would accommodate or even embrace.

The two films discussed here, Kenneth Branagh's *Henry V* (1989) and Ralph Fiennes's *Coriolanus* (2012), are based on plays that preclude simple interpretations and pat resolutions. They may both be set in times and locations in which characters know to which tribe they belong and to which beliefs that tribe is attached, but Shakespeare constantly problematizes any expressed certainty by allowing each side a chance to propagate its views. The directors, however, in their attempt to make their films as accessible and palatable to modern spectators as possible, market their films as having a single aim. Branagh tried to redeem *Henry V* from its reputation as a jingoistic, pro-war, nationalistic play by inverting this impression through imagery. It was billed rather as a coming of age, anti-war film: the young king maturing as a leader, the battle scenes brutal and muddy, as in Orson Welles's *Chimes at Midnight*. This interpretation was inspired by the RSC post–Falklands War production of the play in which Branagh starred under Adrian Noble's direction. The French are rehabilitated as civilized (especially the king, played by Paul Scofield) rather than silly adversaries, as they were in Olivier's version, thus making the war against them seem more questionable. Despite publicity crews' spin-doctoring, however, the fascinating ambiguities in the play survive in the film. It presents the militarist as well as the pacifist viewpoint and is laudatory as well as critical of its eponymous hero. Furthermore, as James Quinn and Jane Kingsley-Smith express it, "Although the ambiguities Branagh discovered in the play might suggest a deconstructionist perspective at work, they were limited in their radical potential by Branagh's insistence ... that Shakespeare's meaning was latent in the text, to be drawn out by the director" (166).

Alexander Leggatt said of *Henry V*, "In criticism and performance it becomes, perhaps more obviously than any other play of Shakespeare's, a way of revealing the biases of its interpreters" (*Political Drama*, 114). This quality makes it ideal for examining the propaganda involved in promoting the film version. Shakespeare himself explores the whole notion of propaganda, or, to use a less modern, loaded term, rhetoric, the art of persuasion, in both plays. In the film of *Henry V*, propaganda works on at least three levels: 1) Shakespeare renders English history entertaining and patriotic for an audience that has just sent soldiers off to Ireland; 2) Henry himself tries to promote his war and his reign after the perceived waste of his youth; and 3) Branagh repackages the play as an anti-war piece rather than a play that glorifies war. Similar levels of propaganda can be discerned in the film of *Coriolanus*: 1) Shakespeare considers the strengths of the absolute monarchy of James I versus a more parliamentary system from the safe distance of Roman history; 2) Coriolanus, at the behest of his friends and family, tries to present himself as a politician (consul, then conciliator) when he is truly only a soldier; and 3) Fiennes transforms the play into an anti-war piece in which personal loyalties and rivalries are paramount.

It is typical of Shakespeare that when he is using a kind of propaganda to sell his subject, he nevertheless deconstructs the whole concept of propaganda in the play. This exploration of spin-doctoring emerges early in *Henry V*, as Henry's reputation is discussed by all the characters, French and English alike. As we have learned from *Henry IV, Parts 1 and 2*, Henry has carefully crafted his public image and is now reaping the rewards. So much of politics, Shakespeare suggests through the play, is orchestrated posturing. The dauphin does not like the image of France as weak and hesitant that his father's decisions have perpetuated. To correct that image, he sends tennis balls to Henry – an irreverent, playful gesture meant to show that the French are utterly unconcerned by Henry's threats. In response, with more posturing, Henry sends Exeter. Branagh heightens the menace in Shakespeare's oration by casting Brian Blessed, a massive presence, in the role, and dressing him in full armour – looking like Robocop, as Michael Pursell observed (119). Later in the play, before the gates of Harfleur, Henry teaches his soldiers how to manufacture the image of the fierce soldier: "Imitate the action of the tiger. / Stiffen the sinews, conjure up the blood, / Disguise fair nature with hard-favoured rage ..." (3.1.6–8). In *Coriolanus*, Volumnia instructs her son in the opposite process, trying to soften his soldier's ways into those of the political candidate:

> Go to them, with this bonnet in thy hand;
> ... Thy knee bussing the stones – for in such business
> Action is eloquence, and the eyes of th'ignorant
> More learned than the ears – waving thy head
> With often, thus, correcting thy stout heart,
> Now humble as the ripest mulberry. (3.2.73–9)

Both Henry and Volumnia use the rhetorical strategy of *"actio"* to wreak political change – both are honest in admitting that politics requires conscious, rehearsed performance from those involved. It is Coriolanus's unwillingness to misrepresent himself by performing that is his most attractive quality and also his downfall: "I will not do't, / Lest I surcease to honor mine own truth" (3.2.120–1).

The Chorus in *Henry V* tends to spout the patriotic Elizabethan line, most obviously by participating in pro-Essex, pro-Irish campaign propaganda with this speech:

> Were now the General of our gracious Empress –
> As in good time he may – from Ireland coming,
> Bringing rebellion broached on his sword,
> How many would the peaceful city quit
> To welcome him! (5.0)

Queen Elizabeth had selected the Earl of Essex, her favourite, to lead the campaign to subdue the Irish. She had sent him off on 27 March

1599, around the time that Shakespeare must have been writing the play. However, Shakespeare was not content merely to let this piece of choric flattery rest. The dialogue following this speech is the absurd leek conflict between Fluellen and Pistol in which members of Henry's army, so far from cheering their victorious leader, are divided along cultural lines. Fluellen objects to Pistol's joke about the leek that Fluellen wears to celebrate the Welsh patron, Saint Davy, and makes him pay for it with blows. Pistol is a lamentable but key representative of the English soldiery in the structure of the play; his encounter with a Monsieur Le Fer essentially represents the Battle of Agincourt. So it is significant when Pistol confides to the audience that he will become a bawd and a thief when he returns to England; he will claim that the bruises he has from Fluellen's beating are wounds honourably received in battle. Branagh cuts this chorus and the leek scene entirely, so the pro-Essex propaganda, a rare topical allusion, and the debunking of it, are lost. This cut is understandable, as the reference to the Irish campaign is obscure to most contemporary viewers, as is the leek-wearing tradition. Branagh explains in the introduction to his screenplay that he found the leek scene "resoundingly unfunny" (xv). The new medium too means that Branagh can show a full battle in realistic detail. By the time Shakespeare writes *Henry V*, he no longer attempts to represent full battle on stage. Perhaps he was stung by Ben Jonson's mocking lines in the prologue of *Every Man in His Humour* that actors "with three rusty swords / And help of some few foot-and-half-foot words, / Fight over York and Lancaster's long jars" (lines 9–11) – a reference to Shakespeare's representation of the War of the Roses in his early history tetralogy.

The patriotism exhibited in the Essex speech, and in the Chorus's speeches generally, contributes to the sense of wistful reminiscence in the play; indeed, patriotism has long been classified by experts as a form of nostalgia. Beardsley Ruml, speaking to the American Psychological Association in the 1930s, "elaborated on this idea, insisting that nostalgic sentiments 'are the foundation of patriotism and nationality'" (Laurence, 1933, 15, in Sprengler, 20). James Quinn and Jane Kingsley Smith summarize the patriotic aspect of Branagh's first film: "It is through its sympathetic, positive and passionate portrayal of the royal figurehead, and through such related extra-textual discourses as those pertaining to the Prince of Wales, that Branagh's film seems to promote the idea of nation" (172). Many British reviewers accused

Branagh of conservatism simply for adapting this particular play. Left-wing British critics particularly excoriated Branagh's consultation with Prince Charles over the role of Henry, viewing this as a kind of endorsement of the class hierarchy. (Kate Kellaway of *The Observer* affirmed that Branagh has suffered "years of toxic press," while Quinn and Kingsley Smith claim that Branagh's relationship with Prince Charles has "impacted on contemporary readings of Branagh's film," 171.) *Henry V* emerged at the tail end of the heritage-film debate in which films like Branagh's, set in Britain's past and seemingly celebrating an English victory, were seen as being ideologically complicit with Thatcherism (Monk, 177). Conversely, some of the hostility aimed at Branagh by the British press may have had diametrically opposed motivations – the right-wing papers disliking the idea of a working-class boy representing Shakespeare to the world (Mark White, 94).

The Chorus provides a constant diet of pro-Henry V, English hero-king propaganda, calling him "this star of England" and "the mirror of all Christian kings" (2.0) and attributing to him "a largess universal, like the sun" (4.0). Most notorious of all in the play is the pro-war propaganda. The Chorus depicts war as an exciting game that every Englishman is eager to play: "Now all the youth of England are on fire ... and honour's thought / Reigns solely in the breast of every man. / They sell the pasture to buy the horse" (2.0). Yet this rhetoric is again undercut by what directly follows. We see the Eastcheap tavern men fighting over Mistress Quickly. The only detail we hear of the glorious enterprise upon which they are about to embark is Pistol's cynical "For I shall sutler be / Unto the camp, and profits will accrue" (2.1.106–7). The first and last revelation we have about the mirror of all Christian kings in this scene is that he has killed Falstaff's heart – this from those who know and love Henry best. Even as early as the preparation period for his assumption of the role of Henry V at the Royal Shakespeare Company, Branagh had viewed Shakespeare's king as complex and tortured by guilt "over his father's seizure of the crown from Richard II as well as his own reckless past" (Mark White, 28).

Branagh maintains his anti-war stance with his version of this scenic arrangement. The Chorus's speech is cut to a mere five lines from forty-three, and Derek Jacobi is directed to deliver them in a "gently ironic" manner (*Screenplay*, 13). The scene that follows is also drastically cut, including Pistol's plans to make money off the war.

However, to his credit, Branagh leaves in the description of the king killing Falstaff's heart. He even interrupts the scene with an added short sequence in which Mistress Quickly looks anxiously at the sleeping Falstaff. Branagh then boldly adds to the ambiguous portrait of the king by interposing a flashback in which Falstaff delivers to his adoring tavern audience some of his best, most endearing lines from *Henry IV, Parts 1 and 2*.

The Chorus before Harfleur in Shakespeare's play continues the glorification of war and Henry's soldiers with lines like: "For who is he, whose chin is but enriched / With one appearing hair, that will not follow / These culled and choice-drawn cavaliers to France?" (3.0). (Branagh shifts the lines to an earlier scene, to introduce the French court.) We have already seen that the English army is filled not with choice-drawn cavaliers but with tavern ne'er-do-wells like Pistol, Nym, and Bardolph – the last of whom the king will execute for stealing from a French church. Shakespeare reminds us of the motley nature of the English troops, bringing them back on stage mere moments after Henry delivers his ultimatum, "Once more unto the breach." Bardolph seems to parody his king's exhortation with his "On, on, on, on, on! To the breach, to the breach!" These lines were delivered in the most overtly mocking, sarcastic tones in the 2016 production at Canada's Stratford Festival (*Breath of Kings: Redemption*), rendering the parody unmistakably obvious. In the original text the lines are followed by the three tavern cronies and their boy avoiding the breach altogether and wishing they were in an alehouse in London instead, until Fluellen comes to chastise them for their cowardice. Branagh cuts this scene, economically suggesting it by having Fluellen chase them towards the breach.

Film critic James Chapman in *Past and Present: National Identity and the British Historical Film* quotes Branagh's intentions, relayed in a *Times* interview, as an effort to liberate *Henry V* from its status as propaganda. Branagh contended that the play needed "to be reclaimed from jingoism and World War Two associations" (140). Despite the cuts mentioned above, he often succeeds in this endeavour. He suggests the ambiguity that exists in the play towards the French campaign and even towards the king, especially with his inclusion of the Williams' scene (*Screenplay*, 72). He reflects that he could have gone even further in problematizing the hero-king: "The way I deal with the King killing the prisoners ... I could have possibly been braver ...

and not ... lost the sympathy of the audience for the central character" (qtd in Cartmell, 172). His bias, however, a contemporary one, is still evident. To appeal to a modern audience, the film must seem to condemn war, whereas Shakespeare's play, emerging from a society that largely equated militarism with manliness, was not under such a constraint. Branagh's way of expanding on the anti-war elements that exist in the play, such as Henry's brutal threats to Harfleur and Burgundy's description of France's ruination, was to present the destruction in gory detail. Branagh also explains his graphic approach to the battle scenes as an attempt to be historically accurate: "All the blood and guts was quite deliberate. In fact, if eyewitness accounts of the Battle of Agincourt are to be believed, we were rather modest in our representation of it" (qtd in Sally Ogle Davis, "Under the Lion's Skin"). Branagh explains the long tracking shot of the corpse-strewn Agincourt battlefield, with the king carrying the boy's body across his shoulder: "After the close-up carnage of Agincourt, I wanted to reveal as much of the devastation as possible" (quoted in Alan Roberts's review of *Henry V*). Branagh clearly indicates that he was intending to propagate, or at least appear to be propagating, an anti-war message by deglamorizing war by showing its catastrophic effects.

Ralph Fiennes claims to have the same anti-war aim in making his film *Coriolanus*. In the DVD commentary, he says, "We wanted to show the horror, the violence" of war. He also explains that he views his warrior-hero, who displays "a weird ecstasy in the middle of all this nightmare," as "psychopathic." This is not dissimilar to the way Branagh describes his Henry V: "I wanted to make [Henry] as human as possible but as vulnerable as possible. Because it was a film that wanted to boost morale, Olivier's performance [in *Henry V*, 1945] presented a tremendously resolved, glamorous, handsome hero. But the text indicates a man of doubt who has to suppress his own innate violence, who is volatile and unpredictable" (Tomlinson, 60).

Both directors' comments again show how much attitudes to war have changed since Shakespeare's day. In Jacobean England, a military hero was a figure deserving admiration; our society, in contrast, tends to use soldiers in wartime and neglect or criticize them in peace, viewing them almost as liabilities. At least one reviewer (Manohla Dargis of the *New York Times*) and Fiennes himself compare *Coriolanus* to *Apocalypse Now* (1979). The implication is that Shakespeare's protagonist has crossed the line from service to his country to killing for bloodlust and power, like Kurtz (Marlon Brando) in Francis Ford Coppola's Vietnam film. The only military man permitted to come across as an unambiguous hero in films today is an Allied soldier in World War II. Contemporary western culture tends to promote tolerance and compassion much more than valour, but Shakespeare's era aped the Romans in the admiration of physical courage. No piece of writing today would include a line like "Valour is the chiefest virtue, and / Most dignifies the haver" (2.2.84–5). However, Jonathan Crewe perceives even in Cominius's encomium of Coriolanus's military prowess "ironies and contradictions that provide much of the play's substance" (Pelican *Coriolanus*, xxxvi). Cominius's mention of the fallen tyrant Tarquin renders equivocal such descriptions of Coriolanus as this one: "As weeds before / A vessel under sail, so men obeyed / And fell below his stem" (2.2.105–7). This is an image of relentless authority ill-suited to a new republic; Fiennes cuts it. As in *Henry V*, the pro- and anti-absolute monarchy and pro- and anti-war sentiments are so intermingled in this play that the impression cannot fail to be ambiguous. Some lines, which must even in Shakespeare's day (long before Wilfred Owen named "*dulce et decorum est pro patria mori*" the "old lie") have come across as unbalanced, seem more extraordinary now. Volumnia's remark about her son's return from the battle in Corioles, which Fiennes maintains, is a prime example: "O, he is wounded; I thank the gods for't" (2.1.119). Even more alienating for a modern audience is Volumnia's comment to Virgilia, also kept in the film: "Hear me profess sincerely: had I a dozen sons, each in my love alike, and none less dear than thine and my good Martius, I had rather had eleven die nobly for their country than one voluptuously surfeit out of action" (1.3.20–5).

The horrified reactions of Virgilia (Jessica Chastain) to these hyperbolic statements provide an alternative discourse that is much more palatable to contemporary audiences. Fiennes also changes the action to make Coriolanus's eagerness for battle seem more idiosyncratic and strange than in Shakespeare's play. In the play, in act 1, scene 7, Martius (he becomes Coriolanus after his victory at Corioles) asks the men "to express his disposition, / And follow Martius." The First Folio stage direction reads: "They all shout and wave their swords, take him up in their arms, and cast up their caps" (line 75, Oxford). In Fiennes's film, however, not one soldier volunteers. They look at him as at a lunatic tempting them to death. Then when he utters the line, "O, me alone," one by one, very slowly and reluctantly, they raise their hands. There is nothing triumphant about the scene. These soldiers are grimly doing their duty in following their bloodthirsty general. Once again, the effect is to make the title character more one-dimensional (even his soldiers do not love him) and to make the film more clearly an anti-war piece. No one but the emotionally crippled Coriolanus, it seems to say, is eager for battle.

Branagh's *Henry V* was linked by British viewers more with "the flurry of low-budget, bitter and oppositional British cinema which also appeared in the late 1980s – including *War Requiem* (Derek Jarman, 1988), *For Queen and Country* (Martin Stellman, 1988) [and] *Resurrected* (Paul Greengrass, 1989) than with heritage cinema" (Quinn and Kingsley-Smith, 168). Similarly, Fiennes's movie bears more resemblance to recent films set in war zones like *The Hurt Locker* (2008), *The Debt* (2010), *Zero Dark Thirty* (2012), and *Blood Diamond* (2006) than to other Shakespeare adaptations. In fact, Fiennes acted in *The Hurt Locker* (Contractor Team Leader), and his director of cinematography, Barry Ackroyd, also worked on that film as well as *Green Zone* (2010) and *United 93* (2006), all involving military or terrorist plots. Fiennes's screenwriter, John Logan, co-created the script for *Gladiator* (2000) and wrote *The Last Samurai* (2003). Furthermore, Fiennes's Virgilia, Jessica Chastain, starred in *The Debt* and *Zero Dark Thirty*. Both these films share with *Coriolanus* torture scenes, which again seem to be characteristic of contemporary films treating war and espionage, even one as mainstream as the Bond film *Casino Royale* (2006). Fiennes's interrogation sequence, which appears very early in the film, was his creation, using lines from other scenes in Shakespeare's play to make up the dialogue. Almereyda took the same approach in his *Cymbeline*; he added a scene in which Cymbeline tortures Pisanio to gain information about Imogen. A thug places a clear plastic bag tightly over Pisanio's face while Cymbeline questions him. Almereyda on the DVD commentary views this as a relevant contemporary touch: "Torture is a little more common and popular than anyone would wish it to be." All these films use a gritty, news-footage approach to violent scenes. In several instances, Fiennes even uses real news clips from the Serbian conflict. Many reviewers noted that the updated setting made the film resonate with the situations in Greece, the Arab Spring, or Bosnia in the 1990s. This resonance again links the film with Branagh's *Henry V*, which was designed to recall World War I in its muddy battle scenes (Quinn and Kingsley-Smith, 168). The overall impression conveyed in these films is that war is hellish, cruel, and utterly regrettable – a sentiment that is part of Shakespeare's two plays but certainly not the whole story. In both *Henry V* and *Coriolanus*, Shakespeare also depicts war as an arena for glory, honour and noble sacrifice, reflecting the views of his cultural moment. In other words, the films flatten out some of the ambiguities regarding war present in the plays. William P. Shaw noted this same effect in earlier adaptations of Shakespeare, regretting "the violence in the Brook *Lear* and Polanski *Macbeth* that 'creates an exaggerated, darker, and less complex vision of humanity than we find in Shakespeare's plays'" (Rothwell, "How the Twentieth," 87).

Another convention of the contemporary war film to which both Fiennes and Branagh adhere is to present the enemy in an egalitarian, respectful manner. Cartmell notes that Branagh's treatment of the "other" is very different from that of Laurence Olivier's 1944 film *Henry V*, which had a mandate to improve British morale. "Not to appear anti-European, [Branagh] turns the French into worthy opponents and even makes the Dauphin a likeable figure" (101). Olivier depicted the French as silly and cowardly, perhaps reflecting the British sense of betrayal at Vichy France's collaboration with the Nazis. The emphasis confirms Leggatt's statement that the play reveals the biases of those involved with its production and is very much affected by the time in which it is produced.

Shakespeare gave his French in this play "a quality of otherness," as Leggatt notes, that they do not have to the same extent in his other English histories (116). For one thing, they slip into French words and phrases, whereas the Frenchmen in the rest of his canon speak only English. Furthermore, when the French are defeated and Montjoy comes seeking permission from Henry to sort the noble dead from the common, Shakespeare still emphasizes their otherness. No band of brothers, the French plebeian soldiers have not found their condition raised by the camaraderie of battle. Montjoy expresses real horror at the thought that "our vulgar drench their peasant limbs / In blood of princes." This treatment of the French has been seen as xenophobic, and certainly, Shakespeare gives to the French nobles remarks like the dauphin's that make the English look good and the French ridiculous:

> Our madams mock at us and plainly say
> Our mettle is bred out, and they will give
> Their bodies to the lust of English youth
> To new store France with bastard warriors. (3.5.28–31)

The remark follows hard upon the scene in which the French princess decides to learn English.

Although Branagh keeps these lines and the scenic order, he makes the French appear civilized and modern in contrast to the English. Throughout, he treats the French seriously, never guying them as Olivier did in his *Henry V*. Their court is airy and well lit, the nobles brightly clad; their council chamber is arranged conference-style, chairs in a circle. By contrast, the English court is dark and sinister, with tall pews as in a church or an old-fashioned schoolroom. Henry appears cloaked in darkness, more like Darth Vader or Count Dracula than the "mirror of all Christian kings."

The French are not the only "others" in Shakespeare's play, however. As mentioned earlier, probably about the same time that Shakespeare was writing *Henry V*, Elizabeth was attempting to conquer the Irish. Shakespeare's one Irish character, MacMorris, is stereotypically fiery and pugnacious, especially when he perceives a slight against his nation. Homesickness, as sociologist Jonathan Matthew Schwartz observes, inspires "cultural defense and identity" (14). As I note elsewhere in this study, soldiers have always been susceptible to homesickness. Henry's motley crew of captains are particularly defensive about their own corners of the British Isles because they have been relocated to France and may die there, far from home. Fluellen, the comic Welsh captain, who plays a sizable role in the play, takes great exception to the Irishman in act 3, scene 3. This scene must have drawn hoots of jingoistic laughter from the original audience, who knew that even as they watched the play, the Irish were fighting desperately to keep their nation their own.

It seems, however, that Shakespeare was also commenting more critically on the Irish campaign. The English historically had a tough time defeating the Irish in battle and keeping them subdued. Rumours suggesting that they were having the same problems under Essex must have circulated in London. Significantly, Shakespeare depicts MacMorris as the only captain getting on with the job, while the English, Scottish, and Welsh captains stand around chatting. Once again, he subtly undermines the propaganda about Essex's venture voiced by the Chorus by showing us a brave Irishman who is ready to fight while the English stand idle. Branagh reinforces this impression. Despite his cuts to the scene, he retains MacMorris's lines "It is no time to discourse, so Chrish save me. The town is beseeched, and the trumpet calls us to the breach, and we talk and, by Chrish, do nothing" (*Screenplay*, 41).

Scholar Curtis Breight argues that if Branagh had really been interested in making an anti-war film, he would have emphasized the cowardice exhibited here by the captains instead of lionizing them (140). Certainly the screenplay describes Fluellen as the "most loyal of the King's soldiers" (39). It is hard to say whether Shakespeare saw him that way, or whether he saw him more as a comic Welshman through whom he could satirize captains who knew more about Roman wars than their own. Certainly, the military pamphlets and handbooks circulating at the time Shakespeare wrote the play were often especially critical of the corruption of English captains. (See Barnabe Riche's *A Pathway to Military Practise*, G1r; and *Allarme for Englande*, J2 r–v, James Purlilia, *The Preceptes of Warre*, G6 v–G7r.) Falstaff's ruthless attitude towards his soldiers in *Henry IV, Part 2*, reflects this reality.

MacMorris's defensiveness about his nation must have raised painful memories for Branagh, born in Belfast and raised half in Northern Ireland and half in England during the worst years of the Troubles. Even though he has spent his adult life in England, he has strong feelings for Ireland; he has chosen to stage the European premieres of all his Shakespeare films in Belfast, and his ongoing commitment to Ulster is well known (Thornton and Wray, 165). When Ramona Wray interviewed him, she asked what his motivation was in having John Sessions play MacMorris "straight," not as a comic stage Irishman as he probably was in Shakespeare's day. Branagh answered:

> I remember a rehearsal discussion when we played [*Henry V*] in London in the theatre, and many of us felt it was politically inappropriate and insensitive to [follow] the broad stage Irishman tradition, the [interpretation] that the part can produce [and sometimes] involves. That's why we went the other way.
>
> Small though that part of the play is, the issue of the four captains is one which it is quite possible to take seriously (I don't mean solemnly) from a dramatic point of view, as [the characters]

all have things that they care about. They all have actions and drives, despite how little they say, and that seems to me to be more interesting as a dynamic and as another little colour in [Shakespeare's] depiction of an army. (166–7)

Reading between the lines, we can see the propaganda game Branagh is playing here. He does not ally himself too closely with his Irishness, because he wants his films to have a global audience, a mandate made clear in the prefaces to all his screenplays. Instead, he plays the "politically correct" card of trying to be sensitive to all cultures.

However, not all spectators felt that the result was sensitive to Irish culture. Film scholar Courtney Lehmann in *Shakespeare Remains* detects in *Henry V* Branagh's working out of his own complex feelings about his nationality. She sees in the image of Branagh as Henry, rearing up on his white horse, sword in hand at the breach of Harfleur, "a tableau of King Billy at the breach of the river Boyne, an image that appears in wall murals all over Ulster" (201). She also notes that he cuts Gower's praise of MacMorris's valiant nature but has him deliver in tones of complaint the fact that he is directing the Duke of Gloucester's tunnel digging (202). Lehmann observes that when Jamy and MacMorris emerge from the mines, only MacMorris's face is "blackened" (although in the screenplay Branagh describes them both as "blackened"). She sees in this the traditional stage association with the Irish, the minstrel tradition, and remembers the slander against them as "white niggers." I think perhaps she overstates the importance of all this. If there is an anti-Irish bent in the film, it may well come from Shakespeare, writing at the time of the Essex campaign, and it may have been subtly pervasive enough in the play that Branagh was unable to eradicate it completely. Granted, Branagh in his screenplay does describe MacMorris as "wild and apparently deranged" (41), and the other captains are not described thus. But a page later in the screenplay, he describes the king as "bloodstained, filthy, and as if possessed by some demon" (42). Could MacMorris's extra-dirty face not just suggest that he has been working harder and longer underground than the other captains?

Curtis Breight makes even more of the Fluellen bias in the film than Lehmann, who sees it as a form of transference for Branagh of his Irishness. Breight cites Branagh's famous interview with the Prince of Wales as a motivating factor for making "the Welsh Fluellen and

Henry such pals." He catalogues a convincing list of scenes in the film in which Fluellen and Henry are mirror images of one another, culminating with the fact that Branagh chose to play Henry in disguise with a Welsh accent (208). Fluellen and the king share a special bond in Shakespeare's play too, but of course it was Branagh's decision whether or not to emphasize this. Breight points out that Henry's Welsh accent suggests that there is a difference, as Bhabha puts it, "between being English and being Anglicized" (90, qtd in Breight, 210). This notion of being Anglicized introduces the issue of imperialism in the film.

One might assume that Branagh, having spent his early years in an "Anglicized" nation, would be sensitive to the distinction. Yet many critics have seen his *Henry V* as a thinly disguised defence of imperialism. For example, Fitter sees the film as whitewashing traditional autocracy and the logic of imperialism. I think any director of the play faces the problem of his interpretation being read this way because of the remarkable effectiveness of Shakespeare's martial rhetoric. His "Once more unto the breach" oration and the "St Crispin's Day" speech are two of the best examples of military rhetoric in the English language, copied by Winston Churchill (his speeches to the House of Commons, 13 May and 4 June 1940) and even by George Bush in more recent conflicts (20 September 2001). Whatever their political persuasion, audience members find themselves caught up in the glory of the language. Branagh aids and abets this effect by delivering these speeches with great passion, and accompanying the words with a rousing soundtrack. It is symptomatic of our nostalgia for great speeches that this film, made in 1989, was both popular and critically acclaimed. In these two speeches, Shakespeare's idealistic portrait of a band of brothers united under an inspiring leader, ready to give their lives for him and his cause, still evokes a powerful response. I see my students, who hail from many cultures, become stirred by it today in the classroom in contemporary Toronto. Our reaction to these speeches reveals a yearning for the idea of a politician who is a gifted speaker and believes in a unifying cause, as Henry, for the duration of his addresses in Branagh's film, seems to do. Even while we can acknowledge that Shakespeare also presents material in the plays that scrutinizes Henry and his cause in a more critical way, and that Branagh includes some of this material, all that is momentarily forgotten as we listen to the two orations. Instead we feel an elegiac longing for a time (real or imagined) when leaders were brave, their causes just, and their people eager to serve them.

It is not surprising that the off-stage audience experiences yearning, when part of the speeches' strategy is to induce it in the on-stage audience: the soldiers. Henry conjures up images of their families and home so that they will fight for them and for their return to them. In the "Once more unto the breach" oration, he mentions "fathers" twice, "mothers" once, and "English" or "England" four times. In the St Crispin's Day address, he vividly describes an English home for ten lines, and a father teaching his son the story of the battle. Quinones argues that "at the heart of the Shakespearean argument of time is the father-son link of generation ... this link forms an important value for Shakespeare and is intrinsically involved with his war against time" (301). Henry promises his soldiers they will never be forgotten because their sons will remember their sacrifice and pass on the story to their sons. Quinones sees in much Renaissance literature that "children and fame are valuable counters in the war against nothingness and oblivion" (346).

Henry, as Elizabethan manuals on the art of war recommended, uses these references to home and family to improve morale. Some later military thinkers have felt that this rhetorical strategy could have the opposite effect:

> On the eve of and throughout the United States' involvement in the Second World War, reports surfaced detailing the causes and even the potential sinister uses of nostalgia. Concern was expressed on several occasions that family members attempting to "pamper" soldiers might inadvertently induce nostalgia (NY Times, 24 August 1941: 57). Letters asking "when can you get home?" and radio programs that "frequently carry the same note of nostalgic sentimentality" threatened morale (NY Times, 15 Feb 1944: 19). Afflicted soldiers serving in Britain were prone to "bragging" about the United States in a way that often offended their hosts. A four page pamphlet targeted at British women working in canteens urged them not to interpret this talk as an attempt to decry Britain nor allow it to "drive a wedge between the nations", for this would only be a "round in the battle for Hitler" (Long 1942). The Germans too seemed fully aware of the effect of nostalgia on American troops and used this as part of their propaganda cam-

paign. Pamphlets dropped near Rome and the Cassino front "recall to the Americans that juicy steaks, swing bands and thrilling movies are fun" (*NY Times*, 13 April 1944: 5). (Sprengler, 20–1)

These reports about the adverse effect of homesickness in war, when set beside Shakespeare's military oration, contribute to the whole larger debate about nostalgia. Is it generally a positive force that encourages people to take lessons from the past and implement them, as Henry V does ("Fathers that like so many Alexanders / Have in these parts from morn till even fought, / And sheathed their swords for lack of argument," 3.1.19–21)? Or does it sap people of their energy and make them live in the past, as the Nazis assumed it would do to the American soldiers abroad?

Despite Branagh's verbal efforts to distinguish his film from Olivier's wartime propaganda adaptation, the movie premiered in the United States three days before Veteran's Day, which in 1989 corresponded with the seventy-fifth and fiftieth anniversaries of the outbreaks of World Wars I and II, respectively. French believes "this display of deference to the latter-day victims of war, and preservers of British autonomy, indicates the reverence towards British institutions of monarchy and statehood that characterizes the marketing of *Henry V*" (69). It seems to me that American distributors would have little interest in promoting British institutions; rather, they seized on a convenient tie-in to promote a small independent film peopled by actors largely unknown to American audiences. Perhaps distributors were also relying on the nostalgia of those who had viewed Olivier's film during the Second World War. When I attended a British showing of the film early in its run in London, it was the film's inception in the theatre that was emphasized rather than wartime tie-ins. I was offered a glossy colour program for £1.50 when I entered.

In the American trailer for *Henry V*, the emphasis is almost entirely on what Hollywood might term Henry's "character arc." The trailer opens in the dark English court with a deep, American voice saying portentously, "It was time of courtiers and kings ... It was a turning point for the English throne." We are treated to shots of the archbishop of Canterbury and the king exchanging significant glances as Henry asks about his claim to France – Henry in deadly earnest, Canterbury conniving. The exchange suggests the court intrigue that audiences have come to expect from screen depictions of Tudor and medieval politics. The voice continues, "It was one of history's great adventures led by a soldier who wouldn't retreat." Meanwhile, we see Henry rearing up on his white horse, filling the fiery gap in the walls of Harfleur, yelling, "Once more unto the breach, dear friends!" The voice then describes him as "a lover who wouldn't give up." We witness the snippet of dialogue in which Princess Katherine doubts that she could love "the enemy of France" and Henry calls himself "the friend of France."

Then, strangely, we are shown a clip from the scene in which Bardolph is hanged, with the words "A leader who upheld justice" read out by the same voice. (Obviously, the marketing team are assuming most viewers will not know that this scene, when Henry decides to execute his old tavern friend for stealing a pyx from a French church, contributes to the profound ambiguity surrounding Henry in Shakespeare's play.) Henry, tears in his eyes, says, "When lenity and cruelty play for a kingdom, the gentler gamester is the soonest winner." The portentous voice adds, "A rebel who wouldn't give up," and we are shown Henry, drinking with cronies in a pub, looking wryly at the two bishops, and then delivering a snippet of his ultimatum to Harfleur. Finally, in ringing tones, the voice tells us that Henry is "a king who defied the odds to prove himself a man," the tagline on the American poster. We then see Henry delivering his best lines from the St Crispin's Day oration, about "the story the good man will teach his son," ending with "the band of brothers" line as a montage of happy, victorious images scrolls past: a laughing Katherine, a cheering crowd of soldiers, and a bloody king and Fluellen tearfully embracing on the field.

The very last image of the trailer is all pomp and circumstance, Henry and Katherine in full royal regalia holding their joined hands aloft behind a table ranged with courtiers. Again, this pageantry promises the audience all the eye-candy of heritage cinema, while the rest of the images in the montage suggest a story of a remarkable man and his camaraderie with his fellows. It is the masculine, action-packed, military qualities of the film that are stressed, as well as more images of Emma Thompson's pretty face than her tiny part would warrant (including an image of her kissing Henry V). This latter is a sop for those spectators who prefer romantic comedies to war movies.

Like Branagh, Fiennes in *Coriolanus* is at pains to persuade the public that Shakespeare's play is relevant today. When he was performing the play on stage, Fiennes recalls in his DVD commentary, he imagined that "with the right adaptation, [the play] would make a very pertinent modern political thriller." Unlike Branagh, he resets the Roman play in contemporary times, shooting in Serbia and thus channelling associations with the recent Balkan war. All the reviewers made comparisons to recent events in the news, not only the ones mentioned above but also the Occupy movement. Fiennes's strategy again differs from Branagh's in that he allowed John Logan to pare Shakespeare's script down to its barest bones. Unfortunately, none of this modernity and filmic quality paid off at the box office. Perhaps the title needed to be updated too.

Nigel Andrews of the *Financial Times* correctly identifies this tragedy, viewed through the window of Fiennes's adaptation, as being essentially about political rhetoric: "Shakespeare's play foresaw the rise of 'spin' and the harlot ways of political popularity. To his hero's scornful, proto-Thatcheresque pride – Coriolanus would surely endorse 'There is no such thing as society' – the play's wise counsel answers, 'What is the city but the people?'" Yet the political content of the play suffers most in the cutting down of the script. The sections of act 4, scene 5, for example, in which three comic Volscian serving men give their perspective on the rivalry between Coriolanus and Aufidius, has been excised. This cut is very revealing of contemporary attitudes to the war narrative. Most war films today are utterly without humour, war being seen as unrelievedly grim. Furthermore, the humour in this scene is at the plebeians' expense. The serving men are dismissive and peremptory with Coriolanus when they think him a random poor man. When his true identity is discovered, however, they all claim to have recognized his stellar quality despite his humble disguise. This scene thus works to confirm the earlier presentation in the play, during and after Coriolanus's solicitation of their voices, of the plebeians as mercurial and easily led. This image of the people would not go over well with audiences in our present, more democratic era.

The two chief relationships, between Coriolanus and Volumnia and between Coriolanus and Aufidius, are also brought into sharp relief by the reduction of the political scenes and the conflation of political characters. Many of Cominius's military lines are given to Titus Lartius (especially in 5.1), whereas Menenius, a politician, is given Valeria's lines of a more intimate, domestic nature (1.3). Scenes in which the tribunes are discussing politics are greatly reduced and often collapsed into one (Sicinius's and Brutus's discussion of Coriolanus in act 1, scene 1, for instance). The dialogue of the citizens is radically edited; for instance, the First Citizen's initial interview with Menenius (1.1) is reduced to a few lines and a televised speech by Menenius.

In Fiennes's *Coriolanus*, the plebeians are definitely signified as "other" – dressed in ragged clothing, all from different ethnic backgrounds, speaking with heavy accents. Fiennes explains in the DVD commentary that he wanted to suggest a diversity in both the population and the ruling class of Rome. Certainly, as Betsy Sharkey of the *L.A. Times* notes, "Belgian actress Lubna Azabal, so memorable in *Incendies*, [is] the defining face of the angry crowd." The two occasions on which Fiennes addresses this issue on the DVD, however, are noticeably the times when his usual articulateness fails him, as if he is anticipating accusations of political incorrectness or at least snobbery. Like Branagh, he suffers in the British press from his association with the upper classes. Fiennes's grandfather was the industrialist Sir Maurice Fiennes (1907–94); he is eighth cousin to the Prince of Wales and was educated at independent Irish and English schools. In the *Guardian* interview quoted below, however, he emphasizes the fact that his parents were "financially challenged."

In the DVD commentary, he claims he "very much wanted to have a black actor playing the highest status part" (Cominius, who in the film is the chief consul, is played by South African actor John Kani). However, Kani is the only exception to a white ruling class. Coriolanus and his family (Vanessa Redgrave, Jessica Chastain) and closest friend Menenius (Brian Cox), in contrast, speak English with "received accents."

Fiennes does, however, create immediate sympathy for the rioting crowd at the beginning, as they are pushed back by policemen in black uniforms with gleaming shields. This image, so common in modern news and topical in England with the Tottenham revolts, suggests a pro-plebeian bias, as one would expect in a contemporary director. In his DVD commentary, Fiennes describes the "extremely aggressive armoured vehicles" the police deploy – obviously the plebeians are outmatched. He comments, "The police are not holding back at all." Fiennes maintains the ambiguity of Shakespeare's play by showing the speed with which, after Coriolanus has secured the people's "voices," the tribunes persuade the crowd to renege on him. Even while we sympathize with the injustice of their situation, we can recognize them as fickle. Coriolanus is by no means the only character in the play who views them in this negative light. Aufidius remarks, "their people / Will be as rash in the repeal as hasty / To expel him thence" (4.7.32–4). These lines are cut in the film, again to sharpen the contrast between the two men. Fiennes speaks politely of the people's "uncertainty," but Peter Debruge's (*Variety*) reference to the plebeians as the "ungrateful rabble he [Coriolanus] fought to liberate" may well be closer to Shakespeare's view. In his history plays, both English and Roman, the general populace are usually shown to be mercurial. Fiennes sees this ambiguity as the strength of Shakespeare's play: "I love this play because Shakespeare tests us with our allegiance ... We may not like Coriolanus's contempt, his arrogance, but he's trying to hold on to who he is" (DVD commentary).

The Volscians are also, of course, signified as "the other" from the first moments of the film. The opening shot shows an ancient dagger, engraved with Celtic-like circles, being sharpened. This primitive weapon provides a sharp contrast with the images of the Romans, en masse and fully equipped with modern weaponry, on Aufidius's television screen. Aufidius seems to be operating out of a basement, whereas the Roman brass and politicians meet in spanking new boardrooms. The Volcians appear bearded, in simple, rumpled green uniforms; the Romans are bald and in the latest "digital camouflage" currently used by American soldiers. Fiennes also underlines contrasts in leaders that are generally positive to the Volsce side. When Coriolanus arrives in Antium, we are shown Aufidius (Gerard Butler) walking casually through the streets with some of his men. He exchanges friendly, relaxed greetings with citizens of all ages. He has the common touch. His ursine appearance and warm Scottish burr make him seem approachable, even cuddly. His accessories are also familiar and gentle; instead of the "lonely dragon" tattoo sported by Coriolanus, Aufidius has a Madonna and child adorning his arm, and he wears a cross around his neck and a Celtic ring on his finger. Fiennes, in contrast, is reptilian, recalling his long-standing role as Voldemort in the Harry Potter films. His bald head and hairless face gleam like snakeskin. When he speaks, his cutting consonants and grey-green eyes reinforce this cold-blooded impression. He seems uneasy and taciturn with people, even his own family. He comes alive only in the thick of battle. He is a damaged individual, raised to excel at killing. Aufidius, on the other hand, seems a complete man. He appears distraught when he encounters a slaughtered Volscian family spilling out of a parked car. He is welcoming and generous with Coriolanus when he takes refuge in his camp. Even after dealing Coriolanus the death thrust with his ancient dagger, Aufidius tenderly cradles him as he dies. Coriolanus is unmoved in the film by anything but his mother's final plea to save Rome. Thus, the film becomes, in contrast to the play, a simple parable in which the more democratic and feeling leader is triumphant in the end.

The sharp contrast between the two men was entirely intentional on the director's part. On the DVD commentary, Fiennes refers to Aufidius as "a man who's popular versus a man who's loathed" (Coriolanus). In fact, it is hard to believe in the film that the Volscian soldiers would embrace Coriolanus as their hero over Aufidius when he displays so little humanity and Aufidius so much. Yet they even erase their own otherness from Coriolanus, shaving their heads to be like him. The iconography, as Fiennes observes, is "fascistic." The soldiers admire him only because he is relentlessly tough and powerful. This sharp dichotomy between the two leaders is also Fiennes's simplification of the play for the sake of a modern film audience. He cuts any scenes in which Coriolanus comes across as warm, such as in his affectionate and courageous farewell to his family on his banishment (4.1), or somewhat reasonable, as in his description of the plebeians' cowardice in war to explain his ill opinion of them (3.1.119–26). Thus, the Coriolanus of the film is much less human than Shakespeare's hero, perhaps an unsurprising consequence of the radical dialogue cuts: when we hear a narrower range of the protagonist's thoughts, he is inevitably more one-dimensional.

In Shakespeare's play, nostalgia for family and home plays a crucial role in the climax in which Coriolanus's mother, Volumnia, reminds him of all the love and duty he owes her, and equates attacking Rome with trampling on the womb that bore him. It is clear throughout the play that Coriolanus has been unable to shrug off an inner pining for his childhood in which his mother reigned supreme. This longing is represented in the film by the extradiegetic scenes in which young Martius appears. Once again, a modern director has added scenes with a child – as Taymor did in *Titus* (1999) and Noble in *A Midsummer*

Night's Dream (1996). We see young Martius shooting at cans in his beautiful garden as his mother looks ruefully on. Later, we see Virgilia enter the boy's bedroom, tidy up the array of military toys scattered on the floor, and then tenderly kiss her sleeping son's cheek. This scene directly follows her witnessing Volumnia bandaging Coriolanus's wounds. Fiennes comments on the DVD extra features that Virgilia displays the "uncomplicated love of mother for son."

Volumnia, of course, has an uncanny hold on Coriolanus still, more powerful than that of his wife and son. Fiennes includes several micro scenes in which Virgilia's appeals to Coriolanus are met with little or no response – when she touches his chest in their bedroom, when she kisses him in the Volscian camp. In the DVD commentary, Fiennes describes Virgilia as very aware of the "power of the bond" Volumnia and her son share, so that she ends up "feeling repelled." The Oedipal aspects of Coriolanus's worship of his mother contribute to his portrayal as a nostalgic. As Sprengler observed, the Oedipal son shares with the nostalgic the desire to return to a place of origin (the womb) and a time before significant change, transformation, and decisive choices (16). The catastrophe of the play is just such a moment of transformation and choice for Coriolanus. This climax also seems to support the newspaper reports quoted above on the role of homesickness in World War II, as Volumnia's presence saps Coriolanus of his strength, diverting his attention away from the alliance with the Volscians and their plans to overthrow Rome, just as it is meant to do. Unfortunately, by appealing to the child in Coriolanus, Volumnia undoes the soldier in him and thus strips him of his identity. He then becomes "the other" to himself ("a kind of nothing," as Cominius earlier observed, 5.1.13) in a way far more self-destructive than when he became Volscian soldier from Roman soldier. Redgrave plays the scene with great intimacy, kneeling directly in front of Coriolanus and placing her hands on his knees (fig. 9). Fiennes expresses it thus: "Shakespeare goes right to the centre of who we are – we are children. The man of war is persuaded by his mother to become a man of peace ... the carapace of military self-regard is broken open" (DVD commentary). In an interview with the star, Xan Brooks of *The Guardian* reports that in the opinion of Fiennes's friend, the theatre director Jonathan Kent, Fiennes's choice of "plays are examinations of him" and thus very revealing of the actor. Brooks observes that Kent directed Fiennes in *Coriolanus, Hamlet*, and *Oedipus Rex*, "all of which hinge

Figure 9 Volumnia (Vanessa Redgrave) kneels at the feet of her son, Coriolanus (Ralph Fiennes), in Fiennes's *Coriolanus*, 2011.

on the fraught relationship between a son and his mother. While I'm wary of attaching too much Freudian baggage to this, I can't believe it's pure coincidence." Brooks's scepticism in this regard may arise from the fact that after playing Hamlet to her Gertrude, Fiennes had an eleven-year affair with Francesca Annis, who is seventeen years his senior. Brooks also notes that despite the radical editing of the text of *Coriolanus*, the mother's part remains virtually uncut. Fiennes explains, "She uses every bit of maternal ammunition that she can lay her hands on, from intimacy, to challenge, to entreaty – 'Speak to me, son, speak to me' – to rejection. So you have to go through it all: it's the nub of the play. What moved me about *Coriolanus* was always that: the mother-son confrontation" (Brooks, 2). Furthermore, Fiennes remembers that it was his own mother who introduced him to Shakespeare by telling him the story of *Hamlet* in her own words when he was eight years old, which left "quite a disturbing impression" (3).

My sense of the film is that, contrary to the images provided by the trailer, the mother-son scenes are indeed at its heart. At the climax, as Fiennes acknowledges in the DVD commentary, Coriolanus recognizes in his mother's erasure of his honour to the Volscians his own ultimate demise, wrought by the very woman who bore him. Volumnia reared him as the ultimate weapon, and in this important scene she disarms him utterly by reminding him of "courtesy" owed her but yet unpaid (5.3.162). She leaves him unsoldiered, with no role to play.

Fiennes reinforces all these elements inherent in Shakespeare's play by transforming Volumnia from Roman matron to contemporary Iron Lady. In his film, it is clear that she herself has had a distinguished army career. When her son returns from Corioles, she appears in a full, decorated military uniform. She has raised Coriolanus in her own image and then, perversely, asks him to alter this image to that of the politician, then, the conciliator – roles that are foreign to both of them.

Volumnia is also shown to infantilize her son. Earlier in the film, as Fiennes remarks in the DVD commentary, she attempts to persuade Coriolanus to be humble with the people, using the family's military flag as a prop, which she reuses during the climax. When that doesn't work, she throws up her hands in the equivalent of "Have it your own way!" which Fiennes regards as a typical mother-child exchange. Aufidius too infantilizes Coriolanus, shaving his head when he accepts his services in a scene that recalls Volumnia tenderly bandaging Coriolanus's wounds on his return from Corioles while his wife shrinks away like an intruder. Volumnia and then Aufidius take care of their military prize, as one might oil and polish a valuable hunting rifle.

The film was marketed very much as a contemporary war movie with an intense rivalry at its heart. The poster features Fiennes's and Butler's faces in profile, each with primitive red paint symbols on their faces. The tagline between their profiles reads: "Nature teaches beasts to know their friends." This line from the play also highlights the relationship between Aufidius and Coriolanus. Arguably, Coriolanus's relationship with his mother is more important to both the play and the film, but the trailer de-emphasizes it, magnifying the masculinity of the adaptation. Opening with a close-up on Coriolanus's dragon tattoo across his muscular, hairless neck, it then focuses on Aufidius's blade. Titles appear: "From the ashes of war, he won glory." Intercut between titles is battle footage from the film and shots of Coriolanus in dress uniform about to accept his honour. The next set of titles states, "At the hands of his people, he was betrayed," intercut with images of protesters bearing crossed-out images of Fiennes's face, and his angry outburst with the tribunes on the steps of the government building. The final set of titles declares, "In the arms of an enemy, he will claim vengeance," intercut with his arrival at Aufidius's headquarters. At the end of the trailer, titles appear advertising that the film was written by John Logan, screenwriter of *Gladiator* and *The*

Last Samurai ; once again, the associations both marketing team and director want the audience to have is with other war movies, not with other Shakespeare films. Jessica Chastain's lovely face appears with more frequency in the trailer than Vanessa Redgrave's, even though Virgilia's part is comparatively tiny. The trailer seems to be particularly targeting a male audience. It is not only a war movie but a movie about fierce opposites who become allies – a buddy action movie like *Lethal Weapon* (1987), if you will. Both the American and international trailers show little of the common people. The trailers make the film seem more personal – the story of one warrior's betrayal.

As Emma French observes in *Selling Shakespeare to Hollywood*, directors often have little say in the making of the trailer. Certainly, this glorification of war does not seem to have been Fiennes's intention in making the film. In the interview with *The Guardian*, he affirms, "It is a part that I should blush in acting," yet he admits to a grudging affinity with the man he plays: the angry ascetic, forced to sell himself to the masses. "Yes, I suppose I do have empathy for him. There's something exhilarating about playing that sort of anger and frustration. And whatever you think of his values, he's trying to hold to his truth; to what he believes in" (Brooks, 2–3). Does this betray Fiennes's own nostalgia for old-style integrity or for patrician values? After all, if Coriolanus' "truth" is snobbery and therefore morally repugnant, should we be impressed that he adheres to it?

The moral ambiguity of the hero, which the trailer glides over, was apparent to all the reviewers. Peter Bradshaw in *The Guardian* observed that Fiennes's "dead-eyed ... face looks very much like Klaus Maria Brandauer in *Mephisto.*" This 1981 German film explores the career of an actor whose performance in a Faust play is so popular with the Nazis that he becomes successful even as his friends flee the regime in terror. Coriolanus too is a character who sells out, abandoning his integrity at several junctures in the play to satisfy his mother's ambitions for him. His personal integrity is in itself an ambiguous concept for a modern audience, as his being true to himself means treating the plebeians with contempt – he is prepared to give his life to protect theirs but will not acknowledge their right to a voice in politics.

As a consequence of the fact that Fiennes cuts the original playscript much more than Branagh does, more of the illuminating ambiguities of *Coriolanus* are lost than in *Henry V*. What Logan's script leaves out are the vestiges of the hero's humanity, which Shakespeare is careful to preserve so that we have some sympathy with him. Both filmmakers engage in a kind of self-promoting propaganda in which they try to convince their audiences that their art is not only relevant to today but politically important – commenting on current issues in a significant way. Whether audience members really needed to see the films of *Henry V* and *Coriolanus* to learn the obvious – that war is hell, and that the poor are people too – is another question. Shakespeare has more complex lessons to teach, but those are better suited for longer evenings at the theatre or watching a televised miniseries. A film has time only for gestures towards these complexities, which Fiennes and, especially, Branagh admirably achieve.

PART FOUR

Music and Memory

10

"Sigh No More Ladies": Shakespeare, Branagh, and Whedon Tackle Issues of Gender and Fidelity in *Much Ado About Nothing*

The four chapters in this section, "Music and Memory," focus on the way in which the music in these adaptations contributes to our understanding of theme and character.

In Shakespeare's *Much Ado About Nothing*, a preoccupation with women's chastity is central to the plot. Many critics have dealt at length with the attitudes expressed in the comedy around Hero's supposed betrayal of Claudio. Some critics have considered the implications of the remarkable number of cuckold jokes, Michael Mangan noting that the play is more obsessed with this idea than any other of its period (183). But Shakespeare is also concerned in this play with *male* chastity, and while this motif is subtler than that of female fidelity, it nevertheless runs through the play. It has its most obvious manifestation in the song, "Sigh No More Ladies," sung by Balthasar at the very heart of the play, act 2, scene 3, before the double gulling scene (lines 61–76). The lyrics of the song serve to remind the audience (if necessary) that relationships between men and women are fraught with difficulties. They suggest that men and women are very different in their attitudes to love. The song portrays men as inconstant, one foot in sea and one on shore, whereas women, by implication, are naturally monogamous. (Beatrice, however, seems to prove the inconstant men's equal in believing herself as incapable of fidelity in marriage as they are. She jokes that God will only send no horns if he sends her no husband, 2.1.24.)

In his 1993 film of the play, Kenneth Branagh makes the song central to his interpretation, privileging it even more than does the play. Music is typically very important to him as a director. For instance, he invited his composer, Patrick Doyle, to play the part of one of the courtiers in his first film, *Henry V*, so that he would, in the composer's words, have "unique insight into the characterisation, construction and requirements of the film" (Mark White, 71). Virgil Thomson notes in "Music for *Much Ado About Nothing*" that Shakespeare's use of music generally takes "no time at all out of the play's dramatic pacing" (qtd in Stevens, 89), yet Branagh breaks cinematic convention to delay the start of the action with the song's recital at the beginning and to pause the narrative in the middle of the film for the song to be heard again. The song's performance in the film takes longer than it would have done in a typical theatrical production, without the lush scenery to captivate the audience. Branagh obviously thought the lyrics important enough to risk tampering with Shakespeare's magical pacing. He even uses the melody as a recurring motif and concludes the film with a leisurely pan out, all the characters dancing to a rousing choral rendition of the same song. I would argue that the song "Sigh No More Ladies" is the most significant representative of the darker commentary on heterosexual relationships in the play left intact in the film, apart from the obvious one provided by Claudio's denouncement of Hero at their wedding. Indeed, the director has acknowledged that his aim was "to emphasise what he regarded as *Much Ado*'s positive message about 'how important love is,' believing that *Much Ado* was the ideal vehicle, as its darker side was less conspicuous than was the case with some other Shakespeare comedies" (Mark White, 143). This comment reinforces the impression given in White's biography of Branagh, that the British director is invested in a nostalgic project of supplying a positive antidote to what he views as an overly negative film industry more interested in serial killers than in love.

Branagh's aim was to convey a clear and emotional narrative to as wide an audience as possible, and so he had compelling reasons to simplify the text. As Stam contends, in the adaptation of a literary novel to the screen, a certain amount of "aesthetic mainstreaming" is commonplace, and this observation is true also of plays: "The recycled, suburbanized Aristotelianism of the screenwriting manuals calls for three-act structures, principal conflicts, coherent (and often sympathetic) characters, an inexorable narrative 'arc' and final catharsis or happy end ... The goal seems to be to 'de-literalize' the text, as the novel is put through an adaptation machine which removes all authorial eccentricities or 'excesses'. Adaptation is seen as a kind of purge. In the name of mass-audience legibility, the novel is 'cleansed' of moral ambiguity, narrative interruption, and reflexive meditation" (43). Through text cuts, Branagh's Benedick becomes a much more sympathetic, loyal, and straightforward man than Shakespeare's. The critical subtext that the song articulates is in the film compromised by Branagh's jolly treatment of it, and by contemporary audiences' tendency to ignore lyrics. Joss Whedon, in his 2013 film adaptation of *Much Ado*, takes the aesthetic mainstreaming even further. The song's lyrics are only heard, not thrown up on screen and repeated several times, as in Branagh's film. The masked party is in progress during the song, so the lyrics are given little chance of being seriously considered.

Much of the play's original subtext contrasts sharply with the jubilant focus on romantic love of the text. Shakespeare achieves this dual focus through references, mostly in the form of humorous banter, to men's and women's difficulty in remaining chaste. Many of these lines are cut in Branagh's and Whedon's films. In Shakespeare's play, the motif of men's fickle nature is introduced early. Beatrice refers to Benedick as Signor Montanto (1.1.30), perhaps a bawdy quibble on the idea of his mounting women. She then compares him to Cupid's challenger, posting handbills to that effect in Messina (1.1.37). This is the first of many references in the play to Benedick as a ladies' man, an aspect of his character that both directors greatly minimize. While both keep the reference to Montanto, obscure enough for a modern audience that it will not besmirch Benedick's reputation, both cut the references to Cupid. Benedick, in Shakespeare's script, is not a celibate bachelor – it is marriage, not sex, about which he is both anxious and cynical. There are at least eight references in the play to Benedick's reputation as a Casanova of sorts (1.1.37, 1.1.52, 1.1.101, 1.1.119, 1.1.237, 3.2.910, 5.2.1–23, 5.3.113). Branagh does away with six of these (1.1.37, 1.1.101, 1.1.237, 3.2.9–10, 5.2.1–23, 5.3.113) and Whedon, three (1.1.37, 1.1.237, 5.4.113). Of the three references that both directors excise, one is quoted above, and here is another: Benedick shows his familiarity with prostitution establishments with the line "Hang me up at the door of a brothel house for the sign of blind Cupid" (1.1.237). The third is explicated below.

In addition, there are at least seven references to Benedick's generally inconstant and changeable nature (1.1.66–83, 2.1.258–263, 2.3.222–35, 4.1.275–9, 5.1.163–6, 5.2.1–23, 5.4.106), two of which Branagh omits in his film (5.1.164–6, 5.2.1–23). Whedon too drops the first, in which Don Pedro quotes Beatrice's summation of Benedick's constancy: "He swore a thing to me on Monday night which he forswore on Tuesday morning. There's a double tongue" (5.1.164–6). He drastically reduces the second instance in act 5, scene 2, when Benedick dallies with Margaret, exchanging bawdy innuendoes. Whedon, unlike Branagh, keeps a few lines of this, but on the DVD commentary he describes himself as working "against the text." This scene in Shakespeare shows Benedick at his most flirtatious and Margaret at her most verbally lewd. Whedon's screenplay notes that Margaret is "nervous and unhappy." His DVD commentary interprets her bantering sexually with Benedick as something she does only "because it's expected of her," but her heart is not in it – the withered flowers she clears away "speak to where she is emotionally." The screenplay also observes that Benedick is just being kind, because he can see that she is upset (171). This gentleness fits with Whedon's other additions to Benedick's character, making him conform better to the ideal screen hero. After the masked party, we witness him helpfully carrying dishes into the kitchen from the garden.

The most significant and obvious of these edited references to Benedick as a Don Juan comes at the end of the play, when Beatrice and Benedick are about to be married. Claudio comments that Benedick will "out of question" prove a "double dealer" to Beatrice unless she looks "exceeding narrowly" to him (5.4.113–15). The double standard of Shakespeare's time is obvious; it is acceptable for Claudio to warn Beatrice on her wedding day that Benedick will be unfaithful to her unless she keeps a sharp watch. This is supposed to be funny, and goes with the "Hey nonny nonny" stoicism urged on women by the song. But the idea of Hero being unfaithful to Claudio is certainly not considered funny by anyone. Why do Branagh and Whedon cut Claudio's line? Both keep the song, which deals in general terms with men's infidelity to women, but Branagh cuts six of the eight references to Benedick's philandering tendencies and Whedon cuts three of them. Perhaps the two directors assume that a modern audience will no longer accept Benedick as the hero of a romantic comedy if he is shown to be fickle, or that it darkens the end of the comedy too much to have this warning that Beatrice's future happiness may be in jeopardy. This is especially true in Branagh's case as the film, as Celestino Deleyto in his article "Men in Leather" suggests, is told primarily from Beatrice's point of view (92). To some extent, these cuts were a result of the two directors conforming to the Hollywood romantic comedy formula. They were probably also made as much to excise jokes that neither further the plot nor are easily comprehended by a modern audience.

The theme of female chastity emerges obsessively in the proliferation of cuckold jokes in the play. Of at least eleven cuckold jests (1.1.187, 1.1.226, 1.1.247, 1.1.251, 2.1.20, 2.1.39, 2.3.59, 3.4.41-45, 3.4.61, 5.2.36, 5.4.122), Branagh omitted eight (5.4.122, 3.4.61, 3.4.42-5, 1.1.187, 1.1.226, 1.1.246, 2.1.20, 2.1.39) and Whedon six (1.1.246, 2.1.20, 2.1.39, 2.3.59, 3.4.42-5, 5.4.122). Here are a few that both directors excised: 1) Benedick says that if he should ever fall in love, "pluck off the bull's horns and set them in my forehead, and let me be vilely painted" (1.1.246); 2) Beatrice describes the devil as "an old cuckold with horns on his head" (2.1.39); and 3) Benedick recommends that Don Pedro find himself a wife because "There is no staff more reverend than one tipped with horn" (5.4.122). Some jokes are quite arcane, of course (like Beatrice's, "Then if your husband have stables enough, you'll see he shall lack no barns" 3.4.42-5), but the omissions do affect our understanding of the play.

Certainly, their absence decreases the atmosphere of paranoia in Messina, centring male insecurity in the figure of Claudio, and to some extent exonerating the other men. In Shakespeare's play, all the men seem anxious about the prospect of their future wives' infidelity, particularly Benedick. Yet in Branagh's film, only Claudio comes across as jealous – first of Don Pedro, wooing on his behalf, then of the man who enters Hero's bedchamber. These cuts to the script effectively make Claudio (in Branagh's film played by Robert Sean Leonard, in Whedon's by Fran Kranz) less sympathetic. In Shakespeare's Messina, it is no wonder that Claudio is quick to think that Hero has deceived him. The banter he exchanges with his male companions is dominated by cuckold jokes. In Messina, as Michael Mangan observes, "to be married is to be cuckolded already" (182). Joseph Westlund in "The Temptation to Isolate" concurs, describing Messina as "a troubling world in which everyone readily suspects everyone else" (69).

The atmosphere of sexual paranoia, like the arms race before a war, leads inexorably to conflict. Hero's undoing in the church is the release of all the pent-up anxiety in the men. In the two films, the concern about women's chastity, and the inconstancy by which men are characterized in the song, rest almost entirely with Claudio. As in the play, first he doubts his best friend, then his fiancée. His love for Hero fluctuates dramatically with his state of mind. He only *likes* her when he must set out for war, but he *loves* her in peacetime when he knows that she is Leonato's sole heir. He scarcely registers her death when he thinks she was unfaithful and then mourns it exceedingly when he hears she was innocent. When, at the end of the film, Benedick defends his own switch from committed bachelordom to committed husband with "man is a giddy thing" (5.4.106–7), it does not seem to apply to his character as much as to his friend's. It is Claudio who has been "to one thing constant never." Indeed, in the Branagh film, the camera focuses at this moment on Robert Sean Leonard's face. Whedon cuts the line, conforming more to typical romantic comedy conventions despite his description of his project as "noir comedy" (*Screenplay*, 24).

But what of the women's unease, expressed indirectly in the song, and in Beatrice's admission that Benedick played for her heart with false dice (2.1.262)? By removing so many of the cuckold jokes, and stressing the song, Branagh evens out the balance between female disquiet over male infidelity and male anxiety over female waywardness in a way that exposes modern attitudes to the subject. Whedon follows suit, in this as in so many other ways. In Elizabethan England, because of the law of primogeniture, women's chastity within marriage was the only guarantee that a man did not leave his estate, name, everything to another man's son. The male anxiety over women's infidelity was thus mostly caused by material concerns: who would inherit all the stuff – one's own son, or a bastard? Women's perturbation over men's disloyalty was more centred on emotions – a fear of being hurt – or on survival – being cast off penniless. Today, in the West anyway, the apprehension over infidelity for both sexes is more often the same, caused by the fear of being emotionally hurt; inheritance is no longer a key issue. It is this modern equality in anxiety that Branagh seems to have aimed for in the film. He emphasizes Beatrice's pain at the past deception practised on her by Benedick, zooming in on Emma Thompson's face as she talks about it wistfully. Branagh also shows that for Claudio,

Hero's supposed betrayal is *personally* hurtful more than offensive to his *honour* by casting a young American with an informal accent in the role. Robert Sean Leonard's young Claudio does not give the impression of deeply considering his family's honour.

Whedon modernizes the attitudes to chastity in the play even more, as befits his contemporary setting. His film opens with a scene in which Benedick leaves Beatrice in bed, presumably after a night of passion (see chapter 3 for a fuller account). Further, he makes it clear in the screenplay that Claudio and Leonato are shocked not that Hero is not a virgin but that she was unfaithful the night before her wedding (18). Inconsistently, all the references to both Hero and Beatrice as "maids" are maintained in the script.

As a consequence of this extradiegetic scene in Whedon's film and the cuts to the dialogue in both, much in the films rests on the lyrics of the song. These have to do more of the work to suggest the rich consideration of the challenges facing couples that makes *Much Ado* such a complex play. Branagh was very conscious of this; in his introduction to the screenplay, he explains that he views the song as an articulation of the play's moral – "a hard-won confirmation of a certain reality in the relationships between men and women" (xiv). Vague as this sounds, it seems to imply that Branagh holds the view of men and women expressed in the song to be accurate – men are deceivers, and since it is their nature, women are best to accept it, and console themselves by not taking it too seriously (an opinion, as Harry Berger Jr argues, that Branagh shares with Don Pedro, 20). Branagh circumvents the double standard inherent in the song and the play so as not to incur the wrath of his female spectators, but also because on some level perhaps he subscribes to it – hence his obsessive use of the song in his film. His choice of setting expresses the same wistfulness for the past as his attitude to the song does: "We made sure that the costumes and period setting did everything they could to release the audience's imagination. We consciously avoided setting this version in a specific time but instead went for a look that worked within itself, where clothes, props, architecture, all belonged to the same world ... anytime between 1700 and 1900" (12–13).

Sprengler writes that recent interior design manages "to create a nostalgic atmosphere and permit reminiscence without reference to specific historical eras. Constructing a look of 'pastness' by rummaging through historical styles is a practice centuries old" (27). This "pastness" was characteristic of the Royal Shakespeare Company's set design during the years Branagh worked for them. The Proustianism of the settings and costumes in his film reflects the regret shown by text choices for a time when men did not have to account for their love-life and were free to do as they pleased.

Branagh very consciously decided to have the lyrics heard three times in the film, and wanted the words themselves up on screen so that the audience would tune in to the language and, he writes, "understand the simplicity, gravity and beauty of the song lyrics" (xvi). "Gravity" seems to me to be the right word for some of the lyrics, and yet this quality is not well served by their presentation in the film, with Beatrice delivering the words wryly, and her on-screen audience laughing uproariously at her conclusion. The film opens with the words of the song appearing one by one, karaoke style, in white on a black screen as Thompson's Beatrice reads them slowly and dryly. Deleyto astutely observes that this technique seems to prompt "the spectator to sing, or at least recite, along and thus identify with the content of what is being said and with the speaking voice. Even before the importance of the message sinks in, the film is, therefore, demanding total identification with Beatrice" (96).

The many close-ups of Thompson throughout the film would seem to support Deleyto's theory. If his supposition is correct, then the song becomes her recommendation to her own sex not to take men or their infidelities to heart but rather to adopt her own blithe, independent stance. By contrast, in the original play, when sung by Balthasar, the song, according to Sheldon Zitner, "suggests the self-serving nature of male counsel: that women reconcile themselves to playing in an unfair game" (203–4). Branagh seems to sit on the fence between these two readings, as we will see: he sees the song both as full of "gravity" (xiv) and as creating a mood of "high romanticism" (xiv) and "deep tranquillity" (41). Perhaps he is just responding to the mixture of the serious and the merry in the play. John F. Cox recognizes this tonal dichotomy in Branagh's use of the song as a key to his film: "The 'fraud of men' (2.3.63) was underscored in the Hero–Claudio–Don John story, but the advice to 'sigh not so, but let them go' (2.3.57) was ironically countered by the film's powerful emphasis on the sexuality that impels women and men together" (83).

The film's light-hearted renditions of the song's lyrics reinforce not only the conventions of romantic comedy but also the Elizabethan double standards inherent in the play. When men betray women, women are to let them go and be blithe about it. However, when women play men false, men are permitted to ruin their reputations in the most painful and public manner, as Claudio and Don Pedro do in making a travesty of Hero's wedding day. Claudio, so far from singing "Hey nonny nonny," throws Hero back to her father as "a rotten orange" (3.5.32). In this scene, Branagh renders Claudio less sympathetic than in Shakespeare's script by directing him to be physically violent with Hero. Yet, through his cuts in the text, Branagh has diminished the motif of men betraying women, except with his emphasis on the song.

Whedon includes the song, although he transposes it to his masked party scene in which the lyrics are all but lost in the barrage of images assailing the viewer. In addition to the distraction of the many party guests dancing, talking, and laughing, Whedon has added two Cirque de Soleil trapeze artists, scantily clad, gyrating in a large tree in his backyard. However, although the audience may not pick up on the lyrics, the melody, which Whedon composed to be reminiscent of Joe Davis and Osvaldo Farres's "Perhaps, Perhaps, Perhaps" as sung by Doris Day (one of many instances of the director's nostalgia for the 1960s in his film), may have served a similar purpose, at least for older viewers (DVD commentary). Davis and Farres's song also treats the theme of fickleness in love:

If you can't make your mind up,
We'll never get started.
And I don't want to wind up
Being parted, broken-hearted.

Whedon has his mellow, jazzy composition sung by a woman rather than Balthasar, which makes the accusations against men in it more pointed. In fact, at one point, we see Whedon's wife, Kai Cole, singing part of the song at the piano (fig. 10). Whedon fans would likely pick up on the theme of uncertainty in love right away, as he cast as his Beatrice and Benedick the actors Amy Acker and Alexis Denisof, who played a couple (Fred and Wesley) who never quite came together on Whedon's cult favourite television show *Angel*. When talk-show host Stephen Colbert asked Whedon "if the Beatrice and Benedick relationship was similar to the formulaic 'will they or won't they' storyline

Figure 10 Kai Cole sings "Sigh No More, Ladies" at Leonato's party in Whedon's *Much Ado About Nothing*, 2012.

of film and TV romance, Whedon responded without hesitation: 'It's the original will they or won't they'" (Lavery, 167).

The song "Sigh No More" is not entirely out of place at the masked ball, the line "men were deceivers ever" being pertinent to Don Pedro's benign deception of Hero and also to Don John's malign trickery of Claudio. Whedon further adds Margaret's longing glance at Borachio to the scene to suggest her vulnerability to Borachio's inclusion of her in the conspiracy to undermine Hero. For the gulling of Benedick, Whedon replaces Balthasar's singing "Sigh No More" with a soft instrumental piece selected by Claudio on his iPod. Despite the contemporary technology, the music, again composed by Whedon, has a retro sound, recalling the 1960s Italian cinema that the director is constantly invoking. Thus this project was for Whedon quadruply nostalgic: wistful for Shakespeare's unique talent (which he addresses in his introduction to his screenplay, 10), elegiac for Whedon's first experience of the play in Regent's Park, London, as a youth (Screenplay, 14), reminiscent of the Shakespeare readings he hosted for over a decade at his house (15), and evocative of films of the 1950 and 1960s. In addition to 1960s Italian cinema, Whedon cites the noir comedy of Billy Wilder and Preston Sturges as influences on his *Much Ado* (DVD commentary).

The song "Sigh No More Ladies" may not be the best vehicle to convey what Branagh views as "the moral" of the play. In reviewing the reactions of critics, students, and scholars – and even characters – to the song, both in the text and in performance, what emerges is that it is generally given less attention than it deserves. Critical commentary on the song tends to be slight. The lyrics treat a major theme of the play, which is betrayal in love, and they offer what Zitner almost uniquely identifies as "hardly reassuring counsel" to women who have suffered from men's deceit (203). Critics and editors alike most often dismiss the song with a remark about it "softening the mood, and preparing for talk of love" (Foakes, 141). Wey writes that "Balthasar is then brought on stage (lines 44–92) to help in the plot which will eventually unite Benedick and Beatrice in love and matrimony" (81). He also notes the conjunction of music in the play with "harmony and happiness and love among the principal characters" (81). Even Branagh, in the screenplay, writes that the song appeals to Claudio's "high romanticism" in the garden (xiv). In what way would a song about men deceiving women, and women letting them go put the audience or Claudio in a romantic mood? W.H. Auden's answer was that Claudio is not paying attention to the lyrics: "Claudio ... is in a dreamy, lovesick state ... he will not notice that the mood and words of the song are in complete contrast to his daydream" (101). So why is it that many critics, who, one assumes, are not similarly infatuated, write about the song's romantic qualities? Is it that critics, reviewers, and editors of Shakespeare plays, when viewing a performance, are lulled by the music of the song to such an extent that, like Claudio, they ignore the lyrics? Certainly, the commentary in most editions concentrates on the settings and the instruments that may have been used, but rarely a word about the way in which the song expands on a central theme of the play and re-examines it from the woman's point of view. Or is it because the song deals only with female sexual insecurity that many male critics can find it romantic and even "soothing"?

To what degree do audiences generally register song lyrics? I asked all the students in my two Shakespeare Comedy and Film classes at University College Dublin, after they had seen and taken notes on Branagh's film, why they thought he had opened the film with the words of the song. They had no answer. I asked them what they thought the song was about, and the lyrics had made no impression on them. It was only when I had them read the song in their texts that they recognized the lyrics' significance. I asked my students what their practice was when they encountered a song in Shakespeare's plays, and some admitted that they tended to skip over the lyrics. I report this not to shame them but to supply evidence for my theory that most spectators, watching a film or play, may remember the tune of a song that breaks up the narrative but will take no particular note of the lyrics, if indeed, they can even hear them clearly. Adrienne L. McLean in *Cinema Journal* contends that songs in non-musical films are apt to be disregarded as sections in which nothing significant occurs (Deleyto, 96). Even critics are not exempt from this tendency to ignore lyrics. Douglas Brode in his book *Shakespeare in the Movies* did not register the name (and refrain) of the song correctly and referred to it as "Cry No More Ladies" (87). What Brecht perceived about the emotional impact of theatre diminishing its intellectual clout seems to be particularly true of songs, even though Brecht himself used them to contribute to his alienation effect. Audiences watching Balthasar sing "sigh no more" in that lovely Tuscan garden in Branagh's film are enjoying the melody and the scenery; they are not thinking about the words. Similarly, Whedon's audience are taking pleasure in the lively party scene, to which the song is a merely pleasant background score. Thomson confirms this primacy of the visual over the musical: "Stylistically speaking, music for a spoken play must always be subservient to the visual element" (qtd in Stevens, 89). Even Branagh's attempt to make the audience aware of the lyrics by having them on screen at the beginning seems to have backfired. Perhaps it takes the audience those opening minutes to adjust to the Elizabethan language, and therefore it is not an ideal place for significant lines to be recited.

It is especially surprising that the lyrics of the song are ignored in this play which so often demands our assessment of words: it is "language, which this play – with the self-conscious verbal wit of Beatrice and Benedick and the malapropisms of Dogberry – keeps uppermost in its audience's attention perhaps more than any other of the comedies" (Davis, 3). This concentrated focus on the way people speak should throw emphasis on the lyrics of the songs in the play, but if my students, who were studying the film after reading the play, paid no attention to the lyrics, what chance has the general public? Barton observed, "I may be cynical but I don't believe most people really listen to Shakespeare in the theatre unless the actors make them do so" (7). This must be even more the case with film audiences, as film is predominantly visual, whereas theatre is still predominantly verbal. In short, we make the same mistake as so many of the characters in the play in not noting words as we should. Perhaps it is a function of the fact that we are now unused to reading anything but credits on a film screen. Words on the screen, especially at the beginning or end of a film, tend to be viewed as details included only for film buffs who actually care about the identity of the best boy, etc. We assume now, in contrast to silent film audiences, that the real information in a film is conveyed in images; the words are mere footnotes.

So if we accept that modern audiences, even modern readers, pay little attention to the lyrics of the song, how important can the lyrics of Shakespeare's songs be? Was Shakespeare, a consummate man of the theatre, aware that his audience might miss the lyrics, or were their ears better able than ours to assimilate both melodic and verbal information? Thomson contends that Shakespeare was "wary of all music's disruptive dangers and ever so careful lest musicians, a powerful and privileged group in [his] ... England, steal the show from poetry" (qtd in Stevens, 88). At the same time, we know that theatregoers went to "hear" a play rather than to "see" one – the arts of rhetoric being at least as important, if not more, than the visual effects.

Shakespeare took great care over the songs in his plays; they were not just random entertainments to break up the narrative. Not only are the lyrics pertinent to his plays' themes and plots but also they are particularly aimed at the group of characters on stage who hear them. This is obvious in *Twelfth Night* in which Feste sings a *carpe diem* song, "O Mistress Mine," to Toby and Andrew, a couple of aging bachelors wasting their lives on drink and immature hijinks instead of getting down to the serious business of comedy: finding a mate (see chapter 11). At first, "Sigh No More, Ladies" seems an odd choice for Balthasar to sing. In fact, John Stevens in the introduction to *Shakespeare in Music* comments: "Balthasar's song, charming though it is, looks rather stuck on to the play. The fusing power of Shakespeare's imagination does not appear, in this play, to have comprehended music; there are no effects that any other Elizabethan playwright could not have contrived" (31). The song certainly seems an odd choice to sing to a group of men. The lyrics directly address women, and seem neither to suit the newly betrothed Claudio, who would rather think about nuptial bliss than betrayal, or the conspirators, who plot to convince the commitment-phobic Benedick to trust love again.

At the same time, the lyrics are also very appropriate for this group of men. Each will make ladies sigh from woe. Benedick has in the past, we learn from Beatrice, played for her heart with false dice. Claudio and Don Pedro will betray and deceive Hero, bringing her to church to rupture the wedding and ruin her reputation. Leonato too will betray her, believing the word of foreign men over his own daughter's confirmation of her innocence. If these men had noted the words to the song, perhaps they would have acted differently. A.R. Humphreys in his commentary in the Arden edition (135) believes that Shakespeare is directing the song to the audience, reminding them of the "fraud of men" set in motion against Hero in the previous scene (2.2). In contrast, Holger Klein in his edition thinks the song functions to "tune Benedick in to what will follow" and to prepare him for the image the conspirators present of "Beatrice's supposed languishing" (192).

Alexander Leggatt voices one plausible theory for the onstage and offstage audience's lack of attention to these lyrics, so contrary to the spirit of romantic comedy. Leggatt observes that Benedick complains about Balthasar's voice and that Don Pedro answers Balthasar's self-deprecatory remarks about his singing with no more than politeness. He sees these lines as inspiring the stage tradition of burlesquing the song. If the song is burlesqued, it cuts through any facile romanticism (173). Furthermore, the audience's attention will be focused on the singer's technique (or lack thereof), and if the lyrics are noted at all, they will be seen as merely one more droll aspect of an absurd performance. However, as Deleyto observes, this is not the route taken by Branagh. The only trace of it appears when Beatrice recites the words ironically to open the film, and her on-screen audience guffaw "in a way that makes us think we must be missing something" (12), as *Independent* reviewer Adam Mars-Jones noted. When the song is later sung in its original place in the play, however, Patrick Doyle as Balthasar renders it beautifully. His *voice* does not draw our attention away from the lyrics and their edgy message, but the *location* does. Branagh's script gives details on the mood the director was hoping to create: "The camera tracks around the circular fountain as BALTHASAR sings and the lounging nobles breathe an image of deep tranquillity. The camera movement is slow. The music is beautiful, melodic, dancing on the late afternoon air. In the background we can see our household servants. Beyond them the vines, the olive groves, the lush countryside" (41).

Not only is the setting distracting but so too are the gentle movements of all the characters. Once again, the song is seen as creating a romantic mood – in complete contradiction to the lyrics that aim to console women for the heartbreak and turmoil in their emotional lives. Branagh indeed seems to be guilty of what J. Hoberman of the *Village Voice* described as "blandly ignoring the play's disturbing undercurrents – the sexual paranoia and the patriarchal cruelty of the social order" (55). Furthermore, the nobles enjoy "deep tranquillity" only at the expense of "our household servants," who continue to work while the lords relax. Once again, the subtext suggests a nostalgia for a time in which men, particularly upper-class men, did not have to account for their behaviour, even when it was characterized by infidelity or sloth.

Of course, in more immediate terms, Balthasar's song seems to anticipate Leonato and Claudio's descriptions in the same scene of Beatrice's anguish over Benedick. While she appears blithe and bonny in society, they claim that, in private, she not only sighs for Benedick but "weeps, sobs, beats her heart, tears her hair, prays [and] curses" (2.3.142–3). If anyone needs the words of consolation provided by the song, it is this absurd, fictional Beatrice created by the old man and the naïve boy, neither of whom know much about a young woman in love. However, Auden noticed the song's parallels with Shakespeare's characterization of Beatrice: "The song is actually about the irresponsibility of men and folly of women taking them seriously, and recommends as an antidote good humor and common sense. If one imagines these sentiments being the expression of a character, the only character they suit is Beatrice" (101). James J. Wey, in a footnote, explains that he sees the song as an extension of the men's plot, carefully chosen to support their description of Beatrice: "This song, like the remaining two songs in *Much Ado*, is admirably suited to the dramatic context. It is a love lament from the woman's point of view in which women deceived by men's inconstancy and indifference are advised to forget the man and be merry. This is good psychological softening of Benedick for it helps convince him that what he overhears his friends saying is true – that Beatrice's gay exterior is evidence that she inwardly sighs for him. In fact, Don Pedro's account in a later scene of Beatrice's state of mind closely echoes the sentiments suggested for the woman in the song (v.i.168–76)" (Wey 85fn9). This is a compelling idea, and while Balthasar gives no indication of being in on the plot, Don Pedro has heard the song before and so would have had a chance to recognize its suitability (2.3.35).

It seems to me that Shakespeare also provides the song to contrast the way men behave when women are unfaithful with the way women conduct themselves when men stray. We see Claudio and Leonato behave very badly indeed in the church scene. Shakespeare, I am convinced, did not mean us to sympathize with them at that point. Leonato's speech about the ruined Hero, with its emphasis on the word "mine," is a study in self-absorption (4.1.121–43). Beatrice's shock at the public nature of Claudio's rejection is also significant (4.2.304–8). F.H. Mares points out in the Cambridge introduction to the play that in Shakespeare's sources none of the Claudio figures rejects the Hero figures in such a humiliatingly public way (5). Shakespeare evidently made this change to render Claudio less sympathetic.

Similarly, Shakespeare altered the Hero character so that she appears younger and more vulnerable than in the sources (Mares, 5). At a time when the ideal woman had a voice that was "ever soft / Gentle and low" (*King Lear*, 5.3.247–8), Hero's silence when Claudio rejects her must have been viewed as virtuous by her original audience. She is barely allowed to speak in the accusation scene, and then she must retreat and pretend to be dead. At the end of the play, she must accept the man who hurt her so dreadfully with good grace, with "Hey nonny nonny."

Did Shakespeare accept the double standard? In *King Lear*, he has his mad king rail brilliantly against two kinds of justice, one for the rich and one for the poor (4.5.147–63), but was he prepared to accept that women had to be chaste while men could be wayward? In *Much Ado About Nothing*, he does not appear to recommend any revolutionary tactics to women. But there is a definite sense of melancholy in the song that seems to suggest, along with the darkening of the Claudio figure and the increased victimization of the Hero figure, that he recognized the unfairness of the system, even while not suggesting how it could be altered. This stance is typical of his comedies. Cesario and Orsino in *Twelfth Night* have a long conversation on the way in which men and women are different in love (2.4), with Orsino contradicting himself in his passion (32–3, 92–101; see next chapter). Once again, Shakespeare seems to promote the idea that women are more constant than men, and more stoical in their suffering. The comedy seems to inspire pity for them because of this. So far from beating their heart and tearing their hair, as Claudio imagines Beatrice doing, really more a reflection of *men's* licence in showing their outrage at female infidelity, women sit "like patience on a monument, / Smiling at grief" (*Twelfth Night* 2.4.114–15).

Shakespeare's *Much Ado About Nothing* is a tremendously complex comedy. Critics who dismiss the play as "all fun ... light as air" (Doyle, 11) seriously underestimate it. The comedy is really about the challenges of monogamy. So far from delivering a conventional happy-ever-after ending, Shakespeare shows us two couples who are about to embark on married lives with considerable emotional baggage. Hero and Beatrice have both been hurt by their spouses in the past, and the forecast is for more of the same, if we read the banter carefully. The only way that the marriages will survive is if the women exercise the stoicism and tolerance urged upon them by the song. Branagh picks up on this in his screenplay, but downplays the double standard: he writes, "*Much Ado About Nothing* ... speaks loudly and gloriously about love ... the cruelty of it, the joy of it. The question of tolerance in love and the danger of judging others" (xvi).

But in Shakespeare's day, it was only dangerous for women to judge men, not the other way round. Beatrice's harsh judgment of men prepares her for nothing but celibacy until her cousin points out her pride to her. Meanwhile, Benedick, similarly harsh in his judgment of women, presumably enjoys the freedom of sowing his wild oats at the brothels he mentions (1.2.236). Claudio and Leonato are forgiven their harsh judgment of Hero, so much so that she is not even given a line of reproach when she welcomes back her former fiancé. Is "Hey nonny nonny" enough to console her?

Shakespeare does give women one other option in the song besides stoicism in the face of male inconstancy; they can let men go. This is an ambiguous line, of course. It could mean that the women should let their husbands go to their mistresses, thus bolstering the double standard. Or it could be a more radical piece of advice, urging the women to let any man who is inconstant depart their lives, and choose rather the independent celibacy that Beatrice makes so blithe. That is why the song fits well in the middle of the play, before Beatrice and Benedick have rejected their single lives. It seems oddly placed at the end of the play, as in the Branagh film, when the couples dance to celebrate their upcoming nuptials. Beatrice and Hero are emphatically not letting their men go at the end; they are taking them on permanently, despite past hurts. They must do this to fulfill the demands of the comic genre that ultimately supports marriage as the basis for a harmonious society. In the film, the song is misplaced at the end because the lyrics urge passive stoicism, and what the end of comedy demands is active commitment. The live-and-let-live attitude of the song is replaced by Claudio's warning to Beatrice to live a life of vigilance to keep her husband constant. Meanwhile, Benedick jokingly seizes on a future of cuckoldry; he quips, "No staff so reverend as one tipped with horn" (5.4.122–3). He has assumed a measure of that stoic tolerance the song urged on the ladies. At the end of the comedy, Beatrice, Benedick, and Hero seem to be accepting suffering in love as part of their lot, which they will lighten with dance, songs, and jokes, as throughout the course of the play.

Other viewers also found the song misplaced at the conclusion. Penny Gay remembers the Bill Alexander Royal Shakespeare Company production in 1990, which I too was fortunate enough to see: "The final dance was performed to a lusty choral reprise of 'Sigh No More, Ladies': it was an imposition of communal harmony which Susan Fleetwood [who played Beatrice] thought inappropriate – the song 'says that men will always be unfaithful, and it completely negates what's gone before.' Whether it was a deliberate irony on Alexander's part or an unthinking attempt to provide the traditional up-beat ending to a comedy, it failed finally to convince: the play itself, in this embodiment, was about a society's loss of faith in the conventions it had created and lived by for so long" (177).

The "Hey nonny nonny" of the song refers us back to the title of the play, *Much Ado About Nothing*. Both title and song seem to urge us not to repeat Claudio's mistake in succumbing to paranoia, or to love only our own wit, like Benedick and Beatrice, whose sins of intellectual pride shut out the possibility of love. Rather, like that same couple reformed, the play urges us to accept the trials of marriage with good humour and to trust and tolerate our partners despite human fickleness.

11

"O Mistress Mine": Intercutting in Trevor Nunn's *Twelfth Night*

In his subtle and intelligent screen adaptation of *Twelfth Night*, English director Trevor Nunn has improved on Shakespeare's original, at least from a twenty-first-century perspective. Nunn's film makes the counterpoint between the main plot and subplot more immediate and explicit, and therefore more effective for contemporary viewers through text cuts and changes, especially through intercutting (alternating shots from two or more sequences to suggest parallel action). Thus, despite its comparative failure in the box office, Nunn has achieved what film directors of Shakespeare strive to accomplish: he has rendered the play accessible to a larger audience by truly translating it to the new medium.

Nowhere is this translation more striking than in act 2, scenes 3 and 4, in which Nunn, through skilful textual editing and intercutting, conveys Shakespearean richness of theme and character in a bare fraction of the dialogue. Nunn cuts between two chief locales: Lady Olivia's kitchen, in which Feste sings "O Mistress Mine" to Sir Toby, Sir Andrew, and, in a significant inclusion, Maria; and Duke Orsino's smoking room, in which Cesario and Orsino are engaged in a game of cards. He also makes quick cutaways to Malvolio's and Olivia's bedchambers. Feste's song provides a connecting tissue, as it is played on the piano in Orsino's smoking room, while Feste's voice from the kitchen floats up in voice-over to Olivia and Malvolio in their respective bedrooms.

Even spectators well versed in the play will not at first recognize how much Nunn has changed these scenes, so true are they to the spirit of the original. He wields his pared-down script and intercutting technique to accelerate and clarify the parallelism that exists in Shakespeare's play from scene to scene. The greater control over audience perception that a film director has compared to a theatrical director also goes some way to explaining the increased clarity of Nunn's version. Shakespeare's original structure and his medium allow the audience to consider any number of aspects when watching these scenes, and the thematic connection between the two scenes may thus be lost. A film controls audience response more tyrannically than a play; semiotician Susan Sontag writes of the "more unrefusable impact on the eye" of film in contrast to theatre (347). Filmmaker Vsevolod Pudovkin reminds us that film editing "builds the scenes from separate pieces, of which each concentrates the attention of the spectator only on that element important to that action. Editing is in actual fact a compulsory and deliberate guidance of the thoughts and associations of the spectator" (84, 87). Yet despite the greater focus and control, Nunn loses little of the rich significance of Shakespeare's scenes; rather, he is able to crystallize some of the key points through the economy exacted by the new medium.

While changes to the text are important in achieving this crystallization, Nunn's use of intercutting is paramount. This technique allows the director to achieve at least four objectives: one, it fulfills a structural function in suggesting that two or more scenes are occurring simultaneously; two, it thus adds to the suspense and pacing of the film; three, it creates dramatic irony by giving the audience more knowledge than any of the characters; and four, it creates parallelism, allowing the intercut scenes to comment on one another. In my chronological analysis of the section, this last effect of intercutting is my primary focus, but the first three are worth considering briefly.

It is the swift movement from setting to setting, sometimes in as little as a few seconds, that suggests simultaneity. Nunn reinforces the impression of concurrence by having the same music played in both locales, starting and ending at the same time. In Paul Thomas Anderson's *Magnolia* (1999), one song, Aimee Mann's "Wise Up," sung by each of the characters in the different plots, also forges a structural link. This method of using music to unify crosscut scenes and enhance the sense of simultaneity calls attention to its own artifice, alerting the audience to their task: they must compare and contrast the different plots. Nunn takes his cue from Shakespeare, who included more songs in *Twelfth Night* than in almost any other of his plays. It is no wonder that the director selects this particular Shakespeare play to adapt, given his long and highly successful experience in directing West End musicals. In the First Folio, a good half of the sparse stage directions call either for music or a catch/song. Several critics have noted the primacy of music in Nunn's film. For instance, Crowl observes in his review: "The film keeps returning to music and song ... to capture the play's lyric quality ... Snatches of 'The Wind and the Rain,' 'O Mistress Mine,' and 'Come Away Death' are interwoven throughout the film, giving it something of the texture of Mozart's *Cozi Fan Tutti*... [and achieving] a quartet of moving ... images of love's perplexing variety" (36). The return to songs already sung can contribute to the nostalgic feel of a film, as scholar Christine Sprengler points out: "A song can function as a mnemonic prompt by calling to mind experiences from the time it was first heard or the time during which it was most often listened to [including within the film itself]" (76).

Shakespeare's structure accomplishes more gradually and less obviously the parallelism that Nunn achieves by cutting between Lady Olivia's kitchen and Duke Orsino's smoking room. The quick cutaways to Malvolio's and Olivia's bedchambers during this sequence once again merely accelerate the process set in motion by Shakespeare's structure. Shakespeare shows us, scene by scene, what love and desire do to characters of different class, sex, age, and temperament. None of his major characters are untouched by love – even Feste (Ben Kinglsey) has his "leman" (according to Sir Andrew, 2.3.24). Nunn suggests all this in one sequence.

Nunn's use of the intercutting technique is very modern. The whole sequence described above lasts no more than seven minutes, yet encapsulates all the narrative information of the first halves of two scenes. Sometimes we are only at one locale for thirty seconds or less of screen time before cutting away. The pace here is what cinema audiences have become accustomed to from rock videos and even another Shakespeare adaptation, Baz Luhrmann's Romeo + *Juliet*, to which Nunn refers in his interview with Crowdus (39). This modernity fits in with Nunn's overall interpretation: "I've always thought that there was something about the play which had an unusually contemporary ring" (Fine Line Features website, 2).

Intercutting also creates a sense of omniscience in the audience – we have an unrestricted knowledge of events to which none of the characters of the play are privy. The omniscience we have as spectators over his characters is similar to the omniscience shared by Shakespeare's original audience – we know Cesario is a girl, which Orsino and Olivia do not; we also know that Sebastian is alive, which Cesario does not. But in Nunn's film, we have a greater sense of omniscience because we do not have to wait long to be given privileged information. In the sequence in question, we learn that Toby and Maria are attracted to each other, because Nunn has included her in the scene, whereas Shakespeare left her out. We compare the (seemingly hopeless) glances exchanged between Maria and Toby with those swapped between Orsino and Cesario – in both cases, Nunn makes it easy for us to compare and contrast the romantic feelings in both plots by connecting the households with swift intercutting and the same love song. His intercutting thus builds suspense. Visually exciting and pacey, it creates expectations in the audience regarding the blossoming love between Orsino and Cesario, and Maria and Toby, expectations that are not immediately fulfilled.

It is worth going through the sequence chronologically to examine the ways in which Nunn composes a visual and musical essay on the encroachment of time on love and beauty – a favourite theme of Shakespeare's sonnets and of many other Elizabethan lyrics. The intercutting makes more evident the fact that Shakespeare's play conducts a kind of survey, airing the opinion of both men and women, lowborn and high, on these eternal subjects. Nunn structures the sequence with great care, cleverly using Shakespeare's lines as sound cues, cutting away to illustrate a line from a song, or to connect the dialogue spoken in one locale with that of the other. This technique is related to one commonly used in adapting Shakespeare to the screen: that of providing images to illustrate difficult passages in the text. For example, Franco Zeffirelli in his *Hamlet* (1990) indulged in a combination of illustration and semaphore for Mel Gibson's delivery of the "to be or not to be" soliloquy.

Nunn opens the sequence with an establishing shot of Orsino's castle and a voice-over. Orsino eulogizes, "O, when mine eyes did see Olivia first" (Nunn, 38), lines taken from act 1, scene 1. Nunn adds to the romantic anticipation inherent in the scene through the composition of his frames and his Pre-Raphaelite decor. We are brought into the drawing room, in which the warm tones of tapestries and carved wood form the background, and a table with a lit candle furnishes the foreground. The duke and his companion appear to be alone. Firelight flickers in the background. Cheroot smoke, weaving between the young, hopeful faces of Orsino and Cesario, seems to emanate from their own smouldering emotions. The image of fire is constantly associated with these two characters in the film, and this is more than the result of historical necessity. The houses are of course heated by fires and lit by candles, but there is no need for these to be included in so many frames. Whenever Orsino and Cesario talk to each other indoors, there is either a candle on the table or a roaring fire in the frame, with smoke (or steam, as in the bath scene) swirling around them. All these signifiers add to the suspense – we want to see all this repressed emotion come to the fore. This "microscopic attention to detail" is seen by theatre critics as a hallmark of Nunn's directorial style (Martin White, 299).

The one action of the short sequence is Orsino lighting a cheroot for Cesario, in a gesture that in cinematic terms has romantic resonance. Film men often light cigarettes for the women they intend to seduce (witness Victor Levin's recent romantic comedy, *5 to 7* (2014) in which the love affair begins in just this way). The gesture is particularly striking because the master lights his servant's cigarette and not the other way round. Perhaps Nunn, in a nostalgic yearning for Shakespeare's more heteronormative society, is suggesting that Orsino unconsciously recognizes Viola's femininity, as he seems to do when he first sends her to woo Olivia ("Diana's lip/ Is not more smooth and rubious," 1.4.29–36).

When Orsino lights Cesario's cheroot, she turns her face away from him, wincing. In this one facial expression, at once comic and poignant, Imogen Stubbs achieves a great deal. She reminds the audience that this role-playing is a terrible strain on Viola for so many reasons. She has, of course, never smoked a cheroot before, so her physical discomfort with her male role is summed up in her nauseated expression. Kenneth Rothwell writes, "As the cross-dressed Viola/ Cesario, Imogen Stubbs interrogates the feminist fantasy that being male can resolve all female problems" (*Shakespeare on Screen*, 239). Smoking is just one of the many challenges expected of males; Cesario must also hunt, fence, shoot pool, play cards, and gracefully reject Olivia's pressing advances. Of course, the most difficult task assigned to her male self is to woo another woman on behalf of the man she loves. The pain of this aspect of her role is palpable as she winces not only from the smoke but also from Orsino's ardent avowal of love for her rival. Nunn here exploits one of the great strengths of cinema – the potential and economy of a single close-up. Yet this attention to the character's face is characteristic of Nunn's work in the theatre also, where he "wanted to put 'chamber' productions of Shakespeare at the core of the RSC," focusing always on the scale of the individual actor (Martin White, 288).

The whole short episode (only five lines of dialogue) is, in a sense, Nunn's creation, as this little scene did not exist in Shakespeare. The play moves directly from Antonio's wistful farewell to Sebastian to Malvolio and Cesario's discussion of Olivia's ring (2.2), and then straight into the subplot with Toby and Andrew asking Maria for a stoup of wine (2.3). In Shakespeare, at the opening of the play, Orsino compares himself to a hart pursued by his own desires before he and the audience have even met Viola. He says these lines not in an intimate tête a tête with Cesario, as in Nunn's version, but publicly to Curio and the other lords. We receive the impression in Shakespeare that he is acting the part of the unrequited lover, wallowing in his own romantic image. Nunn gives us a little of this with Orsino's "Let music be the food of love" speech (Nunn, 13), but Toby Stevens speaks the five lines in question with sincerity and feeling, confiding in his friend. Nunn, in the introduction to his screenplay, explains that he breaks up Orsino's scenes and inserts them at more regular intervals throughout the play (Orsino is offstage in Shakespeare from 2.4 to 5.1) in order to give the cinema audience a sense of getting to know him over time. Nunn ends the short episode with Orsino's voice-over saying, "And my desires, like fell and cruel hounds / E'er since pursue me" (39), while the camera focuses on Stubbs's face, turning green.

The word "pursue" is still lingering in our ears when we see Sir Toby drunk and giggling, scaling, like an ungainly hound himself, the walls of Olivia's estate, trailed by an even clumsier Sir Andrew. This image serves as a kind of establishing shot for the alternate locale. The courtyard they enter is much like an Oxford or Cambridge college quadrangle, Georgian windows set in grey stone walls, the colors cool, age-softened. The dialogue is taken from act 2, scene 3, but is pared down considerably. Nunn chooses to have the two stand under Maria's window to yell, "Marion, I say! A stoup of wine!" (40) while winging pebbles at the glass. The choice is masterly. Not only is the scene reminiscent of undergraduate hijinks – Toby and Andrew as a middle-aged Charles Ryder and Sebastian Flyte (Evelyn Waugh's *Brideshead Revisit-*

ed) drunkenly sneaking into their Oxford colleges after curfew – but it also conjures up romantic associations: a suitor serenading his beloved under her window, Romeo and Juliet, Cyrano de Bergerac and Roxanne. Once again, Nunn's special gift for evoking the unique blend of humour and pathos that runs through the play in a single cinematic image is evident.

All these associations comment ironically on the characters of the subplot. Imelda Staunton's Maria is no Juliet or Roxanne, but a plain spinster fast approaching middle age. Her serenaders seek wine, not love, and are far less romantic figures even than the unsightly Cyrano. For their part, Toby and Andrew are too old to be nostalgic for their undergraduate days and reliving tipsy escapades. The inappropriateness of their climbing into Olivia's estate, and Andrew crashing into a cucumber frame, is at the heart of both the comedy and the poignancy of the scene. All of this is suggested in Shakespeare's own text by Feste's final song ("While tosspots still had drunken heads") and other characters' disparaging comments on the pair.

In the finished film, text is radically cut from this scene. Lines 1 to 12, in which Toby comically equates staying up late with getting up early, and Andrew responds with naive earnestness, are missing. In Nunn's script, only three lines (4, 7, 8) that contain no new material are excised, and the word "betimes" is altered to "early" for greater understanding. In all likelihood, the further cuts are a result of test audience's reactions; a contemporary audience may not have found the joke funny enough to warrant an exchange that in no way forwards the plot. Nunn, whose dictate at the Royal Shakespeare Company had been "we change him at our peril," observes in the introduction to his screenplay that changing and cutting became easier as the film progressed; his published script must then represent a version of the film before final editing.

Nunn treats us to a few quick interior shots of Maria's room as she wraps herself in her dressing gown to go downstairs to meet the men. What little we see of her bedroom confirms her spinster status: a narrow bed with white linen and black bedposts, the colours of virginity and mortality. Out in the garden, a hooded Feste creeps up behind the two drunks and startles them, darkly uttering the line, "Did you ever see the picture of we three?" (40). Nunn then cuts to the kitchen, where Maria waits, looking uneasy and a bit annoyed. Perhaps Nunn's most important change to the scene is his inclusion of Maria at this juncture. In Shakespeare's play, she is not present during Feste's rendition of "O Mistress Mine" but enters seventeen lines after the end of the song, properly roused by the singing of the "catch" (line 68).

The sterile, cool white atmosphere of the kitchen, with the moonlight gleaming on the pale china, provides a dramatic contrast to Orsino's warm smoking room and seems to reflect the bachelor status of Toby, Andrew, Maria, and Feste. The noisy entrance into the kitchen, Sir Toby grabbing Maria for an impromptu spin across the room, inspires a cut to a rosette window, church-like, the establishing shot for Malvolio's room. The steward is engaged in two activities that belie his Puritan stance during working hours – he is reading a magazine called *l'Amour* (Edwardian soft porn?) and drinking something that looks suspiciously like brandy. Once again, this quick cutaway speaks volumes: Malvolio is a hypocrite who in a sense deserves what is coming to him, denying others their drink and women so he can enjoy his quietly in his room. It also suggests the widespread susceptibility of these characters, irrespective of age, gender, or station, to what Olivia describes as the "plague" – love. Malvolio's reading is interrupted suddenly by a voice-over of someone stridently shouting his name. Back in the kitchen, Feste assumes an East-Indian accent (perhaps an allusion to Kingsley's famous role as Gandhi in 1982?) to bellow "Malvolio's nose is no whipstock" (42). By showing us Malvolio at this juncture, with this reading matter, Nunn adds to Shakespeare's suspense. We anticipate seeing him fall under Cupid's arrow just like the others. Conversely, this cutaway, giving a brief insight into Malvolio's point of view, may also inspire a twinge of sympathy for him. In Shakespeare's play, the audience usually begins to feel compassion for Malvolio no earlier than the dark-house scene. It is quite a different experience to hear insults against someone when their image is in front of you (as Malvolio's is in Nunn's intercut sequence) than when it is not (as in Shakespeare's script). For the Elizabethan lawyer and diarist John Manningham, the gulling of Malvolio was clearly the highlight of the play, judging by his diary entry for February 1601 when he saw *Twelfth Night* performed at Middle Temple (I have modernized the spelling): "A good practice in it to make the steward believe his lady widow was in love with him, by counterfeiting a letter as from his lady in general terms, telling him what she liked best in him, and prescribing his gesture in smiling, his apparel etc., and then when he came to practice making him believe they took him to be mad" (Sorlien, 48). Some twentieth-century film critics, sharing Manningham's humour, criticized Nunn for making Malvolio too sympathetic (Crowl, 37; Alleva, 14), and his decision to intercut Malvolio with his insulters no doubt contributed to this noted effect.

Once again, the cuts to the text differ from the published script to the final film. In Shakespeare's original, after Toby's welcome of Feste, Sir Andrew praises Feste's chest, legs, and voice (lines 18–21). Nunn cuts these lines, but, strangely enough, keeps Andrew's obscure references to Pigrogromitus, the Vapians, and Queubus (22–4), phony scholarship no doubt included by Shakespeare to amuse the law students of the Middle Temple, his original audience. Nunn also keeps Feste's elaborate, "I did impetticoat thy gratillity" (25). Then he inserts in his script all the dialogue about "catches" (62–78), which actually follows Feste's song in Shakespeare. In the finished film, all these lines are excised. The catch itself, "There dwelt a man in Babylon," and dancing take the place of the discussion. The repartee of the original is reduced to Feste's lines about the whipstock and the Myrmidons, with the cutaway to Malvolio providing visual interest for the majority of audience members who would not understand the allusions. Then Nunn, in both the script and the final cut of the film, goes back to Sir Toby's request for a song (line 31).

The word "song" cues a cut to Orsino's smoking room. All the men are in uniform, and Viola/Cesario is the only woman present. The smoke and the uniforms, in combination with the cards and drinks that appear later in the scene, create the atmosphere of a men's club. In Nunn's adaptation, Orsino's court is depicted as being highly martial, the men shown regularly maintaining their military training. Orsino's arm is in a bandage, presumably a war wound of recent vintage, so his plangent attitude to music, which famously opens the play and is one of his most consistent characteristics throughout, may in the case of Nunn's version have been acquired on the battlefield. (See especially 2.4.41–7.) This link is consistent with eighteenth-century theories on the role of music in causing homesickness: "In 1720, Theodore Zwinger, another Swiss doctor, upon observing symptoms of nostalgia in soldiers fighting on foreign land, proposed a different explanation for the cause of the disease. Zwinger noticed that nostalgia was preceded, if not triggered, by a rather cheerful state of mind usually created when the soldiers listened to familiar tunes. Recognizing songs from back home, they would be prompted by an associative mechanism of memory to reminisce about the friends and families they had left behind, and soon enough, deadly nostalgia would set in" (Ritivoi, 19). Helmet Illbruck devotes an entire chapter of his recent book to the effect of *ranz des vaches* song on Swiss soldiers.

When Orsino demands "that old and antique song we heard last night" (Nunn, 42), Cesario and an older courtier explain that the singer is not present. The courtier elaborates: it was "Feste, my lord. A fool that the Lady Olivia's father took much delight in" (42). Again, taking his cue from the line, Nunn cuts away to Olivia's kitchen with a close-up of Feste with a concertina. Continuing the script following Shakespeare, Feste asks Toby and Andrew whether they would have "a love song or a song of good life" (43). Maria's inclusion in the scene changes the physical business and the whole thematic import of what follows but not the dialogue, as she is given no speaking lines in the scene. Toby, with a pregnant glance at Maria as he hands her a glass of wine, selects a love song. The song, "O Mistress Mine," clearly composed for a woman who is "sweet and twenty," underscores the middle age of the listeners. Robert Stam observes that this is one of the huge advantages of the medium: "Film's multitrack nature makes it possible to stage ironic contradictions between music and image. Thus the cinema offers synergistic possibilities of disunity and disjunction not immediately available to the novel [or, in this case, play]. The possible contradictions and tensions between tracks become an aesthetic resource, opening the way to a multitemporal, polyrhythmic art form" (20). The song's young, romantic tone makes it a particularly poignant choice for the listeners in Olivia's kitchen – the visual track, with its close-ups on weathered faces showing unmistakeable traces of past disappointments, is thus an ironic comment on the song, and vice versa.

Feste begins "O Mistress Mine," prompting a cut to Feste's own mistress, Olivia, asleep in bed, her dark curls sensuously fanning across the pillow. In contrast to Maria's narrow bed, Olivia's is broad, with warm tawny colours in the bedspread and carved wooden posts. This difference is also, obviously, one of class, but the younger people in the film are definitely surrounded with a warmer, more fertile palette than the older set. The music wakes Olivia, and the feelings Cesario aroused in her at their recent meeting flicker over her face. As she lies in bed hearing Feste's song and we witness her "thriftless sighs" (2.2.39), Nunn intensifies our eagerness for a scene in which she declares her love for Cesario.

Olivia's thoughts return us to Cesario and Orsino, who are now discussing the love song played on the piano. Toby Stephens's Orsino registers surprise at Cesario's eloquence on the subject of love: "Thou dost speak masterly" (45). This line becomes the sound-cue for a cut back to Olivia's kitchen where Feste is singing "Every wise man's son doth know" – the idea of a boy's wisdom on love forming the verbal link between the two scenes. When Feste sings "What is love? 'Tis not hereafter / Present mirth hath present laughter," the camera focuses on Maria, looking sad, reflecting on her own advancing years and the possibly ephemeral nature of Toby's attraction to her (45). Maria and Toby glance at each other throughout Feste's song, suggesting a latent chemistry that the audience hopes to see come to fruition, again adding to the suspense (the close-up ensures that we not only see but take note of these glances). After seeing Nunn's treatment of the scene, Shakespeare's exclusion of Maria from Feste's audience seems a missed opportunity, as the lines seem so pertinent to her. Of course, many stage versions (including the most recent at the Stratford Festival in Ontario in 2011, directed by Des McAnuff,) have cast Maria as a perky girl, for whom the warning lyrics would have little significance.

Nunn then reverts to Orsino and Cesario, still at cards. Viola/Cesario now seems more adept at smoking than in the earlier scene – she is a quick study. Cesario sniffs contemptuously at the hand of cards she has been dealt, and, given that Nunn imbues every cinematic moment with layers of meaning, it is tempting to read into this. Cesario's reaction suggests that she is not happy with the hand life is dealing her right now, forcing her to play messenger and male confidante to the man she wants for herself. Perhaps Nunn is slyly alluding to the adage "lucky in cards, unlucky in love." Cesario's bad hand is a cinematic foreshadowing of the happy conclusion to the romantic comedy.

As they play cards, the piano behind them continues to play a version of "O Mistress Mine." Shakespeare has Orsino and Cesario talk of love, and Cesario is forced into an indirect avowal of love for her master ("Of your complexion," etc.), which the audience hopes to see reciprocated when Cesario becomes Viola once more (45). Nunn cuts only two lines from Cesario and Orsino's exchange (30, 36), lines that merely elaborate on what has already been said. On the whole, the blank verse scenes seem to have endured fewer cuts than the prose scenes, which tend to be more topical and therefore contain many more obscure witty phrases. In addition, there is the whole vexed question of Elizabethan humour – does it still make audiences laugh? Some reviewers found the humour in the film painful (Kauffmann, 40; Coe, 39; Ansen, 74; Lane, 74).

Stevens's Orsino gives his questions an almost jealous edge through his intense delivery. With a conspiratorial air, he urges Cesario to leave his fictional "lady" for a younger woman, admitting that men's affections are transient, and women's beauty short-lived. In so doing, Orsino articulates some common views, still prevalent today, on the difference in the way men and women love: "Our fancies are more giddy and unfirm / More longing, wavering, sooner lost and worn / Than women's are" (Nunn, 46). Here, Cesario lets her cover slip a little as she reveals a profound wistfulness at the thought of women's beauty fading so quickly. Nunn chooses to film this conversation on gender and love very realistically – as he does with the whole film: "I felt the urge to make the content of the play seem real, and not pantomimic or stylized, so that the contrary extremes of sexual behavior in the central characters are seen in a believable social context. The story sets out to provoke both genders in the audience, so it's important that spectators shouldn't be able to get off the hook ... by dismissing [the play] as an improbable, archaic comedy" (Fine Line, 2).

Cesario's lament for the death of female beauty cues a cutaway to Imelda Staunton's Maria, looking sad and worn as we hear Feste's voice-over singing, "What's to come is still unsure" (46). Maria looks at Toby in silent reproach, and he returns her glance sheepishly. Feste's words speak directly to these aging, recalcitrant wooers. Brilliantly, Maria joins Feste on the verse that speaks most about her own situation: "In delay there lies no plenty / Then come kiss me, sweet and twenty / Youth's a stuff will not endure" (46). Kingsley's Feste repeats the last line with great earnestness, as if to hammer the message home to Sir Toby, wasting precious time with his hesitation, and even to Sir Andrew, squandering the vestiges of his youth wooing a woman who will never marry him. Sprengler describes some forms of nostalgia as having "a 'bittersweet' quality, an attachment to a past time as opposed to a place"; she observes that this kind "emerges on the brink of significant change" (21). All the characters listening to Feste's song are on the verge of being too old to find a mate, and their facial expressions seem to suggest that they are fully aware of this sense of "now or never." The significant change approaching is old age.

"These characters are in one way or another trying to parade to the world as young, but each of them is aware that the parade is passing them by," Nunn points out. "Feste is an observer ... what he chooses to sing to people is intentionally relevant and disturbing to them" (Fine Line, 4). Feste's song ends with his on-screen audience looking pensive. The way in which Toby and Maria react to the song is distinct because of gender. Staunton's Maria is close to tears of frustration as well as sadness. She wants her life to change, but as a woman of her time is relatively powerless to change it. The initiative has to come from Sir Toby. Mel Smith's Sir Toby, commitment-phobic, looks at Maria rather guiltily through the song, as if he is aware that he should really have made a move by now. While her suffering is in part caused by having to wait, his is caused by lacking the courage to act. The sequence ends in the film with a quick cut, not in Nunn's script, to Orsino and Viola, still at cards, cheroot smoke swirling round them, smiling wistfully at one another.

Wistfulness is a dominant note in the unique music of the play *Twelfth Night*. All the characters are mourning the loss of some beloved aspect of their life to devouring Time. Viola and Sebastian mourn the loss of their twin siblings. Olivia mourns her brother, and her youth, which has been squandered mourning the dead. Almost all the characters (Antonio, Olivia, Viola, Orsino, Maria, Andrew, Toby, Malvolio) grieve over the stalemate in which they are trapped, unable for various reasons to progress in their love affairs. Sprengler writes that, in non-musical films, "it is arguable that the real force of nostalgia stems almost entirely from the film's visual dimensions, most notably its costumes, sets and props." (25) The pre-Raphaelite setting chosen by Nunn for his film is thus particularly appropriate. The pre-Raphaelite movement pined for the Middle Ages for a kind of purity in art, just as Nunn looks to this play, which he calls "one of those rare phenomena, the perfect work of art" (Nunn, iv), adapting it in order to share Shakespeare's greatness with the larger film audience. The play is an elegy to youth and beauty; the film is also an elegy to Shakespeare's unique achievement. Yet, it is not merely in the "costumes, sets and props" that we perceive nostalgia, but also, even more, in the aching strains of the bittersweet music composed by Shaun Davey. Davey's music seems a living embodiment of Orsino's own dreamy description of the song that dominates Shakespeare's act 2, scene 3, which Nunn intercut in his film (although Nunn places this particular song, "Come Away Death," later):

That old and antique song we heard last night.
Methought it did relieve my passion much,
More than light airs and recollected terms
Of these most brisk and giddy-paced times...
...
Mark it, Cesario, it is old and plain.
The spinsters, and the knitters in the sun,
And the free maids that weave their thread with bones,
Do use to chant it. It is silly, sooth,
And dallies with the innocence of love,
Like the old age. (2.3.3–6, 42–7)

Orsino is chiefly charmed by the song because it speaks to him of a past time that he views as being more innocent, more leisurely, more peaceful, and more honest (plain) than the present.

The intercut segment then returns to Olivia's house where Sir Toby breaks the melancholy mood with a raucous song (the "catch" in Shakespeare's script, line 540) accompanied by loud drumming on pots and pans. The ability to shift moods easily is one of Nunn's acknowledged gifts as a director (Martin White, 297). The four characters move in a kind of conga line to Olivia's drawing room for the "cakes and ale" scene. In Shakespeare, after this scene, Toby and Andrew decide not to go to bed because they have stayed up too late. In the next scene, when Orsino greets his courtiers, it is the same morning but, one assumes, a more civilized hour. Feste is also up and ready to entertain the duke with a different song, "Come Away Death," which in Nunn's film he sings much, much later, after the box tree scene and the second interview between Cesario and Olivia.

As a result of Nunn intercutting these two scenes, the cinema audience is compelled to compare the situations of all the characters and is to led formulate several conclusions about love, gender, and identity earlier in the course of the play than if they were watching Shakespeare's original on stage. This economy is, in part, a result of necessity. An average film is at most half the length of a Shakespeare play, so the film audience must garner information at a fast and steady pace. The cinema audience is bound to be struck by the sense of urgency about love in both locales. Feste's song, played in both households, exhorts its audiences to act on their love now and hesitate only at the peril of their own happiness. The lyrics of the song, heard by Toby, Andrew, and (in Nunn's version) Maria, are explicit about this. Meanwhile, Orsino is revealing to Cesario that he believes men's love lasts only as long as women's youth and beauty. The elements of life that make us happy – love, beauty, laughter – are described in both scenes as extremely vulnerable to time. The cakes and ale of the Yuletide will soon be replaced by more Lenten fare. Twelfth Night marks the end of a season of celebration, and the whole play is tinged with proleptic nostalgia as well as the ordinary kind discussed above. Nunn captures this wonderfully with his autumnal setting; the withered leaves scattered about Olivia's house remind her retainers and herself that the winter of old age and loneliness is just around the corner. Shakespeare concludes his play with four characters still single. Nunn makes Shakespeare's comment on these lonely figures explicit, showing Andrew, Antonio, Malvolio, and Feste separately leaving Olivia's house, a house joyous with a wedding dance in progress. Only Feste seems resigned to his single fate.

Why did Nunn choose to intercut these particular scenes? In one interview, he asserts that they are crucial. They also fall roughly in the centre of Shakespeare's structure. They are especially important because the dialogue in them deals so directly with the themes of gender, love, and identity The parallel editing brings these themes into sharp relief, paring down the unrelated material in which they are embedded in Shakespeare, and drawing together dialogue on the same themes which in Shakespeare is separated by more text and occurrences. Feste's song about the fleeting nature of youth, beauty, and love meshes naturally with Orsino's comments on the same subjects. Feste's song makes Toby, Andrew, and (here) Maria question their own lives, their identities as fun-loving bachelors. Their behaviour no longer suits their age; they need to change to accommodate their advancing years, to take stock of the way they want the remainder of their lives to play out. In a way, the joke they play on Malvolio is their nostalgic farewell to the irresponsible behaviour of youth. Shakespeare captures very well the way that an action that is unworthy of one's age and stage can sour before its completion. Toby admits to being sick of the whole thing – "I would we were well rid of this knavery" (4, 2, 67) – and Nunn seems to have directed his subplot actors to convey a certain queasiness about the Malvolio gulling before its conclusion. Similarly, Orsino and Cesario's discussion about love and time remind both of them about what is at stake. Orsino is wasting his youth pursuing a woman who cares nothing for him. Viola risks losing the man she loves through her disguise.

So much of the play harps on this *carpe diem* theme. By its end, everyone eligible for love has found it, and the characters who are ineligible move on, perhaps to seek love, or at least a better identity, elsewhere. Love, age, and gender are all shown in this sequence to be terribly interdependent. Love makes one utterly vulnerable to the opinion of the beloved. "I prithee, tell me what thou thinkst of me," Olivia entreats Cesario. It is the central question to the lover. Nunn's Maria demands it of Toby with her wistful glances throughout the song. Orsino asks Viola/Cesario that question indirectly by interrogating her about the sort of person she loves. Viola's identity is forever changed by her temporary stint as a man. In her conversation with Orsino, she has had access to privileged male information – his admission that men's love for women is changeable and hugely dependent on their youth and beauty. Viola goes into marriage with open eyes.

In this sequence, then, the audience is simultaneously presented with two seemingly contradictory ideas on love, gender, and identity. From Orsino's words, and Feste's song, and through Maria and Toby's silent exchange of looks, we learn that men and women think differently about love, but from Orsino and Olivia's love for Cesario/Viola, we learn that it is not masculine or feminine anatomy that is critical in love but identity. We can only assume that Olivia accepts Sebastian at the end of the play because she believes his character is as similar to his sister's as his appearance. In other words, she is getting the same essentials in a gender package that suits her better. Orsino's offer of marriage to Viola works on the same principle: he knows he is going to enjoy all the same qualities he loved in his servant, now reparcelled in a female body. Gender is not ignored (Orsino wants a woman, and Olivia wants a man), but it is secondary to identity. All Orsino requires of Cesario to make him/her his bride is a change of clothes.

I have singled this sequence out because it is one of the most brilliant in the film. This intercut sequence is unabashedly filmic, and Nunn was fully conscious of this: "You could never do anything like that [crosscutting] in the theatre. It's only by taking advantage of the instantaneous exchange of location that comes with film editing, and the control of sound, that those two scenes can in some way be brought together and encompassed with the same soundtrack" (Crowdus, 38).

Nunn's *Twelfth Night* is evidence that it is possible to make Shakespeare's plays truly filmic without losing what is Shakespearean about them. Nunn's use of intercutting is a good example in cinema history of interference with Shakespeare's text that renders the play more filmic and yet does not take away from the meaning of the text but rather enhances it. While Nunn viewed Shakespeare's original as so perfect that he could barely bring himself to change it, the scenes in question may well have been changed by Shakespeare first (Mahood, 18–20). Originally, it seems that Viola was to have sung an "old and antique song" to Orsino in act 2, scene 4, but, the theory goes, the boy playing Viola suffered a voice change, and so the song in the scene was transferred to Feste. The song given to Feste in this scene is not "old" at all: "Come away death" was a current air. As a result of the shift from Viola to Feste, the same singer could be heard in Olivia's household and Orsino's, in each case singing of love's transitory nature. This idea was Shakespeare's; Nunn merely took it further, seizing advantage of the technology at his disposal to have the same song sung in one locale, playing in another, suggesting through intercutting simultaneity and thus, parallelism. It is what I suspect that Shakespeare, master of the most popular art form of his day, theatre, would have done when presented with the opportunities of the art form our day, film.

12

Nostalgia in Hoffman's *William Shakespeare's A Midsummer Night's Dream* and Branagh's *Love's Labour's Lost*

It is no mere coincidence that two *fin de siècle* adaptations of Shakespeare's early comedies to the screen are dewy with nostalgia. Michael Hoffman in his *William Shakespeare's A Midsummer Night's Dream* (1999; henceforth *Dream*) celebrates a rural, nineteenth-century Italy that never existed, while Kenneth Branagh in his musical *Love's Labour's Lost* (2000) creates a jazz-era collegiate fantasy that revels in its artificiality. Poised on either side of the turn of the millennium, these directors look back to our recent past with a wistfulness characteristic of postmodern artistic endeavours.

Both directors' films trade to varying degrees on fantasies of home. Hoffman's *Dream* shows us the perfect aristocratic home in festive detail, Duke Theseus's palazzo during wedding preparations, and the ideal home away from home, a rural Italian village in the mountains, with ruined temples in the woods and cafés on the square serving espresso. It is holiday Italy as we (and Merchant/Ivory) imagine it, including lush opera (Rossini, Verdi, Bellini, and Donizetti are featured), steaming pots of pasta, and sunny gardens with classical statues. Branagh's *Love's Labour's Lost* also traffics in idealizations of domestic familiarity in several guises, the primary one the cozy Oxbridge college, with its easy camaraderie, inviting library, weathered walls, and porter's lodge. The French ladies' tent is another idealized familiar image, reminiscent of countless scenes from books and films taking place during summer camp, sleepovers, or boarding school. The ladies appear in one scene in a colourful tent, clad in striped pyjamas, and accessorized with curlers and a teddy bear (the Princess's). They sing Irving Berlin's carefree "No Strings" as they leap joyfully from one trundle bed to another.

With the rejection in the early twentieth century of the definition of nostalgia as a diagnosable disease came a gradual shift away from thinking of it as a weakness. By mid-century, it was thought that homesickness might be eradicated altogether by the effects of technology. People would move from place to place with greater facility and frequency because of the automobile and airplane, and they could stay easily in touch with friends and relatives through the telegraph and the telephone. Yet, as the next century approached, our unimpeded mobility, our rootlessness has instead led to alienation and fragmentation, so thinkers tell us (Ramona Wray, Mark Thornton Burnett, Carolyn Jess-Cooke, Melissa Croteau). Home*sick*ness has not been eradicated but replaced by a sense of home*less*ness. Jan Willem Duyvendak in his book *The Politics of Home* sees this feeling reflected in the politics of western nations: "Politicians across Western Europe champion the ideal of nation-as-home to 'support' native majorities who feel 'overwhelmed' by the arrival of 'strange' new neighbours with unknown habits speaking in foreign tongues ... If we want to understand rising nationalism in Western Europe and its accompanying debates over 'Britishness,' 'Dutchness' and 'Frenchness,' we need to better understand this framing of nations in terms of 'home' and the attendant nostalgia for times past" (2).

Reminiscence has become the tool with which western people fight a sense of homelessness. Television shows and films, our most accessible and popular reflections of ourselves, allude continually to a past idealized as more secure, more rooted, and generally simpler than our present. Shakespeare is an integral part of our efforts to comfort ourselves in a bewilderingly diverse and fast-moving world. He is a constant, unchanging for four hundred years. Grandparents and grandchildren can commiserate on their painful studies of Shakespeare at school or delight in their experience of him on stage or screen. Pierre Bourdieu has argued that "cultural needs are the product of upbringing and education" (1); filmmakers exploit this familiarity and combine it with fantasized images of the past.

Associating nostalgia with fantasy might prejudice the reader against its useful contribution to analysis. Yet a pioneer in this field, Fred Davis, author of *Yearning for Yesterday*, observes that some forms of nostalgia encourage complex analysis. The comparison of the past and present is rendered more profound when the particular memory is carefully evaluated, especially for its relevance. The comparison of one's past and present is obviously related to an exploration of one's identity, so the subjects of nostalgia and identity are necessarily linked. Perhaps we look to Shakespeare for a pre-capitalist sense of identity that was more stable. Capitalism in Shakespeare's day was in its infancy and had not yet wrought the alienating effects on individual identity described by Erich Fromm, for instance (qtd in Marowitz, *Reinventing the Renaissance*, 151). Of course, nostalgia is only possible if the past is available in some representation.

Representing the past is a preoccupation of "heritage cinema" in general and Shakespearean adaptations in particular. Douglas Lanier commented usefully on this fact: "For all their varied approaches to adaptation and their equally varied performances at the box office, the Shakespearean films of the 1990s might be understood in retrospect as participating in a much larger fin de siècle project, the recuperation of traditional literary culture for an age of mass media" ("Nostalgia," 154). I would expand Lanier's statement, enlarging "literary" culture to "high-brow" culture. This is particularly necessary when treating Branagh's film, which traffics in references to "classic" films like *Casablanca* and Busby Berkeley musicals, Astaire and Rogers films, and traditional jazz songs – forms of entertainment now associated with an older generation and slightly rarefied tastes. The target audience of films in general have not seen these "classic" films or heard these songs, but the better informed are aware of them and of their status. They fit the profile of the literary adaptation and the costume drama, and their typical fan: the well-to-do, forty-and-over crowd. As Anthony Guneratne observes, "Branagh is the quintessence of that generation of filmmakers who positively requires their audience's intimate familiarity with cinema ... the Golden Age Musical from audiences of *Love's Labour's Lost*" (216).

Shakespeare's plays are representations of our past, but Hoffman and Branagh in their adaptations foreground other *aides-mémoires*. Hoffman focuses on the phonograph and the bicycle as representations of the past that are intimately connected with technology of the present, such as the CD player (or iPod) and the car or motorbike. Branagh zeroes in on the music and newsreels of the past, again connected to the pop music and DVD of today. These representations of old technology (bike, phonograph, newsreel) and the music that accompanies them are treated in each case with high romanticism. As we can see from Sprengler's work on the subject, romanticizing old technology is a traditional aspect of nostalgia: "As early as 1970 nostalgia was even branded an 'industry', one responsible for marketing and manufacturing products designed to satisfy consumers' appetites for previous eras and, increasingly, the styles of previous decades. These commodities were not limited to cherished objects, the tangible relics associated with the childhood home. They also included the aural and visual fragments of radio, television and film (Slone 1970)" (Sprengler, 29). In an age of iPods and iPads, today's young hipsters celebrate the quaintness and simplicity of old technology by supporting vintage shops, collecting vinyl records, and reading "steam-punk" novels that lovingly describe Victorian machines, invented or real.

Both Hoffman's *Dream* and Branagh's *Love's Labour's Lost* are elegiac in tone, not just for a specific past but for the passing of time in general. In this way, their timbre reflects that of much Renaissance poetry, including Shakespeare's sonnets and plays, in that it centres on a *tempus fugit* theme. The last speeches in both plays are characteristic examples with their elegiac tone. Puck's final speech expresses yearning for our dreams and illusions, lost when we must return to quotidian reality outside the theatre:

You have but slumbered here
While these visions did appear;
And this weak and idle theme
No more yielding but a dream. (5.1.4–7)

The two songs that close *Love's Labour's Lost*, which Branagh excludes, are deeply elegiac for traditional English rural life. In them, Shakespeare catalogues seasonal pursuits in Warwickshire: shepherds piping, maidens bleaching their summer smocks, Tom bearing logs, and Joan keeling the pot (5.2.888–904).

In any elegy, of course, the deceased is idealized. Psychoanalyst Salman Akhtar sees the "process of idealization ... [the] fantasies of 'someday' and 'if only' as integral to nostalgia" (723). The music that Branagh selects uncannily bears out Akhtar's point. Many of the songs have lyrics that include the very phrases Akhtar isolates and others like them, words like "always," "memory," and "never." Holofernia reads out Berowne's verses by singing Jerome Kern's "The Way You Look Tonight," opening with the wistful line, "Someday, when I'm awfully low ..." Most obviously elegiac is the final number, Gershwin's "They Can't Take That Away from Me," which the lords and ladies sing to each other as they get into cars with the ladies' luggage and head to the airstrip, where the ladies depart à la *Casablanca*. The lines are so redolent with Proustian reminiscence they are worth quoting at length:

> Our romance won't end on a sorrowful note.
> Tho' by tomorrow you're gone,
> The song is ended, but as the songwriter wrote
> The melody lingers on.
> They may take you from me,
> I'll miss your fond caress.
> But though they take you from me,
> I'll still possess:
> the way you wear your hat,
> the way you sip your tea,
> the memory of all that,
> No, no, they can't take that away from me ...
> We may never, never meet again on the bumpy road to love;
> still we'll always, always keep the memory of ...

Earlier in the film, Branagh replaced the clumsy Muscovite scene (seen in the outtakes on the DVD) with a Bob Fosse style version of Darius Danesh's "Let's Face the Music and Dance." While the tune is less wistful than the Gershwin favourite, the lines also suggest that the future will never be as delicious as the threatened present moment:

> There may be trouble ahead,
> But while there's moonlight and music ...
> Before the fiddlers have fled,
> Before they ask us to pay the bill,
> And while we still have the chance ...
> There may be teardrops to shed ...
> Let's face the music and dance.

Many of the songs use the same analytic mode as the nostalgic, of contrasting two times: the present (or future) always falling far short of the past. The songs list activities that pale in comparison with memories of spending time with the beloved. Irving Berlin's "Cheek to Cheek" is sung by the lords celebrating that they are all forsworn and in love: "Well I like to go out fishing, / in a river or a creek, / but it doesn't thrill me half as much / as dancing cheek to cheek." Cole Porter's "I Get a Kick out of You" is belted out by Don Armado to explain to Moth his love for Jaquenetta: "I get no kick from champagne ... alcohol doesn't thrill me at all, but I get a kick out of you." Similarly, Irving Berlin's "There's No Business Like Show Business," sung by Costard to replace the Pageant of Nine Worthies (also included in the DVD outtakes), compares all other professions unfavourably to acting:

The butcher, the baker, the grocer, the clerk
Are secretly unhappy because
The butcher, the baker, the grocer, the clerk
Get paid for what they do but no applause ...
Nowhere can you get that happy feeling
Than when you're stealing that extra bow.

Similarly, Branagh sets up unfavourable juxtapositions between other endeavours and dancing in Gershwin's "I'd Rather Charleston" and Will Young's "I Won't Dance." All these comparisons introduce a proleptic nostalgia – the notion that we will regret putting behind us the time spent with the beloved or spent dancing, singing, acting, drinking. These ways of passing time, the songs assert, will create memories that will haunt us.

The occupations referred to in the songs contribute to the sense of yearning throughout *Love's Labour's Lost* for a lifestyle that has died forever, at least in contemporary Hollywood. We get whiffs of pining for the old vices of martinis and cigarettes, both featured prominently in the film: wistfulness for the time before the health craze in California (and across the western world) had everyone drinking vitamin water and eating chia seeds. In other words, the film remembers a time when people seemed less earnest, less interested in staying healthy than in having some fun. At the same time, the fun was more "adult" – it was had without children or video games or family movies, but with liquor, tobacco, and black tie. Adults conversed in bars instead of challenging each other to interactive online games. In the scene that replaces the Muscovites in Shakespeare's script, the lords and ladies drink misted cocktails from martini glasses while dragging on cigarettes glamorously inserted in long holders. These unhealthy habits are associated with uncensored desire (before "safe sex") and with fun. The hugely popular television show *Mad Men* (2007–15) tapped into the same brand of wistfulness. As they sing to the raunchier beat of "Let's Face the Music and Dance" with the ladies clad in furred leotards and fishnet stockings, the dancing takes a much more sensual turn. The lords and ladies run their hands over each other's erogenous zones.

The preoccupations of most of the songs are those of the leisure class – drinking, dancing, singing, sipping tea, snorting cocaine. These activities suggest that the film expresses yearning for a time when the leisure class really did have leisure. The jazz songs are therefore perfectly suited to the lords and ladies of the original play, who have both time and money at their disposal. Branagh's direction also highlights this aspect of the play and the songs. The dance numbers are frothy and fun, but no one sings or dances very professionally (except Adrian Lester). The impression we receive is of a group of people who dabble in the arts while it amuses them. This is another form of nostalgia – Branagh pines for a time when at least the privileged classes could get away with being dilettantes, before the dawning of the age of the specialist, the professional. Even actors could try their hand at many things, like the Edwardian actor/managers, without the disastrous box-office results that Branagh's trifling had when, with this film, he abandoned canonical Shakespeare for uncharted musical territory. Branagh may even be expressing a particular wistfulness for RADA and Footlights at Cambridge where many members of the stable of actors he often draws on cut their teeth as actors, messing about with different forms of theatre. He toyed with these memories earlier in *Peter's Friends* (1992) and *In the Bleak Midwinter* (1995).

Hoffman's music selections in his film also reinforce the Proustian effect. The film opens with Felix Mendelssohn's music for *A Midsummer Night's Dream* (1826), conjuring up in theatregoers the image of countless amateur productions as well as the traditional Victorian and Edwardian productions, equipped with realistic forests, sometimes even live rabbits. Mendelssohn's music went out of style in productions of the play in the 1960s, so Hoffman's use of it immediately cues a sense of wistfulness for the past, particularly the latter part of the nineteenth century.

Mendelssohn shares prominence in Hoffman's film with bel canto music. He uses Giuseppe Verdi's "Brindisi" from *La Traviata* (1853). It is not apparent from the screenplay whether or not Hoffman chose the music merely for its melodies or also for its associations and lyrics, but "Brindisi" in English is the "drinking song," reasonably appropriate to introduce us to the market life in Monte Athena, and to Bottom in particular, finishing off his espresso and flirting with a pretty young redhead. The words of the song also contribute to the overall wistfulness, urging the listener to "adorn" the "fleeting hour" "with pleasure." Less appropriate, and perhaps purposefully ironic, is Gaetano Donizetti's "Una Furtiva Lagrima" from *L'Elisir d'Amore* (1832) which expresses the singer's blissful realization that his beloved returns his passion, to accompany Bottom slinking home, wine-stained and foolish, to his shrewish wife. The lyrics of this song also suggest proleptic nostalgia, however: "For just one moment, the beating / Of her hot pulse could be felt." This could be expressing Bottom's thoughts about the alluring girl in the marketplace, but perhaps I am stretching the point. Vincenzo Bellini's "Casta Diva" from *Norma* (1831), sung while Bottom is entertained by Titania and her fairies, seems utterly inappropriate, as Titania is no chaste goddess, and so far from "tempering" the burning hearts of her people, is bent on inflaming Bottom's heart. "Non Piu Mesta," taken from Gioachino Rossini's *La Cenerentola* (1817), is, on the other hand, very appropriate for Bottom, because it is Cinderella's song recognizing that her suffering is at an end, that an enchantment has changed her fate. Bottom experiences the enchantment of Titania's love, and then his fate is changed by Duke Theseus's reward for his part in *Pyramus and Thisbe*. There is also a verse in the song in which Cinderella forgives her stepmother and sister that suggests both the reconciliation and homecoming that are characteristic of the wistful fantasy: "Fly to my bosom / Daughter, sister, friend / All found in me." Bottom experiences this kind of homecoming when he returns, to the great joy of his artisan friends who had previously abandoned him to his translated state in the dark forest.

Branagh's "trip down memory lane" in *Love's Labour's Lost*, far from being confined to song and dance, extends to many visual allusions to old films. As Ramona Wray has stated, "To pay filmic homage, it might be suggested, is also inevitably to participate in nostalgia" (194). There are pratfalls reminiscent of many old comedies: Abbott and Costello, the Marx Brothers, Laurel and Hardy, the Three Stooges,

Morecombe and Wise (the last couple on whom a show was based, which Branagh, long their fan, directed: *The Play What I Wrote*, 2001). For instance, in the eavesdropping scene during their rendition of "I've Got a Crush on You," the lords walk behind each other, shadowing each other's steps. Similar blocking is used for Nathaniel, Holofernia, and others in the scene in which they read Berowne's verses: "Someday, when I'm awfully low ..." When the king is discovered to be a traitor to his own vows, he lies on the floor writhing, exactly like Bert Lahr's Cowardly Lion in the film *The Wizard of Oz* (1939). In the penultimate number, the camera focuses on a pair of plump, bejewelled hands travelling ostentatiously across the keys, reminiscent of Liberace. The film makes larger, more direct references in the costuming and the blocking to Busby Berkeley musicals, Esther Williams's synchronized swimming films (the "No Strings" number), and Rogers and Astaire films. Katherine Eggert notes the indebtedness of the scene in which the lords float up to the ceiling to sequences in *Mary Poppins* (1964) and *Willy Wonka and the Chocolate Factory* (1971). The suggested yearning for childhood and playing games was also characteristic of Noble's *A Midsummer Night's Dream* and even Taymor's *Titus*. Finally, the obvious homage to *Casablanca* at the end is nostalgia within nostalgia. The original film was dripping with it – the predominant theme of wistfulness for the past – past love especially, emerging in the most [mis]quoted line "Play it again, Sam" and the song "As Time Goes By," with the elegiac chorus "You must remember this." The fact that *Casablanca* has been quoted in so many other films (Woody Allen's *Play It Again, Sam*, 1972, and Peter Bogdanovich's *What's Up, Doc*, 1972, to name just two) makes it even more powerfully Proustian, giving the audience layers of memories of many past experiences. Typical of postmodern filmmaking, it asks audiences to draw not on their own experiences of life but on their experience of viewing other films. Mediated, vicarious experience is being substituted for the more direct form.

Both Hoffman and Branagh draw on the melancholy image of the lone person sweeping the stage after the performance or festivities are over, an image used to close the popular *Carol Burnett Show* (1967–78), for instance. Branagh has Costard sweeping the stage in his "There's No Business Like Show Business" number. Hoffman ends with Puck clad as a sweeper, cleaning the piazza in Monte Athena after the celebrating mechanicals have retired to bed. Hoffman thus

Figure 11 Don Armado (Timothy Spall) kicks at the moon in Branagh's *Love's Labour's Lost*, 2000.

replaces Puck's lines "I am sent with broom before / To sweep the dust behind the door" with this familiar image, taking his cue from the stage directions often added to the play: "Enter Robin Goodfellow with a broom."

Both directors use visual effects that have a hoary history. They both feature artificially oversized moons (Branagh in the "I Get a Kick Out of You" number; see fig. 11), which hearken back to George Méliès's *Le voyage dans la lune* (1902) and have been used in recent films as varied as *Moonstruck* (1987) and *Moulin Rouge* (2001), and in direct homage, *Hugo* (2012). Is it a form of insecurity that modern directors, instead of creating a new image with meaning, fall back on tried and true ones, layered with memory? Or is it merely an efficient way of creating resonant emotion? The oversized moon is a visual reminder of a time that moved more slowly than our own. The directors share a longing for a time when people, we are told, had more leisure – leisure to be aware of nature and amble around on slow vehicles like bicycles, to watch a local amateur thespian strut his stuff in the marketplace, or time to devote three whole years to learning, not with any specific end, like a job, in sight but just for learning's own sake. Of course, this leisure was the privilege only of the rich few, but typical of most film directors, the emphasis is on what people do when they are *not* working.

Pam Cook defines nostalgia as "a state of longing for something that is known to be irretrievable, but is sought anyway. In so far as it is rooted in disavowal, or suspension of disbelief, nostalgia is generally associated with fantasy and regarded as even more inauthentic than memory. Even though memory is tinged with subjectivity, it can still be regarded as authentic, especially ... eyewitness accounts" (3). Hoffman's Monte Athena and Branagh's Navarre are irretrievable because they are imaginary, hybrid places, as are Shakespeare's versions of Athens and Navarre. Branagh's own words to describe the period he evokes in the film sum up his wistful perspective, "the last idyll in the twentieth century ... a stolen, magical, idyllic time which nevertheless had a clock ticking" (Burnett and Wray, 174). It is doubtful whether people alive in the 1930s would have seen it quite this way. Both directors' yearning for the times and places they create in their films is demonstrated by their insistence on realistic details. Hoffman loads his film with props of all kinds to give a substance and particularity to his fantasy. Branagh gives his phantasmagoria the veneer of historical truth with the phony newsreels and the interjection of World War II footage. Even the history that he weaves into his adaptation is idealized and subjective – it is Britain's finest hour that he wants to recall. The wartime scenes show the characters immersed in companionable teamwork and then rejoicing in their reunion at VE Day.

War, after all, is the event most often associated with the diagnosis of "nostalgia" in the past. The term was invented for soldiers experiencing intense homesickness. In fact, eighteenth- and nineteenth-century doctors viewed the condition as potentially fatal. For instance, during the American Civil War, Union doctors confirmed more than five thousand cases of nostalgia among soldiers and reported that seventy-four of those ended in death (Matt, 5). In *Love's Labour's Lost*, Branagh gives us a kind of *Love's Labour's Won* with his montage of the characters, separated by war, joyfully embracing at the peace – their homecoming is represented by their reunion with each other. In the aftermath of World War II, with diasporas everywhere, a sense of belonging was more threatened than ever. Alastair Bonnett writes,

"When one seeks a 'home' in uncertainty, nostalgia is never far from one's door" (22).

The newsreels used in the film, historically "eyewitness accounts," are in Branagh's version addendums to Shakespeare's fictional tale, delivered in the cheery style that characterized the delivery of the light news items in the 1930s and '40s. By using the style and technique employed to convey facts to deliver fiction, Branagh inadvertently compares those early newsreels to creative works. Thus he exposes the newsreels to scrutiny for charges of propaganda. Those newsreels showed to a war-torn country what it needed to see for the sake of morale – a Britain worth fighting for and British men worth looking after (with fresh supplies of food, arms, clothes, etc.).

This is the sly aspect of these films – they are intended as a kind of homage to a certain time and place, but their artificiality inspires us to question our collective memories, our histories of the original. Similarly, in *American Graffiti* (1973), by showing us a perfect 1950s/early '60s America, George Lucas actually leads us to investigate the truth of this image. As Pam Cook astutely observes, "Where history suppresses the element of disavowal or fantasy in the re-presentation of the past, nostalgia foregrounds those elements, and in effect lays bare the processes at the heart of remembrance. In that sense, it produces knowledge and insight, even though these may be of a different order from those produced by conventional historical analysis, and may be experienced in different ways" (4).

If, as I contend, Hoffman and Branagh, like many adaptors working in film, are wistful for the past, which past is it? Neither of them chose to set Shakespeare's comedies in the playwright's own time, or even in his selected locale. Why does Hoffman choose nineteenth-century Italy and Branagh pre-war Britain? Branagh, in his screenplay of *Hamlet*, implies that the nineteenth century is advantageous for two reasons: first, it is close enough to our own time not to be alienating, and second, Shakespeare's more formal, articulate language does not seem out of place (xv). Another advantage is that class distinctions shown in costumes from these eras are more comprehensible to modern spectators than are Tudor (or pre-Tudor) costumes. As Ian McKellen put it about the choice of a twentieth-century setting for his screenplay for *Richard III*, "It is impossibly confusing to try and distinguish between a multitude of characters who are all done up in floppy hats and wrinkled tights" (*Screenplay*, 12). Hoffman may well have learned from previous Shakespeare adaptors like Branagh, Loncraine/McKellen, and Trevor Nunn. In his screenplay for *Twelfth Night*, Nunn described his nineteenth-century setting as a time when women were delicate and decorative, their clothes and manners most unlike men's as compared to any other period. This polarization was useful to him, as it meant that pretending to be a boy was no easy feat for Viola – it was a painful challenge (vii). But Hoffman does not have a cross-dressing heroine. Some of his editing choices and certainly his opening titles suggest that the film expresses a yearning for a time when women "knew their place" and were decorative and fairly silent.

Ostensibly, *A Midsummer Night's Dream* would seem an odd choice of play for a director who is wistful for times when women were subjugated. Titania and Hermia openly defy the men in their life, and Helena is an active pursuer of Demetrius. Hippolyta can also legitimately be played as critical of Theseus. The end of the play reinforces the Elizabethan status quo, but the rest of the play seems to question it. Hoffman cuts many of the speeches in which women express their points of view. For instance, he cuts almost all of Hermia's interjections in act 1, scene 1, lines 135 and following, transforming her dialogue with Lysander into a monologue for him. What's more, earlier in the scene we cannot even read her reactions to Theseus because her face is hidden by a big picture hat, which she only takes off during her tête-à-tête with Lysander. Contrastingly, later in the forest, Hoffman keeps all but one line of Helena's painful speech beginning, "I am your spaniel, and Demetrius / The more you beat me, I will fawn on you" (2.1.203–10). Perhaps Hoffman, an American film director, is responding to what Jan Willem Duyvendak calls "the embattled family household," which he views as "central in the American crisis of 'home'":

> Home at the micro level is in crisis because the custodians of the traditional home – women – have left its bounds to enter the paid workforce ... The American fixation on "family values" – far from hiding the crisis of the nuclear family – is a testament to it and reinforces feelings of nostalgia: while many idealize home in the past as a safe haven ... today it is an unstable and overburdened place for parents working long hours, often combining several jobs and starved for time to spend with their children. American society is deeply nostalgic for better times at home (3).

In Hoffman's introduction to his screenplay, it is clear that he set out to stress a motif of simplicity in love, in itself an old-fashioned goal. He sees Titania's attraction to Bottom as refreshing for her because it is not complicated by politics, as is her relationship with Oberon. Perhaps that is why he reduces Hermia's lines and keeps Helena's most humiliating ones. A doting female simplifies a relationship, whereas a challenging one results in conflict – like his Hippolyta at the opening of the film, flouncing out on the duke on two occasions because she is disappointed that he supports Egeus's controlling ways with Hermia. In his introduction, Hoffman makes much of the fact that Hermia has to learn a lesson in humility by being subjected to the same experiences of rejection as Helena, while Helena has to learn a little dignity by getting used to being loved. On the useful lessons that Lysander and Demetrius might derive from a night of transformation in the forest, Hoffman is silent. Nor does Hermia escape punishment for her defiance of her father; he leaves her wedding feast in a huff. This again is Hoffman's choice, because in Shakespeare's play after Theseus overrules Egeus, Egeus never appears on stage again. In the film, Hermia's happiness on her wedding day is shadowed by her father's anger.

All these directorial choices seem to support Douglas Lanier's argument that one of the director's aims is to "recalibrate heritage film – and heritage culture generally, of which Shakespeare is a part – to a more heteromasculine orientation" ("Nostalgia," 158). At the same time, the film evokes a longing for a time when heterosexual men could show physical affection for one another without it being construed as sexual. The rude mechanicals have a touching camaraderie. When they see that Bottom has returned to town his old self, they run to embrace him. They embrace after the duke sends them a note that their play was "very notably discharged," and once more after their night of revelry in the piazza.

Hoffman was attracted by the nineteenth century for the "simplicity" of dealings not only between the sexes but also between the classes. His film pines for an era when, as he puts it in his introductory inter-titles, "class distinction is a large part of everyday life and to be an aristocrat still means something" (vi). It is important to remember that Hoffman's first film was a student feature starring fellow Oxford scholar Hugh Grant and entitled *Privileged*, about the woes of upper-class youth. Lanier notes that Hoffman keeps the servants in Duke

Theseus's house strictly anonymous – it is the aristocratic viewpoint with which we are meant to identify: "The characters of heritage cinema are often concerned with holding on to their elite class status in the face of its slow loss to modernization, and the viewers of these films are invited to indulge vicariously in the sensual delights of aristocratic finery" (155–6). Of course, as Claire Monk cautions us, the mise en scène is just one of the pleasures offered the viewer, in addition to those of narrative drive, "characterisation, performance, humour, sexuality and so on" (*British Historical Cinema*, 188).

In this case, however, the characterization does seem to fit closely with the pleasure-providing aristocratic setting. The duke, so far from being portrayed as the ruler of Athens, is much more like a lord enjoying his country seat, slightly befuddled by the legal task thrown at him by Egeus. Sophie Marceau's Hippolyta also is aristocratic above and beyond anything else. In *Shakespeare into Film*, the editors find her "a genteel, aristocratic lady, a highly unlikely Amazon queen" (Welsh, Vela, and Tibbetts, 62). Even Bottom, as Lanier observes, is recast in Hoffman's film as a man with pretensions with which we, the audience, are guided to empathize. In other words, the film appeals to aspirational tastes. Martin A. Hipsky in his article "Anglophil[m]ia: Why Does America Watch Merchant-Ivory Movies?" theorizes that these period dramas console graduates of expensive college educations who can no longer rely on their education to guarantee a comfortable lifestyle (101–3). In short, they provide a nostalgic trip to a time when a good education promised social and financial status. Bottom sports a white suit not unlike the duke's and wears his boater at a jaunty angle. His interest in the theatre is also something he is proud of, a mark of refinement. It is just as much Bottom's parvenu inclinations as his hammy acting that are mocked by the boys who tip wine over him. They want to wreck that suit that gives him delusions of grandeur, making him feel superior to the rest of the village artisans.

Lanier comments too on another of Hoffman's additions that stresses the "dream of upper-class privilege": "In a short interpolated sequence he [Bottom] is crowned Titania's consort" ("Nostalgia," 157). Hoffman explains in his introduction to the screenplay that 'it wasn't Bottom the egotist, the clumsy outspoken braggart, not Bottom the buffoon" in which he was interested but "Nick Bottom the dreamer, the actor, the pretender – Nick Bottom sitting at a café in a small Italian town dressed in a white suit, trying his best to look like the gentleman" (viii). Stephen M. Buhler also notes that Hoffman "emphasizes ... Bottom and Titania over all other story elements" (185). Buhler puts this down to the director's wish to foreground the star power of Kline and Pfieffer, but, subtextually, this emphasis just stresses the longing for aristocratic privilege. Hoffman expects his heritage film audience to identify with Bottom; like him, they dream of a life of luxury and refinement and the homage that is due royalty. Hoffman also stresses the royalty of Oberon and Titania over their magical powers. They are seen in state, their powers seeming rather earthbound in contrast to the way they are presented in Peter Hall's (1968) or especially Max Reinhart's (1935) adaptations of *A Midsummer Night's Dream*, in which the fairies' magical feats are stressed. They fly in those two productions; in Hoffman's, they merely revel. Only in their tiny Tinkerbell guise do we see them fly. Hoffman seems to have ransacked world mythology with abandon for their costumes in a veritable frenzy of nostalgia.

It would seem that Hoffman has selected the late Victorian period for his film because he longs for the ostensibly "simpler" relationships between the sexes and the classes: in each case, the upper-class man is at the top of the heap. Branagh selects the pre-war era for his film, and his choice is just as revealing. The pre-war period was the last time in recent history that Britain was the supreme world power. At the same time, I am mindful of Claire Monk's warning not to conflate aesthetic and ideological claims (*British Historical Cinema*, 180). The audience of films like Hoffman's *Dream* and Branagh's *Love's Labour's Lost* may enjoy a two-hour escape into an aristocratic milieu without necessarily supporting a retrograde class hierarchy in their politics. Shakespeare set *Love's Labour's Lost* in Navarre, and Branagh keeps all the references to the name, but he also describes his set as resembling "a kind of fantasy Oxbridge. It's actually inspired by some colleges at Yale University, where in fact, having built their college several hundred years after most of the Oxbridge colleges, they then distressed them. They actually poured acid down the walls and made them all much older looking, so there's a certain ye olde thing which is also redolent of some kind of movie college sets that we wanted to evoke for this musical" (*Screenplay*, 78).

Branagh is honest about his own nostalgia. His "Oxbridge" college is a "fantasy" and connotes the literary image of the Oxbridge college immortalized in book and screen by such works as *Chariots of Fire*

(1981) and *Brideshead Revisited* (1981). He also expresses a dual fascination with Britain's glory days and with America's imitation of them, both in situ at Yale and in Hollywood. Branagh's wistfulness, then, is not only for the days when Britain was the number-one world power but also for the days when the United States imitated and revered Britain and its culture. I am indebted to Katherine Eggert for her concept of *Love's Labour's Lost* as a film that explores the now inverted colonial relationship between the United States and Britain. Emma French expresses the same opinion of Branagh's entire Shakespearean oeuvre: "Branagh's films may be subject to a neo- or post-colonial reading: Shakespeare is ceded by Britain to its stronger partner America" (67). I think these are overstatements. Branagh's *Love's Labour's Lost* is, of course, an homage to American forms of art, the screen musical and jazz. But I would argue that Branagh is honouring the British antecedents to the musical and jazz also, just as he remembers Oxbridge via Yale. Like most Europeans, Branagh is struck by the relatively recent nature of much North American culture, having grown up with the originals on which this culture was largely based; of the buildings at Yale, he says, "the American replicas have finally acquired enough age to amass nostalgia value" (*Screenplay*, 79). This statement could easily be applied to much of the film – the music and the dance, based on art forms that emerged in the 1930s, are themselves descendants of older, European art forms. The musicals of Busby Berkeley and Rogers and Astaire are offspring of Gilbert and Sullivan and music hall. Nathan Lane's vaudevillian Costard certainly owes something to the latter. This is not to deny that jazz is an indigenous American art form, just to suggest that it did not emerge in a vacuum. Furthermore, the jazz classics deployed in the film have long held a quasi-international status. Eggert forgets that they were played constantly on British radio before and during the war. The British assimilated them as part of their own experience. These songs are not now experienced as "American" any more than Shakespeare is digested as restrictively "English." As Brown, Lublin, and McCulloch express it, "Shakespeare is often invoked as an icon of Englishness, yet his works have proved conspicuously portable" (8). Eggert's insistence on Branagh's patriotic possessiveness over Shakespeare as an icon of English culture seems somewhat questionable. Branagh, who is Irish, has been at pains, unlike other Shakespearean directors like Trevor Nunn, Derek Jarman, or

Peter Hall, to cast his films transatlantically, and he has suffered from vitriolic personal attacks from the British press.

At least four of Hoffman's and Branagh's directorial decisions suggest that they were suffering from the fin de siècle malaise of nostalgia. First, they selected Shakespeare to adapt; second, they set Shakespeare in eras different to his own and their own; third, they have opted for musical scores that use existing forms (jazz, musical numbers, and opera) rather than commissioning original music (as Branagh did previously); fourth, they allude to other films through blocking, props, and costumes. Their films *A Midsummer Night's Dream* and *Love's Labour's Lost* are perfect examples of postmodernism. Very little in these films is fresh or new; both rely excessively on quoting other, older works of art. This nostalgia for the art of the past reveals a deep insecurity about the present and the future. It is as though these directors think that to have meaning, art must imitate something that has gone before. But any homage often is most effective at reminding the viewer how much better the original was than the copy. The jazz songs that Branagh uses to replace Shakespeare's poetry, charming though they are, seem slight in comparison. His new versions of the songs and dances similarly pale compared to Astaire and Ginger's initial performance of them. Hoffman's use of Mendelssohn and operatic arias, his recreation of a phony aristocratic lifestyle that has little to do with Shakespeare's ancient Athens or his Renaissance England, also seem like a wild grasping after creativity instead of the genuine article.

13

Ariel's Singing Body as Interpreted by Greenaway and Taymor

Among the last words that ring out from Shakespeare's Ariel are: "Merrily, merrily shall I live now / Under the blossom that hangs on the bough" (5.1.93-4). These unambiguously joyful lyrics were echoed for centuries in equally jubilant settings by composers such as Robert Johnson, Thomas Arne, and Sir Arthur Sullivan (Christopher Wilson, 134-41). The tradition that held sway on stages until our own time cast Ariel as a sprightly apprentice to Prospero, winged like a dragonfly (Ann Field, Drury Lane, 1778) or an angel (Julia St George, Sadler's Wells, 1847). From the 1660s to the 1930s, Ariel was generally played by a young woman who could sing and dance (Orgel, 70).

Ariel was crucial in imparting dazzling spectacle for productions of *The Tempest*. He serves the same purpose in film adaptations today. In their interpretation of the singing body of Ariel, both Peter Greenaway in his 1991 film *Prospero's Books* and Julie Taymor in her 2010 *The Tempest* follow cues furnished by Shakespeare. In both films, Ariel's post-human nature and ability to metamorphose are keys to his depiction. Yet the same variety is not heard in the music given to him to sing. Composers Michael Nyman and Elliot Goldenthal make only minor distinctions in terms of sound and tone between the dirge-like song Ariel sings to Ferdinand ("Full Fathom Five") when he is obeying Prospero's command and his song of freedom ("Where the Bee Sucks"). While Greenaway pays homage to the stage tradition by clothing his Ariels like Baroque cherubs, Nyman's music contributes to a darker trend in interpreting the role. Goldenthal's music too conveys "an introverted, brooding sense of darkness" rather than sprightliness (Clemmensen, 1). The melancholy music provided for Ariel in both films, even in contradiction of some of the sung lyrics, suggests that the directors and composers have absorbed the ambiguity of a postcolonial reading of Shakespeare's play (and how could they not?) even while neither of the directors seems fully vested in developing this reading as their chief interpretation.

The earlier of these films, *Prospero's Books*, premiered almost three years after the emergence of Stephen Greenblatt's seminal *Shakespearean Negotiations* (1988). Yet, in each case, the directors seem, perhaps unsurprisingly given their own career choices, to sympathize more with the artist Prospero than with the enslaved native inhabitants of the island. Ariel is stripped of his voice in *Prospero's Books* and of his body in Taymor's *Tempest*. The moments in each film in which Ariel challenges Prospero's supremacy are fragmentary and unsustained, but the sombre mood prevails, engendered by a sense of the power imbalance, which is now impossible to ignore.

The bittersweet quality achieved by the mixture of joyful lyrics in Ariel's last song and somewhat darker melodies contributes to the nostalgic mood of each film. Psychologist David S. Werman, writing about this complex emotion, described it as "joy tinged with sadness." Moreover, a comprehensive study published in the *Journal of Personality and Social Psychology* (2006) discovered that nostalgic narratives drawn from participants were most often of "redemptive" experiences; that is, they featured disappointment or loss, "mitigated by subsequent triumphs over adversity" (Wildschut et al., 987). This kind of narrative not only fits Ariel's story in the play – which moves from incarceration in the tree to servitude to Prospero to freedom at the conclusion – but to a certain degree, every character. Prospero moves from exile to complete reinstatement as Duke of Milan; Caliban moves from servitude to freedom and power, Miranda from loneliness to full inclusion in her rightful society, and so on.

These "redemption narratives" are inextricably linked to the imperialist material in the play – the adversity that is triumphed over is usurpation of power. The nods to the postcolonial reading of the tragicomedy are stronger in *Prospero's Books* than in Taymor's *Tempest*, perhaps reflecting the fact that the interpretation, still trendy in 1991, had lost some of its gloss by 2010. Greenaway writes in his screenplay that he sees Prospero "not just as the master manipulator of people and events but their prime originator" (9), which is why he is permitted to speak all of the other characters' lines. He is Prospero, Shakespeare, star actor Gielgud, and auteur Greenaway all at once. However, casting Prospero as an all-powerful, manipulative magician is no more than a mere nod. In fact, Lisa Hopkins finds that "the most striking result of its transhistorical perspective is the fact that Greenaway's film, like Jarman's, has no interest in a post-colonial reading" (126). She cites the ransacking of visual history for images as working against a postcolonial reading, as it does not allow the film to be located in a particular political framework. Sarah Martin goes further: "Greenaway questions the now popular postcolonial reading by completely ignoring it" (45).

Just as Prospero takes on four roles – magician, playwright, actor, and director/governor – so Ariel is iterated physically four times also (Cavecchi, 87). Greenaway, always playful with numbers (see his film *Drowning by Numbers*, 1988), seizes on lines in the play that imply that Ariel can "divide" and be seen in many places at once (1.2.198–201). He interprets Ariel with four different actors of four different ages: small child, adolescent, young man, full adult. The Ariels not only embody the four elements but also reflect Greenaway's division of the film, according to the screenplay, into Past, Present, and Future (12–13). This temporal division of the film is echoed in the metronome quality of much of Nyman's music, striking with strong, simple, repetitive rhythms, like a clock. The inexorable passage of time is also highlighted by the contrast between the aged Prospero and the child Ariel, whose bodies often share the frame, especially at the beginning of the film. These comparisons, and the emphasis on time generally, encourage a nostalgic reaction in the viewer. As has been the case with other directors previously considered in these chapters who use children in their films, we are encouraged to remember a time of play, free from worry. Wistful recollection of an anxiety-free period in one's life, especially associated with childhood, is common to many of the narratives cited in Wildshut et al's study of nostalgia mentioned above.

This child Ariel, and the other three, are almost naked, sport blond curly wigs, and resemble Raphael putti, as Greenaway explains in his screenplay (117). He also cites the child figure of Folly in Bronzino's painting "Allegory" as his model. These are just two of the many allusions to Renaissance and Mannerist art and architecture in the film. Greenaway expresses a strong yearning for the art of the past: "I think that every artist dreams of renewing the forms which came before, but I think very few can be considered to have achieved that. We are all dwarves standing upon the shoulders of the giants who preceded us, and I think we must never forget that. After all, even iconoclasts only exist with respect to that which they destroy" (*Peter Greenaway – Quotes*).

In an interview with Marlene Rodgers, Greenaway specifies that his homage adheres particularly to the seventeenth century. *Prospero's Books* is the third film of his oeuvre to draw on that period, one to which he is attracted as he sees it as "transitional" (136). "Transitional" periods are always those that attract most nostalgic attention. Wildschut et al.'s study discovered that it was "momentous occasions" that were most often featured in the narratives solicited from their participants (987). These occasions usually involved a big life change, like graduation, the birth of a child, the death of a relative, or a wedding. The central event in Shakespeare's play is of course a transition – from loss of power and freedom to a restoration of it, not only for Prospero but also for Ariel and Caliban. Ferdinand and Alonso too believe they have experienced the death of a relative (each other), and the play ends anticipating the wedding between Miranda and Ferdinand.

It is not just momentous occasions that inspire nostalgic reactions but momentous language also. Taymor, in her bonus commentary on the *Tempest* DVD, expresses longing for Shakespeare's rhetoric: "We don't actually have the vocabulary, the way of speaking that is quite as visually rich and lush and full of emotion." She, like Greenaway, also demonstrates a yearning for the art of the seventeenth century, particularly that of Diego Velázquez, whose depictions of the Spanish aristocracy influenced the sober costumes of the courtiers shipwrecked on the island. In addition, Taymor's film looks back to the 1986 stage production of the play she directed, which used dark sand, anticipating the black sand of Lanai, Hawaii, and similarly featured a Caliban encrusted with white mud (a symbol of white colonial power imposed on black identity?). Greenaway as well looks back to past theatrical performances of the play by casting Gielgud in the central role and having him voice all the parts. The effect is to conjure up a wistful reaction in viewers of a certain age who may have seen Gielgud on stage or heard him on an LP in their classroom study of Shakespeare.

Nostalgia, as Donald Beecher argues persuasively, is a dominant feature particularly of Shakespeare's romances, as they tell the story of homecomings (281). Beecher's observation is probably most true of *The Tempest*, in which every character seeks and finds home by the end of the play: Prospero regains his dukedom; the shipwrecked Europeans return to their cities; Miranda settles down with Ferdinand; Ariel and Caliban win their freedom; Caliban recovers his island. Shakespeare articulates this sense of general homecoming through Gonzalo's penultimate speech: "All of us [found] ourselves / When no man was his own" (5.1.215–16). Martin Butler points out that "nearly half the screenplay ... is devoted to Shakespeare's first act, and this Greenaway labels 'The Past.' The effect is to underline how much *The Tempest*'s action creates Prospero's story as ... a personal history that he makes or recovers. Greenaway's Prospero is acquiring a virtual subjectivity: his self is, essentially, his power of retrieval" (190). In other words, *Prospero's Books* rewrites Shakespeare's romance so that it is even more a story of recovering or revisiting the past, through Prospero's personal library and through his narration of his past to his daughter, which informs the film's long sections on Prospero's books. The future, represented by Miranda and Ferdinand, is rendered insubstantial by their near-voiceless state until the very end.

Despite Greenaway's use of what was then cutting-edge technology, his fascination in the film is not with the technology of the future but with the arts of the past, represented by the Old Masters' tableaux he creates and the Jacobean quill writing on parchment he reproduces. If the film is, as Jonathan Romney puts it, "the story of a mind reviewing its entire contents" (143), then this mind, characteristic of an older person's, is far more interested in taking a nostalgic journey through the personal past, and the cultural, artistic past of Europe, than in projecting into the future. In Shakespeare's play, the stress is far more on the fecund promise provided by the marriage between the Prince of Naples and the Princess of Milan. The centrality of the wedding masque, which is greatly minimized in Greenaway's and (especially) Taymor's films, signals this shift in emphasis. Greenaway's wedding masque is chaotic with extras, the nuptial couple all but lost in the scrum. Taymor's is a vague interlude in which Prospera shows the signs of the horoscope with brief images of the couple naked – all other images of fertility, with which Shakespeare's masque abounds, left out.

Departing from Shakespeare's text and differing from Taymor's depiction, Greenaway does not evoke Ariel's invisibility. Ariel's only dramatic transformation in Greenaway's film is into a harpy – all black paint and feathers, a costume that seems to have strongly influenced Taymor's rendition. (Ben Whishaw performs this role more convincingly than his antecedent; his head moves stiffly as he surveys the three men of sin, ticking back and forth like those of the owls he mentions in his last song, 5.1.90.) Even though Greenaway follows the original stage tradition of casting a boy (boys) to play Ariel, he suggests Ariel's androgyny or sprite-like asexuality with the blond, curly wig and soprano voice.

Greenaway's division of Ariel's singing body is aptly reflected in the precise, pared-down mathematical quality of Michael Nyman's music, which provides a counterpoint to the rich chaos of images. Ariel's baroque appearance is echoed in the performance of the songs, in which Nyman's "neo-Baroque minimalism" swells into a somewhat "lusher, harmonic" operatic sound (Sanderson 1). Nyman in the liner notes of the CD explains that he did not compose or rewrite any music "remotely contemporary with Shakespeare's play." This is certainly true. Ariel's first two songs, "Come unto These Yellow Sands" and "Full Fathom Five," explicitly call for a "burden," which, as Michael Neill explains, is the old term for a chorus: "[Other] spirits would sing the burden, or recurring line, while Ariel, appropriately, given his name, would sing the 'air' or melody" (42). The lyrics in "Come unto These Yellow Sands" require animal sounds: dogs barking and a cock crowing, or the singers' simulation of these. Nyman does not include any of these elements, keeping the music ethereal and precise.

Nyman also, strangely, describes his singer, Sarah Leonard, as having a "boy soprano," yet the sound seems fairly distinct from the undeveloped purity of a young boy's voice, as she boasts a trained, operatic vibrato. The androgyny of Ariel appearing as a boy but having a woman sing for him is of course concealed to all but the careful observer. We may well believe the young actor, Paul Russell, is singing, despite the inexact dubbing, because our eyes are assailed by so many images at once. This ventriloquism suits Shakespeare's play, in which Prospero is constantly speaking for others: from teaching Caliban to express himself in Prospero's language to rendering Miranda and the recently arrived Europeans mute so that he can speak instead. Greenaway takes this further, having Gielgud speak all the lines of all the characters until the end. In interviews Greenaway affirms that he is not interested in the traditional psychological exploration of character: "Characters for me have to hold a weight of allegorical and personifying meaning" (Rodgers, 139). Thus, it fits perfectly with Greenaway's overall design that Leonard's voice sings for the boy actors playing Ariel. This is a film in which an authority figure (star actor Gielgud/genius playwright Shakespeare) literally talks for everyone, like a parent articulating for a child. A woman's voice emerging from the boy's body is just one more instance of this, whether apparent only to musically knowledgeable spectators or not. This surrogate mother's voice singing through young Ariel is part of Prospero's appropriation of the maternal that Peter S. Donaldson observes throughout the film (111–12), as it is Prospero who sets Ariel warbling in all but his last song.

The androgyny of Taymor's Ariel, in contrast, is always obvious to the viewer. Taymor erases Whishaw's private parts by computer-generated means; and when Whishaw chants "Come unto these yellow sands" as a sea nymph, he grows pubescent breasts, long hair, and a billowing white skirt. He reclines in the water, as if in sympathy with the drowned father he sings about. Later, when he appears as a harpy, Taymor is careful to add breasts again. The androgyny draws special attention to itself as Prospero is here played by a woman (Helen Mirren). Prospera's oppressed status in Jacobean society is fundamental to Taymor's interpretation: "In this gender twist, it is partly because Prospera is a woman that her dukedom could be stolen from her, and the bitterness of this fact infiltrates and heightens the tension of all her interactions with the other characters on the island" (15).

Taymor thus casts the magician much more as the victim than as the cause of exploitation in the world of her film. The gestures towards a postcolonial interpretation (casting the only black actor as Caliban), as in the stage production on which the film is based, are certainly not developed. While it does not seem to engage in any sustained way with a theoretical approach, as reviewers agree (Lacey, Brody, Lanier), the movie comes closest to a feminist reading of the play. Lehmann notes that Prospera and Caliban share a significant moment at the film's end, in which she "identifies with Caliban as a fellow traveler who, like herself, is forever in pursuit of the restitution of lost power" ("Turn Off the Dark," 60). The lost power, in this case, comes from the fact that Prospera returns to Milan society where women hold no sway However, some of the lines maintained in the script sit uneasily with this reading. For instance, Prospera, whose misogynistic society wanted to burn her as a witch (Screenplay, 39), tells Ferdinand that her own daughter is a "gift" and an "acquisition / Worthily purchased" (130). Her subjugation of her daughter, as well as Caliban and Ariel, makes her an even more ambiguous figure than the original Prospero, who, as a man and Duke of Milan, likely had no personal experience of exploitation prior to his brother's usurpation of his city. Prospera seems curiously callous through most of the film to the parallels between her past and her subjects' present situation.

Focus on the self is also characteristic of nostalgic narratives in which the self is always the central character. In fact, these narratives often operate to "increase self-regard ... reinforce one's overall self-adequacy" (Wildschut et al., 986–8). This focus is obvious in all of Prospero's anecdotes, which centre on his heroic status in the past. His first story (1.2.66–169) features him as an innocent victim, devoted to his studies and trusting of his perfidious brother. It is a "redemptive" tale, like most of the accounts in Wildschut et al.'s study, in that Prospero's hardship of being stripped of his power and set to sea in a small boat ends happily, with landing on a hospitable island "by providence divine" (160). Interestingly, Shakespearean directors' accounts of making their films also share this trajectory: they first list the obstacles against them making the film, and then celebrate the fact that they were able to complete the project. Prospero's second narrative, which he must "once in a month recount," presents him as Ariel's saviour: "It was mine art / When I arrived and heard thee, that made gape / The pine and let thee out" (1.2.292–4). Similarly, when Caliban, like Ariel, complains about the work that Prospero has set him, the magician responds with yet another story in which he is shown to be kind and noble: "I have used thee, / Filth as thou art, with human care, and lodged thee / In mine own cell" (1.2.348–50). His accounts always stress his own virtue and the ingratitude with which it is answered by his brother, Ariel, and Caliban. Both directors keep most of the material in these narrative speeches, contributing to their magician-centric rather than slave-centric interpretations of the play.

We have more evidence for Taymor's greater interest in Prospera than in Ariel in the decisions she made in her way of filming him. Taymor makes much of the stage directions that conjure up Ariel as invisible to the on-stage characters while visible to the audience (1.2.302–3; 374; 2.1. 183, 295; 3.2.124; 4.1.193). Through the use of computer-generated images, Ben Whishaw's singing body appears translucent in many of his scenes – again, suitable for the unworldly music written for him by Elliot Goldenthal, who avails himself of eclectic instruments like Japanese flutes and Australian didgeridoos (Bennetts, 225). As Douglas Lanier astutely observes, the clash of allusions to "disparate musical genres ... mirrors the postmodern collision of styles in Taymor's visual design" (*Routledge Companion*, 461). When the cast and crew were shooting on location in Lanai, Hawaii, Whishaw was unavailable. Therefore, his body was never actually present for the other characters – it was literally invisible to them. Thus, Helen Mirren was obliged to act most of her Ariel scenes without Ariel. The fact that Taymor was content to shoot the film in this way suggests that she was more fascinated by the magician's gender and the way that affected her relationship with her daughter than in her exploitation of her servant Ariel. She opens the screenplay with this observation: "It is the mother's protective love for her daughter, Miranda, that fuels the tempest she has conjured and all the subsequent events on the island" (1).

Perhaps the composers choose not to make Ariel's captive songs and his one free song clearly different, in part because they are more interested in creating a recognizable motif for Ariel. Taymor's screenplay indicates as much: "With this [overall] sonic palette [of amplified guitars, and symphonic string orchestra], [Goldenthal] could then ... paint more specific distinctions between individual sets of characters by using additional instrumental colours" (21). In exploiting instruments that western listeners would read as "exotic" to suggest Ariel's otherworldliness and asexuality, Goldenthal is following a path blazed before him by Bach (the string halo for Christ in St Matthew's Passion) and Benjamin Britten (use of the gamelan for non-human and homosexual characters in his operas). Wildschut et al. cite music as one of the most powerful triggers for nostalgia (981); thus, Goldenthal achieves a kind of shorthand in using the same technique to signal difference as his predecessors did.

Creating a motif may also have been important for Nyman because Greenaway uses four actors for Ariel. In contrast to the traditional settings for Ariel's songs that stress his status as a sprite with their light, bouncing melodies, Nyman's music is melancholy. This is the case even for "Where the Bee Sucks," which has a wistful oboe, and, like Ariel's other songs in the film, a dissonance – the singing and accompaniment are often at odds with one another. In this song, there is a definite tension between the jubilant words and Nyman's music, which, while somewhat enlivened by an ascending scale in the background, is still enigmatical in mood. Certainly Nyman was reading postcolonial interpretations around the time he was composing the score. He observes on the liner notes for his recording *Noises, Sounds and Sweet Airs* that he was composing the soundtrack for Greenaway's film at the same time as he was creating music for this album. He explains, "It is Prospero's role as coloniser that interests me most. Stephen Greenblatt's fascinating text 'Learning to Curse' ... draws attention to the resemblance between Shakespeare/Prospero and the dramatist/colonist as outlined by Terence Hawkes in his book *Shakespeare's Talking Animals* (1973). According to Hawkes, a colonist 'acts essentially as a dramatist. He imposes the "shape" of his own culture, embodied in speech, on the new world, and makes the world recognisable.'"

Perhaps the ambiguity that Nyman recognized in Prospero is reflected as well in Greenaway's attitude to the character of Ariel. For Greenaway's "Where the Bee Sucks," Ariel is barely on screen. The four Ariels, while distinguished from the extras by their unique costume, are more often glimpsed as part of the huge crowd of natives or spirits who tend Prospero. This effect is maximized by the fact that Ariel, like the other characters, does not deliver any of his lines until the end; Gielgud recites them all. Even during his songs, the focus is rarely on the singer but is instead on the myriad images crowding the screen, suggesting that Greenaway's interest lies not in his characters but in the effect created by elaborate tableaux. The song's lyrics can barely be heard, although at times Gielgud recites them over the song, or some of the words appear on the screen. Clearly, though, it is not important to Greenaway that the words of the song be closely associated with the actor playing Ariel. Greenaway permitted Nyman to choose an adult woman, Sarah Leonard, to sing his songs. This indicates that the director's focus was not in creating an integral, fully fledged character for Ariel. It is difficult to surmise why, beyond liking Leonard's voice, Nyman would have selected her to render Ariel's songs rather than a boy actor who could also sing. This divorce between the song and the singer is characteristic of the whole film, which bombards the audience with quickly changing images, often one overlaid on the other, and defies any conventional narrative reconstruction. Robert Stam quotes Robert McKee on screenwriting: "Stories should be about realities, not about the mysteries of writing" (Stam and Raengo, 2–3), yet *Prospero's Books* is about exactly that, as was Derek Jarman's *Tempest* (1980) before – both examples of independent films flouting cinematic conventions.

Goldenthal's songs for Ariel are also uniformly pensive in mood. His use of the glass armonica, often exploited to create spooky or suspenseful effects in film (such as his soundtrack for *Pet Semetary*, 1989), and non-western flutes stress Ariel's magical qualities, but we encounter the same disparity between the happy words of "Where the Bee Sucks" and the music. Dissimilar to *Prospero's Books*, however, in this film Ariel and Prospera maintain a developed relationship. Whishaw plays Ariel with a great deal of subtlety, and the complex nature of his bond to Prospera is conveyed despite the disadvantage of his not being on location throughout the shoot. Whishaw is shown regularly in close-up, unlike Greenaway's Ariels, who are mostly exhibited as part of a complex tableau. Ariel as a character thus has more impact on the audience in Taymor's film than in Greenaway's. On the DVD commentary, Goldenthal asserts that he regards songs as "a thumbnail sketch of a character." The haunting quality of Ariel's songs, not only when he is singing of Alonso's death but even when he is trilling of his own freedom, suggests the ambiguity the composer finds in the text. Perhaps Goldenthal (who is Taymor's partner in their private as well as working life and thus is more likely to partake of her vision) was trying to convey a kind of Stockholm Syndrome for Ariel when departing his master – his freedom is tinged with nostalgic regret for the companionship and artistry they shared. He demands, after all, of the magician, "Do you love me master, no?" (4.1.49) – a line Taymor maintains, despite other quite radical cuts (*Tempest* filmscript, 136). As Whishaw's Ariel sings "Where the Bee Sucks," he launches himself backward into the water and appears kaleidoscoped in the splash. The traditional settings of this song imply an ascension into freedom, but this image of Ariel seems more like a descent, a resignation to a kind of death or, at best, oneness with the elements. In this way, Ariel's departure seems to parallel Prospero/a's from the island – "Every third thought shall be my grave" (5.1.311) – a relinquishment of powers rather than an acquisition of liberty.

Taymor films Ariel's songs with a clear focus on the actor's face, and his words dominate the soundscape, which provides atmosphere, a sense of awe, rather than a clear accompaniment. Whishaw's tenor is thus foregrounded, never obscured by vibrato or lush strings like Sarah Leonard's soprano, which contributes to the impression that the lyrics are more assertively present than in Nyman's songs, and more intimately associated with Ariel. They issue from him in a way that is not true of Greenaway's sprite(s). Goldenthal in an interview explains, "The thing is to try and illuminate the language and pin spot the performance, see what's behind the eyes" (Murray, 1). In contrast, Nyman writes in the liner notes for the soundtrack CD, "The musical works ... that I stowed in Peter Greenaway's cutting room became the core of his authority – organizational, illustrational and emotional." The concentration once again in *Prospero's Books* is on serving the central author figure, Prospero/Shakespeare/Gielgud/Greenaway, to the exclusion of other aspects of the play.

Taymor's Ariel is part of a much more naturalistic and natural world than Greenaway's, again, echoing Shakespeare's use of the sprite to convey the sea and animal imagery of an island, and the theme of metamorphosis in the play. This world is reflected in the music, which, as Goldenthal observes in the DVD commentary, "is also the landscape." Whishaw's Ariel appears amongst the trees, in pools of water, as a frog, a swarm of bees. The variety in the presentation of Ariel is true to Shakespeare's multifarious script, from the genre of the play itself (tragicomedy) to the inclusion of a wide diversity of sounds and music. The lyrical, orderly poetry of Ariel's songs is juxtaposed with the chaotic noises of animals, thunder, and wild waves, suggesting the *copia* of Shakespeare's conception and echoing what Robert B. Pierce terms "the pattern of shifting perception" ("Very," 169) that characterizes the play, which "consistently arouses, challenges, and disappoints ... expectations" (Gurr 102).

In her screenplay, Taymor explains that "the character of Ariel was conceived as an actor's fully human performance treated with the use of cinematic visual effects" (15). In contrast, Greenaway objectifies Ariel's body in an almost absurdist, Beckettian way. His prodigious urine session in the Renaissance bathhouse at the opening of the film renders him more like a Baroque fountain than a boy. The sound of his water hitting the pool is "crisply audible," as Greenaway dictates, so that his body is also a kind of music box. Greenaway compares his Ariel to "the figure on a ship's prow" (51). The youngest Ariel rhythmically swings his arms for so long it seems mechanistic, like a windup doll, fitting in with the jerky, repetitive dances of the other native inhabitants or spirits who are under Prospero's reign. These sustained single movements draw attention to the film's artifice. It is rare for any of the characters other than Prospero to seem like live beings, as they are not permitted to speak or to move naturally. The fact that even the Ariels often come across as automatons set in motion by the all-controlling Prospero suggests the influence of postcolonial readings of the play. Greenaway's Prospero has taken enslavement one sinister step further – his spirits, like Stepford wives, are no more than Prospero's machines. Furthermore, as these nameless secondary spirits have no lines in Shakespeare's play, their voices are not even heard at the end when his other characters are finally granted speech by Prospero/Greenaway. Greenaway's film does not seem to offer a sustained criticism of Prospero's tyrannical hold on the other characters. Neither does it develop the pathos of either Caliban's or Ariel's plight. Greenaway admits that his films "are very English. That certain emotional distance" (petergreenaway.org.uk). Moreover, the interest in the film clearly lies with the creator/artist figure, which is consistent with some of Greenaway's remarks about himself as an artist, seeming to overturn Roland Barthes's assertion that the author is dead and rather conferring special powers on the creator. Greenaway maintains, "Creation, to me, is to try to orchestrate the universe to understand what surrounds us" (petergreenaway.org.uk). The director's job, like the playwright's (Shakespeare), and the island monarch's (Prospero), is to orchestrate his world. Greenaway clearly identifies with Prospero, the artist/magician/ruler, and not with Ariel, the servant/production assistant. Robert Stam would term Greenaway's approach to the film as "internal focalization," as all the events of the plot seem to be filtered through Prospero, "a concept close to Henry James's idea of 'center of consciousness'" (Stam and Raengo, 39). Lisa Hopkins implies that Greenaway's identification with Prospero goes further still, "troubling us with gaps and suggestions which seem ultimately to speak more of Greenaway than they do of Prospero" (129).

Greenaway's Prospero figure does not always have control, however. If Prospero's power is demonstrated in the robot-like obedience of his subjects, their insubordination is expressed through Greenaway's more Rabelasian uses of the human body, with the emphasis on the jiggling flesh and bodily fluids. Caliban subversively pees, defecates, and vomits on books belonging to his master, who prized these volumes above his dukedom (1.2.167–8). James Tweedie in his article "Caliban's Books" astutely observes, "As a tradition of postcolonial readings has demonstrated, the play is structured around the relationship between a dominant power and its others, constructing their difference through alterity of language and the body, through the discrepancy between the curses emanating from the 'monster' Caliban and the standards of linguistic and bodily propriety established by Prospero and enforced by his minions" (116).

Tweedie would probably count Ariel amongst Prospero's minions, yet in both the play and each of the films, Ariel is clearly distinguished from other characters by "alterity of language and the body." He is the only character who delivers many of his lines in song, although in Taymor's film he is joined by Ferdinand, who sings "O Mistress Mine" in Miranda's ear (Reeve Carney, who plays Ferdinand, was discovered by Taymor as the lead singer of the rock band Carney) and in Greenaway's, following Shakespeare, by Iris and Juno. Taymor's Ariel, following Shakespeare, is differentiated from the other characters by his ability to shape-shift and his translucency. Greenaway's Ariels are distinguished by their cherubic appearance and the fact that they coexist in four different stages of life. As Greenaway's Prospero has created a Mannerist haven for himself on the desert island, composed of the gems of sixteenth- and seventeenth-century European architecture, it is difficult not to read Ariel's costume as another "insignia of colonial authority" (Bhabha, 144). Shakespeare provides us with no clues as to Ariel's appearance when he was first released from the pine, but it is tempting to assume that Greenaway's Prospero orders Ariel to appear as Bronzino's Folly, just as Marlowe's Faustus bids Mephostophiles to change his form to that of a Franciscan friar (1.3.25–33); in each case, the costume represents the first implementation of power over the servant. However, Greenaway's Ariel uses his alterity subversively at times. While Ariel's initial Herculean pee on the toy galleon representing the shipwreck was commanded by Prospero, later Ariel leaves sooty hand and buttock prints (vestiges of his harpy costume) on the page of the notebook in which Prospero/Shakespeare is composing *The Tempest* (133). Prospero then observes, "These mine enemies are all knit up / In their distractions: they are now in my power." The pubescent Ariel glares at him balefully. Prospero reaches for him gently, but he struggles and flies up, spilling black ink onto the desk (133). His splattering of the ink reads like more desecration of his master's books, another subversive act against the colonial tyrant who has just gloated about his power over others. As all these actions follow the scene in which Caliban befouls

Figure 12 Ariel (Ben Whishaw) sets fire to the king's ship in Taymor's *The Tempest*, 2010.

books, it is hard not to see it as Ariel's own rebellion against his master. If, as James Andreas contends, writing is the source of Ariel's agony (200), then this is another case of what Tweedie terms "the body ... serving as a defense against the book" (118).

Taymor's Ariel also has a sanctioned form of "carnival release," to frame it in Bakhtinian terms, in creating the storm. Whishaw, hair tipped with flames, wildly sets fire to the ship, accompanied by raucous heavy metal guitar, which in its association with transgressive rock bands and teenaged boys, suggests Ariel's rebellious energy, kept just under check by Prospera (fig. 12). We see a similar fiery Ariel again when he sets the spirit hounds on Caliban and his co-conspirators. Earlier, when Prospera reproaches Ariel for demanding his freedom, the scene takes on the form of a headmistress reprimanding a teenaged student, with Whishaw looking just as mulish (remembering his turn playing Hamlet at the Old Vic in 2004, perhaps). The same kind of soundtrack recurs when Ariel emerges as a harpy, slick with black paint and feathers, a costume that would not be out of place in a heavy metal band. Goldenthal comments on the DVD bonus features that his use of "electric guitars" was "messing with a response to specificity of time."

Like Nyman, Goldenthal clearly aimed to avoid creating music that suggested the original time period of the play. His goal was to create a soundscape that "you can't put your finger on or define as a type of music." The association at times between Ariel and rock and roll in this film is palpable, however. One reviewer caught a resemblance between the skinny, spiky-haired Whishaw, and a young David Bowie (Lacey, "*Tempest*"). Taymor in her DVD commentary compared him to Keith Richards, saying "there's a little rock and roll in him." Perhaps it is the sanctioned release provided by Prospero/a's vengeful assignments that allows him to tolerate his enslavement better than Caliban, whose only escape valve, until he meets Stephano, is complaining and cursing. Yet Ariel pities the human beings he is sent to punish; perhaps the audience is meant to read this as his recognition of them as fellow victims of the magician's subjugation.

The complicated bond that Ariel and Prospero share in the play is not really in evidence in Greenaway's film. This is strange as the director planned to highlight, as the turning point in the play, the moment when the servant admonishes the master for his vengefulness. When Prospero then turns to forgiveness, "the characters that his passion for revenge had created out of words now speak for the first time with their own voices, brought to a full life by his act of compassion" (Greenaway, 9). This, of course, does not happen until the last scene of the play. In Greenaway's actual film, the moment of transformation is lost in the usual chaotic frenzy of images. Taymor also pinpoints this scene as crucial to the overall understanding of the play: "This is the scene that finally leads Prospera to understand that 'the rarer action is in virtue than in vengeance.' And it is the spirit, Ariel, as an agent of reconciliation, who signifies this compassion, forgiveness and ultimate redemption" (Screenplay, 17). Thus, Taymor views *The Tempest* as a kind of "redemptive narrative," like those related by participants in the Wildschut nostalgia study. Certainly, Taymor spotlights this scene in her film. It was the one time that Mirren and Whishaw were acting in the same space, instead of Whishaw being added later by CGI. It is also a quiet moment, devoid of flashy special effects. Taymor explains, "I purposefully left Ariel untreated, corporeal" (16). In the DVD commentary, she adds, "It's where he's almost human." It seems strange that in their adaptations of a play which both directors agree is most importantly about forgiveness, the music written for them is predominantly gloomy.

Ariel's singing body, both in the play and the two filmic adaptations discussed here, is above all a body in flux. Shakespeare changes Ariel into a sea nymph, a harpy, an invisible spirit, and Ceres in the wedding masque. In addition, in his final song, Ariel depicts himself as tiny enough to slide into a cowslip's bell. Both directors shift Ariel's real release from Prospero to the end of their films. Taymor, in another homage to her 1986 stage production of the play, moves the song "Where the Bee Sucks" to her movie's final moments. In her DVD commentary, her emphasis is once again on the way this affects the magician rather than the way it affects the sprite: "After everything has happened [Ariel is] the last bit of herself that she lets go."

Greenaway's film minimizes and renders ambiguous Shakespeare's joyful liberation of Ariel in "Where the Bee Sucks," which here merely forms the soundtrack for a chaotic scene in which many spirits/natives dress Prospero. Greenaway creates instead his own version of Ariel's liberation, saving it for the last seconds of the film. The eldest of the four actors starts the run down the corridor, witnessed by applauding native spirits; he quickly morphs into the younger actors until the child Ariel, played by Orpheo, takes the final joyful leap into the camera. The diminution in size recalls the cowslip line from the song. Our emotional engagement here with Ariel, though, is minimal, as he has been depicted throughout as merely one of many spirits who attend on Prospero.

Ariel's form of exit supplies a bookend for Greenaway's film. In the opening scenes, the small body of the youngest Ariel contrasts starkly with Prospero/Gielgud's aging form, both almost naked in the large bath. Lisa Hopkins observes that "the tension between clothes and nakedness provides a recurring motif in the film" (119). In the final scene, Prospero/Gielgud appears at his most elderly, stripped of his magical powers and his fine clothes, talking about death. This aging of Prospero and corresponding regression of Ariel accords beautifully with Greenaway's overarching structure of Past, Present and Future.

The presentation of the spirit Ariel in these two films reflects changing attitudes from periods in which *The Tempest* was viewed as a play chiefly about magic to the postcolonial era when it is seen as a play primarily about exploitation. This shift is echoed in the music composed for Ariel, particularly in the rendition of "Where the Bee Sucks." Shakespeare's lyrics suggest a variety of tones for Ariel's three main songs: coaxing for "Come unto These Yellow Sands," funereal for "Full Fathom Five," and jubilant for "Where the Bee Sucks." While Greenaway and especially Taymor have lived up to Shakespeare's range in their interpretation of Ariel's body, their composers have not followed through with equal variety in the music. The soundtracks for both films are predominantly melancholy, reflecting the composers' and the directors' sense of the play's deep ambiguity, of which directors and composers before the 1980s were generally less aware. Even Greenaway and Taymor, who are clearly more fascinated by the plight of the artist-magician than of his/her servants, cannot escape the ambiguity in Ariel's bond to Prospero. The two film directors' refusal to engage with the postcolonial issues raised by the play in any sustained way betrays a nostalgia for the "simpler" days of production when a theatre could, with impunity, stage *The Tempest* without taking any interest in the politics behind it.

Conclusion

The number of Shakespeare films produced has declined somewhat since the 1990s, but adaptations are still emerging at a rate of at least one every year. I anticipate that this steady output will continue, at least in the near future. Gregory Mikell is slated to come out in 2017 with a low-budget film called *Shakespeare: The Ballroom*. TNT is airing a ten-part series based on young Shakespeare's life entitled *Will*. Steven Berkoff is premiering a film called *Shakespeare's Heroes and Villains*. New filmmakers are encouraged to try their hand at short films based on Shakespeare by the Shakespeare Birthplace Trust Film Festival, a competition patronized by Kenneth Branagh. In addition, the filmed productions from major theatres like the Royal Shakespeare Company and the Stratford Festival in Canada are shown in select cinemas.

Why do we persist in making films of these four-hundred-year-old plays when the box-office returns are generally extremely poor? There are practical reasons. Since the budgets for most Shakespeare adaptations are fairly modest, producers accept the probability of box-office loss – while counting on some later remuneration from DVD sales to educational institutions – in order to gain international prestige for their studio. Shakespeare seems to appeal to some extent to many cultures (see Mark Thornton Burnett's *Filming Shakespeare in the Global Marketplace*; *Shakespeare and World Cinema*), and so, if an adaptation is cast with a few non-English stars, the chances of studios outside of Britain and the United States contributing to the project are improved. And as with any film, there is always a possibility that it may be a hit, like Baz Luhrmann's *Romeo + Juliet*.

The secret behind the box-office success of some Shakespeare adaptations and the failure of others has not yet been uncovered. Emma French theorizes that cinema audiences like their Shakespeare hybridized, which for her explains the popularity of Luhrmann's *Romeo + Juliet* and John Madden's *Shakespeare in Love* (16, 35). Yet one could argue that Branagh's *Love's Labour's Lost* too is a hybrid – half Shakespeare, half musical – and it did not fare well financially. In fact, all Shakespeare films are hybrids, mingling media and genre conventions, juxtaposing the beautiful with the grotesque. Viewers of Shakespearean adaptations, especially those considered here that retain his language, are nostalgic for the classic text but at the same time anticipate with curiosity film directors' new interpretations of that text. Thus, a Shakespeare film straddles past and present, making a new piece of art from an old one and therefore suggesting a reassuring if somewhat circuitous continuity with our cultural history.

Anthony Lane, film critic for the *New Yorker*, propounds a different hypothesis for the success of some plays in adaptation over others: "One of the lasting oddities of Shakespeare movies, in fact, is how frequently they turn to the earliest works. 'Romeo and Juliet,' 'Richard III,' most of the 'Henry' plays and 'A Midsummer Night's Dream' are attributable to the playwright's salad days. Maybe directors warm to the green unsubtlety of that period, as they do to the big-name heroics of the major tragedies ... preferences tied to the orthodoxy that is first encouraged in the classroom" (76). Strictly speaking, the plays that Lane lists, apart from *Richard III*, are not among Shakespeare's earliest efforts, as far as scholars' accepted chronology would have it. Furthermore, no one, as far as I know, has adapted the early *Henry VI* plays into full-length feature films (the BBC adapted them for television). Lane's second point, however, is more convincing. Looking over the span of Shakespeare adaptation to film, we see that his histories and tragedies have tended to be the commercial and/or critical triumphs. (Contrast the fates of Olivier's *Henry V*, *Hamlet*, and *Richard III* with the *As You Like It* in which he was involved, or the far greater financial success of Zeffirelli's *Romeo and Juliet* than his *Taming of the Shrew*.) The stronger narrative drive in the histories and tragedies, coupled with the higher stakes in their plots, may partly explain this phenomenon. Branagh's biographer, Mark White, theorizes, no doubt with the financial failure of *Love's Labour's Lost* (2000) in mind, that the malapropisms and stage devices like the eavesdropping of Shakespeare's comedies generally fail to appeal to modern tastes (162). Furthermore, the plays that get made into films are most frequently the ones taught in school – which may go some way to explaining the dire financial records of such excellent adaptations as Nunn's *Twelfth Night* and Fiennes's *Coriolanus* (the latter almost universally admired by film critics), plays rarely covered in schools, at least in North America.

The above speculations go some distance to explaining continued studio interest in Shakespeare, but do not explain why directors assume the challenge when they know it is unlikely they will make money from it; they, presumably, have little interest in garnering honours for studios. On the other hand, directors may appreciate ready-made, versatile scripts that can be adapted for free. Almost all the directors considered in this book wax lyrical about the adaptability of Shakespeare's works. Luhrmann quotes Benjamin Britten: "If a story is true then there will be many different productions in many different places and it will go on and on" ("Shakespeare in the Cinema," 48). Oliver Parker, who directed *Othello*, concurs: "His plays are colossal things, open to infinite interpretation ... What makes him such a genius is the many layers to his work – his ability to be insightful, moving and profound, while entertaining at the same time" (ibid., 49). And it is not just film directors who pinpoint Shakespeare's flexibility as a crucial element of his unique endurability. A reviewer of Whedon's *Much Ado About Nothing* credits the film with furnishing evidence of "'the incredible versatility of Shakespeare.' [These] 400 year-old works can be endlessly re-interpreted, adapted and updated for amazing new results" (Anderson, 1). Lane, commenting on the explosion of Shakespeare films in the 1990s, eulogizes, "No other writer has been so thoroughly filtered through other eyes and minds; he comes out differently every time, although it is we who are transformed as he passes through" (77). Trevor Nunn, director of *Twelfth Night*, hits the nostalgic note more directly, referring to our rapidly altering society: "Shakespeare is very fruitful territory for personal vision because the plays mean such different things to different people. They also mean different things at different times in history. In our fast-changing world, Shakespeare's plays often change in meaning from decade to decade, sometimes from year to year" ("Shakespeare in the Cinema," 51).

Such adaptability is an unusual characteristic among writers. Compared to his contemporaries, Shakespeare makes fewer references to specifically Elizabethan realities, and those that exist are easily excised as they are generally not wedded to the central concerns of the plays (see chapter 11). His depiction of the past has persisted more than that of other writers of his time and later: witness his characterization of Richard III, for instance. Creative writing of our own period tends to be rooted in the specifics of the period in which it is set, cluttered with the era's accoutrements, and so less likely to speak to future audiences. If we look at the work of a modern/postmodern playwright like Tom Stoppard, we can see how much a play like *Rock and Roll* is studded with references to the objects and politics of a particular epoch. Shakespeare, as Northrop Frye would argue, works instead with archetypes. Ben Jonson's praise "he was not of an age, but for all time" is thus truer than the rival playwright could have foreseen.

Additionally, many of his plays are set in semi-fictional locations like Illyria or a desert island somewhere between Naples and Africa, which makes them ideal sources for screenplays and adds to the fairy-tale quality that makes his plays so appealing to audiences inundated by the minutiae of postmodern life coming at them every second on their smart phones. Even the non-fictional settings are far enough away from the present moment to share the fairy-tale aspect. Modern and postmodern culture has evinced a nostalgia for Shakespeare's era: witness the popularity of mini-series set in Tudor times, the use of Renaissance images in advertising, the prevalence of Renaissance fairs, and references to Shakespeare in popular culture from rock songs to newspaper articles. (See Paul F. Grendler's excellent *The European Renaissance in American Life* for overwhelming evidence of this.) The intrigue of the Elizabethan court seems to be a central aspect of the period's appeal. Branagh's *Henry V* and Fiennes's *Coriolanus* take full advantage of this theme, although they set their films in different times (see chapter 9). Nor is wistfulness for Shakespeare's time a new phenomenon – P.W. Wilson wrote in the *New York Times Magazine* in 1935, "If the screen can rescue Shakespeare from the trammels of the stage ... the Elizabethan urge within us all – boisterous and brave and sentimental and sad – may again encircle the globe" (19). The past century and the present seem to turn to Shakespeare's time more often than other historical periods. The early modern period was the first to focus on "man as the measure of all things"; perhaps we look back to recapture some of the excitement of that discovery, especially when we seem on the verge of making the computer the measure of all things.

The directors considered here cite Shakespeare's language as one of the reasons they chose to adapt his plays, even though it can be an intimidating element for film audiences. Zeffirelli observes that "Juliet Capulet and Romeo Montague in Verona expressed themselves more nobly, more fully than young people do today" ("Shakespeare in the Cinema," 55). Luhrmann too was drawn to Shakespeare's vivid language: "Our philosophy in adapting *Romeo and Juliet* for the screen was to reveal Shakespeare's lyrical, romantic, sweet, sexy, musical, violent, rude, rough, rowdy, rambunctious storytelling through his richly invented language" (48). Whedon concurs, extolling "the energy of the language" (DVD commentary). Kenneth Turan, film critic for the *L.A. Times*, chimes in: "It's hard to go too far wrong with this material. [Shakespeare's] plays are difficult to do superbly but because the language is so good and the situations so delicious, they're forgiving of engaging but not quite perfect attempts" (1). Clearly, adaptors hope that audiences will rise to the challenge of the language, seeing it as a worthwhile enterprise.

Many of those involved in creating entertainment still see Shakespeare as the apex in their field. Returning to him is a going home to our artistic origins. Barton credits Shakespeare with developing realism: "I believe our tradition actually derives from him. In a sense, Shakespeare himself invented it, with his teeming gift for characterisation and his frequent use of naturalistic language" (15). The dominant realism typical of most of the adaptations here, as discussed in chapter 2, contributes to their lasting appeal, as it is a style that dates less quickly than trendier or more avant-garde filmic approaches.

When the editors of *Cineaste* magazine asked film adaptors of Shakespeare to explain his appeal, many of their answers were full of nostalgia for a greatness seemingly missing in present-day works. Zeffirelli, director of the feature films of *Romeo and Juliet* (1968), *The Taming of the Shrew* (1967), and *Hamlet* (1990), as well as television movies of *Much Ado About Nothing* (1967) and the Verdi operas *Falstaff* (1992) and *Otello* (1976) – to say nothing of his career as a stage director – laments lost greatness:

We have to help young people face the past with honesty, courage and greed, because we learn so much from the past. We live in very dry, very poor times, and we have to go back to when our garden was full of flowers and marvelous fruits, because today our poor plants are sterile, they don't produce anything. Children do learn from the past, because only if you know the past can you properly contemplate the present and the future. When you look at the head of David by Michelangelo, that's beyond time, it's an emotion that will last forever. Art has the tremendous advantage of defeating time. François Mitterand, when he opened the Musée d'Orsay, said, "When I look at a work of art, I understand that man can defeat death." ("Shakespeare in the Cinema," 54)

Zeffirelli's reference to our "very dry, very poor times" may be an acknowledgment that digital media have eroded our sense of what is "original" because so much of what we see on the web is copied or pastiched. The assumption underlying his comment is that Michelangelo and Shakespeare lived in a period in which it was still possible to be original (ignoring, for the moment, the fact that most of Shakespeare's plots are lifted from his sources). Zeffirelli yearns, as Susan Bennett would put it, for an "authenticity which is not retrievable," an authenticity which he finds only in early modern masterpieces like the David and *Hamlet*.

Zeffirelli here articulates a good defence of nostalgia's usefulness. If we can look back and remember, and pass that memory on to the next generation, that suggests that we, represented by our art and culture, also might not be forgotten. By adapting *Romeo and Juliet*, *The Taming of the Shrew*, and *Hamlet* to the screen, Zeffirelli ensured that another couple of generations would be familiar with Shakespeare's work. Yet what audiences really became acquainted with was Zeffirelli's idiosyncratic readings of those works. When he passed the baton to Luhrmann and Almereyda, who adapted *Romeo and Juliet* and *Hamlet* respectively, the succession might well have been disputed, especially by Zeffirelli himself. His films, made in the traditions of *resurgimento* – a rebirth of realism – are so very different from the more recent adaptations, especially Luhrmann's. Yet in all their altered forms, Shakespeare's words, characters, and plots resonate.

These issues of memory and succession obsess Shakespeare's Hamlet, the character with whom I opened this book. The amnesia of the Danish court regarding his dead father strikes him as testimony that a human being's life is essentially meaningless. Yet even Hamlet seems to forget the charge his father set him, despite his clearing the tables of his memory to allow his vengeful enterprise to reign alone. Furthermore, his voiced memories of his father – as Hyperion, as a husband who would not beteem the winds of heaven to visit his wife's face too roughly – seem idealized, tinged with the same yearning that makes these directors look back to the Renaissance and assume its art was better than ours, and use it to protect themselves (and their audiences) from what Michael Bristol terms "the cultural abyss ... a ruptured artistic succession" (40). Part of our idealization of the Renaissance is that it was an era, unlike our own, relatively unplagued by nostalgia. In *The Ethnic Origins of Nations*, Anthony Smith writes: "In a 'traditional' society, one was expected to fashion one's life-style and ambitions in terms of collective traditions, so that there was little need to yearn for a past that was being continued" (176). While Shakespeare's era was rapidly becoming less traditional than those preceding it, it still retained a greater degree of continuity with the past than our own era of lightning change. Sociologists Nigel Rapport and Andrew Dawson describe twenty-first-century citizens as "rootless, displaced between worlds, living between a lost past and a fluid present" (qtd in Duyvendak, 7). Shakespeare, for all the myriad interpretations he inspires, is in a way fixed, stable. The texts of his plays, written four hundred years ago, have a polysemic permanence, in spite of, or because of what we do to them. They exist in so many languages, in so many libraries, in theatres, on DVDs and YouTube videos, in bookshops and homes, that they suggest something eternal, immutable. Perhaps this is why film directors continue to turn to them – they are a recognizable locus in a swirling world of change.

Shakespeare's works are familiar to artists whatever their background. Zeffirelli and Luhrmann came to the playwright through opera, as dozens of operas are based on his plays. (A new opera based on *The Tempest* composed by Thomas Ades emerged in 2012.) Peter Greenaway's background is in visual arts, and Shakespeare is there too, supplying subjects for painters as diverse as Fuseli, Millais, Sargent, Waterhouse, Mucha, Delacroix, and Rossetti. Kenneth Branagh grew up with television; he recalls as a child being frightened by the ghost of Hamlet Senior (*Screenplay*, xi). Shakespeare represents a kind of home to many artists, whatever form of art they practise and on whatever entertainment they were raised. He is reassuringly and uniquely common to us all.

Duyvendak in *The Politics of Home* asserts that "the longing for familiarity, for a community that is home, is a central theme in American history" (17). David Morely notes that Americans "use 'the positive language of 'home truths', of the virtues of the 'home-made' – and of the idea of 'settling down' as itself an index of maturity" (430, qtd in Duyvendak, 18). As Americans move on average every five years (Duyvendak, 18), it is no wonder they feel a sense of deep yearning for the concept of "home." Duyvendak observes also that in the United States "the notion of 'homeland' seemed omnipresent following 9/11" (2). Fears of the loss of American identity were whipped up in this last election too, with Donald Trump shamelessly capitalizing on the nostalgic slogan "Make America great again."

The films discussed in this book all passed through the American film industry in one guise or another: if they were not produced by Americans, they were at least distributed by Americans. Perhaps the reason that Shakespeare films continue to make it to the cinema despite usually losing money is that they represent some sense of home. Because Shakespeare is inevitably taught in schools, he can conjure up memories of our youth. Through his use in advertising, popular songs, newspapers, and of course theatre and film, he is all around us. He has "become our 'comfort food,'" Charles Marowitz maintains: "We turn to him as we do to meatballs and mashed potatoes, or fish 'n' chips. That is, to re-experience the pleasurable sensations we had when we first encountered him at school or on the stage or through the medium of doting teachers, critics, and academics. Subconsciously we crave the same thrills, comforts, and insights that were etched into our nature when we were most impressionable, most susceptible to the seductions of art" (72). We identify a place as home largely because of the memories associated with it; or, as sociologist Doreen Massey puts it, "The identity of places is very much bound up with the histories which are told of them, how these histories are told, and which history turns out to be dominant" (1995, 186). Shakespeare is one of the dominant storytellers of all time. His plays have become highly significant elements of the history of the English-speaking peoples. Howard Felperin expressed it thus: "The canon ... is all we finally have to define ourselves" (qtd in Bennett, 13). It is thus no wonder that film directors continue to turn to Shakespeare in this era of rapid change, despite the challenges of his language and culture for mass audiences and his generally disappointing performance at the box office.

Why are film directors drawn to him so much more than cinema audiences seem to be? Perhaps it comes down to an ideal of auteurship – not, obviously, shared by those who are only going to view these films and cannot take any credit for making them. Shakespeare's enduring reputation for greatness confers a little patina of itself on the directors who adapt him. Furthermore, his continued use as an author for school and university study ensures that these films will be seen long after most movies based on original screenplays, or adaptations of lesser literary works, have been largely forgotten. Even when a new adaptation of the same play emerges, the earlier film will likely still be shown for the sake of comparison. What all these directors here considered share is ambition: they want their work to last. Like Ferdinand, Prince of Navarre, these directors of Shakespeare seem to say:

> Let fame, that all hunt after in their lives,
> Live registered upon our brazen tombs
> And then grace us in the disgrace of death;
> When, spite of cormorant, devouring Time,
> The endeavor of this present breath may buy
> That honour which shall bate his scythe's keen edge,
> And make us heirs of all eternity. (*Love's Labour's Lost*, i.i)

Consider the honour garnered by Nunn's *Twelfth Night*. This film, along with Fiennes's *Coriolanus*, was more financially disastrous than any of the other adaptations here discussed, and yet, because it is the only recent big-screen faithful adaptation of this particularly brilliant Shakespeare comedy, academics have written essays on it, and it has been shown and will continue to be shown in countless classrooms. In short, the film has attracted intellectual attention only because it is an adaptation of Shakespeare. No other box-office failure would persist in this way. Sarah Brown corroborates this reality, citing other Shakespearean adaptations: "Texts such as Stoppard's *Rosenscrantz and Guildenstern Are Dead*, Jane Smiley's *1000 Acres* or Peter Greenaway's *Prospero's Books* are, as a direct result of their links with Shakespeare, included on many university syllabuses" (Brown, Lublin, and McCulloch, 5). Shakespeare thus becomes an appealing proposition for film directors who are more interested in having their work last than in making a lot of money. Greenaway, for example, professes, "I sincerely believe that somehow films need to last at least over several generations" (Rodgers, 145). His comment, if representative, speaks volumes about the profiles of directors who choose to adapt Shakespeare. They aim to make a new, lasting work of art out of an existing abiding work of art, and make it accessible to a greater number of people. It is a labour of love, and an attempt to defeat devouring time, not just for Shakespeare, so that his plays are viewed by a larger, less privileged public, but also for the directors' own reputations as artists. As Anthony Smith maintains, "By linking oneself to 'a community of history and destiny', the individual hopes to achieve a measure of immortality which will preserve his or her person and achievements from oblivion" (175). Greenaway admits that his work "does really examine this question, 'Can art make you immortal?'" (Rodgers, 143).

Additionally, these directors who persist in adapting four-hundred-year-old plays may envy Elizabethans their sense of home. Rapport and Dawson assert that the modern "homeless mind is hard to bear, and there is widespread nostalgia for a condition of being 'at home' in society, with oneself and with the universe: for homes of the past that were socially homogeneous, communal, peaceful, safe and secure" (31). It is not that Shakespeare shows us these kinds of homes – even in his comedies filmed recently, home is under siege, as many Americans and Western Europeans consider their own notions of home to be now. In *As You Like It* and *The Tempest*, the rightful dukes and their young daughters are displaced by usurping brothers. In *Much Ado*, Hero's standing in her community and even in her father's eyes is seriously threatened by Don John's conspiracy (see chapter 10). In *Love's Labour's Lost*, the prince's cosy collegial male world is overturned by the arrival of the French court ladies (chapter 12). In *A Midsummer Night's Dream*, patriarchal authority is threatened by Hermia, Hippolyta, and Titania, and even somewhat inadvertently by Puck (chapter 12). In other words, the plays give expression to the homesick.

Shakespeare gives English-speaking peoples (and for some time now, peoples of other language traditions) "a sense of identity," because he was part of their childhood, at least from school if not from other sources: theatre, plays in the park, films, music, art. The saying goes that we only ever meet the world once: in childhood; the rest is memory. The importance of the first encounters with life might partly explain why several of the directors here considered – Greenaway in *Prospero's Books*, Julie Taymor in her *Titus*, Adrian Noble in his *Dream*, and Edzard in her *Dream* – have seized on children as their window into the plays. Children represent fresh experience, for which adults are nostalgic. Childhood also signifies a time when many of us lived at home and felt safe. As Schopenhauer put it, "The years of childhood are so blissful that their memories are always accompanied by longing" (478). Shakespeare becomes connected with all of these positive associations.

Anthony Giddens expands on the current widespread sense of homelessness, writing about people's lack of a "sense of belonging and a sense of purpose in their lives, which is leading to a search for a sense of identity and belonging in the private sphere of the home" (qtd in Clapham, 2005, 137, qtd by Duyvendak, 10). Characters in a drama must have a sense of purpose; that is what drives the play forward. Even someone as conflicted as Hamlet has a mission, though he is uncertain about the morality of this purpose and the method of executing it. This "sense of purpose" that Giddens identifies as lost to postmodern people might suggest a further reason these directors turn to Shakespeare: they are attracted to the faith in humanity and the belief in transcendence expressed by many of his characters. That faith is not generally found in the dysfunctional characters of postmodern texts. The most prolific contemporary adaptor of Shakespeare into film, Kenneth Branagh, maintains that his natural instincts "tend to search for the hopeful, redeeming aspects of the human condition" (Mark White, 140). Nunn concurs (qtd in Russell Brown, 285). These directors may, often inadvertently, be revealing nostalgia for the view that human life, no matter how short, is imbued with meaning and purpose – a reassuring idea for us as we face, through environmental disaster, the eventual loss of our home, the earth.

Works Cited

Ackroyd, Peter. *Shakespeare: The Biography*. London: Chatto & Windus 2005.

Akhtar, Salman. "'Someday' and 'If Only' Fantasies: Pathological Optimism and Inordinate Nostalgia as Related Forms of Idealization." *Journal of the American Psychoanalytic Association* 44 (1996): 723–53.

Alleva, Richard. "Romance Old and New: *Twelfth Night* and *The English Patient*." *Commonweal* 20 (December 1996): 14–15.

Almereyda, Michael. *William Shakespeare's Hamlet: A Screenplay Adaptation*. London: Faber & Faber 2000.

Anderegg, Michael. *Cinematic Shakespeare*. Lanham: Rowman & Littlefield 2004.

– "Shakespeare on Film in the Classroom." *Literature/Film Quarterly* no. 2 (1976): 165–75.

Anderson, Jeffrey M. "Review of *Much Ado About Nothing*." *Combustible Celluloid*. http://www.combustiblecelluloid.com/2013/much_ado_about_nothing.shtml.

Anderson, Jeffrey M., and Lara Sao Pedro. "Oliver Parker Talks about *An Ideal Husband*." *Combustible Celluloid*. http://www.combustiblecelluloid.com. Accessed 22 July 1999.

Andreas, James. "Where's the Master? The Technologies of the Stage, Book, and Screen in *The Tempest* and *Prospero's Books*." In *Shakespeare without Class: Misappropriations of Cultural Capital*, edited by Donald Hedrick and Bryan Reynolds. New York: Palgrave 2000.

Andrews, J.F. "Kenneth Branagh's *Hamlet*." *Shakespeare Newsletter* 46, no. 3 (1996): 62.

Andrews, Nigel. "Reviews of This Week's Films: Ralph Fiennes' 'Coriolanus.'" *Financial Times*, 19 January 2012.

Ansen, David. "It's the '90s, So the Bard Is Back?" *Newsweek*, 4 November 1996, 73–4.
Aristotle. *Poetics*. London: J.M. Dent 1941.
Armstrong, Richard. *Understanding Realism*. London: BFI 2005.
Ascher-Walsh, Rebecca. "'Romeo + Juliet' Preview." *Entertainment Weekly*, 6 September 1996, 27–30.
Ash, Katie. "Computers and Learning, Scaling the Digital Divide: Home Computer Technology and Student Achievement." *Education Week* 28, no. 16 (7 January 2009).
Auden, W.H. "*Much Ado About Nothing*, Act II, Scene 3, Song, Sigh No More, Ladies." In *Twentieth Century Interpretations of Much Ado About Nothing*, edited by Walter R. Davis, 100–1. Englewood Cliffs: Prentice-Hall 1969.
Bakhtin, Mikhail. "Discourse in the Novel." In *The Dialogical Imagination*. Translated by Caryl Emerson and Michael Holquist. Austin: University of Texas Press 1981.
– *Rabelais and His World*. Translated by Helene Iswolsky. Bloomington, IN: Indiana University Press 1984.
Barker, Adam. "A Tale of Two Magicians: Adam Barker Talks with Peter Greenaway about Prospero's Books." In *Film/Literature/Heritage: A Sight and Sound Reader*, edited by Ginette Vincendeau, 109–15. London: British Film Institute 2001.
Barrie, J.M. *Peter Pan, or The Boy Who Would Not Grow Up: A Fantasy in Five Acts*. New York: Dramatists Play Service 1994.
Barton, John. *Playing Shakespeare*. London: Methuen 1984.
Bate, Jonathan. *The Genius of Shakespeare*. London: Picador 1997.
Bayer-Berenbaum, Linda. *The Gothic Imagination: Expansion in Gothic Literature and Art*. Madison: Fairleigh Dickinson University Press 1982.
Beecher, Donald. "Nostalgia and the Renaissance Romance." *Philosophy and Literature* 34, no. 2 (2010): 281–301. http://muse.jhu.edu.myaccess.library.utoronto.ca/journals/philosophy_and_literature/vo34 16/05/2012.
Beckett, Samuel. *The Complete Dramatic Works*. London: Faber & Faber 1990.
Belsey, Catherine. "Shakespeare and Film: A Question of Perspective." In *Shakespeare on Film: A New Casebook*, edited by Robert Shaughnessy, 61–70. New York: St Martin's Press 1998.
Bennett, Susan. *Performing Nostalgia*. London: Routledge 1996.
Bennetts, Leslie. "Two for Tempest." *Vanity Fair* 52, no. 12 (2010): 225.

Berger, Harry, Jr, "Against the Sink-a-Pace: Sexual and Family Politics in *Much Ado About Nothing*." In *Much Ado About Nothing and The Taming of the Shrew: Contemporary Critical Essays*, edited by Marion Wynne-Davies, 13–30. New York: Palgrave 2001.

Berger, Peter. *The Homeless Mind: Modernization and Consciousness*. New York: Vintage 1974.

Bhabha, Homi K. "Signs Taken for Wonders: Questions of Ambivalence and Authority under a Tree outside Delhi, May 1817." *Critical Inquiry* 12, no. 1 (1985): 144–65.

Bonnett, Alastair. *Left in the Past: Radicalism and the Politics of Nostalgia*. New York: Continuum 2010.

The Book of Alternative Services of the Anglican Church of Canada. Toronto: Anglican Book Centre, General Synod of the Anglican Church of Canada 1985.

The Book of Common Prayer. Toronto: Anglican Book Centre, General Synod of the Anglican Church of Canada 1962.

Borrelli, Christopher. "Oscar Nominees Take a Look Back with 'New Nostalgia.'" *Chicago Tribune*, 30 January 2012, 3.

Bourdieu, Pierre. *Distinction: A Social Critique of the Judgement of Taste*. Translated by Richard Nice. London: Routledge & Kegan Paul 1984.

Boyd, Brian. *On the Origin of Stories: Evolution, Cognition and Fiction*. Cambridge, MA: Belknap Press of Harvard University Press 2009.

Bradley, A.C. *Shakespearean Tragedy*. New York: Fawcett World Library 1967.

Bradshaw, Peter. "*Coriolanus* – Review." *The Guardian*, 19 January 2012.

Branagh, Kenneth. *Beginning*. London: Pan Books 1989.

– *Hamlet: Screenplay, Introduction and Film Diary*. New York: W.W. Norton 1996.

– *Henry V by William Shakespeare: A Screen Adaptation*. London: Chatto & Windus 1989.

– *Much Ado About Nothing by William Shakespeare: Screenplay, Introduction and Notes on the Making of the Film*. New York: W.W. Norton 1993.

Breight, Curtis. "Branagh and the Prince, or 'A Royal Fellowship of Death.'" In *Shakespeare on Film*, edited by Robert Shaughnessy, 126–44. New York: St Martin's Press 1998.

Bristol, Michael. *Shakespeare's America, America's Shakespeare*. New York: Routledge 1990.

Brode, Douglas. *Shakespeare in the Movies*. Oxford: Oxford University Press 2000.

Brody, Richard. "Julie Taymor's *The Tempest*." *New Yorker*, 13 December 2010, 1–2. http://www.newyorker.com/online/blogs/movies/2010/12/julie-taymor-the-tempest.html.
Brook, Peter. *The Empty Space*. Harmondsworth: Penguin 1968.
Brooke, Arthur. *The Tragicall Historye of Romeus and Juliet*. Richardi Totelli, 1562 (in the Arden *Romeo and Juliet*).
Brooks, Xan. "Interview with Ralph Fiennes." *The Guardian*, 9 December 2011, 1–15.
Brown, John Russell. *The Routledge Companion to Director's Shakespeare*. New York: Routledge 2008.
Brown, Sarah, Robert Lublin, and Lynsey McCulloch, eds. *Reinventing the Renaissance: Shakespeare and His Contemporaries in Adaptation and Performance*. New York: Palgrave Macmillan 2013.
Brown, Theo. *The Fate of the Dead: A Study in Folk-Eschatology in the West Country after the Reformation*. Cambridge: D.S. Brewer 1979.
Buhler, Stephen M. *Shakespeare in the Cinema*. Albany: SUNY Press 2002.
Bulman, J.C. "*As You Like It* and the Perils of Pastoral." In *Shakespeare on Television*, edited by J.C. Bulman and H.R. Coursen. Hanover: University Press of New England 1988.
Burnett, Mark Thornton. "Fancy's Images: Reinventing Shakespeare in Christine Edzard's The Children's Midsummer Night's Dream." *Literature/Film Quarterly* 30, no. 3 (2002): 166–70.
– *Filming Shakespeare in the Global Marketplace*. New York: Palgrave Macmillan 2007.
– *Shakespeare and World Cinema*. Cambridge: Cambridge University Press 2012.
Burnett, Mark Thornton, and Ramona Wray. *Shakespeare, Film, Fin de Siecle*. London: Macmillan 2000.
Burt, Richard, ed. *Shakespeare after Mass Media*. New York: Palgrave 2002.
Burt, Richard, and Lynda Boose, eds. "Introduction: Editor's Cut." In *Shakespeare, the Movie, II: Popularizing the Plays on Film, TV, Video and DVD*. London: Routledge 2003.
Burton, Robert. *An Anatomy of Melancholy*. Oxford: Clarendon Press 1989.
Bush, George. Speech given 20 September 2001. www.washingtonpost.com/wp-srv/nation/.../bushaddress_092001.htm/. Accessed 26 November 2001.
Butler, Martin. "Prospero in Cyberspace." In *Re-Constructing the Book: Literary Texts in Transmission*, edited by Maureen Bell, Shirely Chew, Simon

Eliot, Lynette Hunter, and James L.W. West, 184–96. Aldershot: Ashgate 2002.

Callaghan, Dympna. *Shakespeare without Women: Representing Gender and Race on the Renaissance Stage*. London: Routledge 2000.

Carnicke, Sharon Marie. "Lee Strasberg's Paradox of the Actor." In *Screen Acting*, edited by Alan Lovell and Peter Kramer, 75–87. London: Routledge 1999.

Carroll, Lewis. *Alice's Adventures in Wonderland*. London: Macmillan 1948.

Carroll, Lewis, and Charlotte B. Chorpenning. *Alice in Wonderland (a Play)*. Toronto: Coach House Press 1959.

Carson, Christie. "Shakespeare Online: An Increasingly Virtual Conversation." In *Shakespeare on Film, Television and Radio: The Researcher's Guide*, edited by Olwen Terris, Eve-Marie Oesterlen, and Luke McKernan. London: British University Film and Video Council 2009.

Cartmell, Deborah. *Interpreting Shakespeare on Screen*. London: Macmillan 2000.

Cassidy, John. "Measuring America's Decline in Three Charts." *New Yorker*, 23 October 2013.

Cavecchi, Mariacristina. "Peter Greenaway's *Prospero's Books*: A Tempest between Word and Image." *Literature/Film Quarterly* 25 (1997): 83–90.

Channel 4 Television Corporation. *Twelfth Night (or What You Will) Online Extra*, 2003. http://www.channel4learning.com/support/programme notes/netnotes/content/docs/twelfth_night.doc. Acessed 1 December 2003.

Chapman, James. *Past and Present: National Identity and the British Historical Film*. London: I.B. Tauris 2005.

Charney, Maurice. *All of Shakespeare*. New York: Columbia University Press 1993.

Churchill, Winston. *Winston Churchill's Speeches: Never Give In*. New York: Random House 2007.

Ciment, Michel. "Interview with Peter Greenaway: *The Baby of Macon*." In *Peter Greenaway Interviews*, edited by Vernon Gras and Marguerite Gras. Jackson: University Press of Mississippi 2000.

The Cinematic Endeavours of Peter Greenaway. http://petergreenaway.org.uk.

Clapham, D. *The Meaning of Housing: A Pathways Approach*. Bristol: Policy Press 2005.

Clemmensen, Christian. "Composer Tribute: Elliot Goldenthal." *Filmtracks*. http://www.filmtracks.com/composers/goldenthal.shtml.

Coe, Jonathan. "Review of Branagh's *Hamlet*." *New Statesman*, 14 February 1997, 41.
- "Twelfth Night." *New Statesman*, 25 October 1996, 39.
Collick, John. *Shakespeare, Cinema and Society*. Manchester: Manchester University Press 1989.
Cook, David A. *A History of Narrative Film*. New York: Norton 1980.
Cook, Pam. *Screening the Past: Memory and Nostalgia in Cinema*. London: Routledge 2005.
Corrigan, Timothy. *A Short Guide to Writing about Film*. New York: Harper Collins College 1994.
Coursen, H.R. *Shakespeare in Space: Recent Shakespearean Productions on Screen*. New York: Peter Lang 2002.
- *Shakespeare Translated: Derivatives on Film and Television*. New York: Peter Lang 2005.
Cox, John F. *Much Ado About Nothing: Shakespeare in Production Series*. Cambridge: Cambridge University Press 1997.
Craig, Cairns. "Rooms without a View." *Sight and Sound*, June 1991.
Crewe, Jonathan. "In the Field of Dreams: Transvestism in *Twelfth Night* and *The Crying Game*." *Representations* 50 (Spring 1995): 101–15.
Croteau, Melissa, and Carolyn Jess-Cooke. *Apocalyptic Shakespeare: Essays on Visions of Chaos and Revelation in Recent Film Adaptation*. London: McFarland & Co. 2009.
Crowdus, Gary. "Adapting Shakespeare for the Cinema: An Interview with Trevor Nunn." *Shakespeare Bulletin* (Summer 1999): 37–40.
- "Recent Shakespeare Films." *Cineaste* 23, no. 4 (Fall 1998): 13–19.
- "Shakespeare Is Up to Date: An Interview with Sir Ian McKellen." *Cineaste* 24, no. 1 (Winter 1998): 46–7.
Crowl, Samuel. "The Golden Girl and a Fistful of Dust." *Cineaste* 24, no. 1 (Winter 1998): 56–61.
- "Hamlet 'Most Royal': An Interview with Kenneth Branagh." *Shakespeare Bulletin* 12, no. 4 (Fall 1994): 5.
- "Julie Taymor's Film of Titus." *Shakespeare Bulletin* 18 (2000): 46–7.
- "Review of Branagh's *Hamlet*." *Shakespeare Bulletin* 15, no. 1 (Winter 1997): 34–5.
- "Review of *Twelfth Night*." *Shakespeare Bulletin* 15, no. 1 (Winter 1997): 36–7.
- *Shakespeare and Film: A Norton Guide*. New York: W.W. Norton & Co. 2008.
- *Shakespeare at the Cineplex: The Kenneth Branagh Era*. Athens: Ohio University Press 2003.

– "A Time for Titus: An Interview with Julie Taymor." *Shakespeare Bulletin* 18 (2000) 33–7.
Dargis, Manohla. "He's the Hero of the People and He Hates It": Movie Review of *Coriolanus*. *New York Times*, 1 December 2011, 1–3.
Davies, J.G., ed. *A Dictionary of Liturgy and Worship*. London: SCM 1972.
Davis, Fred. *Yearning for Yesterday: A Sociology of Nostalgia*. New York: Free Press 1979.
Davis, Walter R. ed. *Twentieth Century Interpretations of Much Ado About Nothing: A Collection of Critical Essays*. Englewood Cliffs, NJ: Prentice-Hall 1969.
Debruge, Peter. "Coriolanus." *Variety*, 14 February 2011.
Deleyto, Celestino. "Men in Leather: Kenneth Branagh's *Much Ado About Nothing* and Romantic Comedy." *Cinema Journal* 36, no. 3 (Spring 1997).
Desmet, Christy. "Teaching Shakespeare with YouTube." *English Journal* 99, no.1 (2009): 65–70.
Desmond, John M., and Peter Hawkes. *Adaptation: Studying Film and Literature*. Toronto: McGraw-Hill 2006.
Dixon, Wheeler Winston. "'Fighting and Violence and Everything That's Always Cool': Teen Films in the 1990s." In *Film Genre 2000: New Critical Essays*, edited by Wheeler Winston Dixon, 125–43. Albany, NY: SUNY Press 2000.
Dollimore, Jonathan, and Alan Sinfield, eds. *Political Shakespeare: Essays in Cultural Materialism*. Manchester: Manchester University Press 1994.
Donaldson, Peter. S. "Shakespeare in the Age of Post-Mechanical Reproduction: Sexual and Electronic Magic in *Prospero's Books*." In *Shakespeare, the Movie, II*, edited by Richard Burt and Lynda E. Boose. London: Routledge 2003.
Doyle, John. "Much Ado About Nothing." *Broadcast Weekly*, *Globe and Mail*, 10 February 1995, 11.
Duyvendak, Jan Willem. *The Politics of Home: Belonging and Nostalgia in Western Europe and the United States*. New York: Palgrave Macmillan 2011.
Eco, Umberto. *Travels in Hyper Reality: Essays*. Translated by William Weaver. San Diego: Harcourt Brace Jovanovich 1986.
"The Effects of Theatre Education." http://www.aate.com/?page=effects.
Eggert, Katherine. "Sure Can Sing and Dance: Minstrelsy, the Star System, and the Post-Postcoloniality of Kenneth Branagh's *Love's Labour's Lost* and Trevor Nunn's *Twelfth Night*." In *Shakespeare, the Movie, II: Popularizing the Plays on Film, Television, Video, and DVD*, edited by Richard Burt and Lynda Boose, 72–88. New York: Routledge 2003.

Eliot, T.S. "Hamlet and His Problems." In *The Sacred Wood*. New York: Alfred A. Knopf 1921.

Erasmus of Rotterdam. *On Copia of Words and Ideas*. Translated by Donald B. King. Milwaukee, WI: Marquette University Press 1963.

Errico, Angie. "William Shakespeare's A Midsummer Night's Dream." *Empire*, April 2000, 110.

Fine Line Features. *Twelfth Night*. http://www.flf.com/twelfth/main.htm. Accessed 1 May 2000.

Fitter, Chris. "A Tale of Two Branaghs: *Henry V*, Ideology and the Mekong Agincourt." *Shakespeare Left and Right*, edited by Ivo Kamps. New York: Routledge 1991.

French, Emma. *Selling Shakespeare to Hollywood: The Marketing of Film Shakespeare Adaptations from 1989 into the New Millennium*. Hatfield: University of Hertfordshire Press 2006.

Fried, Michael. *Realism, Writing, Disfiguration: On Thomas Eakins and Stephen Crane*. Chicago: University of Chicago Press, 1987.

Frye, Roland Mushat. *The Renaissance Hamlet: Issues and Responses in 1600*. Princeton: Princeton University Press 1984.

Gabriel, Yiannis. "Organizational Nostalgia: Reflections of 'The Golden Age.'" In *Emotion in Organizations*, edited by S. Fineman. London: Sage 1993.

Garber, Marjorie. *Vested Interests: Cross-Dressing and Cultural Anxiety*. New York: Harper Collins Perennial 1992.

Gay, Penny. *As She Likes It: Shakespeare's Unruly Women*. London: Routledge 1994.

Genette, Gerard. *Paratexts: Thresholds of Interpretation*. Translated by Jane E. Lewin. Cambridge: Cambridge University Press 1997.

Gerber, Louis. "Richard III." www.cosmopolis.ch, no. 4 (March 2000).

Giddens, A. *Modernity and Self-Identity: Self and Society in the Late Modern Age*. Stanford: Stanford University Press 1991.

Gilmore, Michael T. *Differences in the Dark: American Movies and English Theater*. New York: Columbia University Press 1998.

Gleiberman, Owen. "A Very Palpable Hit." *Entertainment Weekly*, 24 January 1997, 35–6.

– "Wherefore Art? Review of *William Shakespeare's Romeo & Juliet*." *Entertainment Weekly*, 8 November 1996, 46–7.

Graduale Romanae Ecclesiae (Ordinarium Missae). Paris: Tournai 1938.

Greenaway, Peter. *Prospero's Books: A Film of Shakespeare's* The Tempest. New York: Four Walls Eight Windows 1991.

Greenblatt, Stephen. "Martial Law in the Land of Cockaigne." In *Shakespearean Negotiations*. Oxford: Clarendon Press 1988.
- *Will in the World: How Shakespeare Became Shakespeare*. New York: Norton & Co. 2004.
Grendler, Paul F. *The European Renaissance in American Life*. Westport, CT: Praeger 2006.
Guneratne, Anthony R. *Shakespeare, Film Studies, and the Visual Cultures of Modernity*. New York: Palgrave Macmillan 2008.
Gurr, Andrew. "The Tempest at Blackfriars." In *Shakespeare Survey: An Annual Survey of Shakespearian Study and Production*, vol. 41, edited by Stanley Wells, 91–102. Cambridge: Cambridge University Press 1989.
Haldipur, Vrushali. "I Want to Be in Love All the Time." *Times of India*, 5 February 2002. http://timesofindia.indiatimes.com/articleshow/msid-1622947137,prtpage-1.cms.
Harvey, Gabriel. *Four Letters, and Certeine Sonnets*. London: John Wolfe 1592.
Hatchuel, Sarah. *Shakespeare, from Stage to Screen*. Cambridge: Cambridge University Press 2004.
- "Review of Kenneth Branagh's *As You Like It*, or All the World's a Film." *Shakespeare* 3, nos. 1–3 (April–December 2007): 365–8.
Hewison, R. *The Heritage Industry: Britain in a Climate of Decline*. London: Methuen 1987.
Higson, Andrew. "Re-presenting the National Past: Nostalgia and Pastiche in the Heritage Film." In *Fires Were Started: British Cinema and Thatcherism*, edited by Lester Friedman. London: UCL Press 1993.
- *Waving the Flag: Constructing a National Cinema in Britain*. Oxford: Oxford University Press 1995.
Hindle, Maurice. *Shakespeare on Film*. New York: Palgrave Macmillan 2015.
- *Studying Shakespeare on Film*. New York: Palgrave Macmillan 2007.
Hipsky, Martin A. "Anglophil[m]ia: Why Does America Watch Merchant-Ivory Movies?" *Journal of Popular Film and Television* 22, no. 3 (1994): 98–107.
Hoberman, J. "Much Ado About Nothing." *Village Voice*, 11 May 1993, 55.
Hodgdon, Barbara. *The Shakespeare Trade: Performances and Appropriations*. University of Pennsylvania Press 1998.
- "*William Shakespeare's Romeo + Juliet*: Everything's Nice in America?" In *Shakespeare Survey*, vol. 32, edited by Stanley Wells, 88–98. Cambridge: Cambridge University Press 19999.
Hoffman, Michael. *William Shakespeare's A Midsummer Night's Dream: Adapted for the Screen*. New York: Harper Collins 1999.

Holden, Anthony. *William Shakespeare: His Life and Work.* London: Little, Brown 1999.

Holinshed, Raphael. *The Third Volume of Chronicles.* N.p. 1586.

Holleran, James. "Maimed Funeral Rites in Hamlet." *English Literary Renaissance* 19 (1989): 65–93.

Honan, Park. *Shakespeare: A Life.* Oxford: Oxford University Press 2000.

Hopkins, Lisa. *Shakespeare's The Tempest: The Relationship between Text and Film.* London: Methuen Drama 2008.

Howe, Desson. "This 'Romeo' Is Bleeding." *Washington Post,* 1 November 1996. http://www.washingtonpost.com/wp-srv/style/longterm/movies/review97/romeoandjuliethowe.htm.

Howell, Peter. "Stratford's Bard Is Washing Up Everywhere." *Toronto Star,* 27 January 1999, D3.

Hutcheon, Linda. *A Theory of Adaptation.* With Siobhan O'Flynn. New York: Routledge 2013.

Ide, Wendy. Review of *As You Like It. Sunday London Times,* 20 September 2007. http://www.branaghcompendium.com/artic-ayli_times2007.html.

Illbruck, Helmut. *Nostalgia: Origins and Ends of an Unenlightened Disease.* Evanston, IL: Northwestern University Press 2012.

"Interview with Geoffrey Wright, Director of *Macbeth*." *The Movie Show online.* www.youtube.com/watch?V=H2ienX67AmY. Accessed 19 May 2008.

"Interview with Ian McKellen." http://r3.org/onstage/FILM/mckel1.html. Accessed 24 November 2001.

Jackman, Philip. "Hollywood Hears the Bard of Avon Calling." *Globe and Mail,* 15 February 1999, A20.

Jackson, Russell, ed. *The Cambridge Companion to Shakespeare on Film.* Cambridge: Cambridge University Press 2001.

Jameson, Frederic. "Postmodernism and Consumer Society." In *The Anti-Aesthetic, Essays on Postmodern Culture,* edited by Hal Foster, 11–25. Port Townsend, WA: Bay Press 1983.

– *Postmodernism, or The Cultural Logic of Late Capitalism.* Durham: Duke University Press 1991.

Jenkins, Harold, ed. *Hamlet.* Arden Shakespeare. London: Methuen 1982.

Jephson, Robert. *The Count of Narbonne: A Tragedy.* Whitefish, MO: Kessinger Publishing LLC 2009.

Jess-Cooke, Carolyn. *Shakespeare on Film: Such Things as Dreams Are Made Of.* London: Wallflower 2007.

Johnson, Brian D. "Review of Branagh's *Hamlet*." *Maclean's,* 30 December 1996, 101–3.

Jones, Emrys. *Scenic Form in Shakespeare*. Oxford: Clarendon Press 1971.
Jonson, Ben. *Everyman in His Humour: Five Plays*. Oxford: Oxford University Press 1988.
Kauffmann, Stanley. "Blanking Verse." *New Republic*, 2 December 1996, 40–1.
Kendrick, Walter. *The Thrill of Fear: 250 Years of Scary Entertainment*. New York: Grove Weidenfeld 1991.
Kermode, Frank. *Shakespeare's Language*. London: Penguin 2000.
The Killers. "Somebody Told Me." *Hot Fuss*. CD. Hampshire: Lizard King 2004.
Klett, Elizabeth. *Cross-Gender Shakespeare and English National Identity: Wearing the Codpiece*. New York; Palgrave Macmillan 2009.
Knopf, Robert, ed. *Theatre and Film: A Comparative Anthology*. New Haven, CT: Yale University Press 2005.
Kott, Jan. *Shakespeare Our Contemporary*. London: Methuen 1967.
Lacey, Liam. "Bringing Shakespeare to the Masses." *Globe and Mail*, 24 December 1996, C1.
– "*The Tempest*: Taymor Fails to Conjure Much of a Storm." *Globe and Mail*, 16 December 2010. http://www.theglobeandmail.com/arts/film/the-tempest-taymor-fails-to-conjure-much-of-a-storm/article4083167/.
Lane, Anthony. "Tights! Camera! Action!: What Does It Mean That the Bard Recently Hit No. 1 at the Box Office?" *New Yorker*, 25 November 1996, 65–77.
Lanier, Douglas. "Julie Taymor." In *The Routledge Companion to Directors' Shakespeare*, edited by John Russell Brown, 459–75. New York: Routledge 2008.
– "Nostalgia and Theatricality: The Fate of the Shakespearean Stage in the Midsummer Night's Dreams of Hoffman, Noble and Edzard." In *Shakespeare, the Movie, II: Popularizing the Plays on Film, TV, Video and DVD*, edited by Richard Burt and Lynda Boose, 154–73. London: Routledge 2003.
– *Shakespeare and Modern Popular Culture*. Oxford: Oxford University Press 2002.
Larue, Johanne. "James Dean: The Pose of Reality? East of Eden and the Method Performance." *Making Visible the Invisible: An Anthology of Original Essays on Film Acting*, edited by Carole Zucker. Metchuen, NJ: Scarecrow Press 1990.
La Salle, Mick. "This 'Romeo' Is a True Tragedy: Di Caprio/Danes Weak in Shakespeare Update." *San Francisco Chronicle*, 1 November 1996.
Lavery, David. *Joss Whedon: A Creative Portrait*. London: I.B. Tauris 2014.
Leggatt, Alexander. *Shakespeare's Comedies of Love*. New York: Routledge 1987.

- *Shakespeare's Political Drama.* New York: Routledge 1988.
Lehmann, Courtney. "Strictly Shakespeare? Dead Letters, Ghostly Fathers, and the Cultural Pathology of Authorship in Baz Luhrmann's *William Shakespeare's Romeo & Juliet.*" *Shakespeare Quarterly* 52, no. 2 (2001): 189–222.
- "There Ain't No 'Mac' in the Union Jack." In *Shakespeare Remains*, 190–212. Ithaca, NY: Cornell University Press 2002.
- "'Turn off the Dark' : A Tale of Two Shakespeares in Julie Taymor's *Tempest.*" *Shakespeare Bulletin* 32, no. 1 (2014): 45–64.
Lehmann, Courtney, and Lisa S. Starks. "Making Mother Matter: Repression, Revision, and the Stakes of 'Reading Psychoanalysis into' Kenneth Branagh's *Hamlet.*" *Early Modern Literary Studies* 6, no. 1 (May 2000): 21–4.
Levine, Laura. *Men in Women's Clothing: Anti-Theatricality and Effeminization, 1579–1642.* Cambridge: Cambridge University Press 1994.
Lindblom, Kenneth. "Teaching English in the World: Reversing the Decline of Literary Reading." *English Journal* 94, no. 3 (January 2005): 81–4.
Litson, Jo. "*Romeo and Juliet.*" *TCI: The Business of Entertainment Technology and Design* 30 (November 1996): 46.
Litten, James. *The English Way of Death: The Common Funeral since 1450.* London: Robert Hale 1991.
Livingston, E.A., ed. *The Concise Oxford Dictionary of the Christian Church.* Oxford: Oxford University Press 1977.
Logan, John. *Coriolanus: The Shooting Script.* New York: Newmarket 2011.
Loreti, Nicanor. "Interview with Geoffrey Wright." http://www.fearzoneblog. Accessed 15 June 2008.
Lowry, Brian. "Review of *As You Like It.*" *London Sunday Times*, 21 August 2007. http://www.branaghcompendium.com/artic-ayli_times2007.html.
Luckyj, Christina. "Gender, Rhetoric, and Performance." In *Enacting Gender on the English Renaissance Stage*, edited by Viviana Comensoli and Anne Russell. Chicago: University of Illinois Press 1999.
Luhrmann, Baz. *William Shakespeare's Romeo + Juliet: The Contemporary Film, the Classic Play.* New York: Bantam Doubleday Dell 1996.
MacDonald, Michael. "Ophelia's Maimed Rites." *Shakespeare Quarterly* 37 (1986): 309–17.
Mangan, Michael. *A Preface to Shakespeare's Comedies, 1594–1603.* New York: Longman 1996.
Manvell, Roger. *Shakespeare and the Film.* New York: Praeger 1971.

Marlowe, Christopher. *Doctor Faustus*. New York: Signet Classics 1969.
Marowitz, Charles. "Cinematizing Shakespeare." In *Reinventing the Renaissance: Shakespeare and His Contemporaries in Adaptation and Performance*, edited by Sarah Brown, Robert I. Lublin, and Dynsey McCulloch, 63–77. New York: Palgrave Macmillan 2013.
Mars-Jones, Adam. "Much Amiss." *Independent*, 27 August 1993, 12.
Martin, Sarah. "Classic Shakespeare for All: *Forbidden Planet* and *Prospero's Books*, Two Screen Adaptations of *The Tempest*." In *Classics in Film and Fiction*, edited by Deborah Cartmell, I.Q. Hunter, Heidi Kaye, and Imelda Whelehan, 34–53. London: Pluto 2000.
Massey, Doreen. "Places and Their Past." *History Workshop Journal* 39 (Spring 1995): 182–92.
Matheson, Tom. "Franco Zeffirelli." With Russell Jackson and Robert Smallwood. In *The Routledge Companion to Director's Shakespeare*. New York: Routledge 2008.
Matei-Chesnoiu, Monica. *Geoparsing Early Modern English Drama*. New York: Palgrave Macmillan 2015.
Matt, Susan J. *Homesickness: An American History*. Oxford: Oxford University Press 2011.
McKellen, Ian. *Richard III: Notes*. http://www.mckellen.com/cinema/richard/notes.htm.
– *Screenplay*. http://www.mckellen.com/cinema/richard/screenplay/.
– *Writings*. http://www.mckellen.com/writings/8204shakesq.htm.
Meyer, Stephanie. *Twilight*. New York: Little, Brown 2006.
Middleton, Thomas, and William Rowley. *The Changeling*. In *Thomas Middleton: The Collected Works*. Oxford: Clarendon Press 2010.
Miles, Robert. *Gothic Writing, 1750–1820, A Genealogy*. London: Routledge 1993.
Modenessi, Alfredo Michel. "(Un)Doing the Book 'without Verona Walls': A View from the Receiving End of Baz Luhrmann's *William Shakespeare's Romeo + Juliet*." In *Spectacular Shakespeare*, edited by Courtney Lehmann and Lisa S. Starks, 62–88. Madison: Fairleigh Dickinson University Press 2002.
Monk, Claire. "The British Heritage-Film Debate Revisited." In *British Historical Cinema*, edited by Claire Monk and Amy Sargeant. London: Routledge 2002.
– *Heritage Film Audiences: Period Films and Contemporary Audiences in the UK*. Edinburgh: Edinburgh University Press 2011

Monk, Claire, and Amy Sargeant, eds. *British Historical Cinema*. London: Routledge 2002.

Montaigne, Michel de. *On Friendship*. Translated by M.A. Screech. New York: Penguin 2005.

Morely, David. "Belongings: Place, Space and Identity in a Mediated World." *European Journal of Cultural Studies* 4, no. (4 (2001): 425–48.

Morris, Harry. *Last Things in Shakespeare*. Tallahassee: Florida State University Press 1985.

Motion Picture Association of America. *Movie Attendance Study*, 2007. http://www.mpaa.org/Movie Attendance Study.pdf. Accessed 1 May 2009.

Mullan, John. "Ken, Al and Will, Too." *Times Literary Supplement*, 21 February 1997, 19.

Murray, Rebecca. "Interview with Taymor and Goldenthal." *About.com: Hollywood Movies*. http://video.about.com/movies/Julie-Taymor-Tempest.htm. Accessed 15 December 2010

Nashe, Thomas. *The Unfortunate Traveller and Other Works*. New York: Penguin 1972.

Neill, Michael. "'Noises, / Sounds, and Sweet Airs': The Burden of Shakespeare's *Tempest*." *Shakespeare Quarterly* 59, no. 1 (Spring 2008): 36–59.

Nicholl, Allardyce. *Film and Theatre*. London: George G. Harrup & Co. 1936.

Nochimson, Martha. Review of *Hamlet*. *Cineaste* 25, no. 4 (September 2000): 37–8.

Novak, Elaine Adams. *Styles of Acting: A Scenebook for Aspiring Actors*. Englewood Cliffs, NJ: Prentice Hall 1985.

Nunn, Trevor. *William Shakespeare's Twelfth Night: A Screenplay*. London: Methuen 1996.

Nyman, Michael. *Noises, Sounds, and Sweet Airs*. Performed by Hilary Summers and Catherine Bott. Ensemble de Basse-Normandie, Argo Records 1995.

– *Prospero's Books*. Performed by Sarah Leonard, Marie Angel, Ute Lemper, Deborah Conway. Michael Nyman Band. Directed by Michael Nyman. Decca Record Co. 1991.

Ogle Davis, Sally. "Under the Lion's Skin: Young Kenneth Branagh Continues to Defy Critics of His Remarkable Career." *Weekend Australian*, 23–24 December 1989.

Orgel, Stephen. Introduction to *The Tempest*. Oxford: Oxford University Press 1987.

- "Nobody's Perfect: Or Why Did the English Stage Take Boys for Women?" In *Displacing Homophobia: Gay Male Perspectives in Literature and Culture*, edited by Ronald R. Butters, John M. Clum, and Michael Moon, 7–30. Durham: Duke University Press 1989.

Owen, Wilfred. *The Poems of Wilfred Owen*. London: Chatto & Windus 1931.

Packham, Chris. "Joss Whedon Strips *Much Ado About Nothing* to His Signature Elements." *Village Voice*, 5 June 2013, http://www.villagevoice.com/film/joss-whedon-strips-much-ado-about-nothing-to-his-signature-elements-6438557.

Panichas, George A. "Where Have the Readers Gone?" *Modern Age* 47, no. 1 (Winter 2005): 3.

Pearce, Craig, and Baz Luhrmann. *William Shakespeare's Romeo & Juliet: The Contemporary Film, The Classic Play*. New York: Bantam Doubleday Dell 1996.

Perkins, William. *The Workes of That Famovs and Worthy Minister of Christ in the Vniuersity of Cambridge, Mr. William Perkins*. London: I. Legatt 1626–31.

Peter Greenaway – Quotes. http://petergreenaway.org.uk.htm.

Pierce, Robert B. "Understanding *The Tempest*." *New Literary History* 30, no. 2 (Spring 1999): 373–88.

- "'Very Like a Whale': Scepticism and Seeing in 'The Tempest.'" In *Shakespeare Survey: An Annual Survey of Shakespearian Study and Production*, vol. 38, edited by Stanley Wells, 167–73. Cambridge: Cambridge University Press 1986.

Pilkington, Ace. *Screening Shakespeare from Richard III to Henry V*. Newark: University of Delaware Press 1991.

Platinga, Carl. *Moving Viewers: American Film and the Spectator's Experience*. Berkeley: University of California Press 2009.

Prior, Swallow. "What Maya Angelou Means When She Says 'Shakespeare Must Be a Black Girl.'" *The Atlantic*, 30 January 2013.

"Production Notes for *Richard III*." Provided by Mayfair Entertainment International. *Ricardian Register* 10, no. 4 (Winter 1995). http://www.r3.org/wp-content/uploads/2014/03/1995_12.pdf.

Pudovkin, Vsevolud. "From Film Technique: On Editing." In *Film Theory and Criticism*, edited by Gerald Mast and Marshall Cohen. Oxford: Oxford University Press 1985.

Purlilia, James, Earl of. *The Preceptes of Warre*. Translated by Peter Bentham. N.p., 1544.

Pursell, Michael. "Playing the Game: Branagh's Henry V." *Literature/Film Quarterly* 20, no. 4: 268–75.
Quinn, James, and Jane Kingsley-Smith. "Kenneth Branagh's *Henry V* (1989): Genre and Interpretation." In *British Historical Cinema*, edited by Claire Monk and Amy Sargent, 163–75. London: Routledge 2002.
Quinones, Ricardo J. *The Renaissance Discovery of Time*. Cambridge, MA: Harvard University Press 1972.
Rabelais, Francois. *Gargantua and Pantagruel*. Translated by M.A. Screech. New York: Penguin 2006.
Radcliffe, Ann. *The Mysteries of Udolpho*. Edited by Andrew Wright. New York: Holt, Rinehart & Winston 1963.
Rafferty, Terrence. "Solid Flesh: The Prince of Denmark and the King of Sleaze." *New Yorker*, 13 January 1997, 80–1.
Rapport, Nigel, and Andrew Dawson. *Migrants of Identity: Perceptions of Home in a World of Movement*. Oxford: Berg 1998.
Rhodes, Neil. *Elizabethan Grotesque*. London: Routledge & Kegan Paul 1980.
Ribot, Theodule. *Diseases of Memory: An Essay in the Practice of Positive Psychology*. London: Kegan Paul, Trench 1882.
Rice, Anne. *The Vampire Chronicles*. New York: Ballantine 2002.
Richmond, Velma Bourgeois. *Shakespeare as Children's Literature: Retellings from the Victorian and Edwardian Eras*. Jefferson, NC: McFarland 2004.
Riche, Barnabe. *Allarme for Englande*. N.p. 1578.
– *A Path-Way to Military Practise*. London: John Charlewood for Robert Walley 1587.
Ritivoi, Andreea Decier. *Yesterday's Self: Nostalgia and the Immigrant Identity*. Lanham: Rowman & Littlefield 2002.
Roberts, Alan. "*Henry V*: Once More unto the Screen." *Literature/Film Quarterly* 20, no. 4 (1992).
Rodgers, Marlene. "*Prospero's Books* – Word and Spectacle: An Interview with Peter Greenaway." In *Peter Greenaway Interviews*, edited by Vernon Gras and Marguerite Gras. Jackson: University Press of Mississippi 2000.
Rodman, Howard A. "Anatomy of a Wizard." In *Peter Greenaway Interviews*, edited by Vernon Gras and Marguerite Gras. Jackson: University Press of Mississippi 2000.
Rome, Emily. "Shakespeare Meets Biker Gangs and Dirty Cops: Interview with Michael Almereyda." *HITFIX*, 13 March 2015. www.hitfix.com/news/interview-cymbeline-director-michael-almereyda-on-reuniting-with-Shakespeare-and-ethan-hawke.

Romney, Jonathan. "Review of *Prospero's Books*." *Film/Literature/Heritage: A Sight and Sound Reader*, edited by Ginette Vincendeau, 142–5. London: British Film Institute 2001.

Rosman, Lisa. "Tricks and Treats: Michael Almereyda's 'Cymbeline.'" *Signature*, 12 March 2015. http://www.signature-reads.com/2015/03/tricks-treats-michael-almereydas-cymbeline/.

Ross, Lillian, and Helen Ross. *The Player: A Profile of an Art*. New York: Simon & Schuster 1962.

Rostand, Edmond. *Cyrano de Bergerac*. Translated by Anthony Burgess. London: Hutchinson 1985.

Rothwell, Kenneth. *A History of Shakespeare on Screen: A Century of Film and Television*. Cambridge: Cambridge University Press 1999.

– "How the Twentieth Century Saw the Shakespeare Film: 'Is It Shakespeare?'" *Literature/Film Quarterly* 29, no. 2 (2001): 82–95.

– *Shakespeare in Love*: A Review. *Cineaste* 24, nos. 2–3 (1999): 79–80.

– *Shakespeare on Screen: An International Filmography and Videography*. London: Mansell 1990.

Roush, Matt. "Shakespeare with a Twist." *TV Guide* (USA) 55, no. 34 (20 August 2007): 22.

Rowe, Katherine. "'Remember Me': Technologies of Memory in Michael Almereyda's *Hamlet*." In *Shakespeare, the Movie, II: Popularizing the Plays on Film, TV, Video and DVD*. London: Routledge 2003.

Rowell, Geoffrey. *The Liturgy of Christian Burial: An Introductory Survey of the Historical Development of Christian Burial Rites*. No. 59 of the Alcuin Club Collection. London: Alcuin Club 1977.

Rowling, J.K. *Harry Potter and the Philosopher's Stone*. London: Bloomsbury 1997.

Ruskin, John. *The Nature of Gothic*. Portland: Charles Lehman 1975.

Rutter, Carol Chillington. "Looking at Shakespeare's Women on Film." In *Cambridge Companion to Shakespeare on Film*, edited by Russell Jackson. Cambridge: Cambridge University Press 2000.

Sanderson, Blair. "Review of Nyman's Prospero's Books." *Allmusic* 2013. http://www.allmusic.com/album/nyman-prosperos-books-mw0000274323.

Schopenhauer. Arthur. *Parerga and Paralipomena*: *Short Philosophical Essays*. Vol. 1. Translated by E.F.J. Payne. Oxford: Clarendon Press 1974.

Scolnicov, Hannah. "Gertrude's Willow Speech." *Literature/Film Quarterly* 28, no. 2 (2000): 101–10.

Scott, A.O. "Movie Review: Arguing Their Way into Love." *New York Times*, 6

June 2013. http://www.nytimes.com/2013/06/07/movies/much-ado-about-nothing-directed-by-joss-whedon.html.

The Second Shepherd's Pageant. In *Everyman and Medieval Miracle Plays*, edited by A.C. Cawley. London: Dent 1990.

Shakespeare, William. *The Complete Works*. Edited by Stanley Wells and Gary Taylor. Oxford: Clarendon Press 1988.

– *Coriolanus*. In *The Complete Works*. Oxford: Clarendon Press 1988.

– *Coriolanus*. Edited by Jonathan Crewe. Pelican Shakespeare series. New York: Penguin Books 1999.

– *Henry V*. Edited by Gary Taylor. Oxford: Oxford University Press 2008.

– *Much Ado About Nothing*. Edited by R.A. Foakes. New Penguin. New York: Penguin Books 1968.

– *Much Ado About Nothing*. Edited by A.R. Humphreys. Arden Shakespeare. London: Methuen 1981.

– *Much Ado About Nothing*. Edited by Holger Klein. Lewiston, NY: Edwin Mellen Press 1992.

– *Much Ado About Nothing*. Edited by F.H. Mares. Cambridge: Cambridge University Press 2003.

– *Much Ado About Nothing*. Edited by Sheldon Zitner. Oxford: Oxford University Press 1994.

– *Othello*. Edited by Michael Neill. Oxford: Oxford University Press 2008.

– *Romeo and Juliet*. Edited by Brian Gibbons. Arden Shakespeare. London: Methuen & Co. 1980.

– *The Tempest*. Edited by Stephen Orgel. Oxford: Oxford University Press 1987.

– *Titus Andronicus*. Edited by Eugene M. Waith. Oxford: Oxford University Press 1984.

– *Twelfth Night*. Edited by M.M. Mahood. London: Penguin Books 1968.*

"Shakespeare in the Cinema: A Film Directors' Symposium." *Cineaste* 24, no. 1 (Winter 1998): 48–55.

Shakespeare Uncovered. www.pbslearningmedia.org/collection/Shakespeare-uncovered.

Sharkey, Betsy. "'Coriolanus' Review: Ralph Fiennes Directs Shakespeare Update." *Los Angeles Times*, 2 December 2011.

---

* Trevor Nunn does not mention his copy text for his adaptation. The RSC used the Penguin in the 1990s, and since Nunn was artistic director there for many years, I use it in chapter 11.

Shaughnessy, Robert. *Shakespeare on Film: A New Casebook*. New York: St Martin's Press 1998.

Sheppard, Philippa. "'The Difference of Our Spirit': Michael Radford Reconfigures Jewish-Christian Encounters in His Film of Shakespeare's *The Merchant of Venice*." In *Faith and Fantasy in the Renaissance*, edited by Olga Zorzi Pugliese and Ethan Matt Kavaler. Toronto: CRRS Publications 2009.

Shumway, D.R. "Screwball Comedies: Constructing Romance, Mystifying Marriage." In *Film Genre Reader III*, edited by Barry Keith Grant, 404. Austin: University of Texas Press 2003.

Sinfield, Alan. *Shakespeare, Authority, Sexuality*. New York and Abingdon: Routledge 2006.

Smith, Anthony. *The Ethnic Origins of Nations*. Oxford: Blackwell 1986.

Sobczynski, Peter. Review of Almereyda's *Cymbeline*. http://www.rogerebert.com/reviews/cymbeline-2015.

Sontag, Susan. "Film and Theatre." In *Film Theory and Criticism*, edited by Gerald Mast and Marshall Cohen, 249–67. Oxford: Oxford University Press 1985.

Sophocles. *Oedipus Rex*. Edited by R.D. Dawe. Cambridge: Cambridge University Press 2006.

Sorlien, Robert Parker, ed. *The Diary of John Manningham of the Middle Temple, 1602–3* Hanover, NH: University Press of New England 1976.

Sprengler, Christine. *Screening Nostalgia: Populuxe Props and Technicolor Aesthetics in Contemporary American Film*. New York: Berghahn Books 2009.

Stam, Robert, and Allesandra Raengo. *Literature through Film: Realism, Magic, and the Art of Adaptation*. Hoboken, NJ: Wiley 2004.

Stanislavsky, Constantin. *My Life in Art*. Translated by J.J. Robbins. London: Geoffrey Bles 1924.

Stevens, John. "Shakespeare and the Music of the Elizabethan Stage." In *Shakespeare in Music: A Collection of Essays*, edited by Phyllis Hartnoll. London: Macmillan 1964.

Stoppard, Tom. *Rosencrantz and Guildenstern Are Dead*. London: Faber & Faber 1969.

Stubbes, Philip. *An Anatomie of Abuses*. Edited by Margaret Jane Kidnie. Tempe, AZ: Arizona Center for Medieval and Renaissance Studies 2002.

Taylor, Gary. *Reinventing Shakespeare: A Cultural History from the Restoration to the Present*. New York and Oxford: Oxford University Press 1991.

– "Welcome to Bardworld: Any Colour as Long as It's Shakespeare." *The Guardian*, 13 July 2005. https://www.theguardian.com/stage/2005/jul/13/rsc.theatre.

Taylor, Neil, and Robin Richardson. *Seeing and Perceiving: Films in a World of Change.* London: Ikon Productions 1979.

Taymor, Julie. *The Tempest, Adapted from the Play by William Shakespeare.* New York: Abrams 2010.

– *Titus: The Illustrated Screenplay.* New York: Newmarket Press 2000.

"A Teacher's Guide to Websites, Books and Films." http://www.laits.utexas.edu/shakespearekids/winedale/teachers/resources/index.php#watching.

Thompson, Anne. "Swicord on the Map with 'Austen.'" *Variety*, 31 August 2007, 1.

Tomlinson, Doug, ed. *Actors on Acting for the Screen: Roles and Collaborations.* New York: Garland Publishing 1994.

Tookey, Christopher. "As you Like It, Mr. Branagh, but Certainly Not Me." *Daily Mail*, 21 September 2007. http://www.dailymail.co.uk/tvshowbiz/reviews/article-483175/As-YOU-like-Mr-Branagh-certainly-me.html.

Travers, Pamela. L. *Mary Poppins.* London: Harcourt 1982.

Turan, Kenneth. "Movie Review: 'Much Ado About Nothing' a Tasty Snack for Bard Lovers." *L.A. Times*, 6 June 2013. http://articles.latimes.com/2013/jun/06/entertainment/la-et-mn-much-ado-review-20130607.

Tweedie, James. "Caliban's Books: The Hybrid Text in Peter Greenaway's *Prospero's Books.*" *Cinema Journal* 40, no. 1 (October 2000): 104–26.

"The United States Falling Behind." *New York Times*, 22 October 2013. http://www.nytimes.com/2013/10/23/opinion/the-united-states-falling-behind.html.

Varma, Devendra P. *The Gothic Flame.* New York: Russell & Russell 1957.

Vasari, Giorgio. *Lives of the Most Eminent Painters, Sculptors and Architects.* N.p. 1550.

Vincendeau, Ginette, ed. *Film/Literature/Heritage: A Sight and Sound Reader.* London: British Film Institute 2001.

Walker, Elsie. "'Now Is a Time to Storm': Julie Taymor's *Titus* (2000)." *Literature/Film Quarterly* 30, no. 3 (2002): 194–207.

Walpole, Horace. *The Castle of Otranto.* Edited by Andrew Wright. New York: Holt, Rinehart & Winston 1963.

Walworth, Alan. "To Laugh with Open Throate." *Enacting Gender on the English Renaissance Stage*, edited by Viviana Comensoli and Anne Russell. Chicago: University of Illinois Press 1999.

Wasko, Janet. *How Hollywood Works.* London: Sage 2003.

Waugh, Evelyn. *Brideshead Revisited.* Boston: Little Brown & Co. 1945.

Webster, John. *The Duchess of Malfi.* London: A&C Black 1993.

Weissman, Jordan. "The Decline of the American Booklover." *The Atlantic*, 21 January 2014.

Wells, Stanley. Introduction to *Penguin Shakespeare's A Midsummer Night's Dream*. Harmondsworth: Penguin, 1967.

– *Shakespeare: A Dramatic Life*. London: Sinclair-Stevenson 1994.

Welsh, James A., Richard Vela, and John C. Tibbetts. *Shakespeare into Film*. New York: Checkmark Books 2002.

Werman, D.S. "Normal and Pathological Nostalgia." *Journal of the American Psychoanalytic Association* 25 (1977): 387–98.

Westlund, Joseph. "*Much Ado About Nothing*: The Temptation to Isolate." In *William Shakespeare's Much Ado About Nothing*, edited by Harold Bloom. New York: Chelsea House 1988.

Wey, James J. "'To Grace Harmony': Musical Design in *Much Ado About Nothing*." In *Twentieth Century Interpretations of Much Ado About Nothing*, edited by Walter R. Davis. Englewood Cliffs: Prentice-Hall 1969.

Whedon, Joss. *Much Ado About Nothing: A Film*. London: Titan Books 2013.

White, Mark. *Kenneth Branagh*. London: Faber & Faber 2005.

White, Martin. "Trevor Nunn." In *The Routledge Companion to Director's Shakespeare*. New York: Routledge 2008.

Widmark, Richard. *The Player*. Edited by Lillian Ross and Helen Ross. New York: Simon & Schuster 1962.

Wilders, John, ed. *The BBC TV Shakespeare: As You Like It*. London: BBC 1978.

Wildschut, T., C. Sedikides, J. Arndt, and C. Routledge. "Nostalgia: Content, Triggers, Functions." *Journal of Personality and Social Psychology* 91 (2006): 975–93.

Willson, Robert F., Jr. "Kenneth Branagh's *Hamlet*, or The Revenge of Fortinbras." *Shakespeare Newsletter* 47, no. 1 (Spring 1997): 7.

Wilson, Christopher. *Shakespeare and Music*. New York: De Capo Press 1977.

Wilson, Janelle L. *Nostalgia: Sanctuary of Meaning*. Lewisburg: Bucknell University Press 2005.

Wilson, P.W. "Review of 'A Midsummer Night's Dream.'" *New York Times Magazine*, 13 October 1935, 9–19.

Wolpert, Stuart. "Is Technology Producing a Decline in Critical Thinking and Analysis?" *UCLA Newsroom*, 27 January 2009.

Wray, Ramona. "Nostalgic for Navarre: The Melancholic Metacinema of Kenneth Branagh's *Love's Labour's Lost*." In *Shakespeare into Film*, edited by James A. Welsh, Richard Vela, and John C. Tibbetts, 193–200. New York: Checkmark Books 2002.

Yarwood, Doreen. *The Architecture of England*. London: B.T. Batsford 1963.
Zucker, Carole, ed. *Making Visible the Invisible: An Anthology of Original Essays on Film Acting*. Metchen, NJ: Scarecrow Press 1990.

FILMS CITED

Air Force One. Directed by Wolfgang Petersen. With Harrison Ford, Gary Oldman. Columbia Pictures 1997.
American Pie. Directed by Paul Weitz. With Jason Biggs, Chris Klein, Thomas Ian Nicholas. Universal Pictures 1999.
Angel. Directed by Joss Whedon. With Alexis Denisof, David Boreanaz. Twentieth Century Fox Television 1999–2004.
Anna Karenina. Directed by Joe Wright. With Keira Knightley, Jude Law. Universal Pictures 2012.
Anonymous. Directed by Roland Emmerich. With Rhys Ifans, Vanessa Redgrave. Columbia Pictures 2011.
Apocalypse Now. Directed by Francis Ford Coppola. With Martin Sheen, Marlon Brando, Robert Duvall, Laurence Fisburne. Zoetrope Studios 1979.
The Artist. Directed by Michel Hazanavicius. With Jean Dujardin, Berenice Bejo. Studio 37, 2011.
As You Like It. Directed by Kenneth Branagh. With Kevin Kline, Bryce Dallas Howard. BBC Films 2006.
As You Like It. Directed by Basil Coleman. With Helen Mirren, Richard Pasco, Angharad Rees. BBC TV 1978.
As You Like It. Directed by Christine Edzard. With Edward Fox, Emma Croft. Sands Films 1992.
The Avengers. Directed by Joss Whedon. With Robert Downey Jr, Scarlett Johansson. Marvel Studios 2012.
The Bad Sleep Well. Directed by Akira Kurosawa. With Toshiro Mifune, Masayuki Mori. Toho Co. 1960.
Batman. Directed by Tim Burton. With Kim Basinger, Michael Keaton. Warner Bros 1991.
Beauty and the Beast. Directed by Gary Trousdale. With Paige O'Hara, Roby Benson. Walt Disney 1991.
Bend It Like Beckham. Directed by Gurinder Chadha. With Parminder Nagra, Kiera Knightley. Kintop Pictures 2002.
Bewitched. Directed by Nora Ephron. With Nicole Kidman, Will Ferrell. Columbia Pictures 2005.

Bewitched. Directed by Sol Saks. With Elizabeth Montgomery, Dick York. Ashmont Prods 1964–72 (TV).

Blood Diamond. Directed by Edward Zwick. With Leonardo DiCaprio, Djimon Hounsou, Jennifer Connolly. Warner Bros 2006.

Bram Stoker's Dracula. Directed by Francis Ford Coppola. With Winona Ryder, Gary Oldman. Columbia Pictures 1992.

Brave. Directed by Mark Andrews et al. With Kelly Macdonald, Emma Thompson. Walt Disney Pictures 2012.

Buffy the Vampire Slayer. Directed by Joss Whedon. With Sarah Michelle Gellar, Nicholas Brendon. 20th Century Fox Television 1997–2003.

La Cage aux Folles. Directed by Edouard Molinaro. With Ugo Tognazzi, Michel Serrault, Claire Maurier. Da Ma Produzione 1978.

Casablanca. Directed by Michael Curtiz. With Humphrey Bogart, Ingrid Bergman. Warner Bros 1942.

Casino Royale. Directed by Martin Campbell. With Daniel Craig, Eva Green, Judi Dench. Columbia 2006.

Celebrity. Directed by Woody Allen. With Kenneth Branagh, Judi Dench. Sweetland Films 1998.

Charlie and the Chocolate Factory. Directed by Tim Burton. With Johnny Depp, Freddy Highmore. Warner Bros 2005.

The Children's Midsummer Night's Dream. Directed by Christine Edzard. With Jamie Peachey, John Heyfron. Sands Films 2001.

Chimes at Midnight. Directed by Orson Welles. With Orson Welles, Keith Baxter. Alpine Films 1965.

Clerks. Directed by Kevin Smith. With Brian O'Halloran, Jeff Anderson, Marilyn Ghigliotti. View Askew Productions 1994.

Clueless. Directed by Amy Heckerling. With Alicia Silverstone, Paul Rudd. Paramount Pictures 1995.

The Complete Dramatic Works of William Shakespeare. Directed by various. With various. BBC 1978–85.

Coriolanus. Directed by Ralph Fiennes. With Ralph Fiennes, Brian Cox. Hermetof Pictures 2011.

Crush. Directed by John McKay. With Andie MacDowell, Imelda Staunton, Anna Chancellor. Film Council 2001.

The Crying Game. Directed by Neil Jordan. With Stephen Rea, Forest Whitaker. Palace Pictures 1992.

Cymbeline. Directed by Michael Almereyda. With Ethan Hawke, Ed Harris. Benaroya Pictures 2014.

Dan in Real Life. Directed by Peter Hedges. With Steve Carrell, Juliette Binoche, Dane Cook. Touchstone Pictures 2007.

Dead Again. Directed by Kenneth Branagh. With Kenneth Branagh, Emma Thompson. Paramount Pictures 1991.

The Debt. Directed by John Madden. With Helen Mirren, Jessica Chastain, Sam Worthington. Miramax 2010.

La Dolce Vita. Directed by Federico Fellini. With Marcello Mastroianni, Anita Ekberg. Riama Film 1960.

Downton Abbey. Created by Julian Fellowes. With Hugh Bonneville, Elizabeth McGovern. Masterpiece Theatre 2010–15.

Drowning by Numbers. Directed by Peter Greenaway. With Joan Plowright, Bernard Hill. Film Four International 1988.

Le Duel d'Hamlet. Directed by Clement Maurice. With Sarah Bernhardt, Pierre Magnier. Photo-Cinema-Theatre 1900.

The Dukes of Hazzard. Directed by Jay Chandrasekhar. With Johnny Knoxville, Seann William Scott, Alice Greczyn. Warner Bros 2005.

Elizabeth. Directed by Steven Clarke. With David Starkey, Karen Archer. TV Movie, UK, 2000.

Elizabeth. Directed by Shekhar Kapur. With Cate Blanchett, Geoffrey Rush. Polygram 1998.

Elizabeth: The Golden Age. Directed by Shekhar Kapur. With Cate Blanchett, Clive Owen. Universal 2007.

Elizabeth I. Directed by Tom Hooper. With Helen Mirren, Jeremy Irons. Channel 4, 2005.

ER. Creator: Michael Crichton. With Parminder Nagra, George Clooney. Amblin Entertainment 1994–2009.

Family Viewing. Directed by Atom Egoyan. With David Hemblen, Aidan Tierney, Gabrielle Rose. Canada Council for the Arts 1988.

Fantastic Mr. Fox. Directed by Wes Anderson. With George Clooney, Meryl Streep. Twentieth Century Fox 2009.

Fatal Attraction. Directed by Adrian Lyne. With Michael Douglas, Glenn Close, Ann Archer. Paramount Pictures 1987.

Fearless. Directed by Peter Weir. With Jeff Bridges, Isabella Rossellini, Rosie Perez. Warner Bros 1993.

Firefly. Directed by Joss Whedon. With Nathan Fillion, Gina Torres. Twentieth Century Fox Television 2002–03.

5 to 7. Directed by Victor Levin. With Anton Yelchin, Berenice Marlohe. Demarest Films 2014.

Fool's Gold. Directed by Andy Tennant. With Matthew McConaughey, Kate Hudson, Donald Sutherland. Warner Bros 2008.

For Queen and Country. Directed by Martin Stellman. With Denzel Washington, Dorian Healey. Working Title Films 1988.

Frost vs. Nixon. Directed by Ron Howard. With Frank Langella, Michael Sheen. Universal Pictures 2008.

Game of Thrones. Created by David Benioff and D.B. Weiss. With Peter Dinklage, Lena Headey. HBO 2011–.

Gladiator. Directed by Ridley Scott. With Russell Crowe, Joaquin Phoenix, Connie Nielsen. Dreamworks 2000.

Gnomeo and Juliet. Directed by Kelly Asbury. With James McAvoy, Emily Blunt. Dreamworks 2011.

The Godfather. Directed by Francis Ford Coppola. With Marlon Brando, Al Pacino. Paramount Pictures 1972.

Green Zone. Directed by Paul Greengrass. With Matt Damon, Greg Kinnear. Universal Pictures 2010.

Gremlins 2: The New Batch. Directed by Joe Dante. With Zach Galligan, Phoebe Cates. Warner Bros 1990.

Growing Pains. Directed by Neal Marlens. With Alan Thicke, Joanna Kerns. Warner Bros TV 1985–92.

Hallmark Hall of Fame Shakespeare. Directed by various. With various. 1951.

Hamlet. Directed by Michael Almereyda. With Ethan Hawke, Bill Murray. Double A Films 2000.

Hamlet. Directed by Gerard Bourgeois. With Jean Mounet-Sully. Pathé, 1909.

Hamlet. Directed by Johnston Forbes Robertson. With Johnston Forbes Robertson, Gertrude Elliot. Knickerbocker Star Features 1915.

Hamlet. Directed by Svend Gund. With Asta Nielsen, Paul Conradi. Art-Fil GmbH. 1921.

Hamlet. Directed by George Méliès. With George Méliès. Star Film 1907.

Hamlet. Directed by Jean Mounet-Sully. With Jean Mounet-Sully. 1910.

Hamlet. Directed by Laurence Olivier. With Laurence Olivier, Eileen Herlie. Two Cities Films 1948.

Hamlet (Animated). Directed by Natalya Orlova. With Michael Kitchen, Nicholas Farrell. Soyuzmultfilm 1992.

Hamlet. Directed by Franco Zeffirelli. With Mel Gibson, Paul Scofield. Canal Pictures 1990.

The Help. Directed by Tate Taylor. With Emma Stone, Jessica Chastain. Dreamworks 2011.

Henry V. Directed by Kenneth Branagh. With Kenneth Branagh, Paul Scofield. Renaissance Films 1989.

Henry V. Directed by Laurence Olivier. With Laurence Olivier, Leslie Banks. Two Cities Films 1944.

Hugo. Directed by Martin Scorsese. With Asa Butterfield, Chloë Moretz. Paramount 2011.

The Hurt Locker. Directed by Kathryn Bigelow. With Jeremy Renner, Anthony Mackie, Brian Geraghty. Voltage Pictures 2008.

In the Bleak Midwinter. Directed by Kenneth Branagh. With Michael Maloney, Richard Briers. Castle Rock 1996.

The Iron Lady. Directed by Phyllida Lloyd. With Meryl Streep, Jim Broadbent. Pathé Pictures 2011.

Jane Austen Book Club. Directed by Robin Swicord. With Emily Blunt, Kathy Baker, Hugh Dancy. Mockingbird Pictures 2007.

Jules et Jim. Directed by François Truffaut. With Jeanne Moreau, Henri Serre. Les Films du Carrosse 1962.

Julius Caesar. Directed by Joseph L. Mankiewicz. With Marlon Brando, James Mason, John Gielgud. MGM 1953.

The Jungle Book. Directed by Jon Favreau. With Neel Sethi, Bill Murray. Disney 2016.

Juno. Directed by Jason Reitman. With Ellen Page, Michael Cera, Jennifer Garner. Fox Searchlight Pictures 2007.

King John. Directed by Walter Pfeffer Dando. With Herbert Beerbohm Tree, Dora Senior. British Mutoscope 1899.

King Lear. Directed by Peter Brook. With Paul Scofield, Irene Worth, Cyril Cusack, Amanda Rudd. Athena Films 1971.

The Last Samurai. Directed by Edward Zwick. With Tom Cruise, Ken Watanabe, William Atherton. Warner Bros 2003.

Laws of Attraction. Directed by Peter Howitt. With Pierce Brosnan, Julianne Moore, Michael Sheen. Deep River Productions 2004.

Lethal Weapon. Directed by Richard Donner. With Mel Gibson, Danny Glover, Gary Busey. Warner Bros 1987.

Little Dorrit. Directed by Christine Edzard. With Derek Jacobi, Sarah Pickering. Sands Films 1988.

Looking for Richard. Directed by Al Pacino. With Al Pacino, Winona Ryder. Twentieth Century Fox 1996.

Lord of the Rings. Directed by Peter Jackson. With Elijah Wood, Ian McKellen. New Line 2001.

Love's Labour's Lost. Directed by Kenneth Branagh. With Kenneth Branagh, Adrian Lester. Pathé Pictures 2000.

Macbeth. Directed by Justin Kurzel. With Michael Fassbender, Marion Cotillard. Film 4 2015.

Macbeth. Directed by Roman Polanski. With Jon Finch, Francesca Annis. Playboy Productions 1971.

Macbeth. Directed by Geoffrey Wright. With Sam Worthington, Victoria Hill. Mushroom Productions 2007.

MacHomer. Directed by Sean Lynch. With Rick Miller 2011. Filmed live show.

Mad Max. Directed by George Miller. With Mel Gibson, Joanne Samuel. Crossroads 1979.

Mad Men. Created by Matthew Weiner. With Jon Hamm, January Jones. Lionsgate Television 2007–15.

The Magnificent Seven. Directed by John Sturges. With Yul Brynner, Steve McQueen. Mirisch 1960.

Magnolia. Directed by Paul Thomas Anderson. With Tom Cruise, Julianne Moore, Jason Robards, William H. Macy. New Line 2000.

Mamma Mia. Directed by Phyllida Lloyd. With Meryl Streep, Amanda Seyfried. Universal 2008.

Maqbool. Directed by Vishal Bhardwaj. With Irrfan Khan, Pankaj Kapur. Kaleidoscope Entertainment 2003.

Mary Poppins. Directed by Robert Stevenson. With Julie Andrews, Dick van Dyke, David Tomlinson. Walt Disney 1964.

Mary Shelley's Frankenstein. Directed by Kenneth Branagh. With Kenneth Branagh, Robert De Niro. Tristar 1994.

Meet the Parents. Directed by Jay Roach. With Ben Stiller, Robert De Niro, Owen Wilson. Universal Pictures 2000.

Men of Respect. Directed by William Reilly. With John Turturro, Katherine Borowitz. Central City 1990.

Mephisto. Directed by Istvan Szabo. With Klaus Maria Brandauer, Krystyna Janda. Hessischer Rundfunk 1981.

The Merchant of Venice. Directed by Michael Radford. With Al Pacino, Jeremy Irons. Avenue Pictures Productions 2004.

Miami Vice. Directed by Michael Mann. With Colin Farrell, Jamie Foxx. Universal Pictures 2006.

Midnight in Paris. Directed by Woody Allen. With Owen Wilson, Rachel McAdams. Gravier Productions 2011.

A Midsummer Night's Dream. Directed by Michael Hoffman. With Rupert Everett, Kevin Kline. Fox Searchlight 1999.

A Midsummer Night's Dream. Directed by Adrian Noble. With Lindsay Duncan, Alex Jennings. Channel 4 Films 1996.

A Midsummer Night's Dream. Directed by Max Reinhardt. With Olivia de Havilland, James Cagney. Warner Bros 1935.

Miss Pettigrew Lives for a Day. Directed by Bharat Nalluri. With Amy Adams, Frances McDormand, Ciaran Hinds. Focus Features 2008.

Moneyball. Directed by Bennett Miller. With Brad Pitt, Robin Wright. Columbia Pictures 2011.

Monster-in-Law. Directed by Robert Luketic. With Jennifer Lopez, Jane Fonda, Michael Varton. New Line 2005.

Moonstruck. Directed by Norman Jewison. With Nicholas Cage, Cher, Olympia Dukakis. MGM 1987.

La Mort de Jules Cesar. Directed by George Méliès. With George Méliès. Star Film 1907.

Mrs. Doubtfire. Directed by Chris Columbus. With Robin Williams, Sally Field. Twentieth Century Fox 1993.

Much Ado About Nothing. Directed by Kenneth Branagh. With Kenneth Branagh, Emma Thompson. Renaissance Films 1993.

Much Ado About Nothing. Directed by Joss Whedon. With Amy Acker, Alexis Denisof. Bellwether 2012.

Mulan. Directed by Tony Bancroft, Barry Cook. With Ming-Na Wen, Eddie Murphy. Walt Disney Pictures 1998.

Mutant Ninja Turtles. Directed by Steve Barron. With Judith Hoag, Elias Koteas. Warner Bros 1990.

My So-Called Life. Directed by Winnie Holzman. With Claire Danes, Wilson Cruz. ABC Productions 1994–96.

A Nightmare on Elm Street (Freddy's Revenge). Directed by Rachel Talalay. With Robert Englund, Lisa Zane. Warner Bros 1991.

Notting Hill. Directed by Roger Michell. With Julia Roberts, Hugh Grant. Polygram 1999.

O. Directed by Tim Blake Nelson. With Julia Stiles, Josh Hartnett. Daniel Fried Productions 2001.

Omkara. Directed by Vishal Bhardwaj. With Ajay Devgn, Kareena Kapoor. Big Screen Entertainment 2006.

Othello. Directed by Oliver Parker. With Laurence Fishburne, Kenneth Branagh. Castle Rock 1995.

The Other Boleyn Girl. Directed by Justin Chadwick. With Natalie Portman, Eric Bana. Columbia 2008.

The Other Boleyn Girl. Directed by Philippa Lowthorpe. With Natascha McElhone, Jared Harris. BBC TV 2003.

The Parent Trap. Directed by Nancy Meyers. With Lindsay Lohan, Dennis Quaid, Natasha Richardson. Walt Disney 1998.

Peter's Friends. Directed by Kenneth Branagh. With Hugh Laurie, Stephen Fry. Renaissance Films 1992.

Play It Again Sam. Directed by Herbert Ross. With Woody Allen, Diane Keaton, Tony Roberts. Paramount Pictures 1972.

Porky's. Directed by Bob Clark. With Dan Monahan, Mark Herrier, Wyatt Knight. Melsin Simon Productions 1982.

Presumed Innocent. Directed by Alan J. Pakula. With Harrison Ford, Greta Scacchi, Brian Dennehy. Warner Bros 1990.

Pride and Prejudice. Directed by Joe Wright. With Keira Knightley, Matthew Macfadyen. Universal Pictures 2005.

Priscilla, Queen of the Desert. Directed by Stephan Elliot. With Hugo Weaving, Guy Pearce, Terence Stamp. Polygram 1994.

Private Romeo. Directed by Alan Brown. With Hale Appleman, Charlie Barnet. Wolfe 2011.

Prospero's Books. Directed by Peter Greenaway. With John Gielgud, Michael Clark. Allarts 1991.

The Queen. Directed by Stephen Frears. With Helen Mirren, Michael Sheen. Pathé Pictures 2006.

Ran. Directed by Akira Kurosawa. With Tatsuya Nakadai, Akira Terao. Greenway Film 1985.

Regarding Henry. Directed by Mike Nichols. With Harrison Ford, Annette Bening, Michael Healey. Paramount Pictures 1991.

Resurrected. Directed by Paul Greengrass. With David Thewlis, Tom Bell. British Screen 1989.

Richard III. Directed by Richard Loncraine. With Ian McKellen, Annette Bening. Mayfair 1995.

Romeo & Juliet. Directed by Carlo Carlei. With Hailee Steinfeld, Douglas Booth. Swarovski Entertainment 2013.

School of Rock. Directed by Richard Linklater. With Jack Black, Mike White, Joan Cusack. Paramount 2003.

Scotland, PA. Directed by Billy Morrisette. With James Le Gros, Maura Tierney. Abandon Pictures 2001.

The Seven Samurai. Directed by Akira Kurosawa. With Toshiro Mifune, Takashi Shimura. Toho Co. 1954.

Seven Year Itch. Directed by Billy Wilder. With Marilyn Monroe, Tom Ewell. Twentieth Century Fox 1955.

Shakespeare: The Animated Tales. Directed by various. With various. Christmas Films 1992.

Shakespeare in Love. Directed by John Madden. With Joseph Fiennes, Gwyneth Paltrow. Universal 1998.

Shakespeare Retold. Directed by various. With various. BBC 2005.

She's the Man. Directed by Andy Fickman. With Amanda Bynes, Channing Tatum. Dreamworks 2006.

Sleepy Hollow. Directed by Tim Burton. With Johnny Depp, Christina Ricci. Paramount 1999.

The Smurfs. Directed by Raja Gosnell. With Hank Azaria, Katy Perry. Columbia Pictures 2011.

Some Like It Hot. Directed by Billy Wilder. With Jack Lemmon, Tony Curtis. Ashton Productions 1959.

Sweet Home Alabama. Directed by Andy Tennant. With Reese Witherspoon, Josh Lucas, Patrick Dempsey. Touchstone Pictures 2002.

Tall Guy. Directed by Mel Smith. With Jeff Goldblum, Emma Thompson, Rowan Atkinson. Working Title 1989.

The Taming of the Shrew. Directed by Sam Taylor. With Douglas Fairbanks, Mary Pickford. Elton Corp 1929.

The Tempest. Directed by Derek Jarman. With Heathcote Williams, Toyah Willcox. Boyd's Company 1979.

The Tempest. Directed by Julie Taymor. With Helen Mirren, Ben Whishaw. Miramax 2010.

Ten Things I Hate About You. Directed by Gil Junger. With Julia Stiles, Heath Ledger. Touchstone 1999.

Tequila Sunrise. Directed by Robert Towne. With Mel Gibson, Michelle Pfeiffer, Kurt Russell. Warner Bros 1988.

Titus. Directed by Julie Taymor. With Anthony Hopkins, Jessica Lange. Clear Blue Sky Productions 1999.

Titus Andronicus. Directed by Jane Howell. With Trevor Peacock, Eileen Atkins. BBC Television 1985.

Tootsie. Directed by Sydney Pollack. With Dustin Hoffman, Jessica Lange. Columbia Pictures 1982.

The Tudors. Directed by Michael Hart. With Jonathan Rhys Meyers, Henry Cavill. Showtime 2007–10.

Twelfth Night. Directed by Trevor Nunn. With Imogen Stubbs, Helena Bonham Carter. Renaissance Films 1996.

Twelfth Night. Directed by Tim Supple. With Parminder Nagra, Ronny Jhutti. Projector Productions. 2003.

Twister. Directed by Jan de Bont. With Helen Hunt, Bill Paxton, Cary Elwes. Warner Bros 1996.

United 93. Directed by Paul Greengrass. With J.J. Johnson, David Alan Basche, Liza Colon-Zayas. Universal Pictures 2006.

Victor/Victoria. Directed by Blake Edwards. With Julie Andrews, James Garner. MGM 1982.

Le voyage dans la lune. Directed by George Méliès. With Victor Andre, Bluette Bernon, Brunnet. Star-Film 1902.

Warhorse. Directed by Steven Spielberg. With Jeremy Irvine, Emily Watson. Dreamworks 2011.

Warm Bodies. Directed by Jonathan Levine. With Nicholas Hume, Teresa Palmer. Summit 2013.

War Requiem. Directed by Derek Jarman. With Nathaniel Parker, Tilda Swinton. Anglo International 1988.

What's Love Got to Do with It? Directed by Brian Gibson. With Laurence Fishburne, Angela Bassett. Touchstone Pictures 1993.

What's Up, Doc? Directed by Peter Bogdanovitch. With Barbra Streisand, Ryan O'Neill, Madeline Kahn. Warner Bros 1972.

William Shakespeare's A Midsummer Night's Dream. Directed by Michael Hoffman. With Kevin Kline, Michelle Pfeiffer. Fox Searchlight 1999.

William Shakespeare's Hamlet. Directed by Kenneth Branagh. With Kenneth Branagh, Derek Jacobi. Castlerock 1996.

William Shakespeare's Romeo + Juliet. Directed by Baz Luhrmann. With Leonardo DiCaprio, Claire Danes. Twentieth Century Fox 1996.

Willy Wonka and the Chocolate Factory. Directed by Mel Stuart. With Gene Wilder, Jack Albertson. David L. Wolper Productions 1971.

Yentl. Directed by Barbra Streisand. With Barbra Streisand, Mandy Patinkin. United Artists 1983.

Yours, Mine, Ours. Directed by Raja Gosnell. With Dan Quail, Rene Russo, Sean Faris. Paramount Pictures 2005.

Zero Dark Thirty. Directed by Kathryn Bigelow. With Jessica Chastain, Joel Edgerton. Columbia 2012.

WORKS CONSULTED

Allman, Eileen. *Jacobean Revenge Tragedy and the Politics of Virtue*. Newark: University of Delaware Press 1999.

Batson, Beatrice, ed. *Shakespeare's Christianity: The Protestant and Catholic Politics of Julius Caesar, Macbeth, and Hamlet*. Waco, TX: Baylor University Press 2006.

Baumstark, Anton. *Comparative Liturgy*. London: A.R. Mowbray & Co. 1958.

Barber, C.L. "Testing Courtesy and Humanity in *Twelfth Night*." In *Twelfth Night: Critical Essays*, edited by Stanley Wells. New York: Garland Publishing 1986.

Barnes, Alex, et al. *Essays in Audience Perception in Elizabethan and Jacobean Literature*. Salzburg: University of Salzburg Press 1997.

Baruch, Marc. *The American Musical*. Marburg: Tectum Verlag 2003.

Bate, Jonathan, and Russell Jackson. *Shakespeare: An Illustrated Stage History*. Oxford: Oxford University Press 1996.

Beecher, Donald, and Grant Williams. *Ars Reminiscendi: Mind and Memory in Renaissance Culture*. Toronto: CRRS 2009.

Bell, Philip, and Roger Bell. *Americanization and Australia*. Sydney: University of South Wales Press 1998.

Benstioff, Harry M., and Sean Griffin. *America on Film: Representing Race, Class, Gender and Sexuality at the Movies*. Malden: Blackwell 2004.

Berger, Harry, Jr. *Imaginary Audition: Shakespeare on Stage and Page*. Los Angeles: University of California Press 1989.

Besedy, K.S. *Stanislavsky on the Art of the Stage*. London: Faber & Faber 1967.

Bloom, Harold. *William Shakespeare's Much Ado About Nothing*. New York: Chelsea House 1988.

– *The Invention of the Human*. New York: Riverhead Books 1998

– *Major Literary Characters: Hamlet*. New York: Chelsea House 1990.

– *Shakespeare through the Ages: Hamlet*. New York: Infobase 2008.

Blundevill, Thomas. *The True Order and Methode of Wryting and Reading Hystories*. London: William Seres 1574.

Bolton, W.F. *Shakespeare's English*. Oxford: Basil Blackwell 1992.

Bordman, Gerald. *American Musical Revue*. New York: Oxford University Press 1985.

Buchanan, Judith. *Shakespeare on Film*. Harlow: Pearson/Longman 2005.

Buhler, Stephen M. "Camp Richard III and the Burdens of (Stage/Film) His-

tory." *Shakespeare, Film, Fin de Siecle*, edited by Mark Thornton Burnett and Ramona Wray. London: Macmillan 2000.
Bullough, Geoffrey, ed. *Narrative and Dramatic Sources of Shakespeare*. London: Routledge & Kegan Paul 1960.
Bulman, James C. *Shakespeare, Theory, and Performance*. London: Routledge 1996.
Burnely, I.H., S. Encel, and Grant McCall, eds. *Australian Studies: Immigration and Ethnicity in the 1980s*. Melbourne: Longman Cheshire 1985.
Callan, Victor J. *Australian Minority Groups*. North Ryde, NSW: Harcourt Brace Jovanovich 1986.
Campbell, Lily B. *Shakespeare's Histories: Mirrors of Elizabethan Policy*. London: Methuen 1964.
Cartelli, Thomas, and Katherine Rowe. *New Wave Shakespeare on Screen*. Cambridge: Polity Press 2007.
Cartmell, Deborah, I.Q. Hunter, and Imelda Whelehan. *Retrovisions: Reinventing the Past in Film and Fiction*. London: Pluto Press 2001.
Castiglione, Baldassare. *The Book of the Courtier*. Translated by Sir Thomas Hoby (1561). London: J.M. Dent & Sons 1974.
Certain Sermons or Homilies (1547) and a Homily against Disobedience and Wilful Rebellion (1570). Edited by Ronald B. Bond. Toronto: University of Toronto Press 1987.
Comensoli, Viviana, and Anne Russell, eds. *Enacting Gender on the English Renaissance Stage*. Chicago: University of Illinois Press 1999.
Cook, Ann Jennalie. *The Privileged Playgoers of Shakespeare's London, 1576–1642*. Princeton: Princeton University Press 1981.
Coursen, H.R. *Shakespearean Performance as Interpretation*. Newark: University of Delaware Press 1992.
– *Watching Shakespeare on Television*. Rutherford, NJ: Fairleigh Dickinson University Press 1993.
Croall, Jonathan. *Hamlet Observed: National Theatre at Work*. London: NT Publications 2001.
Crompton, Richard. *The Mansion of Magnanimitie*. London: William Ponsonby 1599.
Crowl, Samuel. *Shakespeare Observed: Studies in Performance on Stage and Screen*. Athens: Ohio University Press 1992.
D'Amico, Jack. *Shakespeare and Italy: The City and the Stage*. Gainesville: University Press of Florida 2001.

Daniel, Samuel. *The First Fowre Bookes of the Ciuile Warres betweene the Two Houses of Lancaster and York*. London: P. Short for Simon Waterson 1595.

Dash, Irene. *Shakespeare and the American Musical*. Bloomington: Indiana University Press 2010.

Davies, Anthony. *Filming Shakespeare's Plays*. Cambridge: Cambridge University Press 1988.

Davies, Anthony, and Stanley Wells, eds. *Shakespeare and the Moving Image: The Plays on Film and Television*. Cambridge: Cambridge University Press 1994.

Davison, Peter. *Text and Performance: Hamlet*. Frome, Somerset: Macmillan 1983.

Dawson, Anthony B., and Paul Yachnin. *The Culture of Playgoing in Shakespeare's England*. Cambridge: Cambridge University Press 2001.

Desmet, Christy, and Robert Sawyer, eds. *Shakespeare and Appropriation*. New York: Routledge 1999.

Desmond, John M., and Peter Hawkes. *Adaptation: Studying Film and Literature*. Toronto: McGraw-Hill 2006.

Dika, Vera. *Recycled Culture in Contemporary Art and Film: The Uses of Nostalgia*. Cambridge: Cambridge University Press 2003.

Donaldson, Peter. *Shakespearean Films/Shakespearean Directors*. Boston: Unwin Hyman 1990.

Draper, John W. *The Hamlet of Shakespeare's Audience*. Durham, NC: Duke University Press 1938.

Eckert, Charles W., ed. *Focus on Shakespearean Films*. Englewood Cliffs, NJ: Prentice Hall 1972.

Elsom, J. *Is Shakespeare Still Our Contemporary?* London: Routledge 1989.

Engel, William E. *Death and Drama in Renaissance England: Shades of Memory*. Oxford: Oxford University Press 2002.

Everett, Barbara. "Something of Great Constancy." In *Much Ado About Nothing and As You Like It: A Casebook*, edited by John Russell Brown. London: Macmillan 1979.

The Famous Victories of Henry the Fifth. 1598. Facsimile. Edited by P.A. Daniel. London: C. Praetorius 1887.

Farnham, Willard. *The Shakespearean Grotesque: Its Genesis and Transformation*. Oxford: Clarendon Press 1971.

Findlay, Alison, and Stephanie Hodgson-Wright. *Women and Dramatic Production, 1550–1700*. With Giveno Williams. Harlow, UK: Longman 2000.

Frayling, Christopher. *Nightmare: The Birth of Horror*. London: BBC Books 1996.

Frye, Northrop. *Fools of Time*. Toronto: University of Toronto Press 1967.
- *Northrop Frye on Shakespeare*. Edited by Robert Sandler. Markham, ON: Fitzhenry & Whiteside 1989.
Garber, Marjorie. *Shakespeare, After All*. New York: Pantheon Books 2004.
Garrard, William. *The Arte of Warre*. 1587. Corrected and finished by Captain Hitchcock (1591). London: Roger Warde 1591.
Garson, Barbara. *Macbird*. New York: Grove Press 1966.
Giannetti, Louis. *Understanding Movies*. Upper Saddle River, NJ: Prentice Hall 2002.
Glancy, Mark. *Hollywood and the Americanization of Britain, from the 1920s to the Present*. London: I.B. Tauris 2014.
Greenblatt, Stephen. *Hamlet in Purgatory*. Princeton: Princeton University Press 2001.
Grollman, Earl A. *Concerning Death: A Practical Guide for the Living*. Boston: Beacon Press 1974.
Gross, John. *Shylock: A Legend and Its Legacy*. New York: Simon & Schuster 1992.
Gross, Kenneth. *Shylock Is Shakespeare*. Chicago: University of Chicago Press 2006.
Groth, Helen. *Victorian Photography and Literary Nostalgia*. Oxford: Oxford University Press 2003.
Guernsey, R.S. *Ecclesiastical Law in Hamlet: The Burial of Ophelia*. New York: Shakespeare Society of New York 1885.
Gurr, Andrew, and Mariko Ichikawa. *Staging in Shakespeare's Theatres*. Oxford: Oxford University Press 2000.
Hall, Edward. *The Union of the Two Noble & Illustre Families of Lancastre & Yorke*. N.p. 1550.
Halliwell, Leslie. *Halliwell's Film Guide*. New York: Harper Perennial 1991.
Harbage, Alfred. *Shakespeare's Audience*. New York: Columbia University Press 1941.
Hartnoll, Phyllis. *Shakespeare in Music: A Collection of Essays*. London: Macmillan 1964.
Hays, Michael. *Shakespearean Tragedy as Chivalric Romance: Rethinking Macbeth, Hamlet, Othello and King Lear*. Cambridge: D.S. Brewer 2003.
Hedrick, Donald, and Bryan Reynolds, eds. *Shakespeare without Class*. New York: Palgrave 2000.
Henderson, Diana E., ed. *Alternative Shakespeares 3*. London: Routledge 2008.
- *A Concise Companion to Shakespeare on Screen*. Oxford: Blackwell 2006.

Hill, Charles A., and Marguerite Helmers. *Defining Visual Rhetorics*. Mahwah, NJ: Lawrence, Edbaum Associates 2004.

Hirsh, James. *Shakespeare and the History of Soliloquies*. Madison: Fairleigh Dickinson University Press 2003.

Holden, Anthony. *The Drama of Love, Life, and Death in Shakespeare*. London: Mitchell Beazley 2000.

Holderness, Graham. *Shakespeare Recycled: The Making of Historical Drama*. New York: Harvester Wheatsheaf 1992.

– *The Taming of the Shrew: Shakespeare in Performance*. Manchester: Manchester University Press 1989.

Hornby, Richard. *Drama, Metadrama, and Perception*. Lewisburg: Bucknell University Press 1986.

Howlet, Kathy M. *Framing Shakespeare on Film*. Athens: University of Ohio Press 2000.

Huang, Alexander C.Y., and Charles S. Ross. *Shakespeare in Hollywood, Asia, and Cyberspace*. West Lafayette, IN: Purdue University Press 2009.

Ichikawa, Mariko. *The Shakespearean Stage Space*. Cambridge: Cambridge University Press 2013.

Jackson, Russell, and Robert Smallwood. *Players of Shakespeare 2*. Cambridge: Cambridge University Press 1988.

– *Players of Shakespeare 3*. Cambridge: Cambridge University Press 1993.

Jones, Emrys. *The Origins of Shakespeare*. Oxford: Clarendon Press 1977.

Jones, Maria. *Shakespeare's Culture in Modern Performance*. New York: Palgrave Macmillan 2003.

Jorgens, Jack J. *Shakespeare on Film*. Bloomington: Indiana University Press 1977.

Keller, James R., and Leslie Stratyner, eds. *Almost Shakespeare: Reinventing His Works for Cinema and Television*. Jefferson, NC: McFarland & Co. 2004.

Kerrigan, John. *Revenge Tragedy: Aeschylus to Armageddon*. Oxford: Clarendon Press 1996.

Keough, Peter. *Flesh and Blood: The National Society of Film Critics on Sex, Violence and Censorship*. San Francisco: Mercury House 1995.

Kozintsev, Grigori. *King Lear: The Space of Tragedy: The Diary of a Film Director*. London: Heinemann 1977.

– *Shakespeare: Time and Conscience*. Translated by Joyce Vining. London: D. Dobson 1967.

Krier, Teresa. *Birth Passage: Maternity and Nostalgia: Antiquity to Shakespeare*. Ithaca: Cornell University Press 2001.

Lee, John. *Shakespeare's Hamlet and the Controversies of Self*. Oxford: Clarendon Press 2000.

Lehmann, Courtney. *Shakespeare Remains: Theater to Film, Early Modern to Postmodern*. Ithaca: Cornell University Press 2002.

Lehmann, Courtney, and Lisa S. Starks, eds. *Spectacular Shakespeare: Critical Theory and Popular Cinema*. Madison: Fairleigh Dickinson University Press 2002.

Levin, Carole, and Karen Robertson, eds. *Sexuality and Politics in Renaissance Drama*. Vol. 10, *Studies in Renaissance Literature*. Lewiston: Edwin Mellen Press 1991.

Loehlin, James N. "'These Violent Delights Have Violent Ends': Baz Luhrmann's Millennial Shakespeare." In *Shakespeare, Film, Fin de Siecle*, edited by Mark Thornton Burnett and Ramona Wray. London: Macmillan 2000.

Lovell, Alan, and Peter Kramer. *Screen Acting*. London: Routledge 1999.

Lynch, Stephen. *As You Like It: A Guide to the Play*. Westport, CT: Greenwood Press 2003.

Machiavelli, Nicolo. *The Arte of Warre*. Translated by Peter Whitehorne. London: John Kingston for Nicholas Englande 1560.

– *The Prince*. Edited by Ernest Rhys. London: J.M. Dent & Sons 1935.

Maltin, Leonard. *Movie and Video Guide 1997*. New York: Penguin 1996.

Marlowe, Christopher. *Edward II*. Oxford World's Classics. London: Oxford University Press 1969.

– *The Jew of Malta*. Oxford World's Classics. London: Oxford University Press 1969.

Maskell, William. *The Ancient Liturgy of the Church of England*. Oxford: Clarendon Press 1973.

Mast, Gerald, and Marshall Cohen, eds. *Film Theory and Criticism: Introductory Readings*. New York: Oxford University Press 1985.

Maura, Mary Power. *Shakespeare's Catholicism*. Cambridge: Riverside Press 1924.

Milward, Peter. *The Catholicism of Shakespeare's Plays*. Tokyo: Renaissance Institute 1997.

The Mirror for Magistrates. Edited by Lily B. Campbell. Cambridge: Cambridge University Press 1938.

Moore [sic], Sir Thomas. *The Historie ... of Edward the Fifth and ... Richard the Third*. London: Thomas Payne 1641.

Mullenix, Elizabeth Reitz. *Wearing the Breeches: Gender on the Antebellum Stage*. New York: St Martin's 2000.

Mulvey, Laura. "Visual Pleasure and Narrative Cinema." *Screen* 16, no. 3 (1975): 6–18.
Mulryne, J.R. *Shakespeare: Much Ado About Nothing*. London: Edward Arnold 1965.
Mutschmann, H., and K. Wentersdorf. *Shakespeare and Catholicism*. New York: Sheed & Ward 1952.
Nelson, Benjamin. *The Idea of Usury: From Tribal Brotherhood to Universal Otherhood*. Chicago: University of Chicago Press 1969.
O'Connor, John. *Shakespearean Afterlives: Ten Characters with a Life of Their Own*. Cambridge: Icon Books 2003.
Ovid. *The Metamorphoses*. Translated and edited by Horace Gregory. New York: Viking 1958.
– *Tristia – Ex Ponto*. Translated by A.L. Wheeler and revised by G.P. Gould. Cambridge, MA: Harvard University Press 2002.
Parker, Patricia, and Geoffrey Hartman, eds. *Shakespeare and the Question of Theory*. New York: Routledge 1990.
Paxton, Frederick S. *Christianizing Death: The Creation of a Ritual Process in Early Medieval Europe*. Ithaca: Cornell University Press 1990.
Pearce, Joseph. *Through Shakespeare's Eyes: Seeing the Catholic Presence in the Plays*. San Francisco: Ignatius Press 2010.
Perkins Wilder, Lina. *Shakespeare's Memory Theatre*. Cambridge: Cambridge University Press 2010.
Pittman, Monique. *Authorizing Shakespeare on Film and Television: Gender, Class, and Ethnicity in Adaptation*. New York: Peter Lang 2011.
Poole, Millicent E., Philip R. de Lacey, and Bikkars Randhawa, eds. *Australia in Transition: Culture and Life Possibilities*. North Ryde, NSW: Harcourt Brace Jovanovich 1985.
Puttenham, George. *The Arte of English Poesie*. 1589. Reprint, Louisville: Kent State University Press 1988.
Rackin, Phyllis. *Stages of History*. London: Routledge 1990.
Rank, Sven. *Twentieth Century Adaptations of Macbeth*. Frankfurt: Peter Lang 2010.
Rauchs, Paul. *Du bon usage de la nostalgie: Essai*. Paris: L'Harmattan 2013.
Reeves, Saskia. *Actors on Shakespeare: Much Ado About Nothing*. London: Faber & Faber 2003.
Righter, Anne. *Shakespeare and the Idea of the Play*. Harmondsworth: Penguin 1962.
Roberts, Timothy R. *Gods of the Maya, Aztecs, and Incas*. New York: Metrobooks 1996.

Rose, Mary Beth. *The Expense of Spirit: Love and Sexuality in English Renaissance Drama*. Ithaca: Cornell University Press 1988.
Rosenthal, Daniel. *Shakespeare on Screen*. London: Hamlyn 2000.
Russell Brown, John, ed. *Much Ado About Nothing and As You Like It: A Casebook*. London: Macmillan 1979.
Ryle, Simon. *Shakespeare, Cinema and Desire: Adaptation and Other Futures of Shakespeare's Language*. New York: Palgrave Macmillan 2014.
Sanders, Eve Rachele. *Gender and Literacy on Stage in Early Modern England*. Cambridge: Cambridge University Press 1998.
Sayer, Chloe, ed. *Mexico: The Day of the Dead: An Anthology*. London: Redstone Press 1990.
Schwartz, Jonathan Matthew. *In Defense of Homesickness: Nine Essays on Identity and Locality*. Copenhagen: Akademisk Forlag 1989.
Seifart, Helga. *Shakespeare und die Gothic Novel*. Frankfurt am Main: Peter Lang 1983.
Seger, Linda. *The Art of Adaptation: Turning Fact and Fiction into Film*. New York: Henry Holt 1992.
Senelick, Laurence. *The Changing Room: Sex, Drag and Theatre*. London: Routledge 2000.
Shakespeare, William. *As You Like It*. Edited by Penny Gay. Plymouth: Northcote House 1999.
– *King Henry V*. Edited by T.W. Craik. Arden Shakespeare. London: Routledge 1995.
– *King Henry V*. Edited by Andrew Gurr. Cambridge: Cambridge University Press 1992.
– *The Merchant of Venice*. Edited by Jay L. Halio. Oxford: Oxford University Press 1994.
Shapiro, James. *Shakespeare and the Jews*. New York: Columbia University Press 1996.
Shaughnessy, Robert. *The Cambridge Companion to Shakespeare and Popular Culture*. Cambridge: Cambridge University Press 2007.
Sidney, Sir Philip. *A Defence of Poetry*. Edited by Jan Van Dorsten. Oxford: Oxford University Press 1966.
Skovmand, Michael, ed. *Screen Shakespeare*. Aarhus: Aarhus University Press 1994.
Smallwood, Robert. *As You Like It: Shakespeare at Stratford*. London: Arden 2003.
Spenser, Edmund. *The Faerie Queene*. Edited by A.C. Hamilton. London: Longman 1977.

Spinrad, Phoebe S. *The Summons of Death on the Medieval and Renaissance English Stage*. Columbus: Ohio State University Press 1987.

States, Bert O. *Hamlet and the Concept of Character*. Baltimore: Johns Hopkins University Press 1992.

Steinheimer, Karen. *It's Not the Media: The Truth about Pop Culture's Influence on Children*. Boulder, CO: Westview Press 2003.

Stilling, Roger. *Love and Death in Renaissance Tragedy*. Baton Rouge: Louisiana State University Press 1976.

Stone, Lawrence. *The Family, Sex, and Marriage in England, 1500–1800*. New York: Harper & Row 1977.

Stoppard, Tom. *Dogg's Hamlet, Cahoot's Macbeth*. London: Faber & Faber 1980.

Styan, J.L. *Perspectives on Shakespeare in Performance*. New York: Peter Lang 2000.

Suzman, Janet. *Acting with Shakespeare: The Comedies*. New York: Applause Books 1996.

Swanson, R.N. *Catholic England: Faith, Religion, and Observance before the Reformation*. Manchester: Manchester University Press 1998.

Syme, Holger Schott. *Theatre and Testimony in Shakespeare's England*. Cambridge: Cambridge University Press 2012.

Taranow, Gerda. *The Bernhardt Hamlet: Culture and Context*. New York: Peter Lang 1996.

Terris, Olwen, Eve-Marie Oesterlen, and Luke McKernan. *Shakespeare on Film, Television and Radio: The Researcher's Guide*. British Universities Film and Video Council 2009.

Thomson, Peter. *Shakespeare's Theatre*. London: Routledge 1983.

Thompson, J. Eric. S. *Maya History and Religion*. Norman: University of Oklahoma Press 1970.

Tillyard, E.M.W. *Shakespeare's History Plays*. Harmondsworth: Penguin 1962.

Weiss, Tanja. *Shakespeare on the Screen: Kenneth Branagh's Adaptations of Henry V, Much Ado About Nothing, and Hamlet*. Frankfurt: Peter Lang 1999.

Welsh, James M., and Peter Lev, eds. *The Literature/Film Reader: Issues of Adaptation*. Lanham, MD: Scarecrow Press 2007.

Williams, Anne. *Art of Darkness: A Poetics of Gothic*. Chicago: University of Chicago Press 1995.

Willis, Susan. *The BBC Shakespeare Plays: Making the Televised Canon*. Chapel Hill: University of North Carolina Press 1991.

Wilson, Thomas. *The Arte of Rhetorique*. London: John Kingston 1560.
- *A Discourse upon Usury*. 1572. Reprint, New York: Augustus M. Kelley 1965.
Wollaeger, Mark. *Modernism, Media and Propaganda: British Narrative from 1900–1945*. Princeton: Princeton University Press 2006.
Worthen, W.B. *Shakespeare Performance Studies*. Cambridge: Cambridge University Press 2014.
Wooden, Mark, Robert Holton, Graeme Hugo, and Judith Sloan. *Australian Immigration: A Survey of the Issues*. Canberra: Australian Government Publishing Service 1990.
Wynne-Davies, Marion. *Much Ado About Nothing and The Taming of the Shrew: New Casebooks*. London: Palgrave 2001.
Yaffe, Martin D. *Shylock and the Jewish Question*. Baltimore: Johns Hopkins University Press 1997.

Index

Acker, Amy, 42, 293
Ackroyd, Peter, 155
Across the Universe (film), 119
acting: and celebrity status, 74; computer-generated images of, 353; ensemble, 76; Method, 88; for prestige, 46; realism in, 57–99; screen versus stage, 74; stylized, 21; versus other professions, 325
adaptation to film: aesthetic mainstreaming in, 286–7; appeal to teens, 4, 214, 237, 358; aspirational viewing of, 42–4; cost of Shakespearean adaptations, 18, 54, 97; and creative process, 12, 52, 168; distinctions between Shakespearean and other adaptations, 19, 26, 33, 41; endurance of Shakespearean adaptations, 22, 52, 152, 360, 364; evaluating quality of, 20–2; familiarity in, 74; framing device in, 104–32; frequency of, 15, 25, 31–56, 356; and global devastation, 15; and heritage films, 6, 13, 52, 231, 322; innovativeness of Shakespearean adaptations, 19, 103–4; loose adaptations of Shakespeare, 39, 40, 45, 231; music in, 91, 286; from novels, 9, 41, 252, 286; pleasure principle, 3, 42, 74; profitability of Shakespearean adaptations, 39, 98, 356, 364; publicity for, 92; realism in, 31, 57–99; reflecting society, 30, 264; sales to educational institutions, 33; self-referentiality, 4; settings of Shakespearean adaptations, 14, 174; Shakespeare adaptations before 1989, 4, 17; Shakespeare adaptations since 1989, 7, 33, 34, 48; subplots in, 21; success of, 28, 31–56, 58, 98, 239, 357, 364; theatricality of, 58; vulnerability to criticism, 22
Agincourt, Battle of: in *Henry V*, 6, 256, 259, 262
Allen, Woody, 328
Alleva, Richard, 311
Almereyda, Michael, 26, 60, 91, 116, 124. See also *Cymbeline* (Almereyda's); *Hamlet* (Almereyda's)

Anatomy of Melancholy, An, 190
Anderegg, Michael, 33, 104
Anderson, Wes, 104
Anonymous (film), 130
anti-Semitism: in *Merchant of Venice* (film and play), 105
Apocalypse and Armageddon: fears of in Renaissance, 221; fears of today, 15, 51, 180, 262, 366
Arcimboldo, Giuseppe, 202, 208
Aristotle, 286
Armstrong, Richard, 57; and Channel 4's mandate, 229; and documentary techniques, 90–3; on inserts, 85; on invisible or continuity editing, 79, 83; on narrative structure, 60–5, 76
Arnold, Matthew, 16–17
aspirational motives for interest in Shakespeare, 24, 53, 138, 238–9
Astaire, Fred, 322, 328, 336, 337
As You Like It (BBC adaptation), 19, 27; cross-dressing in, 228, 232, 239, 252
As You Like It (Branagh's), 9, 11, 24, 27; cross-dressing in, 223–53; opening and closing sequences, 121, 131; realism in, 55, 64–5, 73, 79, 94; stage in, 146–9
As You Like It (Edzard's): anti-Thatcherism in, 6, 11, 27, 45, 146, 241; cross-dressing in, 226, 231, 233, 240–1
As You Like It (Shakespeare's), 8, 9, 27, 144, 179; cross-dressing in, 223–54, 365
Austen, Jane, 44, 93; *Pride and Prejudice* (film), 44
auteurship, 59, 95–6, 340, 364

authenticity, 43, 57, 138, 176, 330, 361

Bach, Johann Sebastian, 187
Bad Sleep Well, The (film), 108
Badgley, Penn, 109, 137
Bakhtin, Mikhail, 4, 352
balcony scene, 65, 91, 136
Barthes, Roland, 350
Barton, John, 296; on realism, 46, 49, 58, 70, 360
Bate, Jonathan, 53, 183, 213, 219
Bayer-Berenbaum, Linda, 180–4, 186–7, 189, 191–2, 194
BBC/Time-Life Shakespeare Series, 19, 22, 27, 33, 125, 223–53
Beckett, Samuel, 141, 203–4, 208, 210, 216, 349
Beecher, Donald, 8–10, 181, 341
Beerbohm Tree, Herbert, 17
Bellini, Giovanni, 327
Belsey, Catherine, 60, 67
Bening, Annette, 62
Bergman, Ingmar, 185
Berkeley, Busby, 322, 328, 336
Berlin, Irving, 320, 325
Bernhardt, Sarah, 17
Bible, 144, 157
black-and-white film: use of by Almereyda, 106; by Branagh, 90, 120, 121; by Whedon, 87; by White, 90
Blake, William, 218
Bleinheim Palace, 138
Blessed, Brian: in *As You Like It*, 147, 247; in *Hamlet*, 128; in *Henry V*, 247, 258
blind casting, 236, 238
Bond, Samantha, 145

Bonham-Carter, Helena, 229, 234
Bonnett, Alastair, 13, 15, 330
Boose, Linda, 139
Borrelli, Christopher, 3, 8
Bosch, Hieronymous, 202
Bosworth Field, Battle of, 6
Botticelli, Sandro, 175, 219
Boyd, Brian, 134
Bradley, A.C., 34
Bram Stoker's Dracula (film), 85
Branagh, Kenneth, 11, 33, 40, 44–5, 59, 78, 96, 99, 260, 286, 356, 362, 366; as Iago in Parker's *Othello*, 21, 82, 144; *In the Bleak Midwinter*, 326; *Mary Shelley's Frankenstein*, 43, 182, 192; *Peter's Friends*, 18, 326. See also *As You Like It* (Branagh's); *Hamlet* (Branagh's); *Henry V* (Branagh's); *Love's Labour's Lost* (Branagh's); *Much Ado About Nothing* (Branagh's)
Brecht, Bertolt, 296; and alienation effect, 82, 134, 135, 256, 296
Breight, Curtis, 267, 268, 269
Briers, Richard, 195
Bringing Up Baby (film), 64
Bristol, Michael, 40, 362
British Film Institute, 35
Bronzino, Agnolo, 11, 340, 351
Brook, Peter, 67, 141, 146, 265
Brooke, Arthur, 80, 160
Brown, John Russell, 58, 59, 366
Brown, Sarah, 146, 252, 336, 364
Brown, Theo, 161
Bruegel, Pietr, 202
buddy movies, 26, 66, 280
Bulman, James C., 232
Burbage, Richard, 46, 105

Burnett, Mark Thornton, 145; *Filming Shakespeare in the Global Marketplace*, 356; *Shakespeare and World Cinema*, 17, 356; *Shakespeare, Film, Fin de Siecle*, 15, 51, 321, 330
Burrough, Tony, 72
Burt, Richard, 135, 139, 175
Burton, Robert, 190
Butler, Gerard, 150, 275, 279

canted frame (filmic technique), 87, 121
Carlei, Carlo, 38, 154
Carnicke, Sharon Marie, 74, 88
Carson, Christie, 34
Cartmell, Deborah, 262, 265
Casablanca (film), 322, 324, 328
casting, 52–3, 61, 67, 77, 92, 95, 258, 291, 340, 341, 343, 344; "blind," 226, 238; typecasting, 97, 215
Castle Rock, 54
Catholicism, 153, 154, 155, 168, 169, 173, 176, 187; in Almereyda film of *Hamlet*, 153–76; in Branagh film of *Hamlet*, 191; in *Hamlet* (Shakespeare), 161, 164, 167, 168; in Luhrmann film *Romeo + Juliet*, 40, 153–76; in *Romeo and Juliet* (Shakespeare), 156, 160, 175
celebrity, 16, 46, 47, 207, 214, 215
Changeling, The, 195
Chaplin, Charlie, 204, 235
Charles, Prince of Wales, 56, 260
Charney, Maurice, 49
Chekhov, Anton, 25
children, 124, 140–1, 148, 248; as audience for Shakespeare, 32, 42, 139, 144, 321, 361; books based

on Shakespeare for, 23, 35; in Shakespearean screen adaptations, 115, 120–2, 141, 145, 146, 169, 188, 208, 217, 276–7, 340, 366
Children's Midsummer Night's Dream, The (film). See *Midsummer Night's Dream* (Edzard's)
Chillington Rutter, Carol, 85
Chimes at Midnight (film), 256
Christie, Julie: in Branagh's *Hamlet*, 186, 188; in David Lean's films, 186
Churchill, Winston, 78, 113; as rhetorician, 24, 269
Cineaste, 48, 171, 192, 360
Cirque de Soleil, 151, 293
class, 73, 84, 138, 224–5, 234, 238–9, 241, 254–5, 260, 274, 299, 312, 326, 331–5; and burial rituals, 155, 168; and culture, 24, 41, 53
Clerks (film), 73
Close, Glenn, 93, 127
Clueless (film), 55
Coe, Jonathan (film critic, *New Statesman*), 182, 314
Coen brothers, 59
Coleman, Basil, 9, 228, 232, 240
Collick, John, 180, 183, 194
colonization, 238, 252; and *The Tempest*, 11, 28, 119, 198, 203, 339–40, 341, 344, 346–7, 350, 351, 354–5
commedia dell'arte, 138
continuity or invisible editing (filmic technique), 79, 83
Cook, Pam, 330, 331
Coppola, Francis Ford, 43, 59, 85, 263
Coriolanus: Fiennes's film, 6, 10, 18, 22, 27, 43, 63, 90, 118, 150–1, 179, 254–8, 358–9, 364; Shakespeare's play, 150, 254–80. *See also* Fiennes, Ralph
Corneille, Pierre, 220
corporations, global, 61, 62, 106
Corrigan, Timothy, 59
Cotillard, Marion, 44, 53, 123, 124
Coursen, H.R., 41
Craig, Cairns, 5
crane shot (filmic technique), 87, 195
Cronenberg, David, 59, 220
cross-dressing: in *As You Like It*, 223–53; in *Cymbeline*, 223; in *Merchant of Venice*, 223; in *Twelfth Night*, 153, 223–53; in *Two Gentlemen of Verona*, 223
Croteau, Melissa, 15, 321
Crowdus, Gary, 192, 305, 319
Crowl, Samuel, 33, 38, 46, 47, 105, 127, 128, 184, 204, 208, 235, 305, 311
Crying Game, The (film), 228, 230, 231, 250
Cymbeline (Almereyda's), 10, 21, 43, 50, 51, 52; opening sequence in, 108, 109; realism in, 61, 62, 63, 71, 97; stage in, 136–8, 169, 183, 197, 263, 264
Cymbeline (Shakespeare's), 61–2, 223, 264

Danes, Claire, 39, 55, 98
Darth Vader, 112, 266
Davenant, Sir William, 220
da Vinci, Leonardo, 202
Dead Again (Branagh's film), 18, 182
Dekker, Thomas, 200
De La Tour, Georges, 11, 218

Denisof, Alexis, 42, 293
Desmet, Christy, 34
De Vega, Lope, 53
DiCaprio, Leonardo, 21, 35, 39, 55, 75, 98,
difference: cultural, 254–81; gender, 223–53, 283–319; human and non-human, 346; race, 6, 127, 199, 231, 252; religious, 153–75, 191. *See also* class
Disney Corporation, 220, 248; *Beauty and the Beast*, 104; *Brave*, 248; *Mary Poppins*, 328; *Mulan*, 248
Dollimore, Jonathan, 16, 53
Downton Abbey (TV series), 113
Doyle, Patrick, 92, 130, 286, 298, 301
Drake, Sir Francis, 11, 51
Drowning by Numbers (Greenaway's film), 217, 340
Dryden, John, 220
The Duchess of Malfi (play by John Webster), 195
Le Duel d'Hamlet (film), 17
Duyvendak, Jan Willem, 124, 263, 321, 332, 362–3, 366
Dylan, Bob, 36, 137–8

eavesdropping scenes, 297–302, 328, 358
Eco, Umberto, 57
Edzard, Christine, 59; *The Children's A Midsummer Night's Dream*, 9, 12, 144–6, 228, 266; *Little Dorrit*, 146, 228–9. See also *A Midsummer Night's Dream* (Edzard's); *As You Like It* (Edzard's)
Egoyan, Atom, 59, 90; *Family Viewing*, 91
Elizabeth I, 155, 166, 258, 266

Elizabeth I: film, 51; TV show, 51
Elizabethan theatres, 46, 48, 57, 119, 130, 133, 135–6, 142, 144, 242, 319; staging in, 144, 146, 149, 187, 224–5, 227, 230–1, 297
Entertainment Weekly, 181
environmentalism, 51, 180, 247, 366
Erasmus of Rotterdam, 197
Essex, Earl of, 258–9, 266–8
establishing shot (filmic technique), 87, 89, 110, 117, 126, 127, 128, 306, 308, 310
ethnicity, 25, 237, 274, 362. *See also* difference
extradiagetic scenes, 10, 103, 120–2, 128–9
Eyre, Richard, 70, 143

fade (filmic technique), 86–7
family, 8, 32, 93, 94, 154, 155, 158, 166, 270; depiction in Shakespeare, 9, 10, 11, 77, 103, 157, 164, 254, 270, 276, 291; dysfunctionality today, 51, 62–3, 92, 93, 215, 266, 232; emphasis on in adaptations, 62–3, 68, 89, 111–12, 122, 124, 128, 143, 157, 162, 172, 181, 215, 279
fascism, 6, 67, 276
Fassbender, Michael, 44, 123–4, 149
fast-food analogies, 12
Fellini, Federico, 117
feminism, 61, 225, 248, 307, 344; and chastity, 61, 84, 285–302; in marriage, 61, 225, 285–302
Fiennes, Joseph, 35, 44
Fiennes, Ralph, 59; in *Coriolanus*, 6, 10, 18, 22, 27, 63, 90, 118, 150–1, 179, 254–8, 358–9, 364; family

background, 274, 278; on stage, 150
Fine Line Features, 54, 305, 314
Fishburne, Laurence, 45, 55, 127
flare (filmic technique), 87
Flockhart, Calista, 64
Flynn, Errol, 66
Forbes-Robertson, Johnston, 17
Forster, E.M., 13; *Room with a View*, 110; *Where Angels Fear to Tread*, 110
Fraser, Laura, 99, 206, 220
French, Emma, 16, 40, 229, 271, 280, 336, 357
French Classical drama, 198, 220
Freud, Sigmund, 10, 58, 183; and Oedipus complex, 184, 278
Frida (Taymor's film), 119
Frye, Northrop, 359
Frye, Roland Mushat, 167–8

Game of Thrones (TV series), 14, 43
gangster films, 24, 112
Garai, Romola, 64, 246
gaze, male, 137
genres, 26, 56, 113, 220; action, 66, 70, 280; buddy movie, 26, 66, 280; comedy, 26, 56, 61, 63–5, 68, 77, 94, 110, 131, 226, 229, 236–7, 238, 245, 248, 250, 285–302, 307, 309, 311–14; horror, 181–2, 187, 192, 194, 198, 212, 213, 214–20; thriller, 125, 273; tragicomedy, 339, 349; war, 26, 112, 254–81; western, 56, 78
Gershwin, Ira and George, 324–5
Gibson, Mel, 39, 45–6, 55, 66, 128, 306
Gielgud, John, 35, 168; in *Prospero's Books*, 35, 81, 114–15, 219, 340, 343, 347, 349; reputation as actor, 143, 145, 168, 341, 344, 349, 354
globalization, 17, 61, 226, 229, 253, 356; of culture, 32, 48, 236, 236–8, 268; and nostalgia, 6–7, 8, 51
Globe and Mail, 31, 180
Globe playhouse, 36, 46, 48, 57, 119, 130, 133, 135–6, 142, 144, 242, 319
The Godfather (film), 47, 112, 139
Goldenthal, Eliot, 338, 345–6, 348–9, 352
Graphic Paintbox technology, 89, 114
Greenaway, Peter, 48, 60; and art, 48, 81, 116, 217–19, 340–1, 350, 362, 365; and film, 48, 89, 219, 350–1, 365; and *Prospero's Books*, 11, 15, 20, 24, 26, 28, 37, 45, 71, 81, 89, 99, 114–16, 131, 143, 198–222, 338–55, 364
Greenblatt, Stephen, and *As You Like It*, 241; and *Hamlet*, 161; and religion, 160; and Shakespeare's life, 153, 155, 175; and *The Tempest*, 339, 347
Guardian, 54, 274, 277, 280
Guneratne, Anthony R., 198, 201, 208, 322

Hall, Peter, 335
Hallmark Hall of Fame Shakespeare (TV series), 33
Hamlet (Almereyda's), 9, 21–2, 34; death rituals in, 153–75, 361; filmic techniques in, 87–8, 90, 94; opening sequence in, 105, 106, 107, 108, 115, 124, 128; realism in, 58, 60–1, 67, 71–2, 75, 81,

87–8, 90, 94; stage in, 105–8, 115, 124, 128
Hamlet (Bernhardt's), 17
Hamlet (Bourgeois's), 17
Hamlet (Branagh's), 4–5, 9, 18, 24, 26, 42–3, 56; gothicism in, 172, 179–97; opening sequence in, 108, 128, 130; realism in, 58, 66–7, 73, 75, 77, 79–80, 84–5, 95; stage in, 138–9, 140–4; synecdoche in, 213
Hamlet (Forbes-Robertson's), 17
Hamlet (Gund's, Asta Nielsen's), 17
Hamlet (Kozintsev's), 180–1, 183–4
Hamlet (Méliès's), 17
Hamlet (Noble's), 140, 185;
Hamlet (Olivier's), 82, 133, 180–1, 183–5, 257, 357
Hamlet (Orlova's, animated), 193
Hamlet (Shakespeare's), 249, 254; Fiennes in, 277–8; gothicism in, 182–6, 188–90, 193–4, 196–7; as a masterpiece, 361–2; and memory, 3; method of prince's soliloquies, 25; narrative conventions in, 62, 67, 80, 84, 88, 94; nostalgia for, 56; opening sequence in, 104, 107–8, 128, 139, 143, 161–2, 166–9, 172–3, 175; Ophelia and Hamlet, 42; sense of purpose in, 366; Whishaw in, 352
Hamlet (Zeffirelli's), 9, 12, 16, 24; casting in, 45, 306, cutting of Fortinbras, 185; death ritual in, 172; genre of, 66; neo-realism of, 58–9, 66, 79; Oedipus complex in, 128, 188; opening sequence, 66, 107, 127; selling of, 37–9, 55, 94; setting of, 70–1, 180–1;

shot/reverse shot in, 80, 107, 306, 361
hand-held camera, 87, 123
Hanh, Thich Nhat, 175
Harris, Ed, 108–9, 137
Harry Potter, 37, 50, 275
Harvey, Gabriel, 200
Hatchuel, Sarah, 97, 138, 248
Hawke, Ethan, 87, 153
Henry V (Branagh's), Battle of Agincourt in, 6; catalyst for Shakespearean screen adaptation, 4, 17, 19, 21, 25, 45, 97, 114; continuity editing in, 79; as educational tool, 35; Exeter in, 128; influence of theatre production on, 18; nostalgia in, 9, 27; opening sequence, 111–12, 130–1, 133; propaganda and otherness in, 179, 254–81, 359; realism and accessibility of, 58, 75; selling of, 94; setting of, 24, 70–1
Henry V (Olivier's): morale boosting in, 262, 265–6; nostalgia for, 271; opening sequence, 130; stage in, 133; success of, 357
Henry V (Shakespeare's), 254–81
Heritage Audience Survey, 6, 13, 81
heteronormativity, 226, 307
high-school culture, 19, 35, 36, 214
Higson, Andrew, 5, 43, 138
Hindle, Maurice, 145
Hodgdon, Barbara, 53, 158
Hofer, Johannes, 6
Hoffman, Michael, 12, 59, 99; *One Fine Day*, 64, 79; *Privileged*, 324. See also *A Midsummer Night's Dream* (Hoffman's)
Holden, Anthony, 44, 155

Holinshed, Raphael, 247
Holleran, James V., 155
Hollywood, 12, 18, 37, 43, 201, 229, 325, 336; blockbusters, 48, 58; conservatism, 25, 41, 63, 98, 229–30; narrative structure characteristic of films produced, 60, 63–7, 76, 78–9, 83, 92–3, 98, 104, 107, 112, 124–5, 129, 141, 271; star power, 46, 52, 77; studios that invest in Shakespeare, 54, 280
homoeroticism, 226, 229, 231–2, 241, 243, 245, 251–2
homophobia, 230–1
homosexuality, 223–53, 346
Honan, Park, 155
Hopkins, Anthony, 97, 99, 215
Hopkins, Lisa, 114, 340, 350, 354
Hutcheon, Linda, 3, 12, 52, 74
hybridity, 40, 200, 203–12, 223

Ibsen, Henrik, 58
identity, 4, 366; and capitalism, 322; and cultural tradition, 138, 254–81, 363, 365; and gender, 27, 223–53, 317; and memory, 6, 322, 363; and nationality, 254–81, 363; and race, 127, 341; and romantic love, 317, 318
immigration, 236
intercutting/crosscutting (filmic technique), 27, 83, 304; Almereyda, 106, 109, 137; Branagh, 92, 147; Fiennes, 279; Greenaway, 208, 210; Luhrmann, 117; Nunn, 303–19; Taymor, 119; Wright, 90
International Movie Data Base (IMDB), 24, 34, 40
intertextuality, 22

In the Bleak Midwinter (Branagh's film), 326
Irish campaign under Elizabeth I, 258–9, 266, 268
Irish culture, 11, 255, 258–9, 266–8, 274, 336
Irons, Jeremy, 105
irony, 27, 90, 302, 304

Jackson, Russell, 33
Jacob, Irene, 53
Jacobi, Derek, 130–1, 145, 260
James I, King, 51, 62, 166, 255, 257
Jameson, Frederic, 4, 7, 13
Jess-Cooke, Carolyn, 15, 32, 127
Jewish culture, 12, 105
Johnson, Brian (film critic, *Maclean's* magazine), 192
Johnson, Dakota, 108, 137
Jones, Emrys, 50
Jonson, Ben, 47, 94, 131, 203, 259, 359
Jovovitch, Milla, 108
Jules et Jim (film), 228
Julius Caesar (films), 17, 67
jump-cut (filmic technique), 88
The Jungle Book (Disney), 104
Juno (film), 73

Kabuki theatre, 146–8
Kendrick, Walter, 182–3, 187, 193, 194
Kermode, Frank, 188, 191
King Lear, 8, 53, 121, 125, 300; Brook's film, 67
Kingsley, Ben, 310, 314
Kingsley-Smith, Jane, 35, 257, 259, 260, 264, 265
Kline, Kevin, 55, 111, 149, 335

Kott, Jan, 173, 186
Kozintsev, Grigori, 180, 181, 183, 184, 194
Kurosawa, Akira, 108, 118, 146
Kurzel, Justin, 99. See also *Macbeth* (Kurzel's)
Kyd, Thomas, 46

Lane, Nathan, 336
Lange, Jessica, 215
Lanier, Douglas, 43, 140, 142, 143, 199, 322, 333–4, 344–5
Larue, Johanne, 74
Lean, David, 139, 186
Leguizamo, John, 78
Lehmann, Courtney, 158, 188, 268, 344
Lemmon, Jack, 227, 234–5
Leonard, Robert Sean, 45, 289, 290–1
Leone, Sergio, 78
Lester, Adrian, 326
Lethal Weapon (film), 55, 280
Little Dorrit (Edzard's film), 228, 229
Lodge, Thomas, 200
Logan, John, 63, 264, 273, 279, 280
Loncraine, Richard, 59, 332. See also *Richard III* (Loncraine's)
Looking for Richard (film), 31
Lord of the Rings, The (films), 104
Love's Labour's Lost (Branagh's): borrowing in, 320–37; and box office, 40, 94, 98; and casting, 55; nostalgia in, 27–8, 320–37; and opening sequence, 10, 120; and romantic comedy conventions, 65, 77, 357–8; and setting, 6, 24, 71, 72, 90, 238; and soundtrack, 91, 330–7

low angle shot (filmic technique), 87, 194
Luhrmann, Baz, 60, 358, 360, 361, 362; *Australia*, 12; *Moulin Rouge*, 329. See also *Romeo + Juliet* (Luhrmann's)
Lyly, John, 46
Lynch, David, 59, 220

Macbeth (Kurosawa's), 46
Macbeth (Kurzel's), 10, 12, 14, 18, 24, 34, 53, 59, 63, 68, 71, 122, 123–4, 149, 150
Macbeth (Morrisette's), 12
Macbeth (Polanski's), 17
Macbeth (Reilly's), 32
Macbeth (Wright's), 10, 12, 60, 90; effects of modern setting, 61–2, 71, 88, 96–7; high-def camera use, 88; influence on Kurzel, 63, 123; inserts, 85, 90; nostalgia in, 10, 84, retro camera techniques in, 86–7; success of, 20, 61, 98; witches in, 85–6, 121–2, 149
MacDonald, Michael, 165–6
Machiavelli, Niccolo, 94
MacHomer (play), 12
MacLachlan, Kyle, 87
Madden, John, 45, 357
Mad Max, 66
Magnificent Seven, The (film), 118
Magnolia (film), 304
Mankiewicz, Joseph L., 67
mannerism, 219, 340, 351
Manvell, Roger, 16, 183
Maori Merchant of Venice, The, 17
Maqbool (film), 32
Marlowe, Christopher, 46, 47, 94, 113, 351

Marowitz, Charles, 111, 322, 363
Martin, Catherine, 159, 172
Mary Poppins (film), 328
Mary Shelley's Frankenstein (Branagh's film), 53, 182, 192
Matheson, Tom, 55, 58, 66
Matt, Susan J., 7, 11, 159, 330
McKee, Robert, 130, 347
McKellen, Ian: and *Richard III*, 58, 62, 70, 72, 76–8, 82, 96, 98, 112, 143, 331–2
Méliès, Georges, 17, 329
Mendelssohn, Felix, 110, 139, 326–7, 337
Men of Respect (film), 32, 39, 45
Merchant/Ivory films, 110, 320
Merchant of Venice, The (Maori), 17
Merchant of Venice, The (Radford's), 5, 10, 12, 39, 44, 63, 69, 105, 113, 116
Merchant of Venice, The (Shakespeare's), 223
metatheatre, 139
Method acting, 88
Michelangelo Buonarotti, 219, 361
Middleton, Thomas, 154, 200
Midsummer Night's Dream, A: Brook's, 141; Hall's, 335; Noble's, 9, 139, 141–2, 276–7, 328; Reinhart's, 335; Warner Brothers, 24
Midsummer Night's Dream, A (Edzard's), 9, 12, 144–6, 228, 266
Midsummer Night's Dream, A (Hoffman's): conservative style of, 56; emphasis on Bottom, 111, financial information about, 37–9, 55; influence of Branagh, 98; nostalgia in, 320–37; romantic comedy conventions of, 64; setting, 28, 109, 130; title, 43

Midsummer Night's Dream, A (Shakespeare's), 8–9, 26, 111, 139, 145, 357, 365
Midwinter's Tale, A (Branagh's film). See *In the Bleak Midwinter*
minstrelsy tradition, 268
Miramax, 54, 107
Mirren, Helen, 228, 232, 239, 240, 346, 353
mise en scène, 52, 66, 77, 138–41, 219, 334
Modenessi, Alfredo Michel, 159
Monk, Claire, 6, 13, 41–2, 81, 95, 231, 260, 334–5
Monroe, Marilyn, 206–7, 235
montage (filmic technique), 88–9, 106, 117–18, 124, 137, 272, 330
Montaigne, Michel de, 200
Moonstruck (film), 329
Morris, Harry, 172–3
Moulin Rouge (film), 329
movie merchandising, 37
Mozart, Wolfgang Amadeus, 54, 236, 305
Mrs. Doubtfire (film), 228
Much Ado About Nothing (Branagh's), 9; casting, 21, 39, 52, 77; characterization, 125; fidelity in, 27, 117, 285–302; influence of and on, 18, 70, 76, 117, 129; music in, 117, 283–302; realism in, 58, 62, 70, 75–7, 79, 82; romantic comedy conventions, 64, 91–2, 131; selling, 18, 37–8, 45, 95; setting, 24; stage in, 151; style of, 56, 73, 87, 117, 182
Much Ado About Nothing (Shakespeare's), 285–303, 365
Much Ado About Nothing (Whedon's), 9, 12, 38, 151, 358; and

Branagh's influence, 129; black and white, 87; casting in, 42; characterization in, 9; gender and fidelity in, 27, 283–303; marketing, 38, 42–3, 94; masked ball, 151; music in, 285–303; opening sequence, 128–30; realism in, 59, 79, 87; romantic comedy conventions, 64, 129; setting, 71, 128; sexual double standards in, 27, 283–302; style, 87, 300
Much Ado About Nothing (Zeffirelli's), 360
multiculturalism: in Branagh's *Henry V*, 268; in Channel 4's *Twelfth Night*, 27, 229, 236, 253; inducing nostalgia for heritage, 6, 8, 17, 48, 51, 226; shift to, 134
multiplex cinemas, 33, 105
My Own Private Idaho (film), 19

Nagra, Parminder, 229, 232, 236–7, 245–6
Nashe, Thomas, 200, 201, 215, 219
National Heritage Acts (Thatcher's Britain), 229
National Theatre (UK), 18, 68
New Statesman, The, 233
New Yorker, The, 31, 357
New York Times, 36, 64, 235, 262
Nicoll, Allardyce, 65
Noble, Adrian (director): *Hamlet* (RSC), 138, 140, 185; *Henry V*, 256; *A Midsummer Night's Dream* (film), 9, 24, 139–42, 276, 328, 366
nostalgia: for childhood, 120, 139–42, 182, 293, 340; definitions of, 6, 7, 13, 14, 330; for elevating art, 14, 24, 42, 59, 116, 210, 219, 335, 366; for familiarity, 70, 97, 314, 331; for genius/originality, 49, 53, 369; and the grotesque, 199, 209; for happier/simpler past, 7, 122, 185, 215, 314–17, 321, 323, 355, 359, 362; for homeland, 7, 27, 159, 204, 216, 259, 321; idealization as process of, 323, 325, 330–1, 335; marginalization of, 15; music as trigger for, 346, 312; for non-industrial/technological past, 4, 245, 322; Oedipal (for oneness with the mother/womb), 188, 276; for older films, 327, 328; post-trauma, 191; prevalence of in contemporary culture, 4, 8, 159; for print-based culture, 104, 116, 322; relation to melancholic humour, 189–90; for ritual, 26, 153–78; for sense of belonging, 189, 321, 365; for Shakespeare's language, 48, 196, 221, 250, 269; in Shakespeare's plots/concepts, 9, 25, 68, 185, 199, 341, 353; for Shakespeare's universalism, 6, 46; among soldiers, 270–1, 311–12, 330; for the stage, 26, 42, 133–52, 218; for strong female roles, 231, 262; for traditional culture, 8, 13, 94, 135, 139, 161, 204, 271, 321, 322, 336–7, 355; for traditional family life, 15, 92, 226, 239, 252, 332–3; for upper-class privilege, 229, 248, 280, 299, 326; usefulness of, 321, 331, 361
Novak, Elaine Adams, 57–8
Nunn, Trevor, 75; humanism/optimism of, 59, 358, 366; as theatre director, 18, 56, 62, 68,

141, 307, 319. See also *Twelfth Night* (Nunn's)
Nyman, Michael: and *Prospero's Books*, 37, 115, 209, 211, 338–55

O (film), 19, 33, 39
Oedipus Rex, 51, 277
Olivier, Laurence, 16, 17, 53, 143, 145; on acting, 74; *As You Like It* (film), 357; *Hamlet* (film), 82, 180, 181, 183, 184, 185, 367; *Henry V* (film), 130, 133, 257, 262, 265–6, 271, 367; *Richard III* (film), 111, 367
Omkara, 32
One Fine Day (Hoffman's film), 64, 79
Orgel, Stephen, 250, 338
Osborne, John, 150
Otello (Verdi opera), 360
Othello (Parker's): casting, 21, 55; direct address in, 82; emotions in, 49; family in, 91; financial background, 45, 55; flashbacks in, 85, nostalgia for the stage in, 144, opening sequence in, 125–7, 131; proto-feminism in, 225; race in, 127; realism of, 95; setting, 9, 24, 71; soundtrack, 91; style, 79, 80, 96, 98; travel narrative in, 202
Othello (Shakespeare's), 358
Other Boleyn Girl, The (film and TV show), 51
Ovid, 216–17

Pacino, Al, 44, 46, 105, 105
Padamsee, Alyque, 54
Paltrow, Gwyneth, 41, 229
Parker, Oliver, 19, 53, 59, 95, 99, 358. See also *Othello* (Parker's)
parody, 239, 261
Pasco, Isabelle, 52
pastiche, 4, 8, 28, 56
patronage, 56, 356
Pearce, Craig, 69, 75, 78
Pendleton, Thomas, 193
Perrineau, Harold, 78
Peter Pan (James Barrie's book, play), 140–2
Peter's Friends (Branagh's film), 18, 326
Pilkington, Ace, 66
Pixelvision, 22, 88
plague, 200, 221, 310
Plato, 53, 64, 224
point-of-view shots (filmic technique), 80, 87, 89, 145, 237, 240
Polanski, Roman, 17, 97, 265
Pook, Jocelyn, 91
popular bands which use Shakespeare, 36
post-colonialism, 336, 338–55
Postlethwaite, Pete, 117
Pride and Prejudice (film), 44
Private Romeo (film), 19
Prospero's Books. See *The Tempest* (Greenaway's *Prospero's Books*)
Protestantism, 153–76, 191
Protestant Reformation, 153, 161, 163, 191
Proust, Marcel, 292, 324, 326, 328
Pullman, Bill, 109
Puritanism, 47, 201, 225, 226, 310

Quinn, James, 35, 257, 259, 260, 264–5
Quinones, Ricardo, 14, 25, 49, 68, 190, 270

Rabelais, François, 200, 215
race, 127
Racine, Jean, 220
Rackham, Arthur, 140
Radcliffe, Ann, 180, 182, 184, 191
Radford, Michael, 12, 59, 99, 113, 116. See also *Merchant of Venice*
Raleigh, Sir Walter, 51
Raphael (Sanzio da Urbino), 340
realism: and box-office draw, 54, 56, 360; in Branagh's work, 142; in Channel 4's mandate, 229; conventions of, 26, 31, 57–99; film's drive towards, 57–99, 239, 256; in Shakespeare's *King Lear*, 221; urban, in 1970s film, 17; in Wright's work, 149; in Zeffirelli's work, 361
Redgrave, Vanessa, 274, 277–8, 280
Reeves, Keanu, 39, 45
remakes, of films, musicals, television shows, 8, 22, 41–2
Reinhardt, Max, 335
Rembrandt van Rijn, 116
Renaissance man, concept of, 94
reverse-angle shot (filmic technique), 79
Rhodes, Neil, 200–2, 215, 218, 221
Ribot, Theodule, 6
Rice, Anne, 197
Richard II, 260
Richard III (Loncraine's), 6, 9, 18, 54, 58, 60, 61; and accessibility, 95, 112, 144; and casting, 62, 70, 77, 82, 143; conclusion, 67; direct address of audience, 82; nostalgia for stage in, 143; opening sequence, 111–13, 122, 131; realism of, 72, 82; selling of, 54, 94; setting, 24, 61, 71, 72, 331; soundtrack, 91, 144; stylization, 98
Richard III (Olivier's), 111, 367
Richard III (Shakespeare's), 46, 357, 359
riesumazione, film conventions, 66
Ritivoi, Andreea, 6–7, 189, 312
ritual, 3, 26, 96, 153–76, 215–16
Robinson, Zuleika, 69
romantic comedy: conventions of, 63–6; marketing film as, 94; *Much Ado About Nothing* as, 131, 289, 290, 292, 298; rupturing conventions of, 68; and *Shakespeare in Love*, 56, 229; *Twelfth Night* as, 307, 313
Romeo and Juliet (Carlei's), 38, 154
Romeo + Juliet (Luhrmann's): camera work in, 22, 56, 80, 89, 305; casting of, 21, 40, 55, 75; conclusion, 67, 88; design, 81, 90; hybridity of, 56, 64–5, 69, 78, 98, 99, 136, 357; images of theatre in, 134–6; nostalgia for ritual, 26, 153–76; opening sequence, 89, 117–18, 124; setting, 6, 9–10, 14, 25, 40, 56, 61, 71–2, 131; soundtrack, 17, 35, 56, 89, 91; success, 22, 37–9, 41, 43, 45, 54, 56, 61, 118, 356
Romeo and Juliet (Shakespeare's): allusions to balcony scene in *Twelfth Night*, 309; comic structure until Mercutio's death, 64; connection with Imogen and Posthumous, 138; death rituals in, 153–76; familiarity, 131, 357; Padamsee's production of, 5; puppets, 35; source, 80–1

Romeo and Juliet (Zeffirelli's), 18, 360–1
Rothwell, Kenneth: on adaptations of *As You Like It*, 228, 241; on Branagh's direction, 98, 193; on darkening of Shakespeare's vision in film, 265; on Loncraine's *Richard III*, 143; on Luhrmann's *Romeo + Juliet*, 158; on nostalgia for Shakespeare's language, 48; on number of Shakespeare adaptations, 19; on Nunn's *Twelfth Night*, 307
Rowe, Katherine, 135
Royal Shakespeare Company, 18, 138, 292, 356

St Jerome: paintings of, 218
Scofield, Paul, 66, 128, 256
Scorsese, Martin, 59
Scotland, PA (film), 12, 32
Scott Thomas, Kristin, 98, 112
"screwball" comedy, 64–5
Second Shepherd's Pageant, The, 184
sexual mores: in Hollywood films, 93; in Branagh's *Hamlet*, 42, 84, 187–9; cross-dressing and, 223–54; in films of *Much Ado About Nothing*, 27, 285–302; in Greenaway's *Prospero's Books*, 211; heteronormativity in films, 68, 92, 95, 333–4; in Luhrmann's *Romeo + Juliet*, 172; and male gaze in Almereyda's *Cymbeline*, 137; in Nunn's *Twelfth Night*, 303–20; in Parker's *Othello*, 85, 127, 225–6; in Taymor's *Titus*, 202, 206, 214; today's, 64, 231
Shakespeare: The Animated Tales, 32, 193

Shakespeare, William: ambiguity in works, 275; association with social aspiration, 42–4, 133, 140, 151, 260, 333; business use, 36; *carpe diem* in works, 27, 306; celebrity in, 47; challenges of language to filmmakers, 69–70, 73, 98–9, 103, 117, 134, 217, 256, 296; characterization in works, 46, 111, 146, 272, 274; colonial cultural power of, 17, 53, 210; colonialism in, 203, 338–65; *copia* in, 26, 197–8, 220, 349; cross-dressing in, 223–53; and education, 32–8, 42, 145, 154, 363, 365–6; Elizabethan and Jacobean stage conventions in, 16, 26; endurance of works, 22, 152, 358, 364–5; family in plays, 92–3; film directors' changes to characters, 60, 308, 310; fin de siècle angst in works, 51, genius of, 4, 15, 53, 95, 183, 294, 358, 364; gothic writers' use of, 180–97; grand passions in works, 49, 180, 183; heightened language of, 47–9, 95, 116, 134, 141, 191, 194–5, 199, 204–6, 259, 311, 331; hip image of, 17, 43, 54; homage to, 17, 24, 34, 52, 180, 183–4, 186, 193–4, 196, 207–8; homesickness in works, 8, 11, 276, 342; horror in, 215, 217–18; humanism in, 59, 67, 366; hybridity in, 209; identity in, 27, 225; influences on, 11, 24, 22, 80–1, 154, 184, 201–2, 216–17, 247; leadership depicted in, 61, 212, 269; life of, 25, 53, 94, 131, 155, 259, 275, 297, 356, 357; lost innocence theme in works, 120; martial rhetoric in, 269–70; military life in, 124–5, 199, 260, 267–8; minor characters in, 77; mortality theme in, 119, 153–76, 179, 182, 194–5; nostalgia for language of, 341, 354, 359, 360; originality of, 49–50, 89; redemption in, 345, 354; and religion, 26, 153–76, 191; settings in works, 24, 28, 66, 71–3,126, 330–1; songs in, 285–355; sonnets, 5, 306, 323, 364; as source material, 4, 11, 12, 17–20, 39, 44–5, 55, 60–1, 83, 91–3, 99, 104, 135; structure of works, 66, 83, 103, 105–32, 184, 217, 220, 233, 245, 296, 304–5, 313, 316, 319, 358; as symbol of literary culture, 6–7, 13, 17, 23, 24, 34, 54, 95, 139, 151, 333, 336; time period, 13, 48, 51, 61–2, 68, 84, 93, 113, 153–76, 341, 352, 357, 359–61; theatre of, 119, 133, 136, 139, 141–2, 187, 227, 232, 241; themes of gender and identity, 27, 63–4, 68, 107, 194, 196, 213, 223, 225, 234, 265, 270, 285, 300, 303, 317, 323, 349; ubiquitousness of, 12, 25, 31, 37, 41, 54, 358, 362; unique literary status of, 5, 15–16; universalism of, 6, 46, 96, 122, 134, 146, 336, 356; use of music in, 285–3; violence in, 125, 199, 218, 221, 262, 265

Shakespeare, William, plays of: *As You Like It*, 223–53; *Coriolanus*, 118, 254–81; *Cymbeline*, 136–8; *Hamlet*, 17–18, 128, 130, 139, 153–76, 179–97, 362; *Henry IV, Part I and II*, 19; *Henry V*, 18, 130, 254–81; *Henry VI, Part III*, 111; *Henry VIII*, 93; *Julius Caesar*, 17, 136; *King John*, 17; *King Lear*, 121; *Love's Labour's Lost*, 320–37; *Macbeth*, 17, 20, 86, 121, 124; *Merchant of Venice*, 68–9; *A Midsummer Night's Dream*, 9, 26, 111, 145, 320–37; *Much Ado About Nothing*, 18, 117, 129, 287–302; *Othello*, 125–7; *Richard III*, 18, 68, 72, 76, 111, 113, 144; *Romeo and Juliet*, 19, 117, 153–76; *The Taming of the Shrew*, 17, 19; *The Tempest*, 18, 26, 99, 114–16, 119–20, 131, 198–222, 338–65; *Titus Andronicus*, 10, 125, 143, 198–222; *Twelfth Night*, 19, 20, 223–53, 303–19; *The Winter's Tale*, 141

Shakespeare associations and societies, 36

Shakespeare in Love (film): exclusion from this study, 31; hybridity of, 56, 99, 357; marketing of, 229; nostalgia for Shakespeare's language in, 48; Nunn's influence on, 244; Oscar winning, 45; Paltrow in, 41

Shakespeare Re-Told (TV series), 32

Shaughnessy, Robert, 67

Shepard, Sam, 75, 128, 162

Sheridan, Bruce, 8

She's the Man, 19

silent film, 17, 103,135, 183, 297

Simpson, O.J., trial of, 55

slow motion (filmic technique), 120, 211

social class: in adaptations of Shakespeare, 252; in audience breakdown, 41; in Branagh's *Love's Labour's Lost*, 326; and burial customs, 155, 168; in *Coriolanus* and *Henry V*, 254–5, 260, 274; and Elizabethan pamphlets, 200; in film design, 24, 331; in Hoffman's *A Midsummer Night's Dream*, 333–5; and identity, 224–5; in *Much Ado About Nothing*, 299; in Ophelia's characterization, 84; and Shakespeare's women, 93; in *Twelfth Night*, 305, 312; violation of norms on Shakespeare's stage 230, 236

sonnets, 5, 119, 160, 199, 225, 306, 323

Soulpepper Theatre (Canada), 37

sound, inception of in film, 17, 19, 32

soundtrack: appeal to audiences of, 35, 42; Branagh's typical use of, 269; conservative use of, 91–2; Nunn's use of, 319; postmodernism and, 28; for *Tempest* adaptations, 347–9, 352, 354–5

Sprengler, Christine, 8, 14, 15, 139, 188, 259, 271, 277, 291, 305, 314, 315, 322, 323

Stam, Robert: on conservatism of Hollywood, 230, 286; on derivativeness of all films, 22; on disjunction between visual and sound tracks, 312; on metacinema, 30, 347; on precision of filmic point of view, 240, 286, 350; on retroactive political correctness, 203, 252; on vococentricism of the film medium, 235

Stanislavsky, Konstantin, 58, 76

Starks, Lisa S., 188

steady-cam (filmic technique), 87

Stiles, Julia, 34, 39, 40

Stoppard, Tom, 48, 141, 359, 364

Strasberg, Lee, 88, 98

Stratford Festival, 36–7, 261, 313, 356

Stratford-upon-Avon, 11, 16, 37, 131, 141, 161

Strindberg, August, 58

Stubbes, Philip, 201, 219, 224, 233, 247

Stubbs, Imogen, 40, 229, 232, 235, 237, 242–3, 248, 307–8

Sturges, John, 118

Supple, Tim, 9, 226, 229, 236–7, 242, 245–6, 252. See also *Twelfth Night*

Tall Guy, The (film), 93, 143

Taming of the Shrew, The (films), 16, 17, 19, 39, 232, 257

Tarantino, Quentin, 59, 213, 220

Taylor, Gary, 53–4

Taylor, Neil, 75

Taymor, Julie, 12, 60; and *Across the Universe* (film); *Frida* (film), 119; *The Lion King* (broadway show), 18; *Spiderman* (broadway show), 18. See also *The Tempest* (Taymor's), *Titus* (Taymor's)

Tempest, The (Greenaway's *Prospero's Books*), 45; Ariel in, 28, 338–54; art in, 11, 81, 198–222; casting, 52–3, 143, 366; endurance of, 364; Graphic Paintbox use in, 89; grotesque in, 198–222, 254; hybridity, 96, 210; opening sequence, 114–15, 131; paratexts of, 37, selling of, 94; setting, 24,

71; single-voiced aspect, 81, 99; soundtrack, 338–54; visual imagery, 20
Tempest, The (Jarman's), 60, 336, 340, 347
Tempest, The (Shakespeare's), 18, 26, 99, 114–16, 119–20, 131, 198–222, 338–65
Tempest, The (Taymor's): Ariel's songs and depiction, 28, 338–55; box office, 98; casting, 344; colonialism in, 28; design, 73; influence of stage production on, 11, 18; opening sequence, 118–20; soundtrack, 91, 124
10 Things I Hate About You, 19, 34, 39–40, 47, 232
Thatcherism, 6, 27, 45, 226, 229, 233, 242, 252, 260, 273
Thompson, Emma, 21, 117, 129, 272, 290, 292
Times Literary Supplement, 184
Titus Andronicus (BBC), 125; Shakespeare's play, 125, 198–9, 201–2, 212, 220
Titus (Taymor's): art and the grotesque, 26–7, 198–222; casting in, 97, 99; editing, 99; framing device, 86, 112, 120, 124–5, 276, 328, 366; influence of stage production on, 142; nostalgia for stage in, 142–3; plurality of meaning in, 60; setting, 6, 25, 71–2, 96; soundtrack, 91, 99; surrealism in, 86; violence in, 10, 142
Tootsie (film), 228
Tudors, The (TV show), 51
Tweedie, James, 210, 212, 219, 350–2
Twelfth Night (Nunn's), 19, 20; accessibility of, 58, 95; Branagh and, 98, 147; casting in, 40, 55, 313, 336; concluding scene, 68; cross-dressing in, 89, 223–53; intercutting, 27, 303–19; realism, 58–9, 68, 70, 74–7, 77, 79, 83, 99; setting, 24, 27, 56, 73, 311, 315, 317, 332; song in, 297, 300, 303–19; success of, 20, 21, 39, 55–6, 98, 316, 358, 364; and Supple, 226, 223–53
Twelfth Night (Shakespeare's), 20, 146, 223–53, 301, 303–19
Twelfth Night (Supple's): cross-dressing in, 223–53; multiculturalism in, 27, 223–53; Nunn's influence, 19
Twilight (book and film series), 37, 50, 132, 197

Ulster, 267–8

Variety, 44, 230, 275
Varma, Devendra, 183
Vasari, Giorgio, 200
Venora, Diana, 78, 98, 170
Verdi, Giuseppe, 12, 320, 327, 360
Veronese, Paolo, 11, 116, 214
Victor/Victoria (film), 228
Victorian: cult of death, 169; fiction, 61; setting and costume design, 24, 234–5, 246, 248, 335; social mores, 84, 237; and steam-punk fiction, 323; theatre, 142, 326
Vincendeau, Ginette, 4, 37, 53, 231
violence: anti, 5, 265; in Branagh's *Henry V*, 262; and Croatian-Serbian war, 25, 220; in Fiennes's *Coriolanus*, 262; in Greenaway's

Prospero's Books, 199, 203, 218; media's role in, 124, 214; in our time, 221, 265; in Taymor's *Titus*, 125, 198–9, 203–4, 214–17, 220–1; in Wright's *Macbeth*, 86, 122
Virginia Company, 11, 120
Le voyage dans la lune (film), 329

Wagner, Richard, 158
Walker, Elsie, 211, 220
Walpole, Horace, 180, 182, 186–7, 193–4, 196, 213
Warm Bodies (film), 19, 32, 47
war movies, 26, 112, 272, 279, 280
Warner Brothers, 24
Wasko, Janet, 18, 41
wedding movies, 110
Welles, Orson, 16–7, 53, 266
Wells, Stanley, 25, 145
Welsh, Jim, 334
West, Dominic, 70
westerns, 56, 78
Whedon, Joss, 12, 360; *Angel*, 43; *The Avengers*, 20, 43; *Buffy the Vampire Slayer*, 43; *Firefly*, 43. See also *Much Ado About Nothing* (Whedon's)
Wheeler Dixon, Winston, 38, 50
White, Mark: on Branagh's *Hamlet*, 82, 186, 191, 196; on Branagh's *Henry V*, 260; on Branagh's Irish identity issues, 11; on Branagh's *Love's Labour's Lost*, 35; on Branagh's *Much Ado About Nothing*, 18, 62, 286; on Branagh's wish to convey a hopeful message, 59, 366; on British press attack on Branagh, 260; on Parker's *Othello*, 45; quoting Prince Charles on *Hamlet* as a spiritual comfort, 56; on Renaissance Theatre Company, 45; about Shakespeare's enduring appeal, 52
White, Martin: on Trevor Nunn's work 62, 68, 242, 308, 316
William Shakespeare's Hamlet (film). See *Hamlet* (Branagh's)
William Shakespeare's A Midsummer Night's Dream (film). See *A Midsummer Night's Dream* (Hoffman's)
William Shakespeare's Romeo + Juliet (film). See *Romeo + Juliet* (Luhrmann's)
Wizard of Oz, The (film), 328
Wolf Hall (TV show), 51
Wray, Ramona, 15, 51, 267, 321, 327, 330
Wright, Geoffrey, 12. See also *Macbeth* (Wright's)

Yentl (film), 228

Zeffirelli, Franco: and nostalgia for art of the past, 361; and opera 12, 128, 362; and *Romeo and Juliet*, 17–18, 357, 360; and *Taming of the Shrew*, 16, 357. See also *Hamlet* (Zeffirelli's)
zombie trend, 19, 197